Global Indigenous Politics

This book examines how Indigenous peoples' rights and Indigenous rights movements represent an important and often overlooked shift in international politics – a shift that powerful states are actively resisting in a multitude of ways. While Indigenous peoples are often dismissed as marginal non-state actors, this book argues that far from insignificant, global Indigenous politics is potentially forging major changes in the international system, as the implementation of Indigenous peoples' rights requires a complete rethinking and reordering of sovereignty, territoriality, liberalism, and human rights. After thirty years of intense effort, the transnational Indigenous rights movement achieved passage of the UN Declaration on the Rights of Indigenous Peoples in September, 2007.

This book asks:

- Why did the movement need to fight so hard to secure passage of a bare minimum standard on Indigenous rights?
- Why is it that certain states are so threatened by an emerging international Indigenous rights regime?
- How does the emerging Indigenous rights regime change the international status quo?

The questions are addressed by exploring how Indigenous politics at the global level compels a new direction of thought in IR by challenging some of its fundamental tenets. It is argued that global Indigenous politics is a perspective of IR that, with the recognition of Indigenous peoples' collective rights to land and self-determination, complicates the structure of international politics in new and important ways, challenging both Westphalian notions of state sovereignty and the (neo-)liberal foundations of states and the international human rights consensus. Qualitative case studies of Canadian and New Zealand Indigenous rights, based on original field research, analyze both the potential and the limits of these challenges. This work will be of interest to graduates and scholars in international relations, Indigenous studies, international organizations, IR theory, and social movements.

Sheryl Lightfoot is Canada Research Chair of Global Indigenous Rights and Politics and Assistant Professor in both First Nations and Indigenous Studies and Political Science at the University of British Columbia. Her research interests include global Indigenous peoples' rights and politics, Indigenous diplomacy, social movements, and critical international relations.

Worlding Beyond the West

Series Editors: Arlene B. Tickner
Universidad de los Andes, Bogotá
Ole Wæver
University of Copenhagen, Denmark
David Blaney
Macalester College, USA
and
Inanna Hamati-Ataya
Aberystwyth University, UK

Historically, the International Relations (IR) discipline has established its boundaries, issues, and theories based upon Western experience and traditions of thought. This series explores the role of geocultural factors, institutions, and academic practices in creating the concepts, epistemologies, and methodologies through which IR knowledge is produced. This entails identifying alternatives for thinking about the "international" that are more in tune with local concerns and traditions outside the West. But it also implies provincializing Western IR and empirically studying the practice of producing IR knowledge at multiple sites within the so-called 'West'.

1 **International Relations Scholarship Around the World**
Edited by Arlene B. Tickner and Ole Wæver

2 **Thinking the International Differently**
Edited by Arlene B. Tickner and David L. Blaney

3 **International Relations in France**
Writing between discipline and state
Henrik Breitenbauch

4 **Claiming the International**
Edited by Arlene B. Tickner and David L. Blaney

5 **Border Thinking on the edges of the West**
Crossing over the Hellespont
Andrew Davison

6 **Worlding Brazil**
Intellectuals, identity and security
Laura Lima

7 **International Relations and American Dominance**
A diverse discipline
Helen Turton

8 **Global Indigenous Politics**
A subtle revolution
Sheryl Lightfoot

9 **Constructing a Chinese School of International Relations**
Ongoing debates and sociological realities
Edited by Yongjin Zhang and Teng-Chi Chang

Global Indigenous Politics

A subtle revolution

Sheryl Lightfoot

Routledge
Taylor & Francis Group
LONDON AND NEW YORK

First published 2016 by Routledge

2 Park Square, Milton Park, Abingdon, Oxfordshire OX14 4RN
711 Third Avenue, New York, NY 10017

Routledge is an imprint of the Taylor & Francis Group, an informa business

First issued in paperback 2017

British Library Cataloguing in Publication Data
A catalogue record for this book is available from the British Library

Library of Congress Cataloging in Publication Data
A catalog record for this book has been requested

ISBN: 978-1-138-94668-2 (hbk)
ISBN: 978-1-138-47785-8 (pbk)

Typeset in Times New Roman
by Wearset Ltd, Boldon, Tyne and Wear

For Emma and Chloe

Contents

Figures

Tables

Acknowledgments

I must open by acknowledging the *hən̓q̓əmin̓əm̓*-speaking Musqueam people, on whose traditional, ancestral, and unceded territory I have had the honor of living and working for the past seven years. I am tremendously grateful for your tolerance of me as a long-term visitor in your territory, and I thank you for your hospitality, support, and, especially, your friendship. I also want to acknowledge the Dakota peoples, and my own Anishinaabe (Ojibwe) nation, in whose traditional, shared, and sometimes contested territories of present-day Minneapolis-St. Paul I grew up in and began this work at the University of Minnesota.

A research project spanning ten years involves many people, and I must extend thanks to those who have played a variety of roles in bringing this book to completion. While they all deserve acknowledgment, I remain solely responsible for any errors.

I wish to extend my sincerest thanks to the expert scholars who served as my dissertation committee members: David Wilkins, Kathryn Sikkink, and August Nimtz. A very special thanks to my primary supervisor, Raymond Duvall, for his counsel, patience, and nearly endless intellectual energy and support through every phase of this project.

Special thanks go to my colleagues at the University of British Columbia, in both the First Nations and Indigenous Studies Program and the Department of Political Science. Special thanks go to Daniel Heath Justice, Linc Kesler, Glen Coulthard, Dory Nason, Coll Thrush, Arjun Chowdhury, Barbara Arneil, Laura Janara, Mark Warren, Allan Tupper, and Paul Quirk, who have each provided intellectual and/or emotional support along the way. I also want to thank others from the University of Minnesota who have read various portions of this work in different stages and offered important suggestions, comments, and direction, in addition to support and encouragement, especially Jean O'Brien, Michael Barnett, and Ann Towns, in whose class this project was first imagined. Special thanks as well go to faculty members from Law, Political Studies, and the Native Law Centre at the University of Saskatchewan, who so generously gave their time and energy to a manuscript workshop over two days in February, 2015. I am immensely grateful for your comments and feedback. Huge thanks to Dwight Newman for this invitation. Thanks as well to my colleagues at the University of Victoria – Jeff Corntassel, Taiaiake Alfred, and Heidi Kiiwetinepinesiik Stark – as well as Kevin Bruyneel from Babson College, and Kiera Ladner at the University of Manitoba, who have each offered thoughts, comments, and advice at various junctures.

A number of funders have provided support for the research and writing of this project. I want to acknowledge financial support from the Canada Research Chairs program as well as multiple research grants from the University of British Columbia, an ICGC-MacArthur Fellowship, a Ford Foundation Diversity Dissertation Fellowship, and a University of Minnesota Diversity of Views and Experiences Summer Dissertation Research Fellowship. Pre-dissertation financial support was also generously provided by the University of Minnesota's Graduate Research Partnership Program and a Diversity of Views and Experiences Fellowship.

Deep gratitude also goes out to the numerous individuals and organizations that played a role in my research for this project. Special thanks to the International Indian Treaty Council staff and board, and especially to Bill Means, who helped provide valuable direction and moral support for this project. Thanks to doCip in Geneva for assistance with archives and documentation. Many thanks to the Indigenous Caucus and the United Nations Permanent Forum on Indigenous Issues for allowing me to attend multiple meetings as an observer. I also owe gratitude to board and staff of the American Indian Policy Center for allowing me to serve as your chair for so many years and for extending me the privilege of representing you at international meetings. Huge thanks to all who gave me the gift of their time for interviews and conversations in numerous locations around the world. A special thanks to all those in Aotearoa/New Zealand who shared their time and their country with me for an all-too-short period of time. I am deeply grateful.

I also want to acknowledge members of the American Indian Workshop at the University of Minnesota who painstakingly read and commented on every dissertation chapter, especially Joseph Bauerkemper, David Chang, Boyd Cothran, Jill Doerfler, Robert Gilmer, Laurie Richmond, and Kate Williams. I also want to thank members of the International Relations dissertation writing group at the University of Minnesota for their comments and suggestions, especially Asli Calkivik, Ayten Gundogdu, Mark Hoffman, Isaac Kamola, Denis Kennedy, Jonneke Koomen, David Leon, and Eli Meyerhoff.

I want to acknowledge a number of students at the University of British Columbia whose rich conversations and deep questions pushed my thinking in new directions. Special thanks to graduate students Alison James, Daniel Voth, Corey Snelgrove, Rachel Flowers, and Jessica Rosinski. A very special thanks to graduate students Kelsey Wrightson and Matthew Wildcat for their brilliant organization of Critical Dialogues II, which provided important feedback at such a crucial moment in the development of this manuscript. I am particularly grateful to a group of undergraduate students who always asked the good, hard questions in class, forcing me to think in new ways. Special thanks to Elle-Máijá Tailfeathers, Jordan Wilson, Sarah Robinson, Hannah Butson, Matthew Norris, Jessie McKenzie, Samantha Nock, Chloe Erlandson, and Matthew Ward. It has been my honor to teach and learn from you.

I want to express deep gratitude to the many friends I have made along this decade-long journey – Lauren Wilcox, Jennifer Lobasz, Aaron Rapport, Joyce Heckman, Erin Karski, Krzystof Karski, David MacDonald, Brenda Child, Paula Mohan, Makere Stewart-Harawira, Sarah Hunt, Audra Simpson, Rob Innes, Kim TallBear, and Chris Andersen – and long-time friends Heidi Tucker, Stephanie Pomonis, and Sean Patrick Murphy. Your energy pushes me, your spirits revitalize me, and your support sustains me – thank you always for your friendship.

Most importantly, I cannot find adequate words to express gratitude to my family and my ancestors. I am who I am, and can do what I do, only because of all of you. Special thanks to my mother Kathryn "Jennie" Lightfoot, my sister Julie Hutcheson-Downwind, my nieces Milayka and Alyssa Downwind, my aunt Sharon Edwards, and my uncle the late Donald Edwards, my niece Leslie Edwards Kull, my nephew Brandon Edwards, my great aunt Bertha Lightfoot, and my stepfather Dave Hutcheson. Thank you for your never-ending, unwavering love and support. I also want to thank my grandmother Helen Lightfoot Hanson, my great uncle Raymond P. Lightfoot, and my great grandfather Peter W. Lightfoot. I strive to honor your memory and your legacy through my work. I also want to thank several furry companions – Chaska, Chistina, and Munchy – who each stayed faithfully by my side while I read and typed, all too often into the very late-night hours, through graduate school, dissertation, and the tenure-track.

Most of all, I want to thank my daughters Emma and Chloe Thomas, who have literally grown up with this project. You have always helped keep me in balance and have provided daily reminders of what is most important in life. It has been a sheer delight watching you grow, along with me, and I appreciate all the lessons you have both taught me along the way. I thank you both, from the bottom of my heart, for your unconditional love. I dedicate this book to you, with my deepest love and greatest hopes.

Chi-miigwech!

Abbreviations

AFN	Assembly of First Nations
AIM	American Indian Movement
BBC	British Broadcasting Corporation
BCTC	British Columbia Treaty Commission
CANZUS	Canada, Australia, New Zealand, and United States
CERD	Committee for the Elimination of Racial Discrimination
CIA	Central Intelligence Agency
CISA	Consejo Indio du Sud América (Indian Council of South America)
doCip	Indigenous Peoples' Center for Documentation, Research, and Information
ECOSOC	Economic and Social Council
EMRIP	Expert Mechanism on the Rights of Indigenous Peoples
ICC	Inuit Circumpolar Council
ICCPR	International Covenant on Civil and Political Rights
ICERD	International Convention on the Elimination of All Forms of Racial Discrimination
ICESCR	International Covenant on Economic, Social, and Cultural Rights
IITC	International Indian Treaty Council
ILO	International Labour Organization
ILO 107	International Labour Organization Convention No. 107 – Indigenous and Tribal Populations
ILO 169	International Labour Organization Indigenous and Tribal Peoples Convention No. 169
ILRC	Indian Law Resource Center
INAC	Indian and Northern Affairs Canada
IR	International Relations
IWGIA	International Work Group for Indigenous Affairs
MP	Member of Parliament
NZ	New Zealand
NGO	Non-governmental Organization
UBCIC	Union of British Columbia Indian Chiefs
UN	United Nations

UNDRIP	United Nations Declaration on the Rights of Indigenous Peoples
UNPFII	United Nations Permanent Forum on Indigenous Issues
WAI	Waitangi Tribunal
WCIP	World Council of Indigenous Peoples
WGDD	Working Group on the Draft Declaration on the Rights of Indigenous Peoples
WGIP	Working Group on Indigenous Populations

1 Indigenous politics as global change

The morning of September 13, 2007 was clear and sunny, a beautiful day in New York.[1] At the United Nations, diplomats and representatives from UN member states, dressed in suits and carrying briefcases, looking very serious and businesslike, took their places in the General Assembly behind the nameplates which identified them by country. That morning, dozens of Indigenous delegates also arrived at the UN General Assembly Hall.[2] The Indigenous delegates, however, while also businesslike and carrying large briefcases, were joyful. Many arrived that morning in their traditional regalia, a colorful sea, representing diverse cultures from all over the world, from the Cree in Canada, to the Navajo in the United States, and the Saami in Northern Europe, from the Maasai to the Hmong, to the Quechua. Hugs were freely shared among the Indigenous delegates as they took their places in the back and in the side galleries of the UN General Assembly Hall. There were no official engraved nameplates for the Indigenous nations and organizations these delegates represented, although a few such nameplates began to appear in front of some of the Indigenous delegates, handwritten on pieces of paper, indicating that they represented the Saami Council, Tebtebba, the First Nations Summit, CONAIE, the Navajo Nation, or CISA, the Spanish acronym for the Indian Council of South America. The Indigenous delegates looked truly happy; some had personally labored for more than thirty years to reach this day.

At approximately 10.30 a.m., Sheikha Haya Rashed Al Khalifa, the President of the Sixty-first Session of the General Assembly, announced that the General Assembly had before it a draft resolution entitled the "United Nations Declaration on the Rights of Indigenous Peoples" and that the voting process on the resolution would begin. One by one, the representatives of the UN member states pushed green, yellow, or red buttons on their desktops, indicating their vote on the Indigenous rights declaration ("the Declaration").[3] Green was a vote in favor, while red indicated a vote against, and the yellow button registered an abstention. The Indigenous delegates in the back and on the sides of the room, by and for whom this declaration was written, through whose efforts this day had been made possible, did not have a vote. They could only sit and watch the screen on the wall: a scoreboard of UN member state votes on the Declaration. The scoreboard lit up as the member state votes were tallied. The final vote showed 143 votes for the Declaration, eleven abstentions, and four votes against. After thirty long years of struggle, the Declaration on the Rights of Indigenous Peoples had passed the United Nations General Assembly by an overwhelming margin, and the world's Indigenous peoples now had an international standard that specifically articulated their human rights. Only Australia, Canada, New Zealand, and the USA had registered votes against it. Each of these four countries issued statements immediately following the vote, to clarify the reasons why each, known in Indigenous circles as the CANZUS (Canada, Australia, New Zealand, USA) group of states, had stood in such opposition to the Declaration. All four articulated that while they had various concerns about language, process, and even opposition to collective rights (USA), the primary obstacles for them were land rights and self-determination, including the principle of free, prior, and informed consent.

Even with the predictable opposition from CANZUS states, it did not detract from the absolute jubilation among the Indigenous delegates as handshakes and hugs were again freely shared. Andrea Carmen (Yaqui), Executive Director of the International Indian Treaty Council, described the experience: "I was so privileged to sit in the Chamber that day, on the floor of the General Assembly, to see the voting on the scoreboard go up and realize that, after all of these years, we got the Declaration adopted" (Carmen 2007). The website of the International Indian Treaty Council declared, "History is made for Indigenous Peoples at the United Nations!" as "Treaty Rights, Land Rights and Self-Determination of Indigenous Peoples are recognized internationally with the adoption of the Declaration" (International Indian Treaty Council (IITC) 2007). Les Malezer, Chairman of the Global Indigenous Caucus, declared that "The adoption of the Declaration … marks a momentous and historic occasion for both Indigenous Peoples and the United Nations" (Anonymous 2007). An Indigenous delegate from Guatemala said, "It was great. We really are very happy!" while another Indigenous delegate from Kenya was so moved by the event that he could not speak (Sommer 2007). Grand Chief Edward John from the Canadian First Nations Summit said, "It's a tremendous day. It's all over now, and we have in our hands a declaration we helped construct and one on which we proudly stand. Notwithstanding Canada's 'NO' vote … we should all be proud in our collective achievement" (International Indian Treaty Council (IITC) 2007). In a press release, Victoria Tauli-Corpuz, Chairperson of the UN Permanent Forum on Indigenous Issues, stated:

> The 13th of September 2007 will be remembered as an international human rights day for the Indigenous Peoples of the world, a day that the United Nations and its member states, together with Indigenous Peoples, reconciled with past painful histories and decided to march into the future on the path of human rights.
>
> (Tauli-Corpuz 2007)

Meanwhile, Tonya Frichner (Onondaga), American Indian Law Alliance and member of the UN Permanent Forum on Indigenous Issues, commented in a more muted tone that "It was interesting. It was very interesting" (Sommer 2007).

Over the following year, the Declaration on the Rights of Indigenous Peoples began to have some international impact. Less than five weeks after the passage of the Declaration by the UN General Assembly, the Belize Supreme Court ruled on a case, *Cal v Attorney General* – the world's first legal judgment referencing the Declaration. The court held that the national government recognize the customary land tenure of the Maya in Belize. Chief Justice Conteh's judgment asserted that the Indigenous peoples had collective rights to their lands, resources, and environment and found that the Maya had their own "complex traditional set of land tenure regulations" (*Cal v AG* 2007*)*. More specifically, the Belize Supreme Court found that the Mayan "rights to occupy their lands, farm, hunt and fish pre-date European colonization and remain in force today" (Petersen 2008). In other words, the Supreme Court ruled that land acquisition by the state of Belize did not abrogate primordial Indigenous land rights.

Meanwhile, in Bolivia, President Evo Morales' dream of a "plurinational" state with territorial and administrative autonomy for Indigenous peoples received a significant boost from the passage of the Declaration in the General Assembly. A news article in September, 2007 observed that the Declaration "might call for a reorganisation of the Bolivian state and a reversion to the scheme of self-governing productive communities … and regions, which was in operation at the time of the Spaniards" (Chavez 2007). In fact, on November 7, 2007, President Evo Morales announced the passage of National Law 3760, the Rights of Indigenous Peoples, which incorporated the UN Declaration on the Rights of Indigenous Peoples into domestic law in Bolivia (Kearns 2007). Bolivia was thus the first country in the world to incorporate the Declaration, giving it effect in the national legal system. In his address announcing passage of this law, Morales said,

> From the passage of this declaration, I feel that the Indigenous movement has gone from one of resistance to one of power … a power that, at [its] core, is a way of living in a community … it is the power of resolving problems equally for all, not only in Bolivia but in the entire world.
>
> (Kearns 2007)

The Declaration sets out the individual and collective rights of Indigenous peoples as well as their rights to identity, language, health, education, and regarding a host of other issues. It emphasizes Indigenous peoples' rights to exist, and to maintain and strengthen their own institutions, cultures, and traditions. It prohibits discrimination against them, while simultaneously affirming their right to remain distinct peoples, and to pursue their own visions of development. As it is a United Nations declaration rather than an international treaty or convention, the Declaration is not a legally binding instrument under international law. Nevertheless, it does now form part of the international human rights consensus, and according to the UN, represents a "major step forward towards the promotion and protection of human rights and fundamental freedoms for all … [through] … the General Assembly's important role in setting international standards" (United Nations General Assembly 2007b). In a separate press release, the former UN Special Rapporteur on Indigenous Issues, Rodolfo Stavenhagen, noted the important shift this particular declaration forged in the international human rights system, stating that "the Declaration reflects a growing international consensus concerning the rights of Indigenous peoples" (United Nations General Assembly 2007a). It took more than thirty years of effort by Indigenous peoples at the United Nations to reach this point. These decades of effort included work by numerous working groups and subcommittees, many arguments over definitions and other issues, a hunger strike, and even an eleventh-hour effort by a group of African states to alter the text. Finally, in September, 2007, the Declaration passed the UN General Assembly, to the delight of some, and the continued steadfast opposition of the CANZUS states.

International pressure on the CANZUS states mounted. Within two years, each shifted its official position on the Declaration, eventually issuing formal and official statements of "support" or "endorsement" of it. Each of these official statements also articulated important caveats, qualifiers, and exclusions about how the Declaration should be interpreted and applied domestically. The four CANZUS states expressed their new "support," while each also emphasized that the Declaration was merely an "aspirational" document, and was "non-binding" and would not affect their existing laws or policies. In other words, despite their professed support, the CANZUS states' underlying resistance to the framework of Indigenous rights set out in the Declaration remained firmly intact.

While Indigenous peoples are often dismissed as marginal non-state actors, and Indigenous rights are disregarded as merely aspirational and non-binding, this book argues the contrary. Global Indigenous politics, defined as a project that advances Indigenous peoples' rights, is far from insignificant and is forging major changes in the international system. The implementation of Indigenous rights requires a rethinking and reordering of sovereignty, territoriality, decolonization, liberalism, and human rights. I argue that the United Nations Declaration on the Rights of Indigenous Peoples is more than just a new set of norms emerging and diffusing on the global stage. Indigenous rights, as embodied in the Declaration, represent a moment of revolutionary transformation in global politics, but are often overlooked and under-appreciated, both by international relations theory and in practice. Further, the Indigenous rights movement provides vivid examples of viable, alternative ways of engaging in global politics. Indigenous rights and the Indigenous rights movement thus represent important shifts in both the *structure* and the *practice* of global politics – serving as what I call a *transformational norm vector*, pointing the way toward some alternative ways of doing global politics and new imaginings of political order that can potentially come to exist. For those states that are highly invested in the current international order, these changes represent not only a fundamental threat but also present them with the moral dilemma of how to be world leaders in human rights while also resisting the changes the Indigenous rights regime calls for. States that wish to resist the implementation of Indigenous rights while also maintaining an aura of human rights legitimacy find that they must be careful, calculating, and subversively strategic in their resistance. Their resistance is a defensive struggle to preserve status quo power relations, in the face of the subtle revolution presented by global Indigenous politics.

Global Indigenous politics in international relations

The discipline of international relations (IR) is generally conservative, particularly with regard to concepts of the state, sovereignty, and the Westphalian world order.[4] IR has a set of enshrined, fundamental assumptions that are highly problematic for Indigenous peoples. These assumptions can overlook, silence, or completely erase Indigenous peoples, their political communities, and their alternative ways of being in the world. As J. Marshall Beier (2005) argues, IR is a fundamentally colonial discipline, internalizing many discourses of colonialism in North America, most notably the absence and erasure of Indigenous peoples (Beier 2009). Integrating Indigenous political theory into IR theory can directly address these absences and exclusions. As Franke Wilmer (2009) writes, post-colonial states and Indigenous peoples do share a set of experiences, including cultural, political, and economic marginalization, "othering" of their identity vis-à-vis the West, and being subjected to assimilative forces. Therefore, both post-colonial and Indigenous politics scholarship share a central aim: to "de-center and disturb Western cultural and political hegemomy." Wilmer also correctly notes that the major difference between post-colonial states and Indigenous peoples is the deliberate exclusion of Indigenous peoples from the twentieth-century UN decolonization project, demonstrated by the lack of independent sovereign states for Indigenous peoples. She notes that, as such, the settler colonialism that Indigenous peoples continue to experience is distinct from the post-colonial world, as Indigenous peoples remain "undecolonized."

Post-colonial scholarship in recent years has focused on difference and its accommodation, or lack thereof, in IR. For example, Arlene B. Tickner and Ole Waever (2009) examine the core–periphery nature of IR and find that some of Western IR's fundamental "core" assumptions, especially state-centrism and the primacy of national security, are also firmly in place in the non-Western "periphery" as well as the Western "core." Later work by Tickner and David Blaney (2012) further challenges the core–periphery depiction of the West and others in IR, arguing: "the state remains the nearly singular legitimate form of political organization worldwide and much IR production globally is linked to it." In fact, they argue, IR is not only about explaining state practices, it is even more insidious: it has a normative agenda as "a project connected to a particular political imagination of the world as states." In one of the first political science books ever published about the Indigenous rights movement, Wilmer (1993) pointed out that the marginalization of Indigenous peoples is even greater than peoples of the Third World, as they have not benefitted from self-determination, defined as independent statehood, as have post-colonial states. Since Indigenous peoples remained excluded from the UN decolonization project and are thus "undecolonized" as independent states, IR, even post-colonial IR, has often overlooked them.

A growing number of critical scholars, however, are challenging state-centric IR. For example, Shogo Suzuki and colleagues (2014) challenge the presumption of the Westphalian state form by demonstrating an alternative set of international orders that were in place immediately prior to the rise of Westphalian sovereignty and immediately before the extension of European colonial power over the rest of the world. Thomas Risse (2011) further challenges the primacy of the state form in IR, arguing, "from a global as well as a historical perspective ... the modern nation-state is the exception not the rule." Other scholars consider alternative non-state conceptions of world order as not only legitimate but also currently in operation, in layers either above, underneath, or alongside Westphalian states.[5]

Indigenous political and legal theory intervene

The body of Indigenous political and legal theory that has emerged and blossomed since the late 1990s speaks directly to the colonial assumptions of mainstream IR, and intervenes in openings provided by recent post-colonial IR scholarship. Examining IR through the lens of Indigenous political theory reveals a problematic global state of what we may call *incomplete post-colonialism* resulting from the exclusion and erasure of Indigenous peoples. Indigenous political and legal theory thus calls for *post-colonial completion* through Indigenous inclusion and accommodation. The challenge for post-colonial completion, however, is that Indigenous inclusion and accommodation will ultimately force a rethinking of: (1) the state, (2) decolonization, (3) liberalism, (4) diplomacy, and (5) Westphalian sovereignty. Such challenges of difference and accommodation are not found only among Indigenous peoples, of course, and are common to virtually all of IR's critical spectrum, regardless of where they are situated along the critical spectrum, but Indigenous perspectives do offer some compelling alternative visions of how global politics may be done in a future post-Westphalian world – issues that are not typically explored within state-centric IR.

The State. Canadian political theorist James Tully argues in *Strange Multiplicity* (1995) that conditions of domination and subordination are inherent in the structure of the state form, as this structure is not currently able to accommodate consent, mutual recognition, and cultural continuity for Indigenous peoples. Anishinaabe political theorist Dale Turner (2006) advocates that Indigenous peoples participate in the state's political and legal institutions in order to reshape the Indigenous–state relationship toward greater respect for Indigenous worldviews. However, Dene political theorist Glen Coulthard (2014) adamantly disagrees, arguing that the "politics of recognition" by liberal states is so limiting and problematic for Indigenous peoples that they should reject, and turn away from, the state in favor of traditional, land-based social, political, and economic orders.

Anishinaabe scholar Duane Champagne (in Champagne et al. 2005) agrees that the multicultural nation-state does not work well for Indigenous peoples because they generally wish to preserve their lands and institutions, including culture, religion, and political institutions. The rights to land and self-governance, he writes, "are highly unusual and outside the theory of the formation and growth of nation-states." Further, he states, Indigenous peoples maintain values and institutional organizations that are "alien to those used to construct contemporary nation-states, bureaucracies, and capitalist markets" and Indigenous peoples thus present particular challenges to existing state structures because they make this set of "alternate claims to government, land ownership, land and resource management, community organization and identity, and different institutional patterns for achieving those ends." He concludes with a call for *multinational states* that can accommodate Indigenous rights, territories, institutions, cultures, and self-governance. Champagne argues that such a state formation is the only viable future path to a non-coercive, just, respectful, and consensus-based democratic political order that would better serve the interests of all peoples. American Indian law professor and former UN Special Rapporteur on the Rights of Indigenous Peoples James Anaya (2009) and UN expert Erica-Irene Daes (1993) both agree that Indigenous peoples can potentially achieve self-determination within the state form, although fundamental change is required. Specifically, they both note, states and Indigenous peoples must engage in negotiated and mutually agreed-upon terms and arrangements that accommodate Indigenous difference.

Decolonization. The Doctrine of Discovery is "the theory that guided colonial practice" and state making in colonial and settler colonial contexts (Newcomb 2008). Its underlying assumption is that

> Europeans were higher … in intelligence than the Indians, and also suggests that the Europeans, by virtue of a 'superior' intelligence, possessed a higher position of power in relation to the lands of the (American) continent and in relation to the Indigenous peoples living there.

As Vine Deloria, Jr. (Standing Rock Sioux) wrote (1974 [1985]), "in practice, the theory meant that the discoverer of unoccupied lands in the rest of the world gained a right to the land titles as against the claims of other European nations." Eastern Shawnee legal scholar Robert J. Miller (2006) also writes about property and other rights that Europeans claimed for themselves under the Doctrine of Discovery, which provided that "newly arrived Europeans immediately and automatically acquired property rights in native lands and gained governmental, political, and commercial rights over the inhabitants without the knowledge nor the consent of the Indigenous peoples." Miller also notes that the colonial Doctrine of Discovery remains valid international law today, as it has never been officially and specifically denounced in international law, the seminal USA case articulating it has been cited at various times by courts in Canada, Australia, and New Zealand,[6] and it has been relied upon in a United States Supreme Court case as recently as 2005.[7]

Furthermore, Indigenous peoples were specifically excluded from the UN decolonization project by the 1950s "salt water" or "blue water" thesis. This thesis asserted that only overseas territories, non-contiguous to the colonial power (that is, located across "salt water" from the colonial power), were eligible for decolonization and self-determination, defined under the UN decolonization project as independent, sovereign statehood. The UN Charter and the major human rights covenants each explicitly state that "all peoples have the right of self-determination." However, the question of just who counted as "peoples," and who were therefore entitled to self-determination, remained undefined and subject to contentious politics. The salt water thesis developed in response to efforts by certain colonial powers, especially Belgium, to expand the scope of the UN Charter, and thus the decolonization project, to include Indigenous peoples. This effort was defeated by an unusual (by Cold War standards) coalition of the USA and its allies, along with the Soviet Union and its allies. The salt water thesis was placed into a General Assembly resolution, which passed in 1960 (Anaya 1996).[8] Thus, as the UN decolonization project proceeded over the next several decades, Indigenous peoples were left, as Chickasaw legal scholar James (Sa'ke'j) Youngblood Henderson (2008) describes, as "the unfinished business of decolonization."

Liberalism. Mohawk political theorist Taiaiake Alfred (2005, 2009) argues that the liberal paradigm is not capable of protecting Indigenous nationhood, which requires recovery of the traditional bases of political relations and organization. Another Mohawk scholar Audra Simpson (2014) agrees, noting that liberal democracies have continually attempted to transform Indigenous peoples from sovereign nations into ethnic minority citizens of the state, rather than respect them as nations with land and collective rights.

Both Saami political scientist Rauna Kuokkanen (2009) and American political theorist Courtney Jung (2008) also find an incompatibility between Indigenous peoples' collective rights, and liberal ideology, which is "difference blind" and aims to treat Indigenous peoples the same as any other members of society. Further, Kuokkanen notes that the twin ideologies of social equality and individualism are in direct opposition to the recognition of Indigenous "difference." Thus, there is an ongoing need to question and reject "difference-blind liberalism." Jung argues that Indigenous peoples pose a particular challenge to liberalism because, in order for them to be treated as equals in society, some "difference-sensitive" policies are required, such as tolerance of certain cultural practices or access to bilingual education. In short, Indigenous peoples require not only protection against discrimination on an individual basis, but they also require some protections, as collectives, for their cultures and ways of life. Other Indigenous writers, such as Māori scholar Maria Bargh (2007), Anishinaabe theorist Leanne Simpson (2011), and Cree political scientist Kiera Ladner (2010), articulate the various political, social, and economic components of Indigenous life that need protection, including language, ceremonial and spiritual practices, philosophies, economies, dances, and artistic expression. As Bargh notes, because of the "active difference" of these cultural ways, they "challenge the neoliberal form of world construction and force the neoliberal construction to negotiate a way around it." The failure or outright refusal of liberal states to recognize and accommodate Indigenous difference thus causes a particular type of discrimination and creates a form of assimilationist violence.

Diplomacy. Australian/Canadian political scientist Ravi de Costa (2009) finds that both past and present Indigenous diplomacies are rooted in Indigenous cosmologies. Canadian political scientist J. Marshall Beier (2009) also finds that the diplomatic practices of Indigenous peoples in the contemporary period are not necessarily meaningful only in relation to states but are "meaningful in themselves." Like de Costa, Beier argues that Indigenous peoples' non-state-centric diplomatic practices pre-date European colonialism and hegemony. He finds that Indigenous diplomacy is based on a visceral connection to land and by cultural and social collective rights claims, all of which exist in opposition to state policies, and is also "irreconcilable with ... inherent (state) logics."

Anaya (2004) emphasizes the centrality of mutually respectful negotiations to Indigenous societies, which also hearkens back to the treaty relationships generally entered into by colonial powers and Indigenous nations. Anaya shows how Indigenous peoples' expectations for negotiated, nation-to-nation agreements is now impacting Indigenous–state relations.

Westphalian Sovereignty. The USA is one of a handful of states that recognize a form of "sovereignty" for Indigenous nations, yet as Lumbee political scientist David Wilkins (1997) demonstrates, this is a weakened form of sovereignty and is couched within the wider system of state sovereignty, including a colonial legal system.[9] Wilkins notes that on the one hand federal Indian law in the USA does recognize some measure of Indigenous nations' inherent sovereignty, but on the other hand it limits that sovereignty through various legal doctrines, including "domestic dependent nation" and "plenary power." In fact, as Alfred (2005) argues, sovereignty itself is a foreign and colonial concept for Indigenous peoples, grounded in the European experience, and rooted in notions of dominion that stand in stark contrast to Indigenous forms of political relations, which are based on freedom, respect, and autonomy. Alfred further argues, "the reification of sovereignty in politics today is the result of a triumph of a particular set of ideas over others – no more natural to the world that any other man-made object." Law professor Antony Anghie, in his book *Imperialism, Sovereignty, and the Making of International Law* (2005), likewise finds that there is no inherent logic to sovereignty as it is merely a social construction, with an original imperial agenda that can and should be questioned. Canadian political ecologist Karena Shaw, in her book *Indigeneity and Political Theory: Sovereignty and the Limits of the Political* (2008), builds on this argument, noting:

> [W]hat is new now is that the sovereignty story may no longer be adequate or appropriate, if indeed it ever was.... Perhaps the sovereign state, or indeed sovereignty itself, is either on its last legs or in the process of fundamental transformations.

She finds that Indigenous peoples are at the forefront of this transformation because they stand in opposition to "the modern," and so sovereignty in the "modern" sense does not offer them a resolution to their oppression, which is most often delivered by the state.

Tracing back to the intellectual tradition of Vine Deloria, Jr. (1974[1985]), who argued that the inherent right of self-determination, unbounded by state law and institutions, is a preferable starting point for asserting Indigenous nationhood, political theorist Kevin Bruyneel (2007) finds that Indigenous actors in the USA fight for a "third space of sovereignty." In this third space, Indigenous actors operate neither fully inside nor outside of state structures. This distinguishes this third space from both assimilation and secession, and thus offers "a location of Indigenous postcolonial autonomy that refuses the choices set out by colonial society." Likewise, Audra Simpson (2014) sees the potential for new and better state forms, arguing that various sovereign political orders can be nestled within and between states, although she readily recognizes that such an undertaking will involve significant change and problem solving by both Indigenous and non-Indigenous decision makers.

English School theorist Paul Keal (2003), in one of the few book-length treatments of Indigenous peoples in international relations, and political theorist Jonathan Havercroft (2008) advocate for the international recognition of Indigenous peoples' self-determination in order to reconcile the moral illegitimacies in the current world order. Keal further argues that the concept of self-determination should be decoupled from the state in order for international society to redeem itself from its history of dispossession. Anaya (2009) agrees that self-determination has, to date, been understood to mean statehood, but says the two concepts no longer need to be wedded together; self-determination may take on multiple forms and achieved or advanced with or without independent statehood. Anaya notes that Indigenous peoples are particularly adept at advancing a dual meaning of self-determination: autonomy in governance *and* participatory engagement with the state. However, in the words of Alfred (2005), the real "challenge for indigenous peoples in building appropriate postcolonial governing systems is to disconnect the notion of sovereignty from its Western, legal roots and transform it." Alternatives provided by Indigenous perspectives, he writes, are encompassed in a "regime of respect" which stands in contrast to the presumed superiority of the state. Indigenous forms of political relations, Alfred argues, are based in respectful co-existence "by acknowledging the integrity and autonomy of the various constituent elements of the relationship." The imperative of respect, he writes, "precludes the need for homogenization" and thus promotes the potential for more peaceful relations.

Indigenous political thought thus calls for substantial and fundamental transformations in Indigenous–state relations, a revamp of UN decolonization practices that excluded them, the accommodation of Indigenous collective rights to culture, land and nationhood, acceptance of Indigenous diplomacies, and a shift in the construction of sovereignty itself. As Anaya (1996) articulates, Indigenous thought ultimately promotes unity among diversity and, as a post-colonial alternative, represents a more human-based foundation to political relations than the current Western liberal constructions of states and the international order. I take this argument even further: Indigenous political thought not only informs the future direction of Indigenous–state relations, but because the changes called for in the implementation of Indigenous rights are so substantive and strike at the fundamentals of the current international system, global Indigenous politics is subtly helping to lead the way to an entirely new global political order.

Transformations in the structure and practice of global politics

In order to discuss the transformative nature of global Indigenous politics, it is first necessary to touch upon the question of identity and scope, by specifically addressing questions of who are the world's Indigenous peoples and what brings them together in a unique form of transnational politics. According to data from the International Work Group for Indigenous Affairs (IWGIA), a Copenhagen-based international human rights organization for Indigenous peoples, there are more than 300 million Indigenous peoples in the world, representing approximately 6 percent of the world's population, stretching across six continents. There are more than 5000 distinct peoples living in seventy-two countries who are recognized by the IWGIA as "Indigenous" (International Work Group for Indigenous Affairs (IWGIA)).

A precise and objective definition of Indigenous peoples has been exceedingly difficult to achieve due to the vast diversity of Indigenous peoples in the world, including different historical experiences with colonialism. Furthermore, the question of Indigenous definition has proven to be a constant issue of contention in transnational Indigenous politics. Some Indigenous groups in UN fora have argued that a lack of a formal definition of Indigenous peoples could be used by governments to deny recognition of peoples as Indigenous, while many other Indigenous groups opposed such a definition on the grounds that governments have historically utilized such definitions in discriminatory and problematic ways. For the most part, Indigenous groups in various UN fora have insisted on the right of Indigenous peoples to define themselves and their membership while states have sought a more restrictive definition. After years of heated debate, the UN developed a working definition of Indigenous peoples, based on several prior definitions as well as the statements made by Indigenous representatives. This UN working definition centers on three primary elements: (1) a pre-colonial presence in a particular territory; (2) a continuous cultural, linguistic, and/or social distinctiveness from the surrounding population; and (3) a self-identification as "Indigenous" and/or a recognition by other Indigenous groups as "Indigenous."

Together, these three elements not only comprise the UN's working definition, they also coalesce into a set of common colonial experiences shared by Indigenous peoples all over the world. These shared experiences distinguish Indigenous peoples from ethnic minority groups, and have formed the ways in which Indigenism has constituted itself on a global level (Niezen 2003). First, Indigenous peoples experience discrimination or marginalization. Indigenous peoples are often the poorest and least educated ethnic group in their host states, and the group with the lowest health status. Second, Indigenous peoples are also subjected to dispossession and assimilation as a result of colonialism. Dispossession is the separation of peoples from their ancestral territories through illegal or fraudulent means. Assimilative forces can vary from, at the high end, overt forced assimilation, as was the case in Canadian, American, Australian, and Saami residential/boarding-schools, to more subtle yet insidious pressures to assimilate into the surrounding society, as is often the case with Indigenous peoples in Africa or Asia who are pressured to move into urban centers and assimilate into mainstream cultures under the development paradigm. Linda Tuhiwai Smith (1999) notes that Indigenous identity itself helped create unity in an atmosphere of extreme diversity. The term "Indigenous peoples," she notes:

> has enabled the collective voices of colonized people to be expressed strategically in the international arena. It has also been an umbrella enabling communities and peoples to come together, transcending their own colonized contexts and experiences, in order to learn, share, plan, organize and struggle collectively for self-determination on the global and local stages.

Allison Brysk (2000) describes the Indigenous rights movement as being simultaneously global and local. I take her argument further. This is a global struggle to secure, both internationally and domestically, the right of individual Indigenous nations to exist as self-determining nations within or across the boundaries of existing nation-states.

The human rights regime that grew up after World War II was based exclusively on an individual rights understanding of human rights. As such, it already offered numerous protections to Indigenous peoples under the first experiential category mentioned above: discrimination. However, Indigenous peoples noted that even existing anti-discrimination standards did not adequately protect them. To be effective in Indigenous contexts, the standards needed to be drawn with greater specificity. It is the second experiential category, dispossession and assimilation, where Indigenous peoples had no human rights protection whatsoever under the existing individual-based human rights regime. This category is also where Indigenous peoples met their most continual and fierce resistance from states, indicated visually in Figure 1.1 by the explosion graphic. Based on the collective Indigenous experiences of dispossession and assimilation, the transnational Indigenous rights movement sought a second set of rights, collective rights, to combat these elements of Indigenous colonization. It is the implementation of these rights that will ultimately create fundamental change in both the structure and practice of global politics, which Tully (2000) describes as "a struggle within the structure of domination … with the aim of modifying it in the short term and transforming it from within in the long term." Thus, global Indigenous politics not only seeks the inclusion of Indigenous rights within the existing body of human rights but, in addition, seeks a set of rights that, if implemented, would ultimately bring legal, political, social, and cultural change to the entire international system.

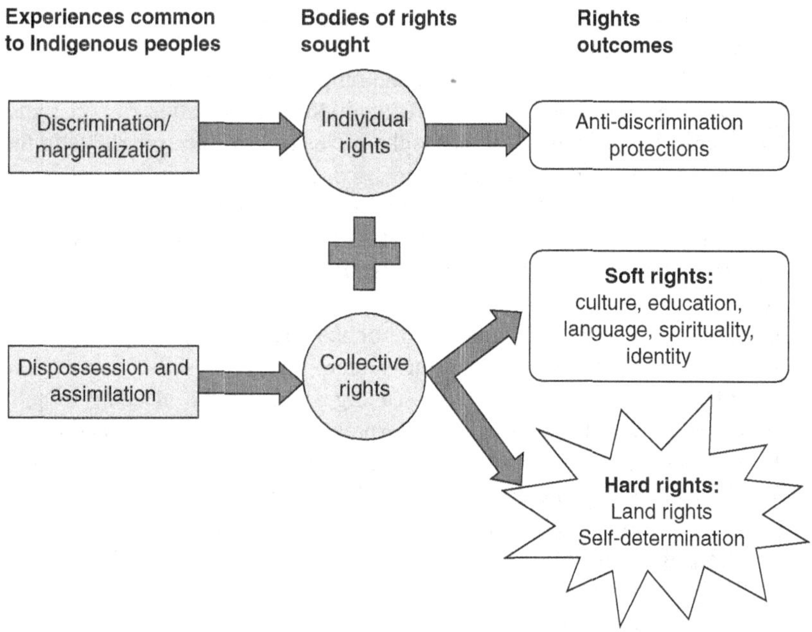

Figure 1.1 Indigenous rights forging changes in human rights.

Prior to the passage of the Declaration in 2007, international human rights law and discourse excluded two elements that are most critical to Indigenous peoples. First, the international human rights regime did not include collective rights to maintain such characteristics as culture, language, religion, identity, or their own educational systems in the face of assimilative pressures. These rights, which I will call "soft rights," are indicated visually in Figure 1.1 by a box with rounded corners. Second, Indigenous peoples' self-determination and their collective right to maintain their lands were specifically excluded from the post-World War II UN decolonization regime by the "salt water" thesis. These were the "hard rights" that states, especially settler colonial states, resist most fiercely. The UN decolonization era's interpretation of self-determination meant independent statehood; the Indigenous rights movement aimed to secure self-determination and land rights for Indigenous nations, with or without statehood. A shift from the former to the latter interpretation ultimately requires a global rethinking of how self-determination and land rights can be successfully decoupled from territorial sovereignty.

In reinterpreting the concept of self-determination, we can better understand state responses to various rights by dividing them into categories of "hard" and "soft" rights. Hard rights strike at certain important fundamentals of the existing international system of states: land, territory, sovereignty, and self-determination. Because Indigenous groups have presented and pushed for certain re-articulations of these concepts, they are termed "hard" rights in order to indicate both difficulty in negotiation but also to expose their perceived threat to the "hard core" of the international system; that is, state territorial sovereignty. "Soft" rights, such as rights to culture, language, education, and religion, are collective rights extensions of existing human rights. While recognition and protection of soft rights involves some change to thinking about the inclusion of collective rights in the international human rights consensus and the complementarity of collective rights to individual rights, the changes required by states and the UN system to secure these rights are not as fundamental as the changes brought forward by hard rights and thus the majority of states accepted soft rights much more readily.

Global Indigenous politics exerts a particular pressure on the international system to accept a new, non-state-centric interpretation of self-determination. Global Indigenous politics is therefore leading a shift in the meaning of self-determination so that it may also be "interpreted as the right of ... peoples to negotiate freely their political status and representation in the states in which they live" (Daes 1993). The quest for rights launched by the transnational Indigenous rights movement ignited a thirty-year battle with states, largely over land and self-determination. While the Indigenous rights movement also demanded a shift in the international consensus on human rights to include collective rights, it was the quest for recognition of land rights and self-determination that proved the most threatening to states and the international system, since they were reshaping the existing meanings of state sovereignty, self-determination, and territoriality.

Global Indigenous politics as a transformational norm vector

The earliest norms literature aimed to show that ideational factors do matter in international politics and these early norms scholars sought to elaborate the mechanisms and processes through which norms influence state behavior (Klotz 1995; Katzenstein 1996). Norms, which are conventions about what behavior is appropriate for actors with a certain identity, have been examined in multiple ways. The first studies which examined the structure of norms, aiming to counter dominant rationalist understandings of strategic, self-interested international behavior, show that "norms matter" (Adler 1997; Kratochwil 1989; Katzenstein 1996; March and Olsen 1998) and demonstrate that states often act in ways that follow a logic of appropriateness (Wendt 1999), based on inter-subjectively shared norms (Risse 2003; Rues-Smit 1997), rather than maximizing their individual benefit. Norms were argued to be constitutive, shaping the interests and identities of state actors (Kowert and Legro 1996; Checkel 1998), yet also regulative and as limiting the range of legitimate action (Barkin and Cronin 1994). Substantial research has been conducted on norm emergence, diffusion, and change (Finnemore and Sikkink 2001), including the "boomerang effect" of transnational advocacy network campaigns on state behavior (Keck and Sikkink 1998), the "spiral model" of human rights norm socialization (Risse et al. 1999), and the study of scope conditions impacting a move from commitment to compliance (Risse et al. 2013). Other studies have examined the reasons why norms emerge and diffuse – for example, Richard Price's (1997) study on the global chemical weapons taboo – or the reasons that they do not, as Charli Carpenter (2007) finds in her study on children born of wartime rape. Later work by Price (2008) moves beyond explanatory agendas to consider ethical dimensions, or the moral limits and possibilities of normative change. More recent studies examine the impact of international norms on domestic law and institutions (Simmons 2009; Sikkink 2011). Others focus on legitimacy in norm production (Brunnée and Toope 2010). Numerous critical scholars have examined the nature of power, structures of domination/subordination, difference and exclusion in international relations through various feminist, post-colonial, post-structuralist and non-Western lenses,[10] although the number of critical scholars who have explicitly studied norms is small.

By examining cross-temporal and cross-national policy changes in women's rights, Ann Towns (2010) argues that norms do not serve to "homogenize states" but rather, norms themselves serve to "rank and set up relations of hierarchy among states," and these very relations of hierarchy can be drivers of normative change by states, since change may occur in either high- or low-ranking states. She finds that normative change tends to occur in clusters of states, and "social hierarchies shape how policies are understood, advocated for and legitimated."

Roxanne Doty (1996) argues that global North–South power relations, or "imperial encounters," result in the denial of "effective agency" to the global South through a process of negation, or "blank spaces waiting to be filled in by Western writing" in the form of such things as "civilization, progress, modernization, and democracy." As she deftly points out, imperial missions are often just as motivated by a civilizing impulse, or the desire to save non-Western people from themselves, as they are by mere conquest over territory. Due to North–South power relations, the North was able to construct "reality" – meaning norms – in a way that created difference and enabled practices of domination and subordination. On the other hand, Amitav Acharya (2014) directly challenges the argument that norms are strictly a global North–South practice. He writes:

> I have been especially uncomfortable with the … tendency to privilege the moral cosmopolitanism of Western transnational actors in explaining norm diffusion in world politics. It is as if all the big ideas come from the West, transmitted mainly by Western transnational movement, with the non-western actors as passive recipients.

Acharya offers examples of norm contestation and variance, including the concept of "norm subsidiarity" that concerns how local actors in the Third World create rules to preserve their autonomy in the face of potential domination by more powerful state and regional actors. In other words, some norms are created and propagated in the global South.

The norms literature, to date, is therefore primarily focused on analyses concerning norm emergence, diffusion, state behavior, and socialization. This literature interrogates norms and behavior within a set space, a particular norm plane as it were, that relies on two important and implicit assumptions. First, Westphalian sovereignty and the state framework are presumed not only to exist, but to define the limits of, and the space of operations for, norms. With few exceptions, norm scholarship does not typically consider antecedents, or the genesis, of the Westphalian system; nor what form(s) of political organization or global political order will eventually succeed it. Second, existing norm scholarship, especially the predominant explanatory literature, presumes that the norms being studied already exist somewhere. For example, in the "boomerang model" of transnational advocacy networks described by Keck and Sikkink (1998), third parties, including non-governmental organizations (NGOs), international organizations (IOs), and at least one State B, utilize pressure and shaming strategies to encourage a behaviorial change in target State A to encourage it to align its behavior with existing norms. Presumably, State B already recognizes and practices the norm(s) in question. Further, the "spiral model" of human rights change and norm socialization presented by Risse et al. in 1999, and reconsidered in 2013, integrates the boomerang model into more dynamic processes. This "dynamic model" presumes "the prior existence of international institutions which regulate human rights norms" as well as the prior existence of the norms themselves. In addition, states are divided into two categories: "repressive states" and "Western powers" which are positioned as part of the "global human rights polity" along with international organizations and human rights organizations. The "spiral model" identifies the phases and mechanisms by which norms become adapted by "repressive states."

These models can account for some aspects of global Indigenous politics, as one objective of the Indigenous rights movement has been to provide specificity within existing individual rights regimes for Indigenous peoples' issues. However, these models cannot account for the second, more complicated and problematic category of Indigenous rights norms: collective rights, and particularly land rights, and self-determination. First of all, these Indigenous rights norms do not yet fully exist in any state, so there is no State B where Indigenous rights are concerned. Further, Western powers are just as repressive in Indigenous rights as other states and cannot therefore be part of the enforcing and enabling "global human rights polity" described by Risse et al. (1999). Finally, the second category of Indigenous rights concerns rights that are deliberately intended to reshape and reformulate the way in which states and Indigenous peoples relate to one another in such a way that the old, state-centric, hierarchical international order that created and enabled colonization is delegitimized and reshaped in favor of a new imagining of global political order.

The norms literature has not yet considered the possibility of such a fundamental transformative shift away from the state-centric norm space – or norm plane A – to a new norm space – norm plane B. Such a shift would represent an entirely new form and means of global politics and political organization – effectively a *post-colonial completion project* of the remnant colonial structures and practices of norm plane A, the current international system. I argue that the nature of global Indigenous rights and politics is dual, operating on the one hand within the existing international order or norm plane A, but, on the other hand, also serving as a transformational norm vector, helping to move global politics from one norm plane to another. The second category of more difficult and problematic Indigenous rights norms and the new ways of doing global politics presented by global Indigenous politics together present challenges to the existing international order that are so fundamental that it begins to break through the constraints of norm plane A, reaching toward a potential future world order of norm plane B (see Figure 1.2).

In addition to specifying protections for Indigenous peoples against discrimination, meaning the emergence, diffusion, and socialization of states into this set of human rights norms, Indigenous global politics seeks a number of radical changes to the structure of the state, the UN's decolonization project, liberal human rights, diplomacy, and the nature of sovereignty itself.

First, Indigenous global politics seeks the inclusion of a broad set of collective rights within the human rights regime, alongside individual rights, for the first time in history. Kulchyski (2013) expresses concerns that universalizing and individualist human rights on the one hand and collective Indigenous rights on the other are fundamentally in conflict, and that human rights may be used as a tool to combat the implementation of Indigenous rights. However, global Indigenous rights are actually trying to create a future where both can exist without disrupting one another. Rhiannon Morgan (2011) has described this line of thinking as a radical "bridging of a paradigmatic gulf" between individual and collective rights. From its earliest beginnings, the Indigenous rights movement has asserted that an exclusively individual rights-focused conception of human rights was insufficient to protect Indigenous peoples. Indigenous peoples also

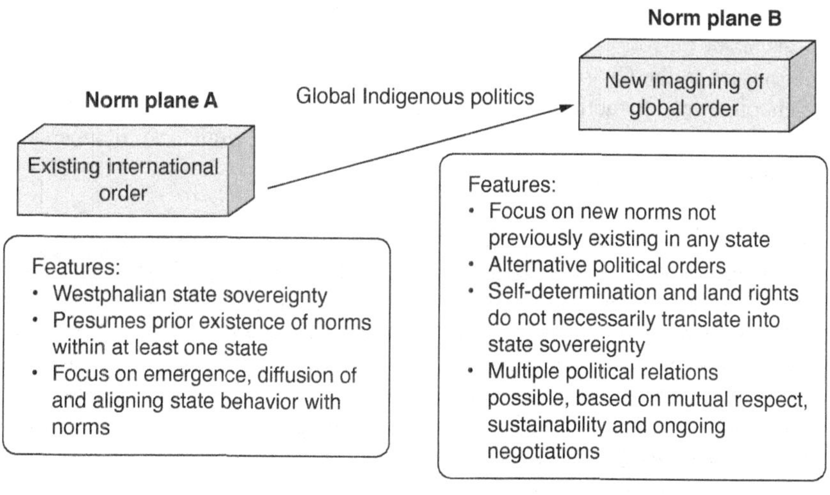

Figure 1.2 Global Indigenous politics as a transformational norm vector.

needed protections as collectives, to protect their cultures, societies, and existence as distinct peoples. The UK and the USA, along with other nations like Australia, New Zealand, and Japan, have all expressed long-standing disquiet about incompatibility between collective rights and individual human rights, concerned that collective rights protections compromise the ability to protect individual members of groups. Yet, the Declaration on the Rights of Indigenous Peoples includes a broad set of collective rights, and passage of the Declaration by an overwhelming majority of UN member states indicates a fundamental global shift in the human rights regime toward the acceptance of collective rights, although how collective rights will be protected alongside and without disrupting individual rights is not yet entirely clear. The last holdout on collective rights was the USA, which, as will be described in Chapter 4, eventually switched its position on the Declaration and reversed its long-held opposition to collective rights. USA support for collective rights means that a global consensus has truly emerged and represents a fundamental normative shift in a new and as yet not fully defined direction.

Second, understandings of decolonization and self-determination have also fundamentally shifted with the passage of the Declaration toward new future constructions. Old colonial doctrines, such as the Doctrine of Discovery, plenary power, and *terra nullius*, have all been delegitimized, Indigenous peoples' exclusion from the UN decolonization project has been corrected, and Indigenous peoples are officially now included as agents of decolonization, since Indigenous peoples are now specified as enjoying the rights of self-determination equal to all other peoples. However, the terms and meaning of decolonization are not as clear as they were in the 1960s era of UN decolonization, since decolonization for Indigenous peoples will not be as independent sovereign states, as Article 46 of the Declaration states:

> Nothing in this declaration may be interpreted as implying for any State, group or person any right to engage in any activity or to perform any act contrary to the Charter of the United Nations or construed as authorizing or encouraging any action which would dismember or impair, totally or in part, the territorial integrity or political unity of sovereign and independent States.

The new challenge, therefore, is to imagine and create means of Indigenous self-determination that do not revolve around or rely on state structures. This necessarily involves a decoupling of sovereignty from self-determination, which will eventually impact not only Indigenous peoples, but also all peoples. The wider implication is that self-determination can now mean something other than independent, territorial, sovereign statehood, although the formidable challenge is to create a new meaning that does not result in a diminished, second-class form of self-determination for Indigenous peoples. The meanings of both self-determination and decolonization are therefore evolving on the global level and Indigenous rights have an important role to play in the global conversation surrounding that evolution. Due to the intervention of global Indigenous politics, a future imagining of self-determination will likely involve sovereignties that may be plural and multiple, and political relations that are grounded in mutual respect and ongoing negotiated power relations.

Third, Indigenous global politics demonstrates that new forms of political relations are possible on the global level. Indigenous global diplomacies have shown that transnational relations can successfully conform to Indigenous ontologies of mutual respect, consensus decision-making, non-hierarchical relations, sustainability, and ongoing negotiations. In other words, these "new" and alternative forms of political practice are actually rooted in very old forms of Indigenous political relations.

This cluster of changes in both the structure and practice of global politics is fundamental enough that Indigenous global politics may be argued to serve as a transformational norm vector; a subtle revolution in global politics. For, if implemented, Indigenous rights involve significant global change not only for Indigenous peoples but change that would alter IR not only in theory, but in practice. These changes could point the way toward a future beyond the current Westphalian international system, the liberal construction of human rights, and state-centric conceptions of diplomacy.

While IR theory has largely been blind to the subtle revolution posed by global Indigenous politics, states, and especially settler colonial states, have detected it, are threatened by it, and have engaged in particular patterns of resistance that are complex and often cunning. States frequently engage in a varied and often internally contradictory range of maneuvers and contortions in order to avoid committing to or implementing Indigenous rights. Revealing these behaviors provides enhanced evidence for the degree of fundamental change that global Indigenous politics ultimately demands. States are fiercely defending the status quo.

Structure of the book

The book is divided into two parts. Part I, "The subtle revolution: Indigenous rights and politics," explores the changes that global Indigenous politics are forging, both in international relations theory and on the ground. Chapter 2 examines how Indigenous rights create structural change. I employ an original historical analysis to demonstrate that the Declaration process took more than thirty years and was so difficult because global Indigenous politics was more than a typical transnational rights movement: by constituting itself in terms of land and self-determination rights, global Indigenous politics represents a real and direct threat to both the existing international system of sovereign states and the contemporary liberal world order.

Chapter 3 explores how the practice of global Indigenous politics forges change. The Indigenous rights movement is grounded in a particular set of transnational Indigenous ways of being that encapsulate shared values and diplomatic traditions of Indigenous peoples worldwide. Global Indigenous politics demonstrates, in both its mission and method, that diplomacy can be successfully conducted in ways that reflect Indigenous values such as equality, dignity, mutually respectful relationships, effective conflict resolution, and consensual decision making.

Part II shifts to an examination and analysis of "State resistance to the subtle revolution of global Indigenous politics." Chapter 4 introduces the concept of "selective endorsement" and argues that by endorsing the Indigenous rights declaration with important qualifications and exclusions, the CANZUS (Canada, Australia, New Zealand, USA) settler colonial states are actually engaging in a nuanced pattern of resistance to the changes being forged by global Indigenous politics.

Chapter 5 examines state compliance with Indigenous rights norms. Through a dataset that demonstrates various types of state compliance behavior, including compliance, partial compliance, under-compliance and non-compliance, I introduce a new concept that I call "over-compliance." This refers to a puzzling pattern of state response that has not yet been explored in international relations or in compliance theory. Over-compliance means that a state's *behavior* counter-intuitively exceeds its *commitments*.

Chapters 6 and 7 aim to explain how and why states might over-comply with Indigenous rights through comparative case studies of Indigenous rights over-compliance in two countries: New Zealand and Canada. Through field research in North America and New Zealand I have identified several mechanisms that create conditions of Indigenous rights "over-compliance" in these states. The conditions are: (1) highly vocal domestic Indigenous movements that are connected to and invoke the principles of global Indigenous politics; (2) a country's concern for its human rights reputation and identity within the international community; and (3) a search for national identity that is shifting to define itself in terms of liberal multiculturalism. These three conditions have propelled these countries toward reconciliation efforts with Indigenous peoples, but these efforts remain firmly rooted in colonial, rather than post-colonial, ideology and thought processes. Therefore, these countries are over-compliant in Indigenous rights not because they are necessarily progressive in Indigenous rights but because they are actually *resisting* the emerging Indigenous rights discourse in favor of the status quo.

Chapter 8 concludes that global Indigenous politics is pushing the international community in a new direction, toward a vision of self-determination, territoriality, and sovereignty that appears to be a new vision of the post-colonial. This new vision moves beyond colonial models and even beyond the state-based models of post-colonialism dominant during the UN decolonization project. Global Indigenous politics is essentially pushing the international system toward *post-colonial completion*, a new vision of what the post-colonial can and should mean. Over-compliant states are actively resisting this shift by attempting to remain firmly rooted in colonial discourses and practices, both domestically and in the international system. Chapter 8 will also explore some of the theoretical and practical implications of global Indigenous politics.

Research methodology

I integrate international relations theory, Indigenous political and legal theory, historical documentary analysis, qualitative case studies in comparative perspective, and Indigenous methodologies in order to investigate the international change brought about by global Indigenous politics, as well as state resistance to such change.

As an Anishinaabe researcher engaged in an emancipatory project involving Indigenous subjects, Indigenous methodology is therefore not only appropriate, but also necessary.[11] The post-positivist turn in political science, and especially in international relations research, has opened up a space for the insertion of Indigenous perspectives (Smith 2005). Integration of these various methodologies in practice means that "we can begin with all the maps of qualitative research we currently have, then draw some new maps that enrich and extend the boundaries of our understandings beyond the margins. We need to draw on all our maps of understanding" (Smith 2005). One of the "maps" that I bring to this project is my experience in Indigenous nations and urban communities, including almost fifteen years of experience working in various volunteer and contract capacities for a number of community-based organizations in the American-Indian community of Minneapolis-St. Paul and more than a decade in a leadership position of an American Indian non-profit research institute that specialized in community-based and Indigenous-driven research.[12] This project thus fuses qualitative international relations research with Indigenous community-based participatory research methods and perspectives.

First, in the spirit of critical constructivism and other critical theories, the goal of this research is to understand the constitutive processes and relations of power of both global Indigenous politics and state resistance. This is therefore a hypothesis-generating study, and so a case study methodology is employed in an exploratory mode rather than a confirmatory/disconfirmatory mode (Bennett 2004; Gerring 2007; Levy 2008).

Second, the universe of cases is small. The transnational Indigenous rights movement is a singular case and, as Chapter 5 will uncover, the universe of countries that exhibit a particular form of resistance called over-compliance is only four, and these four cases deviate substantially from what is expected in extant compliance theory. Because of this small universe, I selected cases in adherence with Mill's method of agreement so that common conditions are located between two cases with the same outcome (Bositis 1990). In other words, I examined the universe of four cases of over-compliance (New Zealand, Australia, the USA, and Canada) and then selected two cases for this study that were most comparable in background variables to achieve as much control as possible (Lijphart 2006). New Zealand and Canada are both treaty-based settler countries in terms of Indigenous–state relations, and both countries have also initiated treaty settlement processes in recent decades.[13] Both countries also find themselves in the "younger, smaller sibling" position to a larger and more powerful English-speaking neighbor. Canada and New Zealand also both assert themselves as world leaders in human rights, so there are many background variables in these two cases that are similar.

Third, the use of qualitative case studies, including fieldwork, is consistent with Indigenous methodologies. The aim here is to integrate Indigenous perspectives into the study of the transnational Indigenous rights movement and into the patterns of state responses to those changes which the Indigenous rights movement is forging in the international order. Experts in Indigenous methodologies advocate qualitative approaches for the study of Indigenous communities because these approaches offer tools that not only insert Indigenous perspectives and alternate storylines into international relations but also decolonize spaces as well as spaces for "dialogue across difference" (Smith 2005) and help understand shifting identities, experiences, and realities.[14] By using Indigenous methodologies, I also aim to keep academic research relevant to the lives of Indigenous peoples and communities, following the path set forth by Vine Deloria (1988 [1969]), who was one of the first to call for academic research in Indigenous contexts to seek not just "knowledge for knowledge's sake" but rather to produce outcomes that are relevant and useful to Indigenous communities.[15]

Notes

1 This narrative of the adoption of the Declaration on the Rights of Indigenous Peoples by the United Nations General Assembly has been compiled from a number of interviews and private conversations with Indigenous delegates who were present at the UN General Assembly on September 13, 2007. I have also relied on draft footage prepared for a documentary film on the Declaration by Rebecca Sommer of Sommer Films.

2 Capitalization or non-capitalization of the term "Indigenous" is an issue that is far from resolved. I prefer to capitalize; however, when the term appears in a quotation, capitalization will conform to the original text.

3 Following the passage of the United Nations Declaration on the Rights of Indigenous Peoples in 2007, a rather unappealing and uncomplimentary acronym, UNDRIP, came into common and scholarly usage. The Indigenous activists who worked on this document for many years do not tend to refer to it as "UNDRIP," and I have even been told that they were quite shocked and somewhat dismayed when this acronym became popular. They always referred to the document as "the Declaration" or "the draft Declaration" while it was in draft form. Out of respect for them and for their many years of struggle, I prefer to utilize their terminology and refer to the document primarily as "the Declaration" or "the Indigenous rights declaration" throughout this text, although I do use the acronym on occasion.

4 The Westphalian system of independent, territorial sovereign states is the norm in international relations (IR) and is one of the central assumptions in all mainstream IR theories. The current international system emanates from the European state system conventionally associated with the Treaty of Westphalia that ended the Thirty Years' War in Europe in 1648. This theory of state sovereignty actually pre-dates the Treaty of Westphalia and so the significance of the 1648 Treaty is more symbolic than substantive.

5 For examples, see Ling (2002), Smith (2012), Khan (2012), Liu (2012), and Shadian (2014).

6 The case referred to here is *Johnson v McIntosh*, 21 U.S. (8 Wheat.) 543 (1823).

7 The case referred to here is the *City of Sherrill v Oneida Indian Nation of New York*, 544 U.S. 197 (2005).

8 The salt water, or blue water, thesis developed in opposition to efforts by some colonial powers (especially Belgium) to expand the scope of the UN Charter to include Indigenous populations. The thesis was placed into G.A. Res. 1541 in 1960. The resolution stated that decolonization was only required for "geographically separate" territories administered by a colonial authority.

9 Other nations, such as Mexico, Bolivia, and Panama, also have autonomous Indigenous areas.

10 See, e.g., Cox (1983), Ashley (1989), Enloe (1990), Mohanty et al. (1991), Tickner (1997), Muppidi (2004), Chowdhry and Nair (2002), Inayatullah and Blaney (2004), Barnett and Duvall (2005), Tickner and Waever (2009), and Acharya and Buzan (2010), with important intellectual forerunners including Said (1979), Fanon (1965, 1967), and Memmi (1965).

11 I am Anishinaabe (Ojibwe), an enrolled citizen of the Lake Superior Band, Keweenaw Bay Community, in what is now commonly known as northern Michigan. I have lived both on and off reservation, but grew up primarily in Minneapolis, the shared and sometimes contested traditional territory of the Anishinaabe and Dakota peoples, during the 1970s and 1980s, and remained active in the American Indian community in the Minneapolis-St. Paul area until I moved to the traditional, ancestral, and unceded territory of the Musqueam people, known commonly now as Vancouver, British Columbia, in 2009.

12 American Indian Policy Center, St. Paul, MN.

13 Australia never signed a treaty with Indigenous peoples, but settled the country strictly on the basis of *terra nullius*, or "empty land."

14 For example, Smith (1999, 2005), Smith (2000), Rigney (1999), Cram (2001), and Bishop (2005).

15 I must acknowledge a set of issues and dilemmas present in this research project. There was a set of clear advantages and privileges I brought to this research project based on my identity and my professional background working in the American Indian community. I had access to meetings and situations that I may not have enjoyed as a non-Indigenous person or solely as an academic. I had personal and professional connections that helped open doors for me. I also possess a set of cultural knowledge, including how to act in certain situations, ethics, and protocols, and the unstated meanings behind particular statements and actions. However, while this set of advantages is substantial in a research project of this kind, I must emphasize that each one of these advantages has an associated set of disadvantages and dilemmas that I also had to work through.

First of all, my presence and participation in meetings presented dilemmas. While I was able to gain access to meetings as a representative of an Indigenous organization, I always had to be clear about who I was and what my agenda was in these meetings. In the spirit of recognizing and acknowledging my biases as a researcher, I did not wish my presence at any of these meetings to disrupt or impede the process in any way, and so I often adopted a quiet and unobtrusive posture in my observations and participations. Such a posture can present a disadvantage in gathering data and seeking out potential interviewees. In addition, since a strong negative legacy is tied to research among Indigenous communities, the most researched people on the planet, participants were often unsure or even suspicious of me, and especially my motivations as an academic researcher. Even though I am Anishinaabe, an Indigenous person, in some instances I was still not able to overcome the legacy of intrusive research that was left behind by researchers that came before me. Finally, even though being Anishinaabe provided some degree of privileged access; it is also important to note that I came to these meetings with a certain set of biases, family histories, and kinship connections that rendered me simultaneously an insider and an outsider to the process, in a highly complex and always dynamic relationship.

Second, during the course of my fieldwork, meeting attendance, and interviewing, I was often provided with information that was confidential, and I was sometimes given information that was completely irrelevant to my research questions. I refer to this as the "gossip factor," and it occurred on more than one occasion, especially during long and detailed interviews and conversations. Broad issues of confidentiality were sometimes difficult to navigate, even outside of the ordinary risks of gossip. The circles in the transnational Indigenous rights movement are small, and it is often easy to identify interviewees by geographic location, date, or even by the interviewee's manner and style of speaking; however, many interviewees did not wish to be publicly identified. I have therefore sometimes been extremely vague in identifying the location and/or the date of an interview.

Fourth, and related to the issues of confidentiality, is that the topics examined in this project are inherently highly political, often controversial, and volatile. Many of these issues are deeply threatening to other actors, particularly to those invested in the dominant world order. In both Canada and New Zealand, outspoken Indigenous activism has been met in recent years by police action and attempted repression, and so issues of confidentiality are extremely salient.

Finally, and most importantly, I have felt the heavy burden of meeting both Indigenous and non-Indigenous criteria for research and performing to multiple levels of accountability: the academy, my home communities, and the larger Indigenous world.

In sum, my research process has attempted to strike a balance between effective qualitative political science research and Indigenous-driven, community-based research methods and procedures. While I make no particular claims about objectivity, I have tried to employ a multitude of methods in order to make my research as complete and informative as possible. My goal is to make simultaneous contributions to international relations theory, to the global political struggle for Indigenous peoples' rights, and, ultimately, to Indigenous communities.

References

Acharya, A., 2014. *The End of American World Order.* Cambridge: Polity Press.

Acharya, A. and Buzan, B., 2010. *Non-Western International Relations Theory: Perspectives on and Beyond Asia.* London; New York: Routledge.

Adler, E., 1997. Seizing the Middle Ground: Constructivism in World Politics. *European Journal of International Relations*, 3(3), pp. 319–363.

Alfred, G.R., 2005. *Wasáse: Indigenous Pathways of Action and Freedom.* Peterborough, Ont.: Broadview Press.

Alfred, G.R., 2009. *Peace, Power, Righteousness: An Indigenous Manifesto*, 2nd edn. Don Mills, Ont.: Oxford University Press.

Anaya, S.J., 1996. *Indigenous Peoples in International Law.* New York: Oxford University Press.

Anaya, S.J., 2004. *Indigenous Peoples in International Law*, 2nd edn. Oxford; New York: Oxford University Press.

Anaya, S.J., 2009. *International Human Rights and Indigenous Peoples.* New York: Aspen.

Anghie, A., 2005. *Imperialism, Sovereignty, and the Making of International Law.* Cambridge; New York: Cambridge University Press.

Anonymous, 9/13, 2007, last update. Indigenous World Celebrates Passage of UN Declaration on Indigenous Rights. Available at: http://bsnorrell.blogspot.ca/2007/09/indigenous-world-celebrates-passage-of.html [last accessed September 20, 2007]..

Ashley, R.K., 1989. Living on Border Lines: Man, Post-structuralism, and War. In J. DerDerian and M.J. Shapiro, eds, *International/Intertextual Relations.* Lexington, KY: Lexington Books, pp. 259–321.

Bargh, M., 2007. *Resistance: An Indigenous Response to Neoliberalism.* Wellington, NZ: Huia.

Barkin, J.S. and Cronin, B., 1994. The State and the Nation: Changing Norms and the Rules of Sovereignty in International Relations. *International Organization*, 48(1), pp. 107–130.

Barnett, M.N. and Duvall, R., 2005. *Power in Global Governance.* Cambridge; New York: Cambridge University Press.

Beier, J.M., 2005. *International Relations in Uncommon Places: Indigeneity, Cosmology, and the Limits of International Theory.* New York: Palgrave Macmillan.

Beier, J.M., ed., 2009. *Indigenous Diplomacies.* New York: Palgrave Macmillan.

Bennett, A., 2004. Case Study Methods: Design, Use and Comparative Advantages. In D.F. Sprinz and Y. Wolinsky-Nahmais, eds, *Methods, Numbers, and Cases: Methods for Studying International Relations.* Ann Arbor: University of Michigan Press, pp. 19–45.

Bishop, R., 2005. Freeing Ourselves from Neocolonial Domination in Research: A Kaupapa Maori Approach to Creating Knowledge. In N.K. Denzin and Y.S. Lincoln, eds, *The Sage Handbook of Qualitative Research.* Thousand Oaks, CA: Sage, pp. 109–138.

Bositis, D.A., 1990. *Research Designs for Political Science: Contrivance and Demonstration in Theory and Practice.* Carbondale: Southern Illinois University Press.

Brunnée, J. and Toope, S.J., 2010. *Legitimacy and Legality in International Law: An Interactional Account.* New York: Cambridge University Press.

Bruyneel, K., 2007. *The Third Space of Sovereignty: The Postcolonial Politics of U.S.–Indigenous Relations.* Minneapolis: University of Minnesota Press.

Brysk, A., 2000. *From Tribal Village to Global Village: Indian Rights and International Relations in Latin America.* Stanford, CA: Stanford University Press.

Cal v Attorney General of Belize (Claims No. 171 and 172 of 2007), October 18, 2007. Supreme Court, Belize.

Carmen, A., 2007. Interview by author. Transcript on file. Mille Lacs Nation, MN.

Carpenter, C., 2007. Studying Issue (Non-) Adoption in Transnational Networks. *International Organization*, 61(3), pp. 643–667.

Champagne, D., Torjesen, K.J., and Steiner, S., 2005. *Indigenous Peoples and the Modern State.* Walnut Creek, CA: AltaMira Press.

Chavez, F., 2007. Bolivia: Morales Gets Boost from UN Declaration on Indigenous Rights, September 19. Available at: http://ipsnews.net [last accessed November 30, 2015].

Checkel, J., 1998. The Constructivist Turn in International Relations Theory. *World Politics*, 50(1), pp. 324–348.

Chowdhry, G. and Nair, S., 2002. *Power, Postcolonialism and International Relations: Reading Race, Gender, and Class.* London; New York: Routledge.

Coulthard, G.S., 2014. *Red Skin, White Masks: Rejecting the Colonial Politics of Recognition.* Minneapolis, MN: University of Minnesota Press.

Cox, R.W., 1983. Gramsci, Hegemony and International Relations: An Essay in Method. *Millennium*, 12(2), pp. 162–175.

Cram, F., 2001. Rangahau, Maori: Tona Tika, Tona Pnon – The Validity and Integrity of Maori Research. In M. Tolich, ed., *Research Ethics and Aotearoa New Zealand.* Auckland, NZ: Longman, pp. 35–52.

Daes, E.A., 1993. Some Considerations on the Right of Indigenous Peoples to Self-determination. *Transnational Law and Contemporary Problems*, 3, pp. 1–12.

De Costa, R., 2009. Indigenous Diplomacies before the Nation-state. In J.M. Beier, ed., *Indigenous Diplomacies.* New York: Palgrave Macmillan, pp. 61–78.

Deloria, J., Vine, 1974 [1985]. *Behind the Trail of Broken Treaties: An Indian Declaration of Independence.* Austin: University of Texas Press.

Deloria, V., 1969 [1988]. *Custer Died for Your Sins: An Indian Manifesto.* Norman: University of Oklahoma Press.

Doty, R.L., 1996. *Imperial Encounters: The Politics of Representation in North–South Relations.* Minneapolis: University of Minnesota Press.

Enloe, C., 1990. *Bananas, Beaches and Bases: Making Feminist Sense of International Politics.* Oakland: University of California Press.

Fanon, F., 1965 [1963]. *The Wretched of the Earth.* New York: Grove Press.

Fanon, F., 1967. *Black Skin, White Masks.* New York: Grove Press.

Finnemore, M. and Sikkink, K., 2001. Taking Stock: The Constructivist Research Program in International Relations and Comparative Politics. *Annual Review of Political Science*, 4, pp. 391–416.

Gerring, J., 2007. *Case Study Research: Principles and Practices.* Cambridge; New York: Cambridge University Press.

Havercroft, J., 2008. Sovereignty, Recognition and Indigenous Peoples. In R.M. Price, ed., *Moral Limit and Possibility in World Politics.* Cambridge: Cambridge University Press, pp. 112–137.

Henderson, J.Y., 2008. *Indigenous Diplomacy and the Rights of Peoples: Achieving UN Recognition.* Saskatoon: Purich Publishers.

Inayatullah, N. and Blaney, D.L., 2004. *International Relations and the Problem of Difference.* New York: Routledge.

International Indian Treaty Council (IITC), 2007. Last update, Treaty Rights, Land Rights and Self-determination of Indigenous Peoples are recognized internationally with the adoption of the Declaration. Available at: www.treatycouncil.org [last accessed September 14, 2007].

International Work Group For Indigenous Affairs (IWGIA). Who are Indigenous Peoples? Available at: www.iwgia.org/culture-and-identity/identification-of-indigenous-peoples [last accessed October 14, 2008].

Jung, C., 2008. *The Moral Force of Indigenous Politics: Critical Liberalism and the Zapatistas.* Cambridge; New York: Cambridge University Press.

Katzenstein, P.J., 1996. *The Culture of National Security: Norms and Identity in World Politics.* New York: Columbia University Press.

Keal, P., 2003. *European Conquest and the Rights of Indigenous Peoples: The Moral Backwardness of International Society.* Cambridge; New York: Cambridge University Press.

Kearns, R., 2007. UN Declaration Becomes Law of the Land in Bolivia, December 12. *Indian Country Today.*

Keck, M.E. and Sikkink, K., 1998. *Activists Beyond Borders: Advocacy Networks in International Politics.* Ithaca, NY: Cornell University Press.

Khan, A., 2012. Social Science Research and Engagement in Pakistan. In A.B. Tickner and D.L. Blaney, eds, *Thinking International Relations Differently.* Abingdon, Oxon: Routledge, pp. 322–341.

Klotz, A., 1995. *Norms in International Relations: The Struggle Against Apartheid.* Ithaca, NY: Cornell University Press.

Kowert, P. and Legro, J., 1996. Norms, Identity, and their Limits: A Theoretical Reprise. In P.J. Katzenstein, ed., *The Culture of National Security: Norms and Identity in World Politics.* New York: Columbia University Press, pp. 451–497.

Kratochwil, F.V., 1989. *Rules, Norms, and Decisions on the Conditions of Practical and Legal Reasoning in International Relations and Domestic Affairs.* Cambridge; New York: Cambridge University Press.

Kulchyski, P.K., 2013. *Aboriginal Rights are not Human Rights: In Defence of Indigenous Struggles.* Winnipeg, Man.: ARP Books.

Kuokkanen, R., 2009. Achievements of Indigenous Self-determination: The Case of Sami Parliaments in Finland and Norway. In J.M. Beier, ed., *Indigenous Diplomacies.* New York: Palgrave Macmillan, pp. 97–114.

Ladner, K.L., 2010. From Little Things.... In L. Simpson and K.L. Ladner, eds, *This is an Honour Song: Twenty Years Since the Blockades.* Winnipeg, Man.: Arbeiter Ring, pp. 299–314.

Levy, J.S., 2008. Case Studies: Types, Designs, and the Logics of Inference. *Conflict Management and Peace Science*, 25, pp. 1–18.

Lijphart, A., 2006. The Comparable Cases Strategy in Comparative Research. In M. David, ed., *Case Study Research, Volume III.* London: Sage, pp. 156–170.

Ling, L.H.M., 2002. *Postcolonial International Relations: Conquest and Desire between Asia and the West.* New York: Palgrave.

Liu, Y., 2012. Security Theorizing in China: Culture, Evolution and Social Practice. In A.B. Tickner and D.L. Blaney, eds, *Thinking International Relations Differently.* Abingdon, Oxon: Routledge, pp. 72–91.

March, J.G. and Olsen, J.P., 1998. The Institutional Dynamics of International Political Orders. *International Organization*, 52(4), pp. 943–969.

Memmi, A., 1965. *The Colonizer and the Colonized.* New York: Orion Press.

Miller, R.J., 2006. *Native America, Discovered and Conquered: Thomas Jefferson, Lewis and Clark, and Manifest Destiny.* Westport, CT: Praeger Publishers.

Mohanty, C.T., Russo, A., and Torres, L., 1991. *Third World Women and the Politics of Feminism.* Bloomington: Indiana University Press.

Morgan, R., 2011. *Transforming Law and Institution: Indigenous Peoples, the United Nations and Human Rights.* Farnham, Surrey; Burlington, VT: Ashgate.

Muppidi, H., 2004. *The Politics of the Global.* Minneapolis: University of Minnesota Press.

Newcomb, S.T., 2008. *Pagans in the Promised Land.* Golden, CO: Fulcrum Publishing.

Niezen, R., 2003. *The Origins of Indigenism: Human Rights and the Politics of Identity.* Berkeley: University of California Press.

Petersen, K., 2008. Indigenous Rights and the Mayan Victory in Belize. *The Dominion*, January 23.

Price, R.M., 1997. *The Chemical Weapons Taboo.* Ithaca, NY: Cornell University Press.

Price, R.M., 2008. *Moral Limit and Possibility in World Politics.* Cambridge; New York: Cambridge University Press.

Rigney, L., 1999. Internationalization of an Indigenous Anticolonial Cultural Critique of Research Methodologies: A Guide to Indigenist Research Methodology and its Principles. *Wacazo Sa Review*, 14(2), pp. 109–121.

Risse, T., 2003. The Euro between National and European Identity. *Journal of European Public Policy*, 10(4), pp. 487–503.

Risse, T., ed., 2011. *Governance Without a State? Policies and Politics in Areas of Limited Statehood.* New York: Columbia University Press.

Risse-Kappen, T., Ropp, S.C., and Sikkink, K., 1999. *The Power of Human Rights: International Norms and Domestic Change.* Cambridge; New York: Cambridge University Press.

Risse-Kappen, T., Ropp, S.C., and Sikkink, K., 2013. *The Persistent Power of Human Rights: From Commitment to Compliance.* Cambridge: Cambridge University Press.

Rues-Smit, C., 1997. The Constitutional Structure of International Society and the Nature of Fundamental Institutions. *International Organization*, 51, pp. 555–589.

Said, E.W., 1979 [1978]. *Orientalism*, Vintage Books 1st edn. New York: Vintage Books.

Shadian, J., 2014. *The Politics of Arctic Sovereignty: Oil, Ice and Inuit Governance.* Abingdon, Oxon: Routledge.

Shaw, K., 2008. *Indigeneity and Political Theory: Sovereignty and the Limits of the Political.* London; New York: Routledge.

Sikkink, K., 2011. *The Justice Cascade: How Human Rights Prosecutions are Changing World Politics.* New York: Norton.

Simmons, B.A., 2009. *Mobilizing for Human Rights: International Law in Domestic Politics.* Cambridge; New York: Cambridge University Press.

Simpson, A., 2014. *Mohawk Interruptus: Political Life across the Borders of Settler States.* Durham, NC; London: Duke University Press.

Simpson, L., 2011. *Dancing on our Turtle's Back: Stories of Nishnaabeg Re-Creation, Resurgence and a New Emergence.* Winnipeg, Man.: Arbeiter Ring.

Smith, G.H., 2000. Protecting and Respecting Indigenous Knowledge. In M. Battiste, ed., *Reclaiming Indigenous Voice And Vision.* Vancouver, BC: UBC Press, pp. 209–224.

Smith, K., 2012. Contrived Boundaries, Kinship and Ubuntu: A (South) African View of "the International." In A.B. Tickner and D.L. Blaney, eds, *Thinking International Relations Differently.* Abingdon, Oxon: Routledge, pp. 301–321.

Smith, L.T., 1999. *Decolonizing Methodologies: Research and Indigenous Peoples.* London; New York: Zed Books.

Smith, L.T., 2005. On Tricky Ground: Researching the Native in the Age of Uncertainty. In N.K. Denzin And Y.S. Lincoln, eds, *The Sage Handbook of Qualitative Research*, 3rd edn. Thousand Oaks, CA: Sage, pp. 85–108.

Sommer, R., 2007. *Adoption of the Declaration on the Rights of Indigenous Peoples.* Sommer Films.

Suzuki, S., Zhang, Y., and Quirk, J., eds, 2014. *International Orders in the Early Modern World: Before the Rise of the West.* Abingdon, Oxon: Routledge.

Tauli-Corpuz, V., 2007. Press Release: Message of Victoria Tauli-Corpuz, Chairperson of the UN Permanent Forum on Indigenous Issues, on the Occasion of the Adoption by the General Assembly of the Declaration on the Rights of Indigenous Peoples, September 13. New York.

Tickner, A.B. and Blaney, D.L., eds, 2012. *Thinking International Relations Differently.* Abingdon, Oxon: Routledge.

Tickner, A.B. and Waever, O., eds, 2009. *International Relations Scholarship Around the World.* Abingdon, Oxon: Routledge.

Tickner, J.A., 1997. You Just Don't Understand. *International Studies Quarterly*, 41, pp. 611–632.

Towns, A.E., 2010. *Women and States: Norms and Hierarchies in International Society.* Cambridge; New York: Cambridge University Press.

Tully, J., 1995. *Strange Multiplicity: Constitutionalism in an Age of Diversity.* Cambridge; New York: Cambridge University Press.

Tully, J., 2000. The Struggles of Indigenous Peoples for and of Freedom. In D. Ivison, P. Patton, and W. Sanders, eds, *Political Theory and the Rights of Indigenous Peoples.* Cambridge: Cambridge University Press, pp. 36–59.

Turner, D.A., 2006. *This is Not a Peace Pipe: Towards a Critical Indigenous Philosophy.* Toronto, ON: University of Toronto Press.

United Nations General Assembly, 2007a. *Press Release: Adoption of Declaration on Rights of Indigenous Peoples: A Historic Moment for Human Rights, UN Expert Says, 14 September 2007.* New York.

United Nations General Assembly, 2007b. Press Release: General Assembly Adopts Declaration on Rights of Indigenous Peoples, September 13.

Wendt, A., 1999. *Social Theory of International Politics.* New York: Cambridge University Press.

Wilkins, D.E., 1997. *American Indian Sovereignty and the U.S. Supreme Court: The Masking of Justice.* Austin: University of Texas Press.

Wilmer, F., 1993. *The Indigenous Voice in World Politics.* Newbury Park, CA: Sage.

Wilmer, F., 2009. Where You Stand Depends on Where You Sit: Beginning an Indigenous–Settler Reconciliation Dialogue. In J.M. Beier, ed., *Indigenous Diplomacies.* New York: Palgrave Macmillan, pp. 187–206.

Part I

The subtle revolution

Indigenous rights and politics

2 The Declaration on the Rights of Indigenous Peoples

Forging structural change

Global Indigenous politics is not a typical human rights movement. Rather than simply engaging in shaming and pressure tactics to get states to conform to a body of rights, global Indigenous politics is more revolutionary, although the changes it is making have not been well noticed or documented in the field of international relations. In this chapter, I will argue that because Indigenous rights ultimately push for a set of fundamental changes in the international order, which can have long-term and extremely broad potential effects, the passage of the Declaration by the UN General Assembly was an important transformational moment in global politics.

The Indigenous rights movement has always, consciously, and purposefully, sought a set of wide shifts in the UN, the human rights system, and the international system itself. Some of these changes are small and align with the current nature of human rights and the international order, but some are much more significant in both theoretical and practical terms, and have the capacity to alter the entire structure of the international order. From its very inception, the Indigenous rights movement has aimed not only to specify human rights in the context of Indigenous peoples, but also to articulate a set of Indigenous rights that move beyond the state-centered, individual rights focus of human rights and the existing international system. The Indigenous rights regime that has been emerging on the global stage, as articulated in the UN Declaration, has added new Indigenous rights to the international human rights consensus. In addition, it also challenges fundamentals of the human rights system and the Westphalian system of sovereign states in two important dimensions. First, the Indigenous rights regime essentially calls on states to recognize and protect not only the rights of Indigenous peoples as individual citizens of states but also as peoples with a broad set of collective rights. Second, implementing these rights ultimately also forces a reinterpretation of the twin concepts of decolonization and self-determination. Indigenous rights shift the meaning of both of these ideas away from an exclusive state-centric construction. Rather than meaning only the right of peoples to independent, territorial, and sovereign statehood as had previously been the case under the UN's twentieth-century decolonization project, a new understanding of decolonizing self-determination is emerging. States are now expected to protect the land, self-determination, and collective rights of

Indigenous peoples, by imagining, negotiating, and recognizing various possible modes of plural sovereignty and power sharing. They are expected to do all this without disrupting states' territorial integrity.

State resistance to Indigenous rights has manifested in issues of definition, participation, and scope. In particular, there has been persistent state concern over self-determination. State opposition to the text of the Declaration itself has also taken on multiple forms. States unilaterally added Article 46 in the last few months before passage, with the aim of protecting state sovereignty and territorial integrity. There was also a last-minute, unannounced, and undetected language change in the text of Article 3 that solidified the legal status of Indigenous peoples' self-determination as "aspirational" rather than already inherently existing – a change that was so small that it even went largely unnoticed, even by the Indigenous Caucus.[1]

A number of scholars and activists have criticized the final text of the Declaration as flawed. Corntassel (2007) argues that the Indigenous rights movement was co-opted during its decades-long participation in the UN system. Watson and Venne (2012), and White Face/Wobaga (2013) all claim that the insertion of Article 46 protecting state sovereignty and territorial integrity undermines the intent and the potential outcomes of the Declaration. Venne (2011) criticizes the lack of enforcement mechanisms and the domestication of implementation efforts. Newcomb (2011) is concerned that the Declaration is not sufficient to undermine colonial doctrines. This chapter argues that while states have indisputably dominated and disrupted the emergence of Indigenous rights in multiple ways, in precisely the ways which these critics point out, the final draft of the Declaration actually does live up to the vast majority of its original intent, as articulated by the Indigenous rights movement in the 1970s. Further, despite ongoing protests and manipulations by especially CANZUS states, the Indigenous rights discourse came to exist by near-global consensus, as was the case with the first Universal Declaration of Human Rights in 1948, the foundational human rights document which likewise had no legal enforceability and was technically constrained by state sovereignty but has come to represent an important global consensus on human rights. However, also like the Universal Declaration, the Indigenous rights declaration, if deployed in a consistent, widespread, and creative manner, could potentially represent the earliest stages of a new way of thinking and doing politics, a new way of being in the world, a new imaging of global politics beyond the constraints of the state system and hierarchical relations of domination and subordination. This chapter's case study of the Declaration process, comprising documentary analysis coupled with interviews, demonstrates several important points about how the final text largely lives up to its original intent, and also represents several important global shifts.[2]

1 The Declaration was always intended to be a *set of guidelines for state implementation* of Indigenous rights, providing a framework for new Indigenous–state relationships grounded in mutual respect, not state domination.

2 The Declaration was always intended to be a *persuasive tool*, a set of international standards that would be utilized morally and politically in Indigenous rights struggles around the world and, like all human rights declarations, was never intended to be a legally enforceable or legally binding document.[3]

3 The Declaration was always seen as a document of *global consensus*, not just among UN member states as had been the case with all previous human rights declarations, but also including the active participation of Indigenous peoples in the consensus-building process.

4 Closely related to its consensual character, the Declaration was necessarily a *compromise* document. As is the case with all international negotiations and treaties, it is rare and generally undesirable for one party to achieve all of its objectives. International agreements, especially ones that take thirty years to negotiate, will end with a compromise text, and the Declaration has always been viewed as such by the Indigenous rights movement. As a compromise document ultimately accepted by both states and the Global Indigenous Caucus, Indigenous peoples' right to self-determination (Article 3) sits alongside the right of states to their sovereignty and territorial integrity (Article 46). The guiding framework of the Declaration therefore expects states to recognize, negotiate, and protect a variety of possible self-government or autonomy arrangements for Indigenous peoples, dealing with them as "peoples," even if not as states. At the same time, it expects Indigenous peoples to negotiate the same with states and not seek secession from or dismemberment of them.

Precursors and preparation: laying the groundwork (up until 1984)

The global Indigenous rights movement was formed in North America during the 1970s at the juncture of a number of domestic and international trends. Indigenous peoples' frustrations over the effects of long-term colonization intensified, resulting in Indigenous movements springing up simultaneously in a number of countries. Due to enhanced communication and transportation opportunities, these domestic Indigenous movements also began to link up transnationally in order to combat both the extreme marginalization of Indigenous peoples within individual nation-states *and also* to protest the current nature of Indigenous–state relations, as states had distanced themselves from the nation-to-nation, treaty-based relationships they had originally established with Indigenous peoples, at least in most of the English-speaking settler colonial world. All of this occurred in a global environment that was increasingly focused on human rights, anti-discrimination, and the decolonization of European empires, which all problematically overlooked or even actively excluded Indigenous peoples. By the mid-1970s in the USA, the militant wave of Indigenous activism that had sprung up in the late 1960s was waning, as most of the American Indian Movement leadership was either jailed or engaged in lengthy court proceedings following a series of direct actions and military-style conflicts. From these early days, the global Indigenous rights movement advanced the idea that Indigenous peoples were "peoples," equal to all others and with the same human rights that all others enjoy. But, in order to be truly equal to all other peoples, their inherent collective rights, as peoples, also had to be secured: most notably their rights to land and self-determination, including a return to nation-to-nation, negotiated political relationships with states.

Historically, there has always been recognition of Indigenous peoples as international actors, particularly by the UK and the majority of English-speaking settler states.[4] As Niezen (2003) writes, "the signing of treaties included a tacit or explicit acknowledgement that the original inhabitants of a territory were 'nations,' to be dealt with through existing mechanisms of international negotiation, conquest, and secession of land and sovereignty through treaties." The treaty-based, nation-to-nation formation of Indigenous–state relationships, became diluted in the mid- to late nineteenth century as power balances shifted, the military and economic power of settler colonial nations increased, and Indigenous populations dramatically declined, often due to diseases imported from Europe. Through most of the twentieth century, Indigenous peoples came to be viewed more as marginalized minority groups than as sovereign nations. During the 1920s, some Indigenous leaders, including Deskaheh of the Haudenosaunee and Māori leader Ratana, approached the League of Nations. Indigenous peoples in Canada and New Zealand were facing rampant treaty violations by those states, and these leaders sought to restore international recognition of their status as treaty-holding nations. However, the League of Nations turned them away and told them to return to their home countries and seek recourse through the domestic courts.

By the 1960s and 1970s, after decades of marginalization and non-recognition as peoples, Indigenous peoples around the world were intensely frustrated. As Vine Deloria wrote in 1974, "The pressure for international recognition has been building up for at least a generation among traditional Indians, and more recently has become intense among the activists." Nations of the Western hemisphere were beginning to consider what relationships should exist between Indigenous peoples and the settler colonial states. Indigenous peoples of the Western hemisphere also began talking to one another and sharing experiences, building a transnational network. Deloria wrote about Wallace "Mad Bear" Anderson, a Tuscarora merchant seaman who, in the mid-twentieth century, made substantial contacts among Indigenous peoples in Mexico and Central America. By the early 1960s, Indigenous peoples in North America were becoming increasingly aware of the situation of Indigenous peoples in Latin America. On both continents, Indigenous peoples became more vocal with their host governments and also increasingly spoke out about the atrocities of other governments. By the early 1970s, Indigenous peoples in the USA began to broadly recognize that the federal government had, for at least a century, neglected to respect its treaties with Indigenous nations. They began demanding that the United States recognize and protect their rights as sovereign treaty peoples. They also began conversing, and then linking with, other Indigenous movements in the Western hemisphere, thus shifting the struggle out of a uniquely domestic framework and into the international community.

The roots of the international Indigenous rights movement are firmly based in the "Red Power" movement of the 1970s. After a seventy-one-day military stand-off between the American-Indian Movement (AIM) activists, and federal officials at Wounded Knee, South Dakota in 1973,[5] a group of elders and traditional leaders in North America decided that seeking justice solely through domestic means was insufficient and ineffectual (Wilmer 1993). During the 1973 Wounded Knee occupation, some representatives from the White House went to Kyle, South Dakota, a small town on the Pine Ridge reservation, to meet with traditional leaders who situated their struggle squarely in terms of the 1868 Treaty and the failure of the USA to uphold its obligations. While the White House representatives agreed to hold periodic meetings in the near future to discuss treaty issues, the Watergate scandal soon erupted, and the Pine Ridge Lakota Treaty issues dropped off the radar. So, traditional leaders decided to hold their own conference to discuss how to restore the political status of their treaties (Deloria 1974 [1985]).

In 1974, a group of more than 5000 elders and traditional leaders representing ninety-eight Indigenous nations from nine countries gathered at Standing Rock Reservation in Lakota territory, what is now commonly known as South Dakota, USA. These elders and leaders decided to take their treaty issues to the international level, especially the UN, and so they officially founded the International Indian Treaty Council (IITC) as their organizational vehicle. With founders that included AIM members Russell Means (Lakota), Bill Means (Lakota), Vernon and Clyde Bellecourt (Anishinaabe), the IITC is sometimes known as the "diplomatic arm of AIM." Later in 1974, the IITC established an office in New York, right across the street from the United Nations. With a small staff headed by Jimmie Durham, the IITC set about its mission of linking Indigenous peoples together and presenting their issues, especially treaty issues, to the international community (Deloria 1974 [1985]).

Following the release of Canada's White Paper in 1969,[6] the Indigenous movement in Canada also ramped up its organizational efforts, led by George Manuel (Shuswap). Others involved included Alex Denny (Mi'kmaw), Oren Lyons (Haudenosaunee Confederacy), Ted Moses and Harold Cardinal (Cree), Marie Smallface Marule (Blackfoot Confederacy), and Dan George (Salish) (Henderson 2008). The first International Conference of Indigenous peoples in Canada convened at Port Alberni, BC in October, 1975 and created the World Council on Indigenous Peoples (WCIP) founded by North American, Scandinavian Saami, New Zealand Māori, and Australian aboriginal groups (Venne 2011). Like the IITC, the WCIP membership included traditional leaders, leaders of newly formed national and provincial organizations, and the first generation of Euro-centric educated Indigenous peoples who all began talking about "rights consciousness and diplomatic strategies" (Henderson 2008). These groups noticed that, in the post-colonial project, self-determination was increasingly viewed within the international community as a necessary and inalienable collective human right. Indigenous groups and leaders also detected a wide and broad international commitment to anti-discrimination. Logically, if self-determination was an inherent and inalienable human right of all peoples and could not be discriminately applied, then there was a fundamental logical and moral inconsistency in the way the United Nations and the international community recognized rights vis-à-vis Indigenous peoples. If all peoples had the right of self-determination, how could this right be denied to Indigenous peoples? Savvy Indigenous leaders decided to expose this inconsistency in international discourse and use it as moral and political leverage to assert themselves as peoples, with treaty rights and the inherent right to self-determination, equal to all other peoples on Earth (Henderson 2008).

Their timing was good. In 1966, the UN General Assembly had adopted the International Covenant on Civil and Political Rights (ICCPR) and the International Covenant on Economic, Social, and Cultural Rights (ICESCR), both of which clearly stated as Article 1 of each document: "all peoples have the right of self-determination" and "by virtue of that right they freely determine their political status and freely pursue their economic, social and cultural development." While the full scope of this set of rights remained unclear, what *was* clear was that the UN had made an important moral statement which Indigenous peoples were going to use as leverage.

There were only two means, however, to gain access to the UN: through official member state representation; or as a non-governmental organization, or NGO, with UN consultative status. Since Indigenous peoples' disputes were with state governments, Indigenous groups in both Canada and the USA began organizing themselves as NGOs in order to approach the United Nations. There is some dispute over which Indigenous organization first sought and/or gained UN consultative status as a non-governmental organization (NGO). The National Indian Brotherhood (forerunner of the current Assembly of First Nations), headed by George Manuel, received this status in May, 1974, which was later transferred to the WCIP, although the WCIP only gained observer status. The IITC also claims to have been the first Indigenous organization to receive UN consultative status, although it received this status in 1977. What is clear from the UN documentary record is that the IITC used its consultative status to get Indigenous peoples included in the first NGO Conference on Discrimination held in Geneva in September, 1977.

NGO Conference in Geneva, 1977

Indigenous politics at the United Nations was born at the International NGO Conference on Discrimination against Indigenous Populations in the Americas held in Geneva from September 20–23, 1977. It was at this conference that the framework for global Indigenous politics was laid, including how the global Indigenous rights movement would function, its founding principles, and its targets. The Conference, which at this point included only Indigenous groups from the Western hemisphere, was sponsored by the UN Sub-Committee on Racism, Racial Discrimination, Apartheid, and Decolonization of the Special Committee on Human Rights that was part of the Economic and Social Council (ECOSOC). Organizers were the International Indian Treaty Council, the American Indian Law Resource Center, and the World Peace Council. Over 100 Indigenous delegates attended, along with sixty NGOs and international organizations, and forty UN member states. Mohawk activist Kenneth Deer described the scene in Geneva when 250 Indigenous delegates arrived for the 1977 conference (2011):

> The presence of "Red Indians" caused a stir in Geneva and the UN itself, and there was talk that the Indigenous representatives might not be allowed into the building. Undeterred, they walked right through the gates in groups. UN staff watched from the windows as delegation after delegation in full regalia walked by their offices and entered the meeting room. These delegates were the ones that opened the doors of the UN to let other peoples follow.

One of the first items on the agenda was a discussion of how the existing international human rights standards, and the anti-discrimination frame, were insufficient for Indigenous peoples. State assimilation projects and the integration of Indigenous peoples into state legal systems were also highlighted early on as issues of discrimination. Indigenous peoples were also noted to be not only victims of specific acts of injustice but also victims of a dominant worldview. The report acknowledges: "it is the human right of all peoples to develop and transmit their own culture." The report also states that Indigenous peoples experience legal discrimination when they are forced to participate in legal structures and systems that are "detrimental to their interests" (International Indian Treaty Council (IITC) 1977).

Indigenous representatives wanted to discuss land, including the spiritual tie between Indigenous peoples and the land as well as their relationship to land that is more about duty and stewardship than about Western conceptions of dominion and ownership. Jose Mendoza Acosta, Representacion de Autoridad Pueblo Indigena de Panama (Representing Authority of Panama's Indigenous Peoples), addressed the states:

> Representatives of all nations of the world, remember one thing and do not forget it. We will not give up our territories. We are not going to abandon them. We are going to defend our territories through all possible means because that territory, recognized as a nation or not, has been ours and will continue to be ours.
>
> (International Indian Treaty Council (IITC) 1977)

The Conference Report notes that "the land question is fundamental to the attainment of the goals of the Indigenous peoples" (International Indian Treaty Council (IITC) 1977) and, as an Indigenous activist later stated in an interview,

"It's all about land. Everything else emanates from that" (Indigenous rights activist #4 2007). Furthermore, since, in many cases, Indigenous peoples prefer to own their land communally, that is a right which should be nationally and internationally protected.

Indigenous delegates from all regions also argued for self-determination and for their recognition as nations. The delegates demanded that states recognize Indigenous peoples and enter into meaningful negotiations, while both the Six Nations Confederacy and the Lakota Nation made their case for immediate recognition as nation-states under international law. UN member states raised two legal issues regarding self-determination. First, they claimed that Indigenous self-determination conflicts with the territorial integrity principle of the UN Charter and other international instruments. Second, they claimed that the international right of peoples to self-determination "has never been authoritatively defined" (International Indian Treaty Council (IITC) 1977). Thus, beginning at this first conference in 1977, states resisted Indigenous self-determination on the grounds of state territorial integrity and began to invoke definitional lines of argumentation.

During this conference, Indigenous peoples drafted a document that represented the broad consensus among Indigenous delegates from the Western hemisphere, the Draft Declaration of Principles for the Defense of the Indigenous Nations and Peoples of the Western Hemisphere. (This document, also referred to as the 1977 Declaration of Principles, is shown in Appendix 2.1.) The 1977 Declaration of Principles, which the Indigenous delegates wrote and presented to the state delegates, represented the first attempt to articulate an international rights standard for Indigenous peoples (International Indian Treaty Council (IITC) 1977). Several dominant themes are evident in this document. First, the exclusive individual rights focus of the international human rights system is inherently discriminatory against Indigenous peoples because it imposes conditions that deny or destroy Indigenous cultures. It emphasizes the need to include collective rights, such as culture, in the international consensus, alongside individual rights. Second, it explicitly calls for recognition of Indigenous nationhood and that even Indigenous groups which do not meet the international territorial, governmental, and populations requirements for statehood should still be recognized as subjects of international law, "provided they are identifiable groups having bonds of language, heritage, tradition, or other common identity." Third, the Doctrine of Discovery is proclaimed invalid, as "no state shall claim or retain, by right of discovery or otherwise, the territories of an Indigenous nation or group, except such lands as may have been lawfully acquired by valid treaty or other cessation freely made." Fourth, Indigenous nation treaties must be accorded the same international rights and respect as other international treaties, and land claims and treaty disputes must be settled in a fair and just manner. Finally, Indigenous–state relations should be conducted with respect for Indigenous self-determination. In addition, "Indigenous nations shall be accorded such degree of independence as they may desire in accordance with international law." In other words, Indigenous nations may choose from a spectrum of autonomy that ranges from establishing themselves as independent states on one end, to total integration with nation-states on the other end, with variations of degrees of autonomy in between. It is important to note that the possibility of the independence of Indigenous nations, that is, secession, was included as a possibility for Indigenous nations. Self-determination was further described as the preservation of national and cultural integrity as well as environmental and resource protection of Indigenous nations. The exclusive right of Indigenous nations to determine their own membership free of state interference, another element of self-determination, is also specifically mentioned.

The 1977 Conference was, up until that point, the "broadest, united representation of the Indigenous nations and peoples that has ever gathered at any international conference" (International Indian Treaty Council (IITC) 1977). But that was not its primary significance. The Draft Declaration of Principles that emerged from this conference "could be characterized as the fundamental political document of the international Indigenous movement" (Dunbar-Ortiz 2006), and it would later provide the backbone of the Draft Declaration process in the Working Group on Indigenous Populations. The 1977 Conference also represented the beginning of an important shift in international relations, forged by global Indigenous politics. With the 1977 Declaration of Principles, the transnational Indigenous rights movement shifted the international conversation on Indigenous peoples from one focused solely on discrimination against Indigenous individuals in a domestic context toward a conversation also based in the rights of Indigenous nations to self-determination, an international conversation that would necessarily and inevitably lead toward discussions of collective rights and plural sovereignty arrangements.

In sum, the 1977 Conference, and the Indigenous-drafted Declaration of Principles, brought forward a series of arguments that would frame the Indigenous rights struggle for the next several decades and on into the future. First, a focus on racial discrimination in domestic contexts was insufficient to protect Indigenous peoples' life ways. Second, land and Indigenous relationships with land are central to Indigenous rights and struggles. Third, Indigenous peoples are equally entitled to the right of self-determination as "peoples" and "nations," even if not as states. Fourth, the individual rights focus of the human rights regime is discriminatory against Indigenous peoples who also need protection of their collective rights to remain viable as peoples. Fifth, Indigenous nation treaties should be recognized internationally as valid treaties. Finally, Indigenous peoples are victims not only of individual states but also of worldviews that emphasize domination and subordination, including such legal principles as the Doctrine of Discovery. Therefore, it is these problematic worldviews that must change in order to accommodate Indigenous rights, Indigenous relationships to land, and Indigenous ways of being in the world.

NGO Conference in Geneva, 1981

In September, 1981, the Sub-Committee on Racism and Racial Discrimination organized a follow-up conference in Geneva focused on Indigenous peoples' issues, particularly the issue of land. This conference, which is described as "giving new confidence and support" to the global Indigenous rights struggle, was much bigger and broader than the 1977 Conference in terms of Indigenous representation. While the 1977 Conference had focused exclusively on Indigenous peoples of the Western hemisphere (Special NGO Committee on Human Rights (Geneva) 1981), the 1981 conference was broader, drawing 130 Indigenous representatives from North America, Central America, South America, Scandinavia, Australia, and New Zealand. Fewer governments participated in the 1981 Conference than in the 1977 Conference, largely due to a government boycott initiated by the USA Reagan administration. Within the Cold War atmosphere that pervaded international politics of the time, the Reagan administration viewed the global Indigenous rights movement as tied to global communism (Dunbar-Ortiz 2006). This had not been an issue in 1977 because the USA Carter administration had a stated commitment to international human rights; this commitment encouraged allied countries to participate in human rights-related international events. Because of the USA-led boycott, only a handful of Western countries attended and participated in the 1981 Conference, namely Denmark, France, Norway, and the Netherlands, while fifteen Latin American, Asian, and African governments participated, along with several national liberation organizations, like the Palestinian Liberation Organization, and more than fifty international NGOs (Special NGO Committee on Human Rights (Geneva) 1981).

In addition to addressing the issue of the insufficiency of existing laws to protect Indigenous peoples, participants at this conference directly claimed that the Anglo-American bias in international law was contributing to the plight of the world's Indigenous peoples and advocated for change in international law to better accommodate Indigenous peoples, including such possibilities as:

> representation in the United Nations, mandatory jurisdiction over Indigenous questions by the International Court of Justice, United Nations supervision of negotiations between Indigenous peoples and the governments concerned, and the international recognition of the validity of treaties and agreements concluded or accepted by Indigenous peoples.
>
> (Special NGO Committee on Human Rights (Geneva) 1981)

Building upon the earlier articulations of the importance of land and self-determination for Indigenous peoples, the 1981 final Conference Report "affirmed that land rights and self-determination are inseparably connected." Indigenous participants made the case that "the root cause of this crisis is the denial of the right to their land" and it is "the constant grabbing of more of their land and the denial of self-determination that is destroying their traditional value systems and the very fabric of their societies." Indigenous delegates further argued, "if the Indigenous peoples were accorded the genuine exercise of their right to self-determination, they would be able to live in their lands and feed their people in accordance with their own traditions, technology and culture." One Māori activist later described the centrality of self-determination to Indigenous struggles: "From the very beginning there was absolute unity on the need for the recognition of the right of self-determination as the baseline from which all other minimum standards would flow" (Jackson 2008). Furthermore, national governments must accommodate Indigenous communal land ownership as "Indigenous nations and peoples have the complete right to determine their own land tenures" (Special NGO Committee on Human Rights (Geneva) 1981).

The 1981 NGO Conference solidified the themes of global Indigenous politics, which first emerged at the 1977 Conference. It also crystallized and extended these themes in several important ways: (1) international awareness of Indigenous issues increased and the Indigenous rights movement broadened its participation from the Western hemisphere to the global level; (2) land rights and self-determination were linked together and asserted to be the solution to the problems of Indigenous peoples; (3) the accommodation of collective land rights for Indigenous peoples was articulated as a necessity; and (4) the recommendation to establish a Working Group on Indigenous Populations for states and Indigenous organizations to together elaborate international standards on Indigenous peoples' rights.

The Cobo Report

In 1970, the United Nations Sub-Commission on the Prevention of Discrimination and Protection of Minorities had recommended that a complete study of the problem of discrimination against Indigenous populations be undertaken, including suggestions about national and international measures that should be taken to eliminate such discrimination (United Nations 1970). A Sub-Commission member, Ambassador José Martinez Cobo of Ecuador, was selected as Special Rapporteur for this study. Completed more than a decade later, in 1982, the final twenty-chapter report, which was the most voluminous document ever produced by the United Nations, was issued in two parts in 1982 and 1983.[7] While the Cobo Report was an official UN undertaking, the process it followed meant that the end report more strongly represented the views of the Indigenous participants in the reporting process than it did those of the UN member states. The Special Rapporteur focused attention on the situation of Indigenous peoples in several dozen countries in the Americas as well as Oceania. The UN study team met with Indigenous groups first, and then gave the governments of these countries the opportunity to clarify and/or correct information and offer their perspectives. Governments were generally slow to respond, if they responded at all. The final chapter of the Report, published in 1987, serves as an accessible and comprehensive summary of the conclusions, proposals, and recommendations of the full Report (United Nations Sub-Commission on Prevention of Discrimination and Protection of Minorities 1987).

The Cobo Report summary presents two major conclusions that lent credence to claims made by Indigenous participants at both the 1977 and 1981 international conferences:

1 The principles in existing international human rights standards are not being adequately applied in all countries where Indigenous peoples are impacted.
2 "It is also clear that the provisions contained in the instruments in question are not wholly adequate for the recognition and protection of the specific rights of Indigenous populations."

The Report summary specifically identifies many areas where existing international standards pertaining to equality and non-discrimination are not adequately applied to Indigenous peoples, including health, housing, education, language, culture, employment, religion, and administration of justice. At the same time, the Report summary also articulates the two main areas where the existing international standards failed to recognize and respect the realities of Indigenous peoples: land and political rights.

The Cobo Report represents the first official acknowledgment within the UN system of a special relationship between Indigenous peoples and land which existing national and international norms and laws did not accommodate:

> It is essential to know and understand the deeply spiritual special relationship between Indigenous peoples and their land as basic to their existence as such and to all their beliefs, customs, traditions and culture. For such peoples, land is not merely a possession and a means of production. The entire relationship between the spiritual life of Indigenous peoples and Mother Earth, and their land, has a great many deep-seated implications. Their land is not a commodity which can be acquired, but a material element to be enjoyed freely.

The Report further made explicit the connection between land, religion, and cultural heritage for Indigenous peoples: "[Indigenous peoples] have the right to the natural cultural heritage contained in the territory and freely to determine the use to be made of it." While there was nothing in the international system that specifically excluded Indigenous individuals from owning land, there was also nothing in the existing international system to adequately protect Indigenous forms of land tenure, including "the use of the resources traditionally generated, or the resources which that land contains." The Report also makes special note of the struggles of many Indigenous peoples to maintain communal or collective rights to land in the face of state efforts to individualize and privatize land ownership.

The Cobo Report also addresses the complexity of Indigenous political rights, which do not align well with current international instruments. Because Indigenous peoples have "their own national identity based on historical realities" and "the natural and original right to live freely on their own territories," the report explicitly states that "respect for the forms of autonomy called for by Indigenous peoples is the necessary condition for guaranteeing and ensuring these rights." Indigenous peoples' self-determination, therefore, is a "basic precondition" to the enjoyment of Indigenous peoples' fundamental rights. The report acknowledged that self-determination has many aspects, but must include political factors. "Internal" self-determination within a nation-state means: "a people or group possessing a definite territory may be autonomous in the sense of possessing a separate and distinct administrative structure and judicial system, determined by and intrinsic to that people or group."

The Cobo Report recommended that the Sub-Commission prepare a "declaration of the rights and freedoms of Indigenous populations." On May 7, 1982, in Resolution 1982/34, the United Nations Economic and Security Council, "believing that special attention should be given to appropriate avenues of recourse at the national, regional and international levels in order to advance the promotion and protection of the human rights and fundamental freedoms of Indigenous populations" (United Nations Economic and Social Council 1982) and in light of the conclusions of the Cobo Report, authorized the establishment of an annual working group on Indigenous populations. The working group's mandate was two-fold: to review developments pertaining to the human rights and fundamental freedoms of Indigenous populations, and "to give special attention to the evolution of standards concerning the rights of Indigenous populations."

Working Group on Indigenous Populations, 1982–1984

The Working Group, made up of five members of the Sub-Commission who are appointed by the Chairman of the Sub-Commission, held its first meeting in Geneva in 1982. Representatives from UN member states and from Indigenous organizations were also encouraged to participate. This was the first time in UN history that the rights holders themselves were asked to participate in the process of writing international human rights standards.

At the first meeting, discussions centered on both definitional issues and standards. The primary areas of concern were: (1) the right to life, to physical integrity, and to the security of Indigenous populations; (2) the right to self-determination; (3) the right to freedom of religion and traditional religious practices; (4) the right to land and natural resources; (5) civil and political rights; (6) the right to education; and (7) various other rights (United Nations Commission on Human Rights, Sub-Commission on Prevention of Discrimination and Protection of Minorities 1982).

Twelve states participated in the first WGIP session: Australia, New Zealand, Canada, the USA, Argentina, Brazil, Nicaragua, Panama, India, Morocco, Yemen, and Sweden; along with the Palestinian Liberation Organization. Three Indigenous NGOs with ECOSOC consultative status also participated: the International Indian Treaty Council (IITC), the World Council of Indigenous Peoples (WCIP), and the Indian Law Resource Center (ILRC).[8] In addition, a number of Indigenous nations and confederations from the United States, Canada, South America, and Australia participated, including the Six Nations Haudenosaunee (Iroquois) Confederacy, the Oglala Lakota, Grand Council Treaty No. 9, Grand Council of the Mikmaq Nation, and the South American Indian Council (CISA). Participation by states, NGOs, and Indigenous nations and organizations grew steadily in successive meetings of the Working Group in 1983 and 1984.

The WGIP agreed on the principles that would guide its work, which would differ in some remarkable ways from all other UN meetings. The first decision made was that the WGIP should be open and accessible to Indigenous peoples, whether or not their organizations held official ECOSOC consultative status. This was a major departure from UN standing rules and procedures. Furthermore, a voluntary fund was set up in order to assist Indigenous peoples to attend WGIP meetings in the future. Like earlier meetings, Indigenous representatives argued that existing international human rights standards, based on the equal rights of individuals, were inadequate to protect Indigenous peoples. Furthermore, the integrationist approach of states and the international system, which encouraged or forced Indigenous people to assimilate into settler societies, had led to the desperate situation of Indigenous peoples. Therefore, there was a need to develop a new international standard on Indigenous rights that would focus on three new priorities: self-determination, land and natural resources, and respect for treaties and international agreements. Governments recommended that the WGIP examine all existing standards and come up with a new draft declaration and, at a later stage, possibly one or more conventions.

In 1982, at the first WGIP meeting, the Indian Law Resource Center presented a document, "The Principles for Guiding the Deliberations of the Working Group" (United Nations Working Group on Indigenous Populations 1982), which closely resembled the Draft Declaration of Principles from the 1977 Geneva Conference. It contained statements on Indigenous peoples' rights to land, natural resources, and self-determination. It specifically invalidated any version of the Doctrine of Discovery that has been relied on by states to deprive Indigenous peoples of their land, natural resources, and self-determination without their "free, prior and informed consent." The document articulated that Indigenous peoples' treaties and other agreements with states be internationally protected. It also argued that Indigenous peoples were eligible for the same protection of their individual rights that all other human beings enjoy, as articulated in the Universal Declaration on Human Rights.

State governments began to argue against Indigenous autonomy, land rights, and self-determination in earnest in the 1984 session of the WGIP, taking positions that such "controversial issues go to the heart of the sovereignty and national integrity of United Nations member states" (United Nations Working Group on Indigenous Populations 1984). In an effort to assuage the fears of some states that these moves necessarily threatened state sovereignty and national integrity, Canada stated that it had recently inscribed Indigenous treaty rights into its 1982 Constitution and had successfully negotiated a major land claim settlement, all without destroying Canada's territorial integrity (United Nations Working Group on Indigenous Populations 1984). This position is ironic given Canada's eventual vote against the Declaration on the grounds that it threatened Canada's national integrity, but it should be noted that, during the first years of the Working Group, Canada was a supporter of the Indigenous movement; its resistance to the Declaration came later as Canada and other members of the CANZUS groups were confronted with the realization that the accommodations they had already made were deemed insufficient.

From its earliest beginnings, the Indigenous rights movement sought a set of fundamental changes in the structure of global politics, including shifts in the construction of human rights, decolonization, and self-determination. The movement argued that unless Indigenous groups' rights as peoples are respected, they remain discriminated against and colonized. Indigenous groups from around the world agreed on a rights structure that revolved around nationhood, land rights, and self-determination. While some states were initially supportive, by the end of this early stage states began to realize the scope of changes that implementation of Indigenous rights would require.

Drafting stage: articulating Indigenous rights, 1985–1994

At its fourth session in 1985, the Working Group on Indigenous Populations determined that the "time had come to begin the preparation of a draft" set of official standards on the rights of Indigenous peoples (United Nations Working Group on Indigenous Populations 1985). The 1985 final report indicated that participants from states, Indigenous organizations, and other NGOs came to "general agreement with this drafting mandate and the need for and expectation of the preparation of new standards and norms on Indigenous rights." Indigenous participants expressed the hope that "precise international standards would also bring into line national legislation and its prompt implementation." One government observer noted that a human rights declaration could be just as or even more important than a convention or a treaty, as a tool of persuasive politics rather than as a legally binding instrument in and of itself:

> A declaration on the basic principles of Indigenous rights could eventually become binding upon all members of the international community, like the Universal Declaration of Human Rights, while a convention would be binding only upon the States that choose to ratify it.
>
> (United Nations Working Group on Indigenous Populations 1985)

Indigenous participants widely agreed with this logic, and so they began working together with governments for a universal human rights declaration rather than a legally binding treaty or human rights convention.

There were two draft texts submitted to the Working Group for consideration as starting points toward elaborating a declaration. The first was a Declaration of Principles adopted at the Fourth General Assembly of the World Council of Indigenous Peoples in Panama, in September, 1984 ("WCIP Draft") (United Nations Working Group on Indigenous Populations 1985). The second text was a Draft Declaration of Principles jointly proposed by the Indian Law Resource Center, Four Directions Council, National Aboriginal and Islander Legal Service, National Indian Youth Council, Inuit Circumpolar Conference, and the International Indian Treaty Council ("Indigenous Organizations Draft") (United Nations Working Group on Indigenous Populations 1985). These two draft texts resembled one another and earlier declarations of principles in some crucial ways, but also differed in certain important respects. While the basic rights and principles expressed in each draft were identical, the drafts varied in terms of how principles were emphasized, and the order in which the principles were set out. The Indigenous Organizations Draft employed a legal UN style, reflecting the international and UN experience and legal expertise that many of these organizations had already gained by this time. The WCIP draft remained firmly rooted in grassroots activism reflective of this organization's original composition.

Both texts place self-determination as the top priority and use generally similar language. One small wording difference may be of crucial importance for implementation: "All Indigenous peoples have the right *of* self-determination" in the WGIP Draft, and "All Indigenous nations and peoples have the right *to* self-determination" in the Indigenous Organizations Draft (emphasis added.) The difference between "of" and "to" may be significant both legally and politically for states, but it is a difference that the Indigenous participants apparently did not notice or fully appreciate at this juncture. As Māori lawyer and activist Moana Jackson (2008) later explained:

> In all other human rights conventions, the wording reads that all peoples have the right of self-determination and the word "of" implies inherency, that as a human, self-determination is something of you; it's within your humanity. What this says is that Indigenous peoples have the right "to" self-determination so that transfers to something, which you might one day be fully entitled or you might one day, aspire to.[9]

This use of the two phrases as synonyms would play a major role in the interpretation of the Declaration, especially by recalcitrant states, during General Assembly passage in 2007.

Both drafts proclaim the importance of land rights and natural resources rights. As the WCIP Draft states, "All States within which an Indigenous people lives shall recognize the population, territory and institutions of the Indigenous people." The Indigenous Organizations draft claims that states must respect the jurisdiction of Indigenous territory and makes a very strong statement regarding land and resources rights:

> Indigenous nations and peoples are entitled to the permanent control and enjoyment of their aboriginal ancestral-historical territories. This includes surface and subsurface rights, inland and coastal waters, renewable and non-renewable resources, and the economics based on these resources.

The WCIP draft mentions culture, language, religion, and educational rights, and other political issues such as participation in the state and respect for treaties and other agreements. The Indigenous Organizations draft includes all of these rights and adds several more important rights to the draft text. The Indigenous Organizations draft proclaims: "Indigenous nations and peoples are subjects of international law." This draft text also includes the possibility of compensation for lost lands as an option where return of land is not possible, while the WCIP draft only states: "lands and resources shall be returned." The Indigenous Organizations draft also stated that disputes between Indigenous peoples and their surrounding states should be adjudicated by an impartial, international authority rather than by domestic courts, and reserved the right of Indigenous nations to "engage in self-defence against State actions" as a part of the right to self-determination.

The Indigenous Organizations draft also included another crucial component that delegitimized the foundation of a number of states and a legal principle still present in international law and politics: "Discovery, conquest, settlement or a theory of *terra nullius* and unilateral action are never legitimate bases for states to claim or retain the territories of Indigenous nations or peoples." The Indigenous Organizations draft then closed with another statement which acknowledged that Indigenous peoples have the same human rights and fundamental freedoms as all other peoples and shall not be subject to discrimination.

States reacted swiftly and immediately to the strong Indigenous claims to self-determination, land, and natural resources rights present in both of these drafts. One state member of the Working Group said that self-determination does not grant the right to independence because the UN international definition of "peoples" remained unclear.[10] Another government observer expressed "concern over proposals relating to the right of self-determination … which would imply a right of secession." He also made the claim that, since they were not states, Indigenous peoples were not in fact subjects of international law.

The UN-appointed Working Group responded to these two drafts by creating a first set of seven draft principles, the 1985 "Working Group on Indigenous Populations Draft Principles" (Appendix 2.2). These principles acknowledged that Indigenous peoples had the same fundamental rights and freedoms as were reflected in existing international instruments and that Indigenous peoples enjoyed individual and certain collective rights. The 1985 Working Group Draft Principles indicated that the UN-appointed members were beginning to accept that Indigenous rights must include collective rights, but it also indicated fierce resistance to Indigenous land rights and self-determination. The 1985 Working Group Draft stated that Indigenous peoples had the "collective right to exist and to be protected against genocide," the right to "religious traditions and practices," education, language, and cultural identity, but there was absolutely no mention of land rights or self-determination in this version.

Prior to the next regular Working Group meeting in Geneva in 1987, a frustrated Indigenous Caucus merged the two 1984 draft documents that had been prepared by Indigenous organizations into a single consensus document and presented it back to the Working Group at its 1987 session. The 1987 Declaration of Principles then served as the basis for the Draft Declaration on Indigenous Peoples' Rights in place of the 1985 Working Group Draft Principles.

This 1987 Declaration of Principles closely resembled the 1984 Indigenous Organizations draft in its style, tone, and content. It opened with an assertion of the equal humanity of Indigenous peoples, followed by assertions of the "hard rights" of self-determination and land rights, and ended with articulations of various "soft rights" of individuals and collectives. When the 1987 Declaration of Principles was presented to the WGIP, states again voiced their objections. Canada argued that the principle of self-determination only applied to colonial or foreign occupation and not to "support secessionist or separatist moves within democratic and independent states" (United Nations Working Group on Indigenous Populations 1987b). A group of states, led by India, reasserted that the international definition of "peoples" entitled to the right of self-determination was "subject to different interpretations" and should not apply to "Indigenous populations" or other minorities. The governments did show support for the cultural, educational, and religious rights of Indigenous peoples, since Indigenous cultures "formed part of humankind's cultural heritage." Given the substantial differences in content between the UN-drafted 1985 Working Group Draft Principles and the Indigenous-drafted 1987 Declaration of Principles, and the desire of both the states and Indigenous organizations to focus discussion on specific proposals, the Working Group members agreed to ask Chair/Rapporteur Erica-Irene Daes to prepare a full draft text of a declaration on Indigenous peoples' rights prior to the next session of the Working Group in 1988.

Chairperson Daes presented her draft to the Working Group at its 1988 session, reflecting compromises between states and Indigenous groups (Daes 1988). First, the term "Indigenous peoples" was used rather than "Indigenous populations." Certain states objected to the use of "peoples," as it may provide a legal right to secession. Some states objected to collective rights but, as one state member noted, "the draft declaration should place emphasis on collective rights and ensure that the exercise of individual rights would not be used to jeopardize the rights of the community." The complementarity of collective rights to individual rights was a particularly important victory for the Indigenous representatives as they had been making their case for years that the recognition of individual rights alone was inadequate to protect Indigenous societies and cultures. The text included land and resources rights for Indigenous peoples, although it was much weaker language than in the earlier texts that had been prepared by Indigenous groups, indicating that the victory of collective rights inclusion was tempered by a continued state and UN resistance to Indigenous land and self-determination rights. Finally, the Daes draft did not include a definition of Indigenous peoples as had been requested earlier by states. Chairperson Daes decided to favor the position of the Indigenous Caucus and leave the issue of definition unarticulated in the draft text, essentially privileging a reliance on the self-definition of Indigeneity as had been advocated by the Indigenous representatives.

There were two striking features of the Daes draft, however, that fell far short of Indigenous peoples' expectations, specifically regarding the issue of self-determination. The order of the articles was reversed from the earlier Indigenous texts. Now placed at the top were soft rights to culture, identity, religion, language, and education, while hard rights to land and resources came second, with only two articles out of twenty-eight mentioning a right to "autonomy" and to "autonomous institutions." The Indigenous Caucus made a statement that while they appreciated Chairperson Daes' standard-setting activities, this draft did not adequately reflect Indigenous peoples' "needs, concerns and aspirations" because it did not include the right of self-determination, and it did not fully address collective rights to lands and resources. The Indigenous Caucus position was that self-determination and land rights should be the fundamental principles of any Indigenous rights declaration.

As expressed by several Indigenous activists in interviews, the Working Group itself (which was composed of government representatives and UN staff), with Daes as its Chair, was interested in maintaining the international status quo or at least minimizing change. Although there was wide acceptance that Indigenous peoples were not being adequately protected under existing international instruments, the Working Group resisted the fundamental changes that Indigenous representatives argued were necessary, especially in the areas of self-determination and land rights. Resistance at this juncture centered on the draft text and questions of what would be included, excluded, and placed in positions of prominence. Several governments, particularly those of the USA, New Zealand, and Australia, voiced continued concern over the use of the term "peoples," which might be thought to imply a right of secession in international law. These states wanted a clear articulation of Indigenous self-determination as being strictly limited to internal interpretations and as excluding the possibility of a right to secession. The USA, in particular, also continued to express concern over the inclusion of collective rights (Daes 1989). Indigenous representatives, on the other hand, stood firm in asserting the importance of self-determination and collective rights.

Given the seeming impasse between states and the UN on the one hand and Indigenous groups on the other, Chairperson Daes recommended to the 1990 session of the Working Group that three drafting groups be established in order to accelerate work on the draft text of the Declaration (Daes 1990). The three groups, which were each open to all Working Group participants, including state representatives, UN staff, and Indigenous representatives, were charged with elaborating the Daes draft, based on the consensus decision-making model advocated by the Indigenous representatives. Drafting Group I was to consider land and resources rights, while Drafting Group II was entrusted with political rights and autonomy, and Drafting Group III considered all other rights (United Nations Working Group on Indigenous Populations 1990).

Drafting Group I on land and resources made a number of changes to the text that enhanced the collective land and resources rights of Indigenous peoples. Drafting Group II recommended that a new paragraph be included at the very beginning of the operative part of the Declaration that would read: "Indigenous peoples have the right to self-determination" in order to represent the fundamental importance of this issue. Drafting Group III made a few non-substantive changes in the wording of several articles. Some governments continued to strongly object to the use of certain terminology, specifically the terms "territories," "peoples," and "self-determination," on the basis that they might imply that Indigenous peoples had a right of secession as was the case for former overseas colonial territories. State governments also expressed continued concern over the reference to collective rights, especially regarding whether the rights were actually collective per se or whether they were a collection of individual rights.

A member of the Working Group observed:

> The time has now come to give some fresh thought to the concept of self-determination.... Legal concepts undergo a constant process of evolution, and that it is the responsibility of the Working Group to help shape the development of those concepts which are of relevance to the continued survival and flourishing of the world's Indigenous peoples.

In other words, there was now public acknowledgment that the process had reached a point where a new conception of self-determination could be emerging. The Working Group drew upon a recent statement made by Professor S. James Anaya at a conference in Moscow that same year in order to help elaborate this emerging and evolving conception of self-determination:

> In that statement, it had been pointed out that the concept of self-determination would only in rare instances imply the right to independent statehood; rather, an Indigenous non-statist conception of self-determination implies substantive rights to the economic, political and social means for Indigenous modes of life, and procedural rights to shape the decisions affecting those modes of life, all of which will vary with the contemporary circumstances of particular Indigenous peoples around the world.... This conception of self-determination would, like many other international human rights standards, condition but in no way deny the principle of territorial integrity.[11]

The emerging conception of self-determination that was developing out of the Working Group process would alter, yet at the same time support, state territorial integrity. While the prevailing understanding of self-determination was based strictly on territorial sovereignty, the Indigenous use of the term in these discussions was different and more complex. This difference required clarification, and Indigenous organizations hoped that such clarification would allay the fears of some governments about the implications of the Declaration.

At the ninth session of the WGIP in 1991, Chairperson Daes presented a further revised Draft Declaration working paper (Daes 1991b) based on the draft proposals of the three drafting groups at the 1990 WGIP session, as well as comments she received throughout the year from governments, Indigenous organizations, international organizations, and others. In accordance with Indigenous groups' requests and the recommendation of the prior drafting group, the first operative paragraph read unequivocally:

> Indigenous peoples have the right to self-determination, in accordance with international law. By virtue of this right, they freely determine their relationship with the States in which they live, in a spirit of coexistence with other citizens, and freely pursue their economic, social, cultural and spiritual development in conditions of freedom and dignity.
>
> (Daes 1991a)

Next came a series of operative paragraphs relating to the equal rights of Indigenous peoples to all other peoples and then three paragraphs that explicitly articulated the "collective and individual rights" of Indigenous peoples to existence, to maintain their distinct cultures, and the freedom to be protected from genocide. The soft rights to education, language, culture, and religion appeared in the middle paragraphs, followed by a series of paragraphs on land rights. Indigenous peoples had the right to "maintain their distinctive and profound relationship with their lands, territories and resources" and had the "collective and individual right to own, control and use the lands and territories they have traditionally occupied or otherwise used." Land restitution was called for, although compensation was indicated where restitution was not possible. This text included "the right to participate fully at the State level" while also maintaining the "collective right to autonomy in matters relating to their own internal and local affairs," and the "right to decide upon the structures of their autonomous institutions." Also included was the "right to maintain and develop traditional contacts, relations and cooperation … across State boundaries." Fair and mutually acceptable dispute resolution with states was also included as a right. Finally, there was a statement that these were the "minimum standards" for Indigenous peoples' survival and well-being.

This draft text was strongly supportive of Indigenous rights as articulated by the Indigenous representatives participating in the Working Group, largely based on scant participation by state governments in the drafting groups at the previous session of the Working Group and the handful of comments and suggestions sent by governments to Chairperson Daes during the year. Yet in the next WGIP session, the text faced familiar strong resistance from states. New Zealand argued that any new international instrument must be consistent with existing international standards. Brazil expressed concern over ambiguity within the text and also warned against adopting text that may be unacceptable to governments. Several governments indicated that self-determination would need to be modified to make the text acceptable to states (Daes 1991a).

The 1992 text represented two important victories for Indigenous organizations. First, there was a return to the language of the "right of self-determination," which indicated this as an inherent right for all peoples in accordance with existing international human rights conventions. As IITC's Bill Means (2008) articulated,

> We had not only our interpretation of self-determination, but we had to go into other documents in the UN system, which talked about self-determination. And so we had to do our homework, and so that's how we began to emphasize the human rights aspect because human rights are inalienable and inherent.

> Once we turned that corner on human rights, we began to emphasize that more, the right of self-determination.

The second notable move in this text on self-determination was its articulation as meaning something other than the right to exclusive territorial state sovereignty. This was in response to a number of government complaints that the earlier text on self-determination implied a right of secession, undermined state sovereignty, and was in conflict with international law. New Zealand and Brazil in particular voiced concern over the inconsistency of Indigenous self-determination with other international standards (Daes 1992). Canada indicated that it was prepared to accept the principle of self-determination as long as it meant solely an internal self-determination and recognized the jurisdiction of existing states. Australia also indicated that it could support this emergent view of self-determination involving a special position for Indigenous peoples within the state, as long as it did not threaten territorial integrity. The USA noted, however, that the current text in paragraph 1 could possibly undermine state sovereignty. Guest scholar Douglas Sanders noted that the Working Group was creating a double meaning of self-determination as international rights standard. Australia noted that self-determination for Indigenous peoples should be "an aspirational concept that provided a firm basis for progressively increasing the decision-making powers of Indigenous peoples."

At the 1993 session of the Working Group, states and Indigenous groups reached agreement on a final text that was to be sent to the Sub-Commission on Prevention of Discrimination and Protection of Minorities for approval (Daes 1993). This text, now called the Draft Declaration on the Rights of Indigenous Peoples, closely resembled the 1992 WGIP draft. While there were some cosmetic changes, the only major substantive change concerned self-determination. The article on self-determination was moved down from first to third, behind a new Article 1 that mentioned specifically the UN Charter and the Universal Declaration of Human Rights as well as a new Article 2 that articulated the equality of Indigenous individuals with all other individuals and their equal right to be free from discrimination. The addition of these two articles was a direct result of concerns expressed by certain governments, most notably the USA, Canada, New Zealand, and Australia, regarding the consistency of this Declaration with existing international instruments (Indigenous rights activist #7 2007). These two articles functioned as preliminaries, attempting to balance Indigenous self-determination within the context of equality of all citizens. Following them, the text of Article 3 now read: "Indigenous peoples have the right of self-determination. By virtue of that right they freely determine their political status and freely pursue their economic, social and cultural development." No specific clarification was offered about whether Indigenous self-determination meant autonomy or self-government. The preceding articles already implied that this version of self-determination fully respected the territorial integrity of sovereign states as established in the UN Charter. At the same time, the use of the term "the right *of* self-determination" rather than "the right *to* self-determination" retained the meaning of inherency. Chairperson Daes further advocated for drawing a distinction between:

> "External" self-determination, by which peoples liberated themselves from imposed alien rule, and "internal" self-determination, by which collective groups of Indigenous peoples sought to preserve and develop their cultural and territorial identity within the political order of the State in which they lived.

Even with these clarifications, Canada, New Zealand, and Chile still withheld support for Indigenous self-determination.

The USA also remained opposed to the collective rights provisions in the Declaration which went "far beyond the limited collective rights recognized in international law." Canada raised concerns that the final draft was unclear about the issue of land rights. Did Indigenous land rights mean all traditional lands and territories? This interpretation would be highly problematic for states like Canada, and so it proposed some sort of a "reasonable limits" clause on land rights.

Despite these remaining concerns and reservations by states, the Working Group on Indigenous Populations celebrated the fact that, after eleven years, it had achieved a final consensus text that it sent to the Sub-Commission for consideration in 1994 (Appendix 2.3). The Sub-Commission on Prevention of Discrimination and Protection of Minorities in resolution 1994/45 adopted the Draft Declaration on the Rights of Indigenous Peoples on August 26, 1994 (United Nations Sub-Commission on Prevention of Discrimination and Protection of Minorities). It then also created a new inter-sessional working group on the Draft Declaration on the Rights of Indigenous Peoples (WGDD) in order to move the Declaration process into its next phase: elaboration (United Nations Economic and Social Council 1995).

During the drafting phase, Indigenous rights activists worked together with a small set of states to articulate Indigenous rights, fully cognizant that Indigenous rights implied significant structural change. Sensitive to this, the Indigenous rights movement approached discussions in a manner that emphasized consensus among Indigenous groups but also between states and Indigenous groups. They attempted to negotiate respectfully with states in order to achieve acceptable compromises and, ultimately, consensus. States, however, showed some initial resistance, using small maneuvers of language and process to counter Indigenous rights articulation, especially where self-determination was concerned.

Elaboration phase: the fight for change, 1995–2006

The highly volatile and often hostile elaboration phase of the Declaration on the Rights of Indigenous Peoples began in 1995 with the first meeting of the inter-sessional working group (WGDD). Sixty-one governments and sixty-four Indigenous and non-Indigenous NGOs attended the first meeting of the WGDD;

participation by both NGOs and governments had grown substantially since the earlier WGIP meetings in which only a handful of governments participated (United Nations Working Group on the Draft Declaration 1996). Apparently, the circulation of the 1994 Draft Declaration to all UN member states had sparked additional government interest in the Indigenous rights process. It is important to note that, in contrast to the WGIP meetings, the WGDD officially comprised only governments and UN organizations; Indigenous representatives were technically only "observers," not participants.

During the first session of the WGDD, state resistance to Indigenous rights was readily apparent, and the creative and cunning maneuvers which state governments, especially the CANZUS states, were prepared to deploy against Indigenous rights began to emerge in earnest. State governments consistently advocated for "clarification," "streamlining," and "consistency" with existing international instruments; they relied on the primary tactic of "creatively using language to obscure rather than resolve some of the underlying issues" (Indigenous rights activist #7 2007). Some states, especially the USA, argued that Indigenous peoples were already adequately protected under existing human rights standards and that additional collective rights were not necessary and could be problematic with respect to the principles of equality and universality of human rights. The USA, New Zealand, and Australia all advocated that there should not be any special rights that adhered to Indigenous peoples, but other governments (such as Canada and the Netherlands) did not object to the inclusion of collective rights "as long as their contents were clear and they were compatible with international law" (United Nations Working Group on the Draft Declaration 1996). Some governments, notably the USA and Australia, stated that the Draft Declaration be viewed as an aspirational document and not as an articulation of existing rights. Other governments requested clarification of certain terminology, especially "peoples," "Indigenous peoples," and "self-determination." The majority of the time, however, was spent on discussions of self-determination. Many governments argued that the Draft Declaration unacceptably moved the meaning of self-determination beyond its historical context of decolonization and expressed their greatest level of "concern" about the implications for state territorial integrity and unity.

At the second meeting of the WGDD in 1996, a dramatic conflict arose between the Indigenous representatives on the one hand and the states and UN organizations on the other. The session opened with a statement from the highly frustrated Indigenous Caucus. The statement called for the immediate

> adoption of the Draft Declaration on the Rights of Indigenous Peoples in its current text, as approved by the WGIP and the Sub-Commission, in its entirety and with no changes, amendments, or deletions as a minimum standard protecting, promoting and recognizing the rights of Indigenous peoples.[12]

Rather than accepting this call from the Indigenous Caucus, the Chairman/Rapporteur José Urrutia proposed instead that the WGDD begin a re-examination of the Draft Declaration article by article. The Indigenous Caucus immediately rejected this proposal outright, standing by their position that the Sub-Commission text already comprised a minimum standard of Indigenous rights that represented more than ten years of article-by-article work by both Indigenous and state parties. Fearing that the draft would be weakened by states if opened to article-by-article consideration, the Indigenous Caucus, in a consensus statement read by Moana Jackson, then requested open debate on the Draft Declaration as a whole with the full participation of Indigenous representatives in order to bring a "sense of dignity to the proceedings" (Indigenous Caucus 1996b). The Indigenous Caucus stated that "the need for a cooperative approach is crucial to building consensus" and if Indigenous peoples were merely observers in the process, "then many have no desire to subject themselves to such a low standard of recognition." The rules of the WGDD were flawed, the Caucus said, and violated "the spirit of cooperation and consensus that should guide this process." Chairman/Rapporteur Urrutia reacted with indifference to the requests by the Indigenous Caucus, refusing repeatedly to recognize Indigenous delegates who raised their hands wishing to speak. The Indigenous representatives then staged a "walkout in protest of the agenda and the lack of response to their collective proposals for change" (Indigenous Caucus 1996a). As Haudenosaunee activist Kenneth Deer (2011) states, "We had some leverage in this because without Indigenous participation, the WGDD lacked credibility." The challenge, Deer says, "was how to get back in the room."

The Indigenous delegates negotiated with states to establish an Indigenous co-chair of the WGDD. Other process changes were made to increase Indigenous participation, meaning that consensus would have to be achieved between states and Indigenous peoples before votes could be called. As Deer (2011) describes, "this was a significant victory for Indigenous peoples, which those who entered the process after 1996 may not fully appreciate: if we had not been part of the consensus, we would not have the Declaration we have today."

The Indigenous representatives wanted to defend the Draft Declaration in its entirety, as a holistic document, not discuss articles one by one, viewing this as another tactic by governments to alter and diminish the text one piece at a time (Indigenous rights activist #2 2007). At their request, the Chair agreed to allow a general debate on the Draft Declaration, and so Indigenous representatives returned to the plenary session to defend the Draft Declaration against amendments, especially to Article 3 concerning self-determination. The Indigenous representatives were still gravely disappointed that they held only "observer" status, even though they were allowed to make statements for the record. Some Indigenous delegates from Australia, New Zealand, and North America went home and never returned to the UN because the "observer" status did not allow for full and equal participation. As Moana Jackson (2008) stated, "because of the implacable opposition of states to self-determination, the Māori delegation that year withdrew from the process." Other Indigenous representatives stayed on. Yet, according to the Indigenous Caucus, all Indigenous peoples remained united in their commitment to defend the current Draft Declaration (Indigenous Caucus

1996a) and to the principle that a group's decision to stay or leave was itself a reflection of that group's inherent self-determination.

This walkout protest was a success for the Indigenous rights movement in two important ways (Indigenous rights activist #2 2007). First, it succeeded in gaining a partial change in the agenda, even if the participation of Indigenous peoples in the WGDD remained incomplete. Second, it helped sort out which governments supported Indigenous peoples and which were attempting to use rules to limit consensus building. The governments supporting the return of Indigenous representatives to the plenary were: Canada, Denmark, Sweden, Finland, Norway, Mexico, Chile, Bolivia, South Africa, and Venezuela. However, Brazil and Argentina requested that the session continue with a discussion of individual articles, supported by the USA, China, Colombia, Australia, and New Zealand (United Nations Working Group on the Draft Declaration 1996).

A general debate on the Draft Declaration was held, followed by a discussion of the articles, organized into twelve thematic clusters. As before, there was the least concern about or resistance to the articles that dealt with soft rights such as education, language, religion, and culture, although certain states (e.g., the USA) still regularly voiced opposition to the inclusion of collective rights, concerned that collective rights violated the spirit of citizen equality, non-discrimination, and rights of the individual. Government opposition grew as discussion moved to the articles that dealt with lands, resources, territories, treaties, and cross-border activities. Canada and Brazil joined the USA in its opposition to such articles, although they usually articulated this opposition in terms of "needing clarification" on the articles in question. The final cluster discussed were the articles dealing with self-determination. At this point, the USA expressed complete opposition. Canada also voiced its "concerns" about these articles. During the discussion of each cluster of articles, Indigenous representatives strongly and tenaciously made almost the same statement each time: "the Indigenous Caucus supports immediate adoption of the existing Sub-Commission text without changes or amendments."

At the next WGDD meeting in 1997, the Chair/Rapporteur again decided to hold a general debate before moving on to a specific discussion of articles. Importantly, the Chair also announced that the WGDD would operate on a consensus decision-making basis (Carmen 2007). At this meeting, two articles were adopted by consensus without changes or amendments: Article 43, a guarantee of equal rights to male and female Indigenous individuals, and Article 5, which stated that every Indigenous individual has the right to a nationality, defined as citizenship in a state (United Nations Economic and Social Council 1998). Discussion was held on eleven other articles, and Australia, New Zealand, Canada, Brazil, France, Japan, and the USA proposed substantial changes to the text.

No further articles were adopted in the WGDD for the next seven years. Year after year the WGDD held a general debate, but there was a stalemate. Indigenous delegates argued for immediate adoption of the Sub-Commission text and considered it a victory that there was no qualification of "peoples" or of the right to self-determination (Carmen 2007). States (especially the USA, Canada, New Zealand, and Australia) repeatedly attempted to make amendments and alterations to the text, particularly in the areas of land rights and self-determination. These proposed changes almost always took the form of clarifications, or enhancements of issues of definition. Discussions were held and changes in text were proposed each year, but there was only minimal progress and no consensus.

Beginning in 2001, the Indigenous Caucus stated that it could consider changes to the text as long as the core principles and the integrity of the original text were maintained. This "cracked the egg" and there was no going back to the original hardline Indigenous position on pure and unwavering support for the Sub-Commission text, according to Andrea Carmen, Executive Director of the International Indian Treaty Council (2007).

On the first day of the 2004 session of the WGDD, New Zealand, supported by Denmark, Finland, Iceland, Norway, Sweden, and Switzerland, introduced an amended Draft Declaration text (United Nations Working Group on the Draft Declaration 2004). The Indigenous Caucus argued that this text introduced a number of changes that weakened the rights of Indigenous peoples, especially in the area of land rights, and so they opposed it in favor of the original Sub-Commission text (United Nations Economic and Social Council 2005). The Chair and many states, however, decided to use the new amended text as the basis for WGDD discussion for the following two weeks.

On November 29, 2004, the first day of the third week of the 2004 WGDD session, six Indigenous delegates began a hunger strike and spiritual fast "to call the world's attention to the continued attempts by some states, as well as the UN process itself, to weaken and undermine the draft declaration developed in the UN Working Group on Indigenous Populations and adopted by the UN Sub-commission" (Indigenous Peoples' Representatives at the United Nations 2004).[13] The hunger strikers called for the Sub-Commission text to be sent back to the Human Rights Commission with the message that no consensus had emerged in the WGDD process in ten years. They rejected any attempt to represent a newly amended text as a consensus document. They also protested that "a handful of States" had "the opportunity to weaken the human rights of Indigenous Peoples" and they insisted that the process must include the voices of Indigenous peoples themselves. The process that had been implemented in the WGDD, they argued, encouraged

> openly discriminatory proposals for changes by States that weaken the Declaration, but does not allow us to defend the position of the vast majority of Indigenous Peoples of the world by calling for adoption of the text approved by the Subcommission.
>
> (Indigenous Nations and Organizations 2005)

The hunger strike ended on December 2, 2004 following a meeting between the hunger strikers, the UN High Commissioner on Human Rights, and the Vice President of the UN Commission on Human Rights. The High Commissioner promised that the Human Rights Commission would adopt no document different from the Sub-Commission text if such a text was not produced by a consensus of Indigenous peoples (Carmen 2007). In response, the WGDD Chair/Rapporteur decided to ask four groups of facilitators to consult with all participants on proposed changes of language.

During 2005, the government of Mexico held a workshop intended to discuss, in an informal manner, the major outstanding issues of self-determination, lands, territories, and resources. Indigenous experts had also held a meeting during the year and noted that the Indigenous Caucus was ready to provisionally adopt many articles. In the 2005 meeting of the WGDD, Chair/Rapporteur Luis-Enrique Chavez indicated that there was a need to show progress to the Commission on Human Rights, and therefore, in the spirit of moving forward, he presented a Chairman's Proposal (United Nations Working Group on the Draft Declaration 2005) on all articles that had been previously discussed.[14] He proclaimed that this text was "as close to the original text as possible, while including proposed amendments where they seemed to be required."

Even though many states expressed disagreement with the text of the Chairman's Proposal on self-determination, lands, resources, and collective rights, this was the last meeting of the WGDD, and a consensus on the text was needed. The USA, Australia, and New Zealand submitted a proposal on December 13, 2005, which was intended to weaken Article 3 on self-determination by restricting the meaning of Indigenous self-determination to self-management. However, this wording was immediately rejected by Indigenous representatives and their small group of allied states (especially Mexico and Guatemala). Some changes were made to the Chairman's text, most notably the addition of an article that added protections for state territorial integrity, some changes to articles on land rights and collective rights, all intended to provide additional protections to state sovereignty vis-à-vis Indigenous peoples' self-determination. The Chairman's Proposal was presented to the Human Rights Council in June 2006 as a final compromise text, even though language in the areas of self-determination and land rights could not be agreed upon. The USA, Canada, New Zealand, Australia, and the Russian Federation still objected to the key provisions on land and self-determination. The majority of states, however, along with Indigenous organizations and international organizations, voiced support for this compromise text.

During the elaboration phase, the extreme level of threat felt by states, especially English-speaking settler states, by Indigenous rights became clear; states were becoming increasingly aware of the depth and breadth of structural change that would be expected if Indigenous rights as articulated by the Indigenous rights movement were implemented. While tensions between states and Indigenous groups had been simmering since first appearing in earlier phases, they now exploded into open conflict. Indigenous activists faced the heavy task of defending the Draft Declaration against unilateral state diminution of Indigenous rights, especially against attacks on land and self-determination. While their defensive action was not a complete victory, they were able to maintain the vast majority of their preferred text.

Passage and implementation stage: forging change, 2007 going forward

The Human Rights Council passed the Draft Declaration on the Rights of Indigenous Peoples on June 29, 2006 (United Nations Human Rights Council 2006) by a vote of thirty for, two against, with twelve abstentions, and forwarded it to the UN General Assembly for adoption. Of the states that had raised the majority of the opposition to the Draft Declaration in the WGDD, only four were voting members of the Human Rights Council at the time. Brazil voted in favor, Canada and the Russian Federation voted against, and Argentina abstained.

On December 20, 2006, a non-action resolution was put forward by a group of African states (led by Namibia) to defer action on the Draft Declaration in the General Assembly, arguing that, since the African countries had not been involved in the working groups, more time was needed for further consultation (United Nations General Assembly 2006a). African countries have had long-standing issues with how to define "Indigenous peoples" and with the implications of Indigenous rights on the African continent. Notwithstanding this, Indigenous groups had expected support from formerly colonized states and were so taken aback by the response of the African Group that they widely charged that the African Group was being manipulated behind the scenes by the USA and Canada.[15] Amnesty International issued a statement accusing the Canadian government of being "obstructionist and exploitative in its efforts to block discussion" by encouraging states in Africa, Latin America, and Asia to oppose the Draft Declaration (Canada Press 2007). However, Dwight Newman (2010) argues that the African Group's concerns with Indigenous rights were their own and rooted in a "number of historical-structural characteristics of the post colonial African state" associated with "persisting colonial legacies," including such issues as state building and identity formation, developmental aspirations, and reactions to international interference. While there is little hard evidence as to the reality of Western manipulation of the African Group, the frequency with which it is alleged by Indigenous activists testifies to the depth of suspicion that had built up over the years against the USA and Canadian governments.

Between January and August, 2007, a group of states supportive of the Draft Declaration (led by Mexico, along with Peru, Guatemala, and Fiji) worked with the African Group on a "package" proposal of amendments to resolve the impasse without reopening negotiations on the Declaration itself (African Group 2006). The Mexican delegation was of the opinion that if negotiations on the text were reopened, the entire Declaration would fail (Martinez 2007). At the request of the African Group, Indigenous representatives were excluded from all discussions, even as observers.

On August 31, 2007, the African Group, along with Mexico, Guatemala, and Peru, presented the Indigenous Caucus with yet another new draft of the

Declaration. The African Group package, which proposed nine changes (five deletions and four additions) to the text, did maintain about 95 percent of the original language and kept the following provisions intact: self-determination, treaties, lands, territories, and resources (Malezer and Trask 2007). The major changes involved enhanced protections for state sovereignty and territorial integrity, most notably Article 46.1, which states:

> Nothing in this Declaration may be interpreted as implying for any State, people, group or person any right to engage in any activity or to perform any act contrary to the Charter of the United Nations or construed as authorizing or encouraging any action which would dismember or impair, totally or in part, the territorial integrity or political unity of sovereign and independent States.

The African Group also reported that, although a few states had indicated their intention to oppose the Declaration, the Group still felt they had sufficient votes to pass it. The African Group told the Indigenous Caucus that it would block any additional amendments (Indigenous rights activist #3 2007).

Beginning on Saturday, September 1, 2007, urgent faxes and emails went out from the Indigenous Caucus to Indigenous nations and organizations around the world asking for consultation on the proposed African Group amendments. The Indigenous Caucus regional coordinators collected responses up until noon on Tuesday, September 4, 2007. Clearly, there was no time for the Indigenous Caucus to seek consensus on this new text. Les Malezer, Chair of the Indigenous Caucus, stated: "these urgent consultations will determine whether or not we can live with the amendments, and the Declaration is adopted OR whether we cannot accept the agreed version and the Declaration will not be adopted" (Malezer 2007).

While some Indigenous organizations opposed the amendments and some elected to simply "not support" yet "not oppose" the African Group amendments, the Indigenous Caucus held a press conference on September 6, 2007 to endorse the amendments to the text (UN Department of Public Information 2007).[16] Again, the Indigenous representatives accused Canada and the USA of manipulating the African Group by trying to use aid as a tool. The Indigenous Caucus called for the adoption of the Declaration by the General Assembly of the UN the following week.

On September 13, 2007, Mr. Luis Enrique Chavez, Chair of the Working Group on the Draft Declaration, introduced to the General Assembly, on behalf of Peru, Draft Resolution A/61/L.67, to adopt the Declaration on the Rights of Indigenous Peoples (Appendix 2.4). Australia, New Zealand, and the USA requested a recorded vote. There were 143 votes in favor, eleven abstentions and four votes against.[17] The votes against were: Canada, New Zealand, Australia, and the USA. Even with these abstentions and "no" votes, the Declaration enjoyed wide support; more than 74 percent of UN member states voted in support, although it should also be noted that thirty-four UN member states (17.7 percent of membership) were absent from the vote, primarily African, Central Asian, and Pacific Island countries.[18]

The Indigenous Caucus celebrated the vote as a victory and expressed that it looked forward to the Declaration being implemented as international customary law. Les Malezer, Chair of the Indigenous Caucus, stated:

> The Declaration does not represent solely the viewpoint of the United Nations, nor does it represent solely the viewpoint of the Indigenous Peoples. It is a Declaration which combines our views and interests and which set the framework for the future. It is a tool for peace and justice, based upon mutual recognition and respect.
>
> (Indigenous Peoples' Caucus Regional Steering Committee 2007)

The USA issued a statement that same day, articulating its position on the Declaration (United States Mission to the United Nations 2007). The USA noted that, since it had participated in negotiations in Geneva over the years, it was "fully aware of what participants intended in its drafting" and so it was in a position to "provide an understanding of the intent of participating states on the core issues." The USA stated that the Declaration "was an aspirational declaration with political and moral, rather than legal, force." The USA also rejected outright "any possibility that this document is or can become customary international law." It also expressed its opposition to reproducing the Article 1 common to both the ICCPR and the ICESCR, which states: "all peoples have the right of self-determination." Canada, Australia, and New Zealand each issued very similar statements, highlighting almost exactly the same reservations.

What most Indigenous organizations had not noticed was that the text of the resolution that had passed the General Assembly on September 13, 2007 had undergone a critical, subtle, and unannounced change at the last minute. While the Spanish-language version of the text remained unchanged, the English version had a newly (but silently) altered Article 3 on self-determination – an unannounced editorial change that has potential significance for implementation.[19] The adopted text reads: "Indigenous peoples have the right *to* self-determination" (emphasis added), which differed from the agreed-upon African Group text that had circulated the weekend prior: "Indigenous peoples have the right *of* self-determination" (emphasis added.) As Māori lawyer and activist Moana Jackson (2008) explained:

> That prepositional change was deliberately engineered by the UN and by the states and in a deeply legal sense and a philosophical sense I think it changes and diminishes self-determination. It is not accorded to Indigenous peoples as it is accorded to other peoples.

This last-minute, unannounced, and subtle yet important change to the English text likely indicates that, even with the added protections for state sovereignty, the Declaration represented a change in the conception of self-determination that was still too revolutionary for certain states, especially English-speaking settler states, to accept.

Conclusion

While many Indigenous scholars, lawyers, and activists decry the inclusion of Article 46 and at least a few are concerned about the "of/to" distinction in self-determination, and some have even called the Declaration a complete failure, this chapter has argued that the thirty-year odyssey to achieve an Indigenous rights declaration was, for the most part, successful. The text, as passed by the UN General Assembly in 2007, largely lives up to its original intent, as defined by early Indigenous rights organizations in the 1970s. The final text: (1) represents a set of guidelines and a framework for state implementation of Indigenous rights; (2) is meant to be used as a persuasive moral and political tool to push state actors toward a new vision and new global imaginings that can accommodate Indigenous ways of being, and thinking beyond the existing international law and the constraints of state sovereignty; (3) represents a broad global consensus of both Indigenous and state actors; and finally (4) as is the case with all multilateral international agreements, it represents a compromise.

The four main arguments (goals) articulated by the Indigenous rights movement throughout their thirty-year journey were left intact in the final text. The final text provides specificity on the rights of Indigenous peoples that did not previously exist in anti-discrimination human rights instruments. It includes a broad spectrum of collective rights to protect Indigenous cultures, languages, social relations, educational systems, political relations, and lands. It corrects the "salt water" exclusion of Indigenous peoples and nations from the UN decolonization regime and self-determination. It also establishes a framework of "best practices" for Indigenous–state relationships; a minimum standard of human rights that all states are now expected to recognize and protect.

This is not to argue that the success was complete or that state actions along the way have been accommodating, honorable, or even that they have consistently met minimum reasonable standards of good faith. Quite the contrary. As this chapter and Part II demonstrate, state behavior regarding Indigenous rights takes on new and noteworthy patterns – some patterns not previously seen in human rights campaigns – because states, especially certain settler colonial states like Canada, Australia, New Zealand, and the USA, treat Indigenous rights implementation as a direct threat. They are not entirely incorrect. The Declaration on the Rights of Indigenous Peoples is an indicator of global consensus that the ways in which these countries were founded, the ways in which they have ruled over Indigenous peoples, and the ways in which they continue to deal with Indigenous peoples today are now recognized as illegitimate human rights violations. Just as slavery and overseas colonization were once features of the international system that were taken for granted, only to later become delegitimized through global normative change, the Declaration now signals the end of the era when state domination over Indigenous peoples can be considered acceptable. Even with the addition of Article 46 to protect state sovereignty and territoriality, even with a change in language to indicate that the self-determination rights of Indigenous peoples are aspirational rather than inherently existing, states still recognize that implementation will require significant domestic and international change. Because Indigenous rights activists had not centered their struggle around a legal right of secession or even a state-centric construction of self-determination, Article 46 was viewed more as symptomatic of the pervasive sense of threat routinely expressed by states during the drafting, elaboration, and passage processes. In short, these last-minute, non-consensual, behind-the-scenes manipulations and almost desperate moves by certain state actors did not take these activists by surprise. Indeed, these state maneuvers exemplify the fundamentally oppressive and illegitimate presumptions upon which such states are founded.

Indigenous rights activists knew from the beginning that they were seeking no small set of changes. This was not like other human rights movements that sought mere inclusion for new populations in an already-existing human rights system. This was not like other human rights campaigns that challenged a few states to change their internal behavior toward particular populations. Rather, Indigenous rights activists have known from the beginning that they were ultimately delegitimizing colonization of Indigenous peoples as it has been practiced by settler colonial states and mimicked by other states around the world whose territories include Indigenous peoples. They knew they were attempting to do more than add themselves to the larger human rights regime. They knew they were countering a pattern of conquest, domination, and exploitation that has been routinely practiced for hundreds of years. They knew they were shaking up the status quo because the status quo was lethal to Indigenous peoples and Indigenous ways of life. They knew, from the very beginning, that the journey would be long and fraught with difficulty because of the depth, breadth, and strength of the very systems they were challenging. Onondaga Faith Keeper Oren Lyons captures these sentiments in a video called *Why We Came to Geneva in 1977*:

> When we arrived in Geneva, the Swiss official looked at me....
>
> And as we looked at each other, we realized that this was going to be a long encounter.... They weren't prepared for our intelligence, for our intensity, and for our mission.
>
> And so when we greeted each other, and we looked across the table for the first time, we both knew that this was going to be a long encounter.

Notes

1 I offer here only a handful of examples of the patterns of state resistance to the Declaration and to Indigenous rights. More forms of resistance will be elaborated in Chapters 4 and 5, but even these patterns should not be considered an exhaustive list. I interviewed numerous individuals who have been involved in Indigenous rights advocacy and heard stories of creative state resistance that are too numerous to relate here. Some activists have expressed the view that in the current age of Indigenous rights implementation, it is not politically wise or expedient to rehash all these stories. I do feel, however, that an analysis of some of the most common and egregious state resistance behaviors is central to the argument that states, especially settler colonial states, are deeply imbedded in the current international order and severely threatened by the scope and depth of changes that Indigenous rights implementation requires.

2 This case study is predominantly based on original archival and field research in Geneva, New York, and other locations in North America, and relies on three sources of data. First, I used United Nations documents, which are found in the collection of doCip, the Documentation Centre for Indigenous Peoples, located in Geneva. This archive holds the full set of documents associated with the development and passage of the Declaration on the Rights of Indigenous Peoples, from 1977 through 2007. I supplemented these documents with a set of interviews with key individuals involved in the Declaration process, as well as my direct observations of UN meetings and Indigenous Caucus meetings in both New York and Geneva. Because there have been individuals in the past who have infiltrated the Indigenous Caucus on behalf of states in order to disrupt the process, the Indigenous Caucus and other transnational Indigenous meetings are typically closed to outsiders. Indigenous individuals active in the international system are often reluctant to speak to academics or others who may or may not have their best interests in mind. Because maintaining consensus and solidarity has been so critical to the success of the Indigenous rights movement at the UN, the Indigenous Caucus and individuals associated with the movement do not easily trust outsiders. In order to maintain trust, identifying information from almost all interviews and transcripts has been removed. With only a few exceptions, the Indigenous activists that were interviewed will remain anonymous. Many identities could be easily ascertained by the inclusion of specific dates and locations of interviews, so anonymous interviews are typically cited only by an interviewee number and by the year of the interview, although the location and date of interviews will be cited where doing so would not divulge the identities of the individuals who gave the interview. All transcripts of both named and anonymous interviews are on file.

3 As a United Nations declaration and not a convention, the Declaration on the Rights of Indigenous Peoples is not legally binding on states, but rather, it is a political document that became part of the international human rights consensus and its principles are, in some sense, morally binding on all state conduct whether or not an individual state voted for it. The distinction between conventions and declarations is noted throughout United Nations documents. For example, Pamphlet No. 1 of the UN Guide for Minorities states:

> neither the UN General Assembly nor other UN bodies have the authority to create rules of law that are legally binding on States, but they have adopted a wide range of declarations, proclamations, recommendations, guidelines, and principles. These statements, particularly when they are adopted unanimously or by consensus, represent important political and moral commitments by States that may influence their conduct of international relations.
>
> (http://ohchr.org/Documents/Publications/GuideMinorities1en.pdf)

4 The notable exception is Australia, which was settled by the British without any form of treaty relations.

5 The Wounded Knee occupation began in February, 1973 when about 200 Oglala Lakota and American Indian Movement (AIM) members seized and occupied the town of Wounded Knee, South Dakota on the Pine Ridge Reservation. This was a grassroots protest against the USA government's failure to fulfill its treaty obligations as well as against the Richard Wilson tribal government at Pine Ridge. The site carried historical significance since it was the location of the Wounded Knee Massacre in 1890, when the Seventh Calvary massacred 300 Lakota women, children, and elders in the last military confrontation between the USA government and the Lakota. Both sides were heavily armed, gun battles were frequent, and a number of individuals on both sides were injured and killed. The siege ended on May 4, 1973 after the Nixon administration sent a letter to the activists promising that administration officials would meet the Lakota to discuss the 1868 Fort Laramie Treaty. The months following the siege saw massive violence, including the murder of sixty-nine AIM activists. Most activists were also arrested and tried in federal court.

6 The White Paper was an integrationist and assimilationist policy proposal made by Prime Minister Pierre Trudeau and Indian Affairs Minister Jean Chrétien. It proposed to abolish the Indian Act and Indian status in Canada, dissolve the Department of Indian Affairs, and dismantle the legal relationship between Indigenous peoples and the federal government in favor of equality. The Canadian government released the White Paper without having consulted Indigenous peoples.

7 Each of the twenty chapters is an individual UN document, but the full report was issued in a consolidated form in both English and Spanish in 1986 as E/CN.4/Sub.2/1986/7 and Add.1–3.

8 The Indian Law and Resource Center (ILRC) was founded as a US-based non-profit law and advocacy organization in 1978 and gained UN NGO consultative status shortly thereafter. Its mission is to provide legal assistance to American Indian and Alaska Native nations. According to the organization's website (http://indianlaw.org/), it brought the first Indigenous rights case to the Inter-American Commission on Human Rights in 1979, submitted the first human rights complaint against the USA to the UN Commission on Human Rights, and led the effort to establish the UN Working Group on Indigenous Populations. The ILRC's founder and executive director is attorney Robert "Tim" Coulter, an enrolled member of the Citizen Potawatomi Nation.

9 The UN Charter includes the fundamental principle of self-determination, but Articles 1 of both the International Covenant on Civil and Political Rights and the International Covenant on Economic, Social and Cultural Rights state that "All peoples have the right of self-determination," implying inherency. However, the Declaration on the Granting of Independence to Colonial Countries and Peoples, General Assembly Resolution 1514 (XV) of December 14, 1960 states: "all peoples have the right *to* self-determination," indicating aspiration (emphasis added).

10 Every attempt has been made to specify countries and individuals who contributed particular statements in the Working Group; however, many such details are often not recoverable based on existing documentation. The Working Group reports often do not list specifics of which country or which individual in the Working Group made a particular statement. The reports typically refer to "one state" or "a group of states" or "one member of the Working Group" rather than specify them by name. I have examined the numerous official statements submitted by governments and NGOs to doCIP, in order to decipher the source of statements, but in some cases these details were not possible to reconstruct. In these instances, I have followed UN Working Group practice as executed in their reports and refer simply to "a state," "some states," and "a member of the Working Group." This practice reflects only a paucity of detailed information in the documentary record, and does not reflect any attempt on my part to hide identities.

11 Professor Anaya was later named UN Special Rapporteur on the Rights of Indigenous Peoples, the first Indigenous person to hold this position. He served in that capacity from May, 2008 until May, 2014.

12 This handwritten statement dated October 25, 1996, issued by the International Indian Treaty Council on behalf of the Indigenous Caucus, is on file with doCip in Geneva.

13 The hunger strikers were: Adelard Blackman (Buffalo River Dene Nation, Canada), Andrea Carmen (Yaqui Nation, Arizona, USA), Alexis Tiouka (Kalina, French Guyana), Charmaine White Face (Oglala Tetuwan, Sioux Nation Territory, North America), Danny Illie (Traditional Independent Seminole Nation of Florida, United States), and Saul Vincente (Zapoteca, Mexico).

14 The Human Rights Commission was being dissolved and replaced with a new body called the Human Rights Council.

15 Most African and Asian states argue that there are no "Indigenous peoples" in their countries since everyone is "Indigenous." The tendency in these regions is for governments to refer to "tribal populations" or even "backward peoples." I heard the accusation of CANZUS state manipulations of African states numerous times in interviews and during attendance at meetings of the Indigenous Caucus in Geneva.

16 Some Indigenous organizations (e.g., the IITC) decided to not support yet also not oppose the amendments. As the IITC's Executive Director Andrea Carmen (2007) explained, "It was either this or worse."

17 Abstentions were: Azerbaijan, Bangladesh, Bhutan, Burundi, Columbia, Georgia, Kenya, Nigeria, the Russian Federation, Samoa, and Ukraine.

18 Chad, Côte d'Ivoire, Equatorial Guinea, Eritrea, Ethiopia, Fiji, Gambia, Grenada, Guinea-Bissau, Israel, Kiribati, Kyrgyzstan, Marshall Islands, Mauritania, Montenegro, Morocco, Nauru, Palau, Papua New Guinea, Romania, Rwanda, St. Kitts and Nevis, São Tomé and Príncipe, Seychelles, Solomon Islands, Somalia, Tajikistan, Togo, Tonga, Turkmenistan, Tuvalu, Uganda, Uzbekistan, Vanuatu.

19 Tēnā rāwā atu koe (many thanks) to Moana Jackson who brought this issue to my attention.

References

African Group, 2006. *Draft Aide Memoire: United Nations Declaration on the Rights of Indigenous People 9 November 2006*. New York: African Group.

Canada Press, 2007. Last update, Press Report. Available at: http://ca.news.yahoo.com/s/capress/070606/national/cda_un_native_rights [last accessed July 14, 2010].

Carmen, A., 2007. Interview by Author with Andrea Carmen, Executive Director, International Indian Treaty Council, September 24, 2007. Transcript on file. Mille Lacs Nation, Minnesota.

Corntassel, J., 2007. Partnership in Action? Indigenous Political Mobilization and Co-optation During the First UN Indigenous Decade (1995–2004). *Human Rights Quarterly*, 29, pp. 137–166.

Daes, E.A., 1988. *Report of the Working Group on Indigenous Populations on its Sixth Session UN Doc E/CN.4/Sub.2/1988/24*. Geneva: United Nations.

Daes, E.A., 1989. *Report of the Working Group on Indigenous Populations on its Seventh Session UN Doc E/CN.4/Sub.2/1989/36*. Geneva: United Nations.

Daes, E.A., 1990. *Report of the Working Group on Indigenous Populations on its Eighth Session UN Doc E/CN.2/Sub.2/1990/42*. Geneva: United Nations.

Daes, E.A., 1991a. *Report of the Working Group on Indigenous Populations on its Ninth Session UN Doc E/CN.4/Sub.2/1991/40*. Geneva: United Nations.

Daes, E.A., 1991b. *Working Paper on the Revised Draft Declaration on the Rights of Indigenous Peoples UN Doc E/CN.4/Sub.2/1991/36*. Geneva: United Nations.

Daes, E.A., 1992. *Report of the Working Group on Indigenous Populations on its Tenth Session UN Doc E/CN.4/Sub.2/1992/33*. Geneva: United Nations.

Daes, E.A., 1993. *Report of the Working Group on Indigenous Populations on its Eleventh Session UN Doc E/CN.4/Sub.2/1993/29*. Geneva: United Nations.

Deer, K., 2011. Reflections on the Development, Adoption, and Implementation of the UN Declaration on the Rights of Indigenous Peoples. In J. Hartley, P. Joffe, and J. Preston, eds, *Realizing the UN Declaration on the Rights of Indigenous Peoples: Triumph, Hope, and Action*. Saskatoon, SK: Purich, pp. 18–28.

Deloria, J. Vine, 1974 [1985]. *Behind the Trail of Broken Treaties: An Indian Declaration of Independence*. Austin: University of Texas Press.

Dunbar-Ortiz, R., 2006. The First Decade of Indigenous Peoples at the United Nations. *Peace and Change*, 31(1), pp. 58–74.

Henderson, J., 2008. *Indigenous Diplomacy and the Rights of Peoples: Achieving UN Recognition*. Saskatoon, SK: Purich.

Indigenous Caucus, 1996a. *Press Release: Indigenous Peoples' Caucus Calls for Change to UN Rules*, October 28. Geneva: Indigenous Caucus.

Indigenous Caucus, 1996b. *Statement of 25 October 1996.* Geneva: Indigenous Caucus.
Indigenous Nations And Organizations, 2005. Open Letter to the President of the UN Commission on Human Rights from 130 Indigenous Nations and Organizations, March 15.
Indigenous Peoples' Caucus Regional Steering Committee, 2007. Press Release: United Nations General Assembly Adopts the United Nations Declaration on the Rights of Indigenous Peoples, September 13. New York.
Indigenous Peoples' Representatives at the United Nations, 2004. *Press Release: Hunger Strike by Indigenous Peoples' Representatives at the United Nations*, November 29.
Indigenous Activist #2, 2007. Interview by author. Transcript on file.
Indigenous Activist #3, 2007. Interview by author. Transcript on file.
Indigenous Activist #4, 2007. Interview by author. Transcript on file.
Indigenous Activist #7, 2007. Interview by author. Transcript on file.
International Indian Treaty Council (IITC), 1977. *The Geneva Conference: International NGO Conference on Discrimination Against Indigenous Populations in the Americas.* New York: International Indian Treaty Council.
Jackson, M., 2008. Interview by author. Transcript on file. Wellington, Aotearoa/New Zealand.
Lyons, O., 2015. Why We Came to Geneva: Indigenous Peoples' First Time to the UN in Geneva. Available at: https://youtube.com/watch?v=NLNMEbzm4WM [last accessed July 16, 2015].
Malezer, L., 2007. Urgent Message – Indigenous Peoples – Global Consultation – Important Notice. Sent out by Les Malezer, Chairperson, Indigenous Peoples Caucus at the UN, September 1. New York.
Malezer, L. and Trask, M., 2007. Urgent Request and Update Relating to Final UN Action on the Declaration on the Rights of Indigenous Peoples, Pacific Regional Coordinators on the Draft Declaration on the Rights of Indigenous Peoples, September 2. New York.
Martinez, E.J.O., 2007. Statement by First Secretary, Humanitarian and Social Issues, Permanent Mission of Mexico to the United Nations at a Progress Report on the Declaration on the Rights of Indigenous Peoples, April 12, Church Center at the UN. New York.
Means, B., 2008. Interview by author. Transcript on file. St. Paul, MN.
Newcomb, S.T., 2011. The UN Declaration on the Rights of Indigenous Peoples and the Paradigm of Domination. *Griffith Law Review*, 20(3), pp. 578–607.
Newman, D.G., 2010. Africa and the United Nations Declaration on the Rights of Indigenous Peoples. In S. Dersso, ed., *Perspectives on the Rights of Minorities and Indigenous Peoples in Africa.* Pretoria, SA: Pretoria University Law Press, pp. 141–154.
Niezen, R., 2003. *The Origins of Indigenism: Human Rights and the Politics of Identity.* Berkeley: University of California Press.
Office of the High Commissioner For Human Rights, 2011. Last update, Pamphlet No. 1: Minorities, the United Nations and Regional Mechanisms. Available at: http://.ohchr.org/Documents/Publications/GuideMinorities1en.pdf [last accessed July 10, 2015].
Special NGO Committee on Human Rights (Geneva), 1981. International NGO Conference on Indigenous Peoples and the Land, organized by the Sub-Commission on Racism, Racial Discrimination, Apartheid and Decolonisation, Final Report. Available from doCIP, Avenue de Trembley 14-CH 1209, Geneva, Switzerland.
UN Department of Public Information, 2007. *Press Conference on Indigenous Rights Declaration*, September 6. New York: United Nations.
United Nations, 1970. Sub-Commission on Prevention of Discrimination and Protection of Minorities Resolution 4B (XXIII), August 26.

United Nations Commission on Human Rights, Sub-Commission on Prevention of Discrimination and Protection of Minorities, 1982. *Report of the Working Group on Indigenous Populations on its First Session UN Doc E/CN.4/Sub2/1982/33.* New York: United Nations.

United Nations Economic and Social Council, 1982. *Study of the Problem of Discrimination Against Indigenous Populations Resolution 1982/34.* New York: United Nations.

United Nations Economic and Social Council, 1995. *Establishment of a Working Group of the Commission on Human Rights to Elaborate a Draft Declaration in Accordance with Paragraph 5 of General Assembly Resolution 49/214.* Economic and Social Council Resolution 1995/32.

United Nations Economic and Social Council, 1998. *Report of the Working Group Established in Accordance with Commission on Human Rights Resolution 1995/32 of 3 March 1995 UN Doc E/CN.4/1998/106.* Geneva: United Nations.

United Nations Economic and Social Council, 2005. *Report of the Working Group Established in Accordance with Commission on Human Rights Resolution 1995/32 of 3 March 1995 UN Doc E/CN.4/2005/89.* Geneva: United Nations.

United Nations General Assembly, 1960. *Declaration on the Granting of Independence to Colonial Countries and Peoples UN Resolution 1514 (VX)*, December 14.

United Nations General Assembly, 2006a. *Namibia: Amendments to Draft Resolution A/C.3/61/L.18/Rev.1 Working Group of the Commission on Human Rights to Elaborate a Draft Declaration in Accordance with Paragraph 5 of General Assembly Resolution 49/214 of 23 December 1994 UN Doc A/C.3/61/L.57/Rev.1.* New York: United Nations.

United Nations General Assembly, 2006b. *Report of the Human Rights Council, Report of the Third Committee UN Doc A/61/448.* New York: United Nations.

United Nations General Assembly, 2007. *Report of the Human Rights Council: United Nations Declaration on the Rights of Indigenous Peoples UN Doc A/61/L.67.* New York: United Nations.

United Nations Human Rights Council, 2006. *Working Group of the Commission on Human Rights to Elaborate a Draft Declaration in Accordance with Paragraph 5 of the General Assembly Resolution 49/214 of 23 December 1994 UN Doc A/HRC/RES/1/2.* Geneva: United Nations.

United Nations Sub-Commission on Prevention of Discrimination and Protection of Minorities, 1987. *Study of the Problem of Discrimination Against Indigenous Populations by Jose R. Martinez Cobo (Special Rapporteur of the Sub-Commission on Prevention of Discrimination and Protection of Minorities) UN Doc E/CN.4/Sub.2/1986/7/Add.4.* New York: United Nations.

United Nations Sub-Commission on Prevention of Discrimination and Protection of Minorities, 1994. *Draft United Nations Declaration on the Rights of Indigenous Peoples Sub Commission Resolution 1994/45.* Geneva: Office of the United Nations High Commissioner for Human Rights.

United Nations Working Group On Indigenous Populations, 1982. *Principles for Guiding the Deliberations of the Working Group UN Doc WGIP82/AME/2.* Geneva: United Nations.

United Nations Working Group On Indigenous Populations, 1984. *Report of the Working Group on Indigenous Populations on its Third Session UN Doc E/CN.4/Sub.2.1984/20.* Geneva: United Nations.

United Nations Working Group On Indigenous Populations, 1985. *Report of the Working Group on Indigenous Populations on its Fourth Session UN Doc E/CN.4/Sub.2.1985/22.* Geneva: United Nations.

United Nations Working Group On Indigenous Populations, 1987a. *Declaration of Principles Adopted by the Indigenous Preparatory Meeting, held at Geneva 27–31 July 1987. UN Doc E/CN.4/Sub.2/1987/22, Annex V.* Geneva: United Nations.

United Nations Working Group On Indigenous Populations, 1987b. *Report of the Working Group on Indigenous Populations on its Sixth Session UN Doc E/CN.4/Sub.2/1987/22.* Geneva: United Nations.

United Nations Working Group on Indigenous Populations, 1990. *Report of the Informal Drafting Groups Established to Consider the First Revised Text of the Draft Universal Declaration on Indigenous Rights UN Doc E/CN.4/Sub.2/AC.4/1990/7/Add.1.* Geneva: United Nations.

United Nations Working Group on the Draft Declaration, 1996. *Organization of Work (Participation) UN Doc E/CN.4/1996/WG.15/CRP.7.* Geneva: United Nations.

United Nations Working Group on the Draft Declaration, 2004. *Amended Text United Nations Draft Declaration on the Rights of Indigenous Peoples UN Doc E/CN.4/2004/WG.15/CRP.1.* Geneva: United Nations.

United Nations Working Group on the Draft Declaration, 2005. *Revised Chairman's Summary and Proposal UN Doc E/CN.4/2005/G.15/2.* Geneva: United Nations.

United States Mission to the United Nations, 2007. *News Release: Observations of the United States with Respect to the Declaration on the Rights of Indigenous Peoples, 13 September 2007.* New York: United Nations.

Venne, S., 2011. The Road to the United Nations and Rights of Indigenous Peoples. *Griffith Law Review*, 20(3), pp. 557–577.

Watson, I. and Venne, S., 2012. Talking up Indigenous Peoples' Original Intent in a Space Dominated by State Interventions. In E. Pulitano, ed., *Indigenous Rights in the Age of the Declaration.* Cambridge: Cambridge University Press, pp. 87–109.

White Face, C. and Wobaga, Z., 2013. *Indigenous Nations' Rights in the Balance: An Analysis of the Declaration on the Rights of Indigenous Peoples.* St. Paul, MN: Living Justice Press.

Wilmer, F., 1993. *The Indigenous Voice in World Politics.* Newbury Park, NJ: Sage.

3 Practicing global politics in Indigenous ways

The enactment of Indigeneity at the United Nations has always been an enigma for states, the UN bureaucracy, NGOs, grassroots Indigenous communities, and scholars. Confusion abounds about how and why the Indigenous movement behaves the way it does at the UN and in other international fora. Is this movement, as many state representatives say among themselves, a bunch of agitating Indigenous activists in colorful garb making excessive, impractical, and unreasonable demands on states and the UN system? Or, as some Indigenous community members, activists, and scholars charge, have the members of the Indigenous rights movement become a co-opted elite, "selling out" to the states and the rules of the UN, fashioning careers for themselves by writing speeches to deliver at the UN to no practical end?

This chapter will argue that, contrary to both of these divergent views, the Indigenous rights movement is a unique force in global politics and is, in fact, reshaping how politics can be done at the UN and in other international fora. Grounded in transnational Indigenous ways of being, with grassroots activist origins, the movement is deeply anti-colonial in both nature and practice, and consistently and in multiple ways challenges international structures of domination and subordination. At the same time, Indigenous political actors are intelligent, strategic, creative, and articulate diplomats on the global stage, seeking a global space of dignity for Indigenous peoples. Global Indigenous politics is bringing forward ways of practicing global politics that fundamentally differ from predominant state-centric practices. By drawing on Indigenous ontologies, values, and commitments, global Indigenous politics offers a new (old) method of practice in international politics.

My qualitative research approach draws heavily upon Indigenous methodologies, which are approaches to research that privilege Indigenous voices, experiences, knowledge, reflections, and analyses. These approaches are deliberately and unapologetically activist, and counter-hegemonic in the tradition of critical theories and emancipatory research (Rigney 1999; G.H. Smith 2000; L.T. Smith 2000, 2005, 2012; Cram 2001; Bishop 2005). Linda Smith (2012) describes these methodologies as "involving the unmasking and deconstruction of imperialism … in its old and new formulations," as well as the transformation of colonial relations. Indigenous methodologies situate research programs and approaches firmly within a decolonization framework while attempting to build and maintain connections between the academy, Indigenous communities, and wider political struggles. Indigenous approaches to research recognize that research is never neutral but reproduces a certain set of power relations, and so Indigenous methodologies attempt to channel their transformative agenda to the benefit of Indigenous communities.

Indigenist approaches to research require particular sets of ethics, protocols, and methodologies. Three principles are central. First, reciprocal and respectful relationships must be established and maintained. Second, trustworthiness and integrity must be absolute. Third, researchers need to be accountable to the Indigenous communities being researched and engage in "culturally responsive research practices." This also means that research questions should emanate from the Indigenous community and results reported back to the community in a comprehensible way. These are the guiding values and principles I adopt in my research. While I am asking research questions relevant to international relations theory, I am merging those questions with those I have also heard voiced in Native American and First Nations communities, questions that are relevant to Indigenous activism and politics not only in my communities but at the global level as well.

I rely upon numerous sources of data for this chapter. First, as in the historical analysis in Chapter 2, I utilized United Nations documents that are housed in the collection of doCip in Geneva. I supplemented these documents with a set of interviews with key individuals involved in the Declaration process and in the transnational Indigenous rights movement more generally. I also integrate my own direct observations of numerous meetings in New York, Geneva, and other varied locations over nearly a decade.[1] Interviews, direct observations, and participant observations of international Indigenous activity took place between mid-2007 and mid-2015. Interviews with participants in the transnational Indigenous rights movement were conducted between September, 2007 and early 2014. In total, thirty-five interviews were conducted during this time period in a variety of locations around the world. These interviews were semi-structured, with a focus on a particular set of questions, but interviewees were encouraged to talk about global Indigenous politics as they saw and understood it.

Some of the transnational Indigenous political activity I was able to directly observe is closed to outsiders, and I was able to gain access only because of the leadership position I held in an Indigenous organization at the time. I thus sometimes became a participant observer in the transnational Indigenous rights movement and part of the process, rather than remaining simply an academic observer outside the process (Bositis 1990; Schuler and Namoika 1993). While I always disclosed my university affiliation and my academic research agenda, there were several meetings where I was allowed to attend only as a person holding a leadership position in an Indigenous organization. I also needed permission from the Board of Directors of my home organization to travel and represent them while I was doing field research. Because of the delicate issues of representation and accountability involved in this process, and in an effort to maintain the confidentiality of the Indigenous Caucus, I tend toward explaining generalities I observed over time rather than detailed specifics of meetings. While I do include some quotations from these meetings, I never identify the speaker or the date, or the location of the meeting. As in Chapter 2, some interviewees have chosen to be identified, while others have preferred to remain anonymous. I have made every attempt to preserve their anonymity and the integrity of their decision.

The foundation: transnational Indigenous ways of being

I refer to the character of the Indigenous rights movement as "transnational Indigenous ways of being." No monolithic "Indigenous" culture exists, and there is obviously vast diversity among the world's more than 300 million Indigenous peoples making up 5000 distinct Indigenous nations spanning seventy-two countries.[2] Even so, as Niezen (2003) observed, the Indigenous rights movement is centered on the concept of a globally shared Indigenous identity that largely emerged as a result of the movement. This is a supranational layer of Indigenous identity added to the already complex web of kinship, tribal, and national identities that Indigenous people maintain. It is important to note that this Indigenous identity, while global in scope, is not intended as a universalizing force. Rather, it deliberately aims to collectively secure the distinctiveness and singularity of individual Indigenous nations, cultures, and communities. One unifying force is what Māori lawyer and long-time Indigenous rights activist Moana Jackson (2008) describes as "an Indigenous worldview in which there are similarities of perceptions about the Earth as the mother and the importance of *whakapapa*, or relationships" among human and non-human entities and spirits. The other unifying force is what anthropologist Andrea Muehlebach (2001) notes is a common experience of colonial oppression coupled with "a discourse of global indigeneity founded on the centrality of self-determination." In sum, the movement is grounded in a unifying (as distinct from unified) vision of Indigenous ontologies and composed of thoughtful and creatively strategic Indigenous political actors who represent the diversity of Indigenous peoples and enact common Indigenous values in their transnational activities. The very first official document of the Indigenous rights movement, the 1974 Declaration of Continuing Independence by the First International Treaty Council, makes these unifying forces clear:

> Might does not make right. Sovereign people of varying cultures have the absolute right to live in harmony with Mother Earth so long as they do not infringe upon this same right of other peoples. The denial of this right to any sovereign people, such as the Native American Indian Nations, must be challenged by *truth* and *action*. World concern must focus on all colonial governments to the end that sovereign people everywhere shall live as they choose; in peace with dignity and freedom.

While Indigenous cultures vary widely, there does seem to be a broad tendency toward a shared vision of life and the universe as interconnected, and respectful relationships must therefore be cultivated and maintained. This type of vision also characterizes the Indigenous rights movement. In every internal meeting I have observed over nearly a decade, members of the movement begin their remarks with "brothers and sisters" and in Spanish "hermanos y hermanas." Some Indigenous individuals and groups extend this practice into meetings with states, although, given the depth of anger, resentment, and suspicion many Indigenous peoples hold against state governments due to the nature and length of their oppression at the hands of nation-states, this issue is more contentious. Nevertheless, the norm of respectful relations prevails. For example, at the Seventh Session of the United Nations Permanent Forum on Indigenous Issues (UNPFII) in 2008, a representative from a large Latin American Indigenous organization rose and expressed his frustration with the state-centric nature of the UN, speaking harshly of states and accusing them of using Indigenous peoples as mere puppets in their relations among themselves. UNPFII Chair Victoria Tauli-Corpuz encouraged restraint and respect, saying,

> This is an organization of states, IOs, and Indigenous peoples. It will not be acceptable to cast aspersion on members of the Secretariat or even on states. We must show respect to all others who are engaging with us in this dialogue.
> (Author's personal notes)

Also reflecting widespread Indigenous philosophies, the Indigenous rights movement takes a holistic approach that is firmly grounded in culture and spirituality. As one activist said in an anonymous interview:

> I think it's a basic philosophical difference between the modern world and Indigenous people – modern governments I should say and Indigenous peoples – is that there is no separation of our culture and government, or our rights. So in many cases we don't even attempt to make that distinction.
> (Indigenous activist #4 2007)

Both the current practice and revitalization of Indigenous cultures is a priority. Long-time activist and International Treaty Council Board Member Bill Means (2008) describes it as

> part of our cultures, and certainly the idea is that our culture is still practiced and we haven't put it aside into a university or a history book and so we're basically – we're not doing anything new for our people, we're carrying out our culture and our history.

The movement finds unity and solidarity in the expression of individual Indigenous cultures. At every international movement meeting I have ever observed, greetings are exchanged in a cross-cultural manner. Individuals greet one another in their own Indigenous language and then also use the other person's language if possible. For example, both Māori and non-Māori people greet one another with "kia ora" (the Māori term of greeting) and the *hongi*, which is a form of Māori greeting where the noses of the greeting persons are touched together so that each person can share the breath of the other. Ojibwe and non-Ojibwe people greet one another with "Boo-zhoo," the Ojibwe word for "hello," and likewise, both Hawaiians and non-Hawaiians say "aloha."

Living culture is also expressed in the way individuals dress for meetings and events, representing simultaneously unity and diversity as well as helping keep people grounded in who they are and whom they represent. Indigenous cultures are always manifested in dress and ornaments worn for meetings. From the very first WCIP conference in 1975, Indigenous participants have worn traditional regalia and have included song, dance, and ceremony as a part of both formal and informal meetings. As Sanders (1980) describes,

> The Sami delegates and observers wore their richly coloured costumes [*sic*] during the conference. Certain of the Latin American delegates wore typical ponchos. There was a rich pride in culture, which showed most clearly at the evening gatherings in the auditorium – with singing, dancing and ceremonies. The richness and diversity of the gathering was hard to absorb.

While clearly political, the Indigenous rights movement remains intensely spiritual. One activist stated unequivocally that "a spiritual foundation laid the groundwork" for global Indigenous solidarity. He said,

> At a lot of these meetings I've participated in a lot of ceremonies around the world where Indigenous peoples have come together in that way, and I think that's strengthened us and made the movement a little bit different than other movements.
>
> (Indigenous activist #6 2007)

Another activist stated that this tradition began at the 1977 Geneva Conference and that this "phenomenon introduced by Indigenous people is a recognition of culture at least in terms of reminding ourselves where we come from" (Indigenous activist #4 2007).

My research confirms this practice. Every meeting, whether an International Indian Treaty Council (IITC) Board meeting, an Indigenous Caucus meeting in Geneva, or the Permanent Forum on Indigenous Issues (UNPFII) at UN headquarters in New York, begins with an opening prayer and/or song, always conducted in the Indigenous language of the person invited to do so. In addition, the people of the territory where the meeting is being held will lead the prayer, or, if they are not present, they will be acknowledged before opening the meeting. Even the IITC logo demonstrates the spiritual grounding of the organization. It includes a map of the Western hemisphere shown without any borders overlaid by "the symbol of the sacred pipe uniting the hemisphere [which] was chosen for IITC by the elders to represent the common bonds of spirituality, ties to the land and respect for traditional culture and spirituality which is common to all

Indigenous Peoples" (International Indian Treaty Council (IITC) 2015). Ron Lameman (2007) of the Beaver Lake Cree Nation, Confederacy of Treaty Six Nations, and one of the early members of the Working Group on Indigenous Populations, expressed the centrality of spirituality to the movement:

> The work at the UN was a spiritual movement. Our elders used to come to the UN. We remember them, and it makes us stronger. We forge ahead for our children and grandchildren. It's like witnessing a prayer unfold before our eyes.

Another characteristic of the Indigenous rights movement is a tendency toward long-term thinking that decisions should be made with the impact of multiple generations in mind. The idea is that actions taken in the past have a direct impact on peoples today and decisions made in the present will likewise have a direct future impact. Māori activist and law professor Claire Charters (2007) spoke of the long-term vision on Indigenous rights implementation:

> It's not necessarily about what happens in the short-term, as is the case within the structure of democratic states, but the Indigenous perspective is much more long-term and is seeking to protect our rights for generations to come – not just in the next one, two, five, or ten years.

As a result, Indigenous peoples have a responsibility to make decisions that are sustainable and will not cause harm in the future. The late Tonya Gonnella Frichner (2011), Onondaga lawyer, activist, president and founder of the American Indian Law Alliance, and expert member of the UNPFII, emphasized this approach as central to the transnational struggle for Indigenous rights:[3]

> As we say from the community that I'm from, the Haudenosaunee, when our leaders sit in deliberation, when they are in counsel, their decisions are going to be made with the seventh generation in mind.... So that we don't stick with a quick fix, or something that will only last for fifteen years. No, it must be until that seventh generation has arrived. The world needs to be intact for them when they arrive and are here to take on the challenges of this world.

Frichner explained that this approach traces back to the Great Law of Peace, the seventeenth-century constitution of the Iroquois, or Haudenosaunee, Confederacy. While many people associate seventh-generation thinking with ecology and environmental concerns, it is more than that. Since everything is interconnected in Indigenous thought, the ecological cannot be separated from any other form of human and non-human relations without thinking about how it affects other parts of the interconnected world, necessitating both holistic and long-term perspectives.

The approach: strategies, tactics, and processes of the Indigenous rights movement

The individuals who represent Indigenous organizations at the global level display very high levels of strategic and pragmatic thinking as well as a deep commitment to common goals. Many are trained and practicing lawyers while others have years of experience as activists, community leaders, and in NGO management. Niezen (2003) identified secondary education as a key factor in the emergence of the movement, especially its timing. Bill Means confirmed this observation, noting that education and the increasing expertise of global Indigenous actors has been an important characteristic of the movement:

> As Indigenous people had more access to education, the movement for our rights grew – should we say right alongside of that access to education. Because we could go into the legal documents, we could go into the historical documents and read and understand them; and most importantly we could produce our own – our own studies to counter and to document why we're questioning certain things, and policies, and laws, and demanding our rights.
>
> (Means 2008)

From the earliest days of the Indigenous rights movement, its founders recognized that the UN offered political opportunity, and a certain space to assert Indigenous rights using a moral leverage strategy made possible through human rights regimes. In other words, the UN and human rights were and are viewed as useful tools for domestic Indigenous struggles, not the end game in and of themselves. Implementation of Indigenous rights, Bill Means explained (2008), was to be a two-track process, both with standard setting at the UN followed by country-by-country implementation: "Now that we have a standard, all governments where Indigenous people live will be continuously challenged to uphold that standard whether that country voted or their government voted for it or not." As another anonymous IITC Board Member put it at a meeting in 2007, "Instead of only scrapping with these guys domestically, let them know that there is an additional level that can be used."

Mohawk activist Kenneth Deer explained that by framing Indigenous rights as human rights,

> we have the moral high ground. And that's why we can't support terrorism or certain kinds of actions that might abandon that moral high ground. You don't do that.... We have to maintain the moral high ground on the fundamental issues over the long term.

The only leverage, he explained, lies in the collective conscience of the larger society; "But it's not a question of guilt, it's a question of reason. And, people say, we shouldn't feel guilty. It's not about guilt, it's about justice. And also, it's reasonable to do that" (Deer 2012). At the same time, members of the movement were and remain keenly aware of the inherent tensions involved in framing Indigenous rights as human rights, as scholar Peter Kulchyski (2013) has also noted. Moana Jackson (2008) clarifies that

> our people have never been naively optimistic about the international human rights process and we are very aware of what I guess are the philosophical shortcomings in that construct … and so we see it not as a panacea but as another tool that can be used.

One individual in an Indigenous Caucus meeting in Geneva also demonstrated consciousness of these complexities by stating: "Indigenous rights are *more* than just human rights. The human rights mechanisms are not adequate to protect Indigenous rights. So, we prefer to talk about Indigenous rights, which are now protected by an international standard, rather than human rights."

This consciousness traces back to the beginning of the movement:

> The contradictions between theory and practice in western European colonialism suggested to indigenous populations that they could influence the European powers by political and legal agitation. It was, at best, an uncertain alternative to other forms of resistance. This type of indigenous political activity began within particular colonial systems. It expanded to the sphere of international organizations when the League of Nations and the United Nations were formed. In the last decade it has led to the formation of an international organization, the World Council of Indigenous Peoples, which has established a formal relationship to the United Nations and is seeking to have concepts of aboriginal rights accepted internationally as basic economic and political rights of indigenous peoples.
>
> (Sanders 1980)

For many Indigenous peoples around the world, conflict resolution typically occurs through open discussion of issues (which can often become quite heated) but where all viewpoints are heard and then consensus positions reached through discussion and persuasion rather than majority vote. Often, an elder who rises to tell a story does the most effective persuasion. Contained in that story is a metaphor or central message that convinces the group of the best course of action. Examples of this storytelling technique will appear throughout the remainder of this chapter, where lengthy quotes are often included in their entirety, to demonstrate this form of consensus seeking in action. While consensus does not necessarily mean unanimity and individuals remain free to defect, this model of conflict resolution tends to lead to stronger solidarity and unity among Indigenous peoples. Among the Indigenous delegates at the UN, there has been a "genuine and agreed commitment to seek consensus" (Jackson 2008).

The search for unifying Indigenous positions through consensus appeared at the first global Indigenous conferences in the 1970s. The 1977 IITC Geneva

Conference report notes that "nightly meetings were held during which consensus was reached concerning the content and structure of the next days [*sic*] work." An Indigenous delegate from the 1977 Geneva Conference explained how the traditional model of consensus works in his North American Native community:

> The whole idea of consensus is that all viewpoints are heard, and if there's a disagreement then we have to deal with the particular aspects, points of that disagreement and not just make some kind of blanket decision. As Indian people we do that, have consensus or try to go by consensus. I've been to meetings as a young person where the elders appoint – and the English word they use is critic – after people have their say then this person we call critic, has the right to limit the debate and then to ask people or a council of chiefs depending on the situation, a number of people, a smaller number of people I should say agree on how to go forward. Usually it's not even a vote, it's just a smaller group of elders – in our ways.
>
> (Indigenous activist #1 2007)

Since the 1977 Geneva Conference was one of the first to bring together diverse Indigenous delegates, NGOs, and governments, one would not expect to see strong consensus among them. Such events are likely to be characterized by discussions about the diversity of interests which individual groups bring to the meeting. However, contrary to such expectations, this conference demonstrated how such a diversity of Indigenous groups could come together in strong consensus positions. Two issues emerged immediately in the Indigenous Caucus[4] that met ahead of the full conference with governments and NGOs, which Indigenous groups needed to resolve prior to the actual conference so as to present a stronger and more unified position. The resolution of these issues helped pave the way for Indigenous transnational solidarity and consensus building.

The first of these issues was self-identity, or what the disparate groups were to call themselves in the conglomerate. IITC Board Member Bill Means (2008) tells the story:

> The first part is what do we call ourselves?
>
> Some people said, "Well I'm Mayan." Other people said "I'm Quechua." They didn't want to certainly be identified by the nation state they came from – the whole hemisphere agreed on that. Well, what do we call ourselves? Indigenous people? Do we call ourselves Mestizo? Do we call ourselves Indians? And finally one of the elders from South America, an organization called CISA, Indian Council of South America, got up and said, "If Indian was a name under which we were oppressed, then Indian will be the name under which we will rise." That settled that argument. So we identified as Indian, and, believe me, this was a difficult decision, especially for Latin America, because to call someone *indio* in Spanish, more so in those days but, even today, is a very derogatory term, and so this

> coming – emanating from South America where there is so much discrimination, as much or more than America, that it had particular significance; and so that was the beginning.

While the terminology used by the transnational Indigenous rights movement would later change from "Indian" to "Indigenous peoples" in order to draw in groups from outside the Western hemisphere, the method used by the movement to resolve the issue laid the groundwork for how future issues would be resolved within the movement.

IITC's Bill Means continues the story by talking about the resolution of the second major issue among Indigenous groups – who would speak first at the upcoming conference:

> Another phenomenon happened on who would speak first, that was the next item on the agenda. So, of course, the Haudenosaunee, the Six Nations, they said "Well, we sent Deskaheh here in ... the era of the League of Nations," which was housed in Geneva. "Therefore as a reminder of that history, we should go first."
>
> Us Lakotas, we said, "Well, we've got a strong treaty and this mandate of the Treaty Council to put forth the issue of treaties, and because of that we should go first because treaties represent the legal foundation of nation to nation."
>
> The Central Americans said that their civilization, the Mayan civilization, is the oldest recorded history in this part of the world. South Americans said, "We represent millions, we're not just one million, we're not just two million, we're many millions, and so we should go first."
>
> Then a great thing happened. Phil Deere, who is Muskogee Creek, and board member, and one of the founders of Treaty Council, got up when it came his turn to speak, and said, "Many years ago before we had electricity we had fire-keepers, people who kept the flint and the stone. It was their responsibility to start the fire. Before they prepared the fire, they would get all the wood and the kindling and everything together, and then they would get around in a circle, and each one then would start from a different point around that kindling using their flint and stone to make the spark. Nobody really knew who made the first spark that created the fire. They all were given credit as fire-keepers for starting the fire. Today we are starting a fire in the United Nations, it doesn't matter who goes first."
>
> That ended that argument.

As they had in 1977, Indigenous groups met in Caucus prior to the 1981 Geneva Conference, as well as during the conference, in order to reach consensus positions that would give them stronger and more unified positions vis-à-vis states during the conference.[5] The 1981 final Conference Report notes that the success of the conference was "particularly due to the very thorough preparations prior to the conference on the part of Indigenous peoples' organizations" who had produced more than fifty papers in advance of the conference, all by consensus.

In the Indigenous Caucus meetings I observed, consensus has been the primary objective and process focus. Since the Indigenous Caucus is constrained by time and resources as much as any other political decision-making body in any context, a vote is sometimes required in order to reach a final decision, although in the Indigenous Caucus this is viewed as a highly undesirable last resort. One activist (2010) described the difficulties of using consensus within the UN structure, noting that "the UN itself uses that word consensus and it's fairly close to Indigenous peoples' view," although the UN prefers voting methods. She continued,

> But again, we call on our history and our culture, we just experience it and say "We got to give everybody a voice." So it's accepted, it's not discouraged where I think in the UN circles it's discouraged to try to reach consensus.
>
> (Indigenous activist #12 2010)

As I have heard many Indigenous Caucus members say, "Consensus does not mean unanimity" and sometimes, in the end, a consensus document means that discussions were held for long enough that opposing viewpoints were able to be heard and compromises made, and on a rare occasion, a vote was taken.

The tradition for Indigenous Caucus meetings is to have two co-chairs: one English speaking and one Spanish speaking. Chairs are not elected but the decision is made by consensus among the English- and Spanish-speaking representatives present. Consensus decision-making processes then continue throughout the meeting. In one meeting I attended, the Chair asked for approval on a small portion of text. He asked the room, "Do we agree?" Heads around the room nodded, and in the absence of any vocal dissent the Chair announced that the text was approved. Next, the Chair asked for the removal of certain text because it duplicated other text and may have also been overly controversial for states. Again, the Chair asked the Caucus, "Do we agree?" Heads nodded around the room and, again with no vocal dissent, the text removal was approved. When there was dissent on a topic, a discussion would be held. These discussions could be contentious and emotionally charged as different peoples from varied regions, interacting with different types of governments and with vastly different priorities, were likely to disagree on issues both large and small. Yet, consensus is the overriding goal both for ideological reasons – to enact Indigenous ways of doing politics – and for practical and strategic reasons. In the midst of one intense discussion, a member of the Caucus demanded that the Chair call for a vote. The Chair responded:

> Voting is not what I want to do. As Indigenous peoples, we need to reach consensus and make compromises. Voting is about winning and losing, and I don't want to do things that way. What's important here is to come to a consensus, then we can move forward with states. I don't want any hurt feelings when we come out of here.

Broad and open participation by Indigenous peoples has also been a core objective of the movement. Strong attention is paid to balanced geographic inclusion among delegates, especially to avoid North American domination due to advantages in fundraising and institutional development. Achieving a mix of community-based people, tribal governments, and political organizations has also been a goal. Elders and youth have always been included and often play a central role in meetings:

> We allowed the elders to speak and make the final say after we all had our opinions because the base of our fight for our human rights has to be cultural and spiritual.... So in that sense when it came down to the actual decisions ... we depend on the elders there to make the final say.
>
> (Indigenous activist #4 2007)

Both the credentialing process and UN speaking rules have presented huge challenges to the open participation model over the years, but the movement has successfully advocated for important alterations in UN rules to permit openness in both attendance and speaking rights. UN standing rules clearly state that only NGOs with UN consultative status may exercise the right to speak in UN meetings, but through bold and consistent advocacy by the movement, the UN ultimately made particular concessions to accommodate Indigenous ways of doing politics. The movement was also able to successfully advocate for the creation of a UN Voluntary Fund for Indigenous Populations in 1985 to financially assist Indigenous representatives to attend UN meetings in Geneva and, later, New York (Office of the High Commissioner for Human Rights).[6] As a result of these efforts, Indigenous meetings at the UN have broader and more open participation than any other issue area. There is some early evidence that the open participation norm forged by the Indigenous rights movement is permeating other areas of the UN, pointing toward a new way of conducting UN business. On December 29, 2014, in accordance with General Assembly Resolution 69/244, the UN announced that the United Nations Summit for the Adoption of the Post-2015 Development Agenda would have more open participation rules than usual at the UN. The Summit also included a credentialing process specifically for organizations not already accredited through the usual UN channels.

Early activist movements that formed the roots of the global Indigenous rights movement, especially the American Indian Movement (AIM) in the USA and the National Indian Brotherhood (NIB) in Canada, were male dominated in both leadership and participation, often with a certain warrior ethos. This pattern began to shift at the first Treaty Conference in 1974 as the direct action approach to activism gave way to a more global diplomatic approach. This newer approach was grounded in a wide base of traditional Indigenous ways that included participation and leadership by elders, youth, and community leaders, many of whom are women. Women have been central to the Indigenous Caucus meetings I have attended in Geneva and New York as well the UNPFII sessions and Indigenous organization meetings and community consultations I have observed. Formal speakers include nearly equal proportions of men and women. At the IITC Board Meeting I observed in 2007, only four of the thirteen board members were female, but their voices were disproportionately strong. When they spoke, the men listened. As Māori activist Hinewirangi Kohu (2007) stated, "It's good to have plenty of women on the IITC Council, strong women … and then the men too, who can put up with me, I'm the worst. But you know, I can't be ignored either, and they know it." Andrea Carmen (Yaqui) started working at IITC as a student intern in 1976, joined the staff in 1983, and has served as executive director since 1992 (Carmen 2007). She has a consistently strong and vocal presence in global Indigenous politics. Of the thirteen IITC staff, including program consultants, legal representatives, and trainers, eleven are female (International Indian Treaty Council (IITC)). Many organizations that regularly participate in the Indigenous rights movement have been founded and headed by women, and Indigenous women often hold high leadership positions within UN Indigenous bodies. For example, the American Indian Law Alliance was founded and headed by Tonya Gonnella Frichner (Onondaga) who also served as expert member of the UNPFII from 2008 to 2010. Na Koa Ikaika o Ka Lāhui Hawai'I, a Hawaiian sovereignty NGO, was founded by Mililani Trask, and Tebtebba, a Philippines-based international Indigenous advocacy organization, was founded and headed by Victoria Tauli-Corpuz (Kankanaey Igorot), who was also Chair of the UNPFII from 2005 to 2010 and was appointed UN Special Rapporteur on the Rights of Indigenous Peoples in May, 2014.

In addition to resisting UN rules on participation and speaking rights, Indigenous representatives began another struggle as early as the 1977 Geneva Conference through the insertion of Indigenous culture and spirituality into official conference proceedings. The day before the conference opened, the Iroquois Chiefs presented the Mayor of Geneva with invitation wampum in an opening ceremony (International Indian Treaty Council (IITC) 1977). In the closing conference ceremony, Larry Redshirt of the Lakota Treaty Council addressed the cultural and spiritual significance of the Lakota Pipe and why he had brought it into this international political conference:

> This Pipe is a symbol of peace and as such we have offered it to many of our brother nations. We have even offered it to the United States of America, and they have accepted. We made agreements in good faith and blessed it with this Pipe and their Bible. When we were sent here on behalf of myself, my brothers, relatives, from the Lakota Nation, they told us to bring the Pipe.… As we come with this Pipe, also we come with the Treaty, the 1868 Treaty.… As we talked among ourselves we said this is just a beginning, and the process of understanding had just begun. In due time, this Pipe we will offer to the world.… Together, our leaders, our chiefs, our governments will smoke with leaders of the world, with the United Nations. This morning we prayed and smoked it among ourselves, and the Indians of the nations know what it means, what it represents.… We'll pray with it … and I am sure the Creator will hear us. I can already feel his presence among us.
>
> (International Indian Treaty Council (IITC) 1977)

Multiple Indigenous participants in the 1977 and 1981 Geneva conferences have testified to the importance of cultural and spiritual grounding in achieving solidarity. Bill Means (2008) described how difficult it was to engage in cultural and spiritual practices at UN meetings with states: "sometimes at the UN they don't know how to react, but other times, they feel good about it. It's just that they're taught, all taught to keep that separate, and we're taught that it can't be separated." In the 1977 and 1981 Geneva conferences, Indigenous participants insisted on opening and closing meetings with Indigenous prayers and ceremonies in direct opposition to standing UN rules and procedures – a tradition that has continued to this day.

The issue of Indigenous prayer and ceremony emerged during the Working Group on Indigenous Populations (WGIP) in the early 1990s. Indigenous representatives had insisted, as they had in earlier international and UN meetings, that the WGIP sessions be opened and closed with an Indigenous prayer and/or a ceremony. Chair Daes had allowed this practice since she took over the Chairperson position in 1984. During one session (either 1991 or 1992, according to the memory of Indigenous delegates who were present), Ms. Daes suddenly decided to uphold UN rules and forbade the prayer.[7] She was met with such an angry reaction by the Indigenous delegates that she left the room. When she returned, the Indigenous delegates were just finishing their prayer. Thus the centrality of a spiritual and cultural foundation for unity and solidarity in the global Indigenous rights movement was confirmed in the WGIP, even if in protest.

The Indigenous rights movement has internationalized from its grassroots origins but has always tried to stay grounded and connected to its activist and community base of support. At the 1974 Treaty Conference, elders, traditional leaders, and the AIM activists present deliberately shifted away from the AIM's direct action activist model and into the international diplomacy model of the IITC, the "international arm of AIM" as it is sometimes called. On the Canadian side of the forty-ninth parallel, the leadership of George Manuel was also rooted in activism. It began with the National Indian Brotherhood where Manuel served three terms as head (1970–1976). In 1971, he traveled to Australia and New Zealand and then to the Saami areas of northern Sweden in 1972. On the same 1972 trip, he also traveled to Copenhagen and Geneva, met with various transnational NGOs and the International Labour Organization, and began work on an international Indigenous conference that he insisted must be organized and conducted by Indigenous peoples themselves. In August, 1972, the General Assembly of the National Indian Brotherhood endorsed the idea of an international conference of Indigenous peoples and authorized the National Indian Brotherhood to apply for Non-governmental Organization (NGO) status at the United Nations (Sanders 1980). As a result of these origins, the Indigenous Caucus is made up of numerous activists, which translates into strong personalities and individuals who are deeply committed to their cause.

The Indigenous rights movement does not hesitate to utilize collective action techniques to challenge the UN system to provide them with fair and just access and accommodations. During the past three decades, the Indigenous Caucus, or portions thereof, have engaged in protests, walkouts, and even a hunger strike at critical junctures to draw attention to whatever UN structures and/or practices were creating an unjust situation. For example, during registration for the Eleventh Session of the UNPFII in 2012, participants were told, without any advance warning, that due to renovations in the main UN building, this session of the UNPFII would be held in a satellite building that did not have sufficient space to accommodate all of the delegates attending the forum. Entrance to the UNPFII room would require an additional security pass in addition to the usual blue UN grounds pass worn by all participants. Only one additional pass would be provided to each organization, and so only one person from each organization would be allowed access to the meeting room at a time. On the first day of official meetings, UN guards strictly enforced this rule, turning away individuals who did not possess the second pass. Indigenous delegates were outraged. Not only did this violate the long-standing tradition of open participation, but it was also seen as fundamentally unjust that organizations from around the world had flown in multiple representatives to New York, including elders and youth, only to be told once they arrived at UN headquarters that all of these people would not be allowed to observe or participate in the meeting, except one at a time. Furthermore, the pass was widely interpreted by Indigenous delegates as a structural means by the UN or UN member states to deny access. This impression was heightened by the fact that the discussion theme of the Forum that year was the Doctrine of Discovery, an international legal principle that has enabled colonialism and especially settler colonialism; discussion of this doctrine could be viewed as a threat to the foundation of countries like the United States, Australia, or Canada.

On the second morning of the UNPFII, the Indigenous Youth Caucus held a silent protest, lining up shoulder to shoulder near where security was refusing access to people without the second pass. They also uploaded video footage of their protest to YouTube. After a few minutes, UN security removed all of the protesters from the property and revoked all of their credentials. A representative from the Indigenous Youth Caucus (who still had his credentials) addressed the UNPFII later that afternoon, telling the story of the Youth Caucus protest and also revealing that for the rest of that day, youth wearing traditional Saami clothing were being denied entry to the Forum, based on their appearance and under the presumption that they were protesters. As a result of this presentation, several Indigenous representatives from the UNPFII made a formal complaint to the UN. The following morning, the youths' credentials were restored, the additional pass requirement disappeared, and everyone with a UN grounds pass was able to attend all of the remaining days of the meeting.

While protest and collective action are sometimes important tactics to bring attention to an unfair situation and force change, the default approach of the Indigenous Caucus is careful, thoughtful, dignified diplomacy. As one activist put it, "You have to act like diplomats to be treated equally as diplomats" (Indigenous activist #12 2010). Diplomacy necessarily means negotiations, and since the movement itself emerged in part from an Indigenous conference on treaties, it is natural that the movement would gravitate toward negotiated agreements as standard practice, including a future vision that involves ongoing negotiations between Indigenous peoples and states.

It has been widely reported by Indigenous activists that although Indigenous peoples share a common history of oppression and dispossession, it is the taking and holding of a strong position that helps keep consensus and unity within the Indigenous groups: "A hard position attracts consensus, a soft position drives it away. Changes can come later" (Indigenous activist #7 2007). For this reason, there was a tradition beginning in 1977 of "presenting your ideal situation – your strongest position – you have to maintain that. Otherwise the other side will never move off their position" (Means 2008). In 1977, this meant including the right to independence for Indigenous nations, including the right of secession, among the principles for which Indigenous delegates argued. Over time, the "realities of the UN system" convinced the Indigenous delegates to place "lesser emphasis on independence" (Means 2008). Independence and secession never featured as an objective in any official document following the 1977 Geneva Conference.

As is the reality of any international negotiation, the Indigenous rights movement is keenly aware how diplomatic compromise operates. For example, during the end stage of the WGIP, Indigenous groups recognized that they would likely lose all input into the Declaration process once the Working Group handed the text back to the UN Sub-Commission, where only UN member states could change and make decisions regarding the text (Indigenous activist #1 2007). Therefore, the Indigenous Caucus aimed to create a document that was as strong as possible, since it would likely be weakened later in the process. One activist said, in an anonymous interview (2007): "The objective of the Indigenous Caucus is that we decide what we should propose to governments, not the other way around. We, the Indigenous peoples, need to decide what we want." She went on to mention the pragmatic realities of compromise and calculated risk inherent in all international negotiations: "Our strategy must be to take the strongest position that we want – it should reflect what we want. We will be bargained down regardless."

I have observed that there seems to be a particular tension at work within the Indigenous Caucus: how to take the strongest possible position while also framing text in terms that will not be rejected outright by states? The task of drafting individual documents takes on a particularly high level of difficulty because of the need to work within existing international institutions in order to work against the structures of domination and subordination that persist within states and the international system (Tully 2000). For example, the Indigenous Caucus feels a need to craft the language of documents very carefully, because, as any document moves through the UN process and concomitant negotiations, the language will likely be substantially weakened. Meanwhile, the strategy is to make positions as strong as possible while also being sensitive to the possibility that states could reject the document outright. Therefore, the Indigenous Caucus tries to be diplomatic and prepare for later negotiations but, at the same time, to stand firm as resolute representatives of their home communities and organizations, many of whom are on the edge of physical and cultural survival. These two impulses are often in competition, without there being any clear way to resolve this tension. Frustrations are often apparent within the Indigenous Caucus, as these are emotionally charged issues for many Indigenous representatives who have a sense of urgency for strong and immediate action: "We have leaders and elders disappearing all over the world" (Indigenous Caucus n.d.).

It was this urgent need to act as a global collective of Indigenous peoples to save Indigenous peoples that originally sparked this movement in the 1970s, and that has sustained it over three difficult decades of work at the UN. The mission and principles of the movement were clearly articulated from the beginning and embodied in many early documents, including the WCIP Declaration from its first global Indigenous conference in Port Alberni, British Columbia in 1975. The 1975 WCIP Declaration continues to be poignant with respect to the Indigenous rights movement's contemporary mission and traits. As such, it is worth quoting it here in its entirety:

> We the Indigenous Peoples of the world, united in this corner of our Mother the Earth in a great assembly of men of wisdom, declare to all nations:
>
> We glory in our proud past: when the earth was our nurturing mother, when the night sky formed our common roof, when Sun and Moon were our parents, when all were brothers and sisters, when our great civilizations grew under the sun, when our chiefs and elders were great leaders, when justice ruled the Law and its execution.
>
> Then other peoples arrived: thirsting for blood, for gold, for land and all its wealth, carrying the cross and the sword, one in each hand, without knowing or waiting to learn the ways of our worlds, they considered us to be lower than the animals, they stole our lands from us and took us from our lands, they made slaves of the Sons of the sun.
>
> However, they have never been able to eliminate us, nor to erase our memories of what we were, because we are the culture of the earth and the sky, we are of ancient descent and we are millions, and although our whole universe may be ravaged, our people will live on for longer than even the kingdom of death.
>
> Now, we come from the four corners of the earth, we protest before the concert of nations that, we are the Indigenous Peoples, we who have a consciousness of culture and peoplehood on the edge of each country's borders and marginal to each country's citizenship. And rising up after centuries of oppression, evoking the greatness of our ancestors, in the memory of our Indigenous martyrs, and in homage to the counsel of our wise elders:
>
> We vow to control again our own destiny and recover our complete humanity and pride in being Indigenous People.

In sum, global Indigenous politics is simultaneously a destabilizing and a transformative force in global politics. It unabashedly reveals and confronts colonial structures in the current world order. At the same time, it offers a transformative vision of alternative global political relations. While global Indigenous politics is grounded in a particular set of what I call transnational Indigenous ways of being, it also offers many lessons to non-Indigenous peoples, organizations, and institutions about the possibility of alternative global political relations. The Indigenous movement, in both its mission and practice, has shown that global politics can be done in a different way. Rather than focusing on the accumulation of wealth or the balancing of power among nation-states, global Indigenous politics has effectively demonstrated, in both its mission and method, that global politics can be done in a way that values equality, human dignity, sustainability, mutually respectful relationships, effective conflict resolution, and consensual decision making.

As global political relations move into an unknown future, presumably away from colonial or even post-colonial relations of power, Indigenous global politics offers some important lessons to a future world:

1 *Marginal global actors can forge change in international systems* by exposing structural injustice, and boldly, tenaciously demanding change. Sometimes these changes start out small, like changing discriminatory rules and practices of UN bodies, but those small changes can become new global norms with wider impact over time.
2 *Rights cannot be disassociated from responsibilities.* For the Indigenous rights movement, the sole purpose of attaining "rights" over land, culture, and self-determination is to attend to Indigenous responsibilities to protect lands and cultures, to care for the elders, the youth and the community at large, to live in a self-determining way, and to be respected as such by states and other cultures and societies.
3 *Different styles of political relations are possible on the global level.* Global politics may be viewed in terms of balance, sustainability, equity, justice, and interconnectedness. Furthermore, Indigenous rights, self-determination, and sustainability are all interconnected. I was given a poster during a trip to an Indigenous community in Guatemala that says simply, "Los pueblos indigenas no son parte del problema … son parte de la solución," meaning, "Indigenous peoples are not part of the problem, they are part of the solution."
4 *Indigenous rights do not need to be seen as zero-sum vis-à-vis states.* As the past two chapters have argued, implementation of Indigenous rights is not a threat to the existence of states. In actuality, implementation of Indigenous rights provides a roadmap to more peaceful, more just relationships not only between Indigenous peoples and states but also between other global political actors. Fierce state resistance to Indigenous rights does remain palpable however, and the following four chapters will highlight some of the curious, complex, and cunning patterns of state – especially settler colonial state – responses to Indigenous rights.

Notes

1 I observed a number of official UN meetings: an Informal Meeting to Discuss the Most Appropriate Mechanisms to Continue the Work of the Working Group on Indigenous Populations, December 6–7, 2007, Palais des Nations, Geneva; the Seventh Session of the United Nations Permanent Forum on Indigenous Issues, April 21 to May 2, 2008; the Ninth Session of the United Nations Permanent Forum on Indigenous Issues, April 19–30, 2010; the Eleventh Session of the United Nations Permanent Forum on Indigenous Issues, May 7–18, 2012; the Thirteenth Session of the United Nations Permanent Forum on Indigenous Issues, May 12–23, 2014; and the Fourteenth Session of the United Nations Permanent Forum on Indigenous Issues, April 20 to May 1, 2015, all held in New York.

I was a participant observer at Indigenous Caucus meetings. These closed meetings of the Indigenous Caucus were held either at the Palais des Nations, Geneva or in New York. Out of respect for confidentiality and anonymity, I will not reveal particular dates or speakers from these meetings.

I attended two community consultations by the United Nations Special Rapporteur on the Rights of Indigenous Peoples during his official visit to the USA in 2012 and to Canada in 2013. The first was held at Sinte Gleska University at Sicangu Lakota Oyate, also known as the Rosebud Sioux reservation, South Dakota in 2012, and the second was held at the Musqueam Nation near Vancouver, British Columbia in 2013.

I was also able to directly observe a number of meetings of Indigenous rights organizations. I attended a Board of Directors' meeting of the International Indian Treaty Council as well as several human rights training sessions for Indigenous nations and organizations conducted by the International Indian Treaty Council, one session hosted by the Mille Lacs Band of Ojibwe, located near Onamia, Minnesota, in September, 2007, and another session co-hosted by the First Nations Summit, the Assembly of First Nations, the International Indian Treaty Council, and the Confederacy of Treaty 6 First Nations in Ottawa, Ontario in December, 2011, as well as an Indigenous Rights Implementation workshop for tribal leaders hosted by the Indian Law Resource Center in Portland, Oregon in October, 2011, and a UNDRIP implementation workshop in Vancouver, British Columbia in November 2011, hosted by the Indigenous Bar Association.

2 Data provided by IWGIA, the International Work Group for Indigenous Affairs.

3 Tonya Gonnella Frichner passed away on February 14, 2015.

4 Meetings of the Indigenous delegates in Caucus are also documented by Roxanne Dunbar-Ortiz (2006). I have witnessed multiple meetings of the Indigenous Caucus in Geneva and New York.

5 Records do not exist for many early Indigenous Caucus meetings, for several reasons. First, often careful notes were not taken during these early meetings. Second, the Indigenous Caucus did not have language translation services available at this time, so the Caucus was constantly preoccupied with correctly translating conversations and documents into Spanish and English. Third, there was a suspicious fire at the doCip document depository in Geneva in 1982 that destroyed many early records of the international activities of the Indigenous rights movement. I have conducted eleven interviews with individuals who were involved with the global Indigenous rights movement since its inception and each interviewee testified to the existence and the strategic importance of the Indigenous Caucus. Transcripts of these interviews are on file.

6 The name of this fund was changed in 2013 to the UN Voluntary Fund for Indigenous Peoples. UN Doc A/C.3/68/L.30/Rev.1.

7 This story is told by several Indigenous activists who were present at both the 1991 and 1992 meetings.

References

Bishop, R., 2005. Freeing Ourselves from Neocolonial Domination in Research: A Kaupapa Maori Approach to Creating Knowledge. In N.K. Denzin And Y.S. Lincoln, eds, *The Sage Handbook of Qualitative Research*, 3rd edn. Thousand Oaks, CA: Sage, pp. 109–138.

Bositis, D.A., 1990. *Research Designs For Political Science: Contrivance And Demonstration In Theory And Practice.* Carbondale: Southern Illinois University Press.

Carmen, A., 2007. Interview by author. Transcript on file. Mille Lacs Nation, MN.

Charters, C., 2007. Personal communication, November 8, 2007. New York.

Cram, F., 2001. Rangahau, Maori: Tona Tika, Tona Pnon – The Validity and Integrity of Maori Research. In M. Tolich, ed., *Research Ethics and Aotearoa New Zealand.* Auckland, NZ: Longman, pp. 35–52.

Deer, K., 2012. Interview by author. Transcript on file. Vancouver, BC.

Dunbar-Ortiz, R., 2006. The First Decade of Indigenous Peoples at the United Nations. *Peace and Change*, 31(1), pp. 58–74.

First International Treaty Council, 1974. *Declaration of Continuing Independence.* Standing Rock, SD.

Frichner, T.G., 2011. Interview by author. Transcript on file. New York.

Indigenous Caucus, n.d. Meeting.

Indigenous Activist #1, 2007. Interview by author. Transcript on file.

Indigenous Activist #4, 2007. Interview by author. Transcript on file.

Indigenous Activist #6, 2008. Interview by author. Transcript on file.

Indigenous Activist #7, 2007. Interview by author. Transcript on file.

Indigenous Activist #12, 2010. Interview by author. Transcript on file.

International Indian Treaty Council (IITC), 1977. *The Geneva Conference: International NGO Conference on Discrimination Against Indigenous Populations in the Americas.* New York: International Indian Treaty Council.

International Indian Treaty Council (IITC), 2015. About IITC. Available at: www.iitc.org/about-iitc/ [last accessed July 17, 2015].

Jackson, M., 2008. Interview by author. Transcript on file. Wellington, Aotearoa/New Zealand.

Kohu, H., 2007. Interview by author. Transcript on file. Mille Lacs Nation, MN.

Kulchyski, P., 2013. *Aboriginal Rights are Not Human Rights: In Defence of Indigenous Struggles.* Winnipeg, Man.: ARP.

Lameman, R., 2007. Presentation at IITC's Human Rights CERD Training Session, September 27.

Means, Bill, 2008. Interview by author. Transcript on file. St. Paul, MN.

Muehlebach, A., 2001. "Making Place" at the United Nations: Indigenous Cultural Politics at the U.N. Working Group on Indigenous Populations. *Cultural Anthropology*, 16(3), pp. 415–448.

Niezen, R., 2003. *The Origins of Indigenism: Human Rights and The Politics of Identity.* Berkeley: University of California Press.

Office of the High Commissioner for Human Rights, UN Voluntary Fund for Indigenous Peoples. Available at: www.ohchr.org/EN/Issues/IPeoples/IPeoplesFund/Pages/IPeoplesFundIndex.aspx [last accessed July 17, 2015].

Rigney, L., 1999. Internationalization of an Indigenous Anticolonial Cultural Critique of Research Methodologies: A Guide to Indigenist Research Methodology and its Principles. *Wicazo Sa Review*, 14(2, Emergent Ideas in Native American Studies), pp. 109–121.

Sanders, D., 1980. *Background Information on the World Council of Indigenous Peoples, The Formation of the World Council of Indigenous Peoples.* Vancouver, BC: World Council of Indigenous Peoples.

Schuler, D. and Namoika, A., 1993. *Participatory Design: Principles and Practices.* Hillsdale, NJ: Lawrence Erlbaum Associates.

Smith, G.H., 2000. Protecting and Respecting Indigenous Knowledge. In M. Battiste, ed., *Reclaiming Indigenous Voice and Vision.* Vancouver, BC: UBC Press, pp. 209–224.

Smith, L.T., 2000. Kaupapa Maori Research. In M. Battiste, ed., *Reclaiming Indigenous Voice and Vision.* Vancouver, BC: UBC Press, pp. 225–247.

Smith, L.T., 2005. On Tricky Ground: Researching the Native in the Age of Uncertainty. In N.K. Denzin and Y.S. Lincoln, eds, *The Sage Handbook of Qualitative Research*, 3rd edn. Thousand Oaks, CA: Sage, pp. 85–108.

Smith, L.T., 2012. *Decolonizing Methodologies: Research and Indigenous Peoples*, 2nd edn. London; New York: Zed Books.

Special NGO Committee on Human Rights (Geneva), 1981. International NGO Conference on Indigenous Peoples and the Land, organized by the Sub-Commission on Racism, Racial Discrimination, Apartheid and Decolonisation, Final Report. Available from doCIP, Avenue de Trembley 14-CH 1209, Geneva, Switzerland.

Tully, J., 2000. The Struggles of Indigenous Peoples for and of Freedom. In D. Ivison, P. Patton, and W. Sanders, eds, *Political Theory and the Rights of Indigenous Peoples.* Cambridge: Cambridge University Press, pp. 36–59.

United Nations General Assembly, 2014. *Organization of the United Nations Summit for the Adoption of the Post-2015 Development Agenda Resolution 69/244.* New York: United Nations.

World Council of Indigenous Peoples, 1975. *WCIP Declaration.* Port Alberni, BC: WCIP.

Part II

State resistance to the subtle revolution of global Indigenous politics

4 "Selective endorsement" of the Declaration on the Rights of Indigenous Peoples

Human rights theorists typically interrogate commitments to international regimes in a binary fashion – either a state commits to a rights regime or it does not. This binary remains the dominant standard largely because existing scholarship focuses on ratification of treaties (Simmons 2009; Hathaway 2002; Moravcsik 2000; Farber 2002). However, when analyses include instruments other than treaties (e.g., human rights declarations), we find that many nuanced behaviors exist in the gray zone between commitment and non-commitment. Despite the dearth of scholarship which seeks to expand that dichotomy, acknowledging more nuanced positions advances our understanding of state behavior. For example, states exhibit wider varieties of behavior when commitments are defined more broadly than ratification and non-ratification, and instead include public endorsements and expressions of support for human rights declarations. This chapter aims to identify and discuss one such nuanced behavior: the practice of selectively endorsing Indigenous rights.

Selective endorsement

Existing scholarship defines state commitment as a "government's decision to ratify a particular treaty text" (Simmons 2009). This chapter seeks to expand that definition to include national endorsements and public expressions of support for human rights declarations. Unlike treaties, declarations are not legally binding; commitments to human rights norms expressed in declarations are less enforceable than treaty obligations. Yet when a state endorses or expresses support for a declaration, it makes a powerful public statement. While they do not carry the same weight as treaties or conventions in international law, declarations hold states morally and politically accountable.

Typically, commitment to a cluster of rights matches a state's intended implementation – whether through domestic policies or legal and institutional changes that align with the emerging norms (Raustiala and Slaughter 2002). This means that when a country commits to a rights regime, it intends to follow that commitment with domestic changes that move it toward compliance.[1] (Sometimes states commit to regimes that already align with their domestic practices, requiring no further implementation or making implementation easy.) But Beth Simmons has identified several other behaviors, which she calls "false positives" and "false negatives" (2009). A false positive can happen when an ambivalent government strategically ratifies a treaty in order to avoid international or domestic criticism. A false negative can occur when a country's ratification procedures prevent its government from publicly endorsing a treaty that aligns with its existing values and behavior. For example, the USA has stringent ratification procedures which often prevent it from formally committing to treaties that reflect existing values and domestic practices.

In analyzing state commitment, rationalist scholars might argue that states are strategic, and follow norms and international regimes that align with their interests (Chayes and Chayes 1993; Downs et al. 1996; Moravcsik 2000). Constructivist scholars, on the other hand, may observe a process of norm socialization, wherein a country's commitment to human rights gradually aligns with global norms and results in de facto implementation and compliance (Kratochwil 1989; Checkel 2001; Franck 1990). Such alignment occurs not only because the state fears the consequences of non-alignment, but because a logic of appropriateness pushes it toward international benchmarks.

How would a liberal, democratic country that publicly advocates for human rights behave when an emerging international regime directly conflicts with its interests? For example, the global community declares in the Declaration that Indigenous peoples have the right to freely determine their political status with the state, including autonomy if they wish, but that right interferes with the state's unitary governance structure, as is the case in New Zealand. When the implementation of that regime would require significant, expensive, and politically challenging alterations to existing legal, economic, and political institutions? A rationalist might predict that such a state would be strategically instrumental and not commit to the norms. A constructivist might predict that norm socialization would encourage the state to conform to the rights regime over time, not only because of negative consequences but because it comes to align its identity and interests. But I argue that there is a third possibility, one that lies at the intersection of rationalist and constructivist approaches. When an international rights regime emerges and a liberal democracy perceives norms to be at odds with its own interests, the state may resolve the dilemma through a practice that I call "selective endorsement."

In a selective endorsement situation, a state engages in strategic logic while maintaining its position in the global community, where complying with human rights norms is constitutive of belonging. Because compliance does matter to many nations, states shrewdly express support for internationally recognized rights (as constructivists might expect). However, when a state makes a selective endorsement, it "writes it down" – or commits to its own watered-down version of a set of rights in such a way that its compliance occurs automatically. Additional implementation is thus unnecessary. In effect, the state undersells its commitment, while at the same time avoiding the international and domestic political costs of under-commitment, and preserves its reputation as supportive of human rights.

This chapter explores the phenomenon of selective endorsement through the history of the United Nations Declaration on the Rights of Indigenous Peoples, specifically within the anglosphere community.[2] Since the Declaration's adoption in the General Assembly in 2007, the anglosphere has simultaneously advocated human rights that it recognizes and avoided implementing international Indigenous rights norms. This is selective endorsement. As I demonstrate below, selective endorsement comprises several elements. First, a state belatedly affirms the process by which the norms emerged as legitimate. Second, it underscores the normative importance of the rights contained within the accord, while at the same time qualifying them. Finally, it strategically, collectively, and unilaterally writes down the recognized rights, so that they conveniently align with existing policies and practices. Combined, these elements assure that a state complies, without having to pursue further implementation.

Indigenous rights and the anglosphere

The United Nations General Assembly passed the Declaration on the Rights of Indigenous Peoples on September 13, 2007, with 144 out of 192 UN members voting for it. The Declaration affirms the right to maintain and strengthen Indigenous cultures, traditions, and institutions, and prohibits discrimination against individuals, while simultaneously asserting such collective rights as remaining socially and politically distinct, pursuing unique visions of development, and promoting full and effective participation in pertinent decision-making processes.

With its passage, the document joined the ranks of other key statements, including the UN Charter and the Universal Declaration of Human Rights, that articulate the global standard for respecting and promoting human rights – both morally and politically. According to a UN press release, it represented "a major step forward towards the promotion and protection of human rights and fundamental freedoms for all." In a separate press release, the Special Rapporteur on the Rights of Indigenous Peoples, Rodolfo Stavenhagen, hailed it as representing "a growing international consensus concerning the rights of indigenous peoples."

Like the Universal Declaration of Human Rights, the Declaration on the Rights of Indigenous Peoples is not legally binding. However, as the UN Permanent Forum on Indigenous Issues observed in 2007, such agreements "represent the dynamic development of international legal norms and reflect the commitment of states to move in certain directions, abiding by certain principles." And as UN Special Rapporteur James Anaya observed in 2010, the Declaration's technical legal significance matters less than its normative legitimacy:

> Whatever its legal significance, the Declaration has a significant normative weight grounded in its high degree of legitimacy. This legitimacy is a function not only of the fact that it has been formally endorsed by an overwhelming majority of United Nations member States, but also the fact that it is the product of years of advocacy and struggle by indigenous peoples themselves.

Normative changes can alter a state's human rights practices (Risse-Kappen et al. 2013), and it is incumbent to understand how the emerging Indigenous rights regime impacts state behavior. As Chair of the UN Permanent Forum on Indigenous Issues in 2007 Victoria Tauli-Corpuz predicted, the Declaration "will become the major foundation and reference" for UN agencies, and will serve "as the main framework to guide States." She also noted that the Declaration is intended to serve as a "key instrument and tool for raising awareness on and monitoring progress of indigenous peoples' situations and the protection, respect and fulfilment of indigenous peoples rights."

Four prominent UN members, however, publicly rejected the normative changes implicit in the Declaration. Despite having reputations for being committed to human rights, Australia, Canada, New Zealand, and the USA – the anglosphere's four largest settler states – worked as a bloc to oppose the new global standard for Indigenous rights. Shestack observed that human rights law is now a globalized phenomenon and carries such a strong moral force that "nations who have not assented to [human rights] standards are compelled to explain their departure from the world view" (1997). That was certainly the case for the only four countries to vote against the Declaration.

Within minutes, the countries issued simultaneous public statements, complaining that the Declaration was incompatible with their constitutional democracies. They expressed similar misgivings about the document's language (especially its provisions on self-determination, and land and resource rights), the transparency of the Declaration's drafting and deliberation processes, and the final text's incompatibility with domestic laws and the equality of all citizens. They also announced that they would not be bound by it.

Over the next few months, Australia, Canada, New Zealand, and the USA all faced international pressure and diplomatic criticism, as well as angry Indigenous constituents at home. Indigenous organizations in all four countries spoke out publicly against the governments that voted against the Declaration. Editorials were placed in newspapers and brochures printed to draw public attention to the fact that these were the only countries that had voted no. Both Indigenous and non-Indigenous NGOs in Canada publicized the fact that this was the first human rights document ever rejected by Canada. At the UN, other countries and UN bodies repeatedly called upon these four states to change their position. In the November 2007 federal election in Australia and the November 2008 election in New Zealand, it became an election issue.

Indeed, what followed the vote may be characterized as a full-blown international moral persuasion campaign, intended to embarrass and pressure the anglosphere into changing its position on Indigenous rights (Keck and Sikkink 1998). To varying degrees, human rights groups chastised the four countries: the UN Committee on the Elimination of Racial Discrimination reviewed the USA in 2008, the Human Rights Council's Universal Periodic Review included Canada and New Zealand in 2009, and the USA in 2010. UN reports specifically mentioned the four countries' opposition to the Declaration and recommended they change their positions. In annual and country reports, the UN's Special

Rapporteur on the Rights of Indigenous Peoples, Rodolfo Stavenhagen, also called for change, and for several years the four countries were subjected to a virtual barrage of public criticism at the UN Permanent Forum on Indigenous Issues. At the same time, Indigenous and non-Indigenous NGOs around the world initiated letter-writing campaigns to the USA president and the prime ministers of Australia, Canada, and New Zealand, calling on them to support the rights articulated in the Declaration.

This moral persuasion exposed unresolved colonial ambivalence within the anglosphere. While normally held up as human rights champions, the four countries opposed international standards by clinging to the status quo. For example, the 2009 Report of the Working Group on Universal Periodic Review on Canada noted that Canada was resisting the Declaration and had confined its commitment to "fulfilling its existing human rights obligations and commitments to Aboriginal peoples." The report called on Canada to

> support and fully implement … the United Nations Declaration on the Rights of Indigenous Peoples … [and] take the provisions of the Declaration into account in the national legislation, because the Declaration is a United Nations document and represents guidelines for the conduct of States.

Eventually, the pressure got to the anglosphere. Between April, 2009 and December, 2010, the four countries changed their official positions on the Declaration and issued formal statements of "support" or "endorsement." Australia was the first, in April, 2009, when Indigenous affairs minister Jenny Macklin announced the change in Parliament House. A year later, on April 19, New Zealand's minister of Māori affairs Pita Sharples surprised the world at the opening ceremony of the UN Permanent Forum on Indigenous Issues, saying his country would now support the Declaration. Canada took a less public approach on November 12, 2010, when Indian and Northern Affairs Canada announced the country's formal endorsement online. Finally, the USA changed its position on December 16, 2010, after extended review and tribal consultations. Addressing the White House Tribal Nations Conference, President Barack Obama briefly mentioned that the USA would be "lending its support" to the Declaration it had previously rejected as flawed and not implementable.

Positions shifted between 2007 and 2010; the text and the content of the Declaration on the Rights of Indigenous Peoples stayed the same. If the Declaration stood as such a fundamental contradiction to anglosphere democracy in 2007, can moral persuasion alone explain the quick reversals? Or, on a more theoretical level, do the eventual anglosphere endorsements reveal anything new about how states commit to human rights norms?

As Harold D. Lasswell famously articulated in 1936, a fundamental question in the study of politics is to decipher who says what, to whom, why, in what context, and to what effect? Below I present a content analysis of anglosphere statements regarding the Declaration, to understand more precisely when and how Australia, Canada, New Zealand, and the USA shifted positions on a document they initially deemed problematic. Specifically, I compare their 2007 comments with their later expressions of support, describe and categorize trends in their statements, and illustrate how selective endorsement of human rights can work. Finally, I discuss some implications of selective endorsement—for human rights commitment theory and for Indigenous political movements on the ground.

A comparative content analysis of anglosphere statements on the Declaration

In 2007, the Chair of the Global Indigenous Caucus, Les Malezer, observed in a public statement,

> The Declaration on the Rights of Indigenous Peoples contains no new provisions of human rights. It affirms many rights already contained in international human rights treaties, but rights which have been denied to the Indigenous Peoples.

Nevertheless, the Declaration is a holistic document and standard-setting tool – one intended to guide action based on justice, and to serve as a framework for mutual recognition and respect among states and Indigenous peoples. The Declaration is comprehensive; many states have expressed confusion and misgivings about implementing it. Addressing those concerns in 2010, Special Rapporteur Anaya offered concrete expectations for initial implementation efforts: training for state officials and Indigenous leaders, a comprehensive review of existing legislation and administrative programs, legal and programmatic reforms in consultation with Indigenous peoples, and technical and financial implementation assistance from the UN to states.

These are high expectations for any nation, but for anglosphere states, which were founded and settled on the basis of a legalized dispossession of lands and resources, the expectations are extraordinary. In fact, the Declaration calls for resetting entire settler state–Indigenous frameworks – moving away from colonial models and toward new relationships based on mutual respect, compensation for lost lands and resources, and self-determination, including self-governance and control over their Indigenous lands and resources (Lightfoot 2010). Because the Declaration calls for significant changes to the anglosphere's political and legal status quo, a certain amount of resistance was expected; the four votes against the Declaration were not particularly surprising. What did come as a surprise, however, was the speed with which Australia, Canada, New Zealand, and the USA moved to "support" or "endorse" the Declaration, and the nuanced way they offered such endorsement.

A nation-by-nation content analysis, which compares 2007 statements with statements of support or endorsement issued in 2009 and 2010, illuminates this about face.

Australia

Explanation of opposition

Australia's ambassador and permanent representative to the UN, Robert Hill, explained his country's 2007 vote against the Declaration, in a statement that expressed concerns over the document's content and the negotiations behind it. Hill began by noting that Australia was actively involved in the drafting stage in the 1980s and 1990s, and had hoped that the document would be "universally accepted, observed and upheld." In its final form, however, the Declaration failed "to meet this high standard." Hill then expressed disappointment that all states could not participate in the text's final negotiations.

Hill also commented on the Declaration's non-binding status. He stated, unequivocally, that the document was "*not in itself legally binding* nor reflective of international law," and "it was the clear intention of all states that it be an *aspirational* declaration with political and moral force, but not legal force" (emphasis added). Furthermore, because the final version did not conform to current Australian practices and because states were legally obligated to act in accordance with it, the Declaration did not "provide a basis for legal actions, complaints, or other claims in any international, domestic, or other proceedings."

Australia objected to specific rights outlined in the Declaration. First among them was Indigenous self-determination. Hill noted that "self-determination applies to situations of de-colonisation and the break-up of states into smaller states with clearly defined population groups." In an effort to distance his country from decolonization expectations, as well as pull Indigenous issues back into domestic politics, Hill noted that Australia

> supports and encourages the full and free engagement of Indigenous peoples in the democratic decision-making processes in their country, but it does not support a concept that could be construed as encouraging action that would impair, even in part, the territorial and political integrity of a state with a system of democratic representative government.

Next, Hill outlined Australia's objection to territory and resource provisions, because "they could be read to require recognition of Indigenous rights to lands without regard to other legal rights existing in land, both indigenous and non-indigenous." Rhetorically, Hill attempted to domesticate land and resources issues, stressing that "any right to traditional lands must be subject to national laws" and that "Australia will read the lands and resources provisions … in line with its existing domestic laws." Indigenous rights to territory and raw materials, as articulated in the Declaration, would simply be "impossible to implement."

Australia also objected to the principle of free, prior, and informed consent, which asks states to obtain consent from Indigenous peoples before implementing various policies and measures that may affect them. In its view the principle was overly broad, and therefore "unworkable" on a practical level, because it would give a subset of the Australian population veto power over the "legitimate decisions of a democratic and representative government."

Hill commented on intellectual property rights as well as the rights of third parties in different ownership arrangements. In another move to domesticate Indigenous issues and affirm the superiority of Australian law, he raised concerns about the Declaration as customary law, or unofficial law, and stated that *opinio juris* "should never override national laws and should not be used selectively to permit the exercise of practices by certain Indigenous communities which would be unacceptable in the rest of the community."

Hill concluded his statement with a somewhat derisive reminder that the Declaration was merely an aspirational document, and, due to concerns over its content, status, and process, Australia would not support it.

Statement of support

On April 3, 2009, the Indigenous affairs minister Jenny Macklin addressed Parliament House in Canberra, saying Australia would now give its "support" to the Declaration, as the country "takes another important step in re-setting the relationship between Indigenous and non-Indigenous Australians and moving forward towards a new future." Macklin wove throughout her speech the theme that Australia's flawed Indigenous policies lie in the past – and that her announcement was part of new policies and efforts to "close the gap," "build trust," and "re-set relations."

Far from critiquing the negotiations behind the Declaration, Macklin complimented decades of hard work on the part of Indigenous peoples, which culminated in the passage of a "landmark document." She even highlighted the contributions of five prominent Indigenous Australians, whose "leadership and efforts were central to the development of the Declaration."

Macklin addressed the Declaration's legal status with the same terminology that Hill used in 2007, though she was more oblique. Rather than devote an entire section of her speech to the issue, she peppered her remarks with subtle assertions that the Declaration's status remained limited. Macklin used the word "aspirational" five times, in sharp contrast to the UN's position that the Declaration represents a minimum standard which all states should recognize and protect. Midway through her address, Macklin repeated that Australia was separating itself from the "flawed policies of the past," and noted that because the Declaration is "non-binding," the country's belated support of it "does not affect existing Australian law."

Macklin referenced Australia's 2007 concerns about content, and addressed the issues of self-determination; lands and resources; and the principle of free, prior and informed consent. On self-determination, she stated that "the Declaration recognizes the entitlement of Indigenous peoples to have control over their destiny and to be treated respectfully," while quickly adding that nothing in the document would be "used to impair Australia's territorial integrity or political unity." In an attempt to domesticate Indigenous issues, she said that "we want Indigenous peoples to participate fully in Australia's democracy," as well as manage their own affairs and maintain their identities and cultures.

Macklin also domesticated land and resource issues – framing them as matters of local concern and cultural heritage. Disputes over land rights, she stated, would be resolved through the Australian courts, or preferably through mediation. No domestic laws concerning land rights and title would be altered by the Declaration. She noted the "distinctive spiritual relationship" that Indigenous peoples have "with land and waters," and pointed out that the Indigenous Land Fund would continue to purchase freehold land "to further the social, cultural and economic aims of Indigenous peoples."

On the issue of free, prior, and informed consent, Macklin carefully maintained the argument that all Australian citizens, Indigenous and non-Indigenous, have equal rights; in order to "close the gap," Indigenous Australians must have full access to the "building blocks of economic and social prosperity – healthy living, a decent house, the skills and training to get a job." After a lengthy articulation of the importance of citizen equality, she noted that "free, prior and informed consent" gave Indigenous peoples a voice in domestic political decision making. Even while voicing support for the Declaration, Macklin implicitly reiterated Hill's 2007 concern that free, prior, and informed consent should not grant any group the right of veto, even over matters that directly concern them.

Despite Australia's change in position, differences in tone between 2007 and 2009 are minor. The country no longer objected to process behind the Declaration, but it maintained its position on the document's qualified status. The main differences lie in how Australia framed content, specifically provisions for self-determination; land, and resources rights; and the principle of free, prior, and informed consent. Rather than use these provisions to justify opposition to the Declaration as a whole, as it had in 2007, Australia rhetorically shifted these issues into the realm of domestic politics in 2009, and attempted to frame them as cultural heritage issues within its existing institutional and legal framework. With its carefully couched revised position, Australia expressed support for Indigenous rights, generally, while qualifying the legal status of those rights, and it effectively wrote down the content of international Indigenous rights norms to fit the domestic status quo.

New Zealand

Explanation of opposition

Following the General Assembly vote, New Zealand's permanent representative to the UN, Rosemary Banks, explained her country's opposition to the Declaration on the Rights of Indigenous Peoples. New Zealand objected to the negotiation process and the Declaration's legal status, Banks explained. It also took issue with some of the document's content, particularly areas the country deemed "fundamentally incompatible with New Zealand's constitutional and legal arrangements."

Banks opened her statement by noting that "New Zealand has an unparalleled system for redress" and asserting that Indigenous rights "are integral to our identity as a nation State and as a people." She continued: "New Zealand is one of the few countries that supported the elaboration of a declaration that promoted and protected the rights of indigenous peoples from the start." And her government forcefully articulated its objections to how the Declaration was negotiated. "Lest there be any doubt," Banks explained,

> we place on record our firm view that the history of the negotiations on the Declaration and the divided manner in which it has been adopted demonstrate that this text … does not state propositions which are reflected in State practice or which are or will be recognized as general principles of law.

Ultimately, Banks contended, the Declaration did not reflect the "constructive and harmonious" partnership with Indigenous peoples that New Zealand required.

In her statement, Banks placed the Declaration in the larger body of international law and clarified its applicability to New Zealand. She emphasized its forward-looking, non-binding character while maintaining that her country "fully supports the principles and aspirations of the Declaration." Throughout, she commented on the high status of Māori, as well as highly evolved institutions and structures that distinguish New Zealand from the many countries where "indigenous peoples continue to be deprived of basic rights."

Banks strongly objected to language pertaining to land and resources, redress, and informed consent. While she took issue with the Declaration's intellectual property provisions, she deemed them less egregious than the rest. In terms of land and resources, New Zealand found the Declaration's provisions impractical; they would result in inequality among Māori and other citizens. When it came to redress and compensation, it found the provisions "unworkable," especially in light of the "unparalleled and extensive processes that exist under New Zealand law." Concerning the principle of informed consent, which Banks likened to a veto, it insisted that Māori were already well represented in government institutions, including Parliament, and that the Declaration would create "different classes of citizenship, where indigenous have a right of veto that other groups or individuals do not have."

Statement of support

In April, 2010, at the opening ceremony of the UN Permanent Forum on Indigenous Issues, New Zealand's minister of Māori affairs Pita Sharples was called to the rostrum. He approached the microphone and began to speak in Te Reo Māori, working through the usual protocols of acknowledgment that Māori culture requires: acknowledging the land, the people of the land they were meeting on, the spirits and the people in the room, along with the mountains, the rivers, and the ancestral lands of those present. He said that he "came with a humble heart to celebrate the Declaration on the Rights of Indigenous Peoples."

The New Zealand government, he proclaimed, had "recently decided to support it." Then he repeated himself in English.

Sharples spoke positively about the negotiations behind the Declaration, noting that the document was a "historic achievement: the result of many years of discussions – twenty-two years in fact – and of hard work and perseverance by many people." His comments suggest that New Zealand completely reversed its opinion of the negotiations, but not of the Declaration's legal status or content. Like his Australian counterpart, Sharples attempted to rhetorically domesticate Indigenous rights, by framing them as issues of cultural heritage and reiterating the institutional status quo.

Sharples strongly asserted that the Declaration is an aspirational, non-binding document – one that was already consistent with New Zealand's record on Indigenous rights. Immediately after announcing New Zealand's change in position, he said,

> In keeping with our strong commitment to human rights, and indigenous rights in particular, New Zealand now adds its support to the Declaration both as an affirmation of fundamental rights and in its expression of new and widely supported aspirations.

He then described the centrality of the Treaty of Waitangi to his country's constitutional arrangements, noting that the "Treaty establishes a foundation of partnership, mutual respect, cooperation and good faith between Māori and the Crown."

Far from being the "fundamentally incompatible" document that Banks described in 2007, the Declaration now contained "principles that are consistent with the duties and principles inherent in the Treaty, such as operating in the spirit of partnership and mutual respect." Sharples also noted that the Declaration "acknowledges the distinctive and important status of indigenous peoples, their common historical experiences and the universal spirit that underpins its text." But while he called the Declaration "an affirmation of accepted international human rights," he also said it "expresses new, and *non-binding*, aspirations" (emphasis added.) Due to the purported aspirational and non-binding nature of the Declaration, New Zealand could affirm the rights contained therein without creating conflict within the "legal and constitutional frameworks that underpin New Zealand's legal system." In his five-minute statement, Sharples used some form of the word "aspirational" six times. (Again, the United Nations considers this document to be not merely aspirational, but as a set of minimum standards.)

Sharples also addressed previous concerns about content. Regarding land and resources, he made it clear that his country had "developed its own distinct approach" and would determine land and resources rights, along with restitution, "through its well-established processes for resolving Treaty claims." Furthermore, it would "continue to maintain [its] existing legal regimes for the ownership and management of land and natural resources."

The Māori affairs minister continued by addressing issues of redress: "New Zealand acknowledges and understands the historic injustices suffered by Māori in relation to their land and resources and is committed to addressing these through the established Treaty settlement process." In a nod to practicality, equality among all New Zealanders, and economics, he then said that "redress offered in Treaty settlements is, however, constrained by the need to be fair to everyone and by what the country can afford to pay."

When it came to Indigenous involvement in decision making, Sharples nodded to existing institutional structures and practices – as Banks had two years earlier. New Zealand, he said, "has developed, and will continue to rely upon, its own distinct processes and institutions that afford opportunities for Māori for such involvement."

The Māori affairs minister ended by acknowledging and restating "the special cultural and historical position of Māori as the original inhabitants – the *tangata whenua* – of New Zealand," and by offering platitudes of "possible paths forward" and "encouragement and inspiration for the future."

New Zealand's 2010 support of the Declaration, like Australia's, differed most from its 2007 position in terms of negotiations and contextual framing. Whereas it voiced concerns over the legitimacy of process in 2007, it struck a celebratory tone in 2010. Whereas it considered the Declaration's provisions on land, resources, redress, and Indigenous decision making to be "fundamentally incompatible with New Zealand's constitutional and legal arrangements," it reframed the document as aspirational and non-binding. As such, the once-offensive provisions could be interpreted within a domestic cultural heritage framework. New Zealand did not drop its concerns about the formation of international Indigenous rights norms. In fact, it emphasized the normative importance of Indigenous rights, while at the same time qualifying the legal status of those rights and writing down the norms themselves so that they aligned with existing domestic policies and institutions.

Canada

Explanation of opposition

Canada's permanent representative to the UN, John McNee, explained his country's position against the Declaration on September 13, 2007, the day of the General Assembly vote. Striking similar chords to Australia's and New Zealand's representatives, the Canadian ambassador noted problems with the process behind and content of the Declaration, while emphasizing its aspirational and non-binding legal status. Like them, he attempted to highlight the strength of his country's existing institutions for resolving disputes with Indigenous peoples, and aimed to separate Canada from less progressive states.

McNee began by noting how Canadians had "long demonstrated our commitment to actively advancing indigenous rights at home and internationally" and already recognized that "the situation of indigenous peoples around the world warrants concerted and concrete international action." Despite the fact that Canada had initially supported a declaration related to Indigenous peoples, and "continues to make further progress at home," McNee expressed great "disappointment that we find ourselves having to vote against the adoption of this Declaration as drafted."

McNee pointed to negotiations behind the document. Although Canada "had long been a proponent of a strong and effective text that would promote and protect the human rights and fundamental freedoms of every indigenous person without discrimination and recognize the collective rights of indigenous peoples around the world," the final text "did not meet such expectations and did not address some of our concerns." Specifically, McNee and his government objected that:

> the few modifications presented at the last minute to this Assembly, prepared by a limited number of delegations, do not arise from an open, inclusive or transparent process, and do not address key areas of concern of a number of delegations, including Canada.

Like the other anglosphere states, Canada went to great pains to show the Declaration's aspirational qualities – which stood in sharp contrast to the evolution of customary law. To emphasize this point further, McNee concluded his remarks: "For clarity, we also underline our understanding that this Declaration is not a legally binding instrument. It has no legal effect in Canada, and its provisions do not represent customary international law."

Like Australia and New Zealand, Canada rejected provisions on lands and resources – on the grounds that they were, in McNee's words, "overly broad, unclear, and capable of a wide variety of interpretations." Crucially, however, the ambassador noted Canada's existing pride in recognizing Indigenous land and resource claims. Almost perversely, the Declaration could put "into question matters that have been settled by treaty."

McNee also pointed out that provisions requiring "free, prior and informed consent are unduly restrictive." Such provisions could enable the "establishment of a complete veto power over legislative and administrative action for a particular group," which would be "fundamentally incompatible with Canada's parliamentary system." As did his Australian and New Zealand counterparts, the ambassador asserted that existing rights in Canada, along with domestic processes already in place, were already far superior to what the Declaration offered.

Statement of endorsement

Canada's 2010 endorsement of the Declaration stands apart in several respects. Unlike the other anglosphere states, Canada handled its change of position relatively quietly. Its formal announcement was not delivered at a large public event. Rather, on the morning of November 12, 2010, McNee met with the President of the United Nations General Assembly, Joseph Deiss, to inform him that Canada would officially endorse the Declaration (Windspeaker 2011). Later that afternoon, a press release appeared on the website of Indian and Northern Affairs Canada (now Indigenous and Northern Affairs) which outlined endorsement of the Declaration. This followed a brief announcement in March, 2010, when Governor General Michaëlle Jean mentioned in her Speech from the Throne that Canada was reconsidering its position.

The November, 2010 announcement consisted of six concise paragraphs – by far the shortest, least detailed explanation among the anglosphere states. Despite its brevity, the press release made Canada's views quite clear. It made no mention of negotiations, but it did make clear Canada's position on the Declaration's legal status: Canada had "formally endorsed the United Nations Declaration on the Rights of Indigenous Peoples in a manner fully consistent with Canada's Constitution and laws," despite it not being "legally binding." Nevertheless, it had chosen to support the Declaration "as an important aspirational document [in] a significant step forward in strengthening relations with Aboriginal peoples."

Unlike other statements, Canada's online endorsement did enumerate previous content complaints, in an attempt to reconcile those issues by reframing them as domestic, cultural heritage concerns. Canada simply stated that the Declaration "sets out a number of principles that should guide harmonious and cooperative relationships between Indigenous peoples and States, such as equality, partnership, good faith and mutual respect" and that the country "strongly supports these principles and believes that they are consistent with the Government's approach to working with Aboriginal peoples."

In a background statement that also appeared on the INAC website, Stephen Harper's government indicated that while concerns remained – regarding land and resources, as well as the principle of free, prior, and informed consent – it had decided to endorse "this document because it has the potential to contribute positively to the advancement of Indigenous rights around the world." Thus, in similar fashion to Australia and New Zealand, Canada asserted that it could now comfortably interpret the Declaration as being in line with existing domestic practices, and would now endorse it because Indigenous peoples in *other* parts of the world would benefit from it. The eventual endorsement, then, represented diplomatic and rhetorical moves on multiple levels – moves that at once reduced the Declaration's significance in Canada, domesticated Indigenous issues, maintained the legislative and institutional status quo, and separated the country from others "around the world." This was especially true because Canada aimed to "further reconcile and strengthen our relationship with Aboriginal peoples."

United States of America

Explanation of opposition

Robert Hagen, USA Advisor to the UN, presented his country's opposition to the Declaration; a second, longer, and more detailed document, "Observations of the United States with Respect to the Declaration on the Rights of Indigenous

Peoples," circulated within an hour of the General Assembly vote. Hagen's short statement concentrated on USA objections to the negotiation process and briefly mentioned objections to content, while "Observations" said more about the status of the Declaration and Washington's objections to its content.

Like its anglosphere allies, the USA objected to how the Declaration was negotiated; Hagen claimed that his government "had worked hard for eleven years in Geneva for a consensus declaration, but the document before us is a text that was prepared and submitted after the negotiations had concluded." The process, he explained, "was unfortunate and extraordinary" and set "a poor precedent with respect to UN practice." Furthermore, the adopted text was "confusing" and risked "endless conflicting interpretations and debate about its application." Therefore, the USA found it not "capable of implementation."

While Hagen made no mention of the Declaration's status, the supplementary statement made clear the USA's position, which was in keeping with the anglosphere trend. "Observations" described the Declaration as an "aspirational" list of recommendations that "is not in itself legally binding nor reflective of international law." It had "political and moral, rather than legal, force." The USA also rejected the possibility that the Declaration was, or could ever become, customary international law. Furthermore, the final document did "not provide a proper basis for legal actions, complaints, or other claims in any international, domestic or other proceedings."

USA concerns about content echoed those of other anglosphere states. Predictably, the USA objected to provisions on self-determination; lands, and resources; redress; and the principle of free, prior, and informed consent. Like Australia, it noted that Indigenous self-determination was intended only to mean self-government or autonomy within a nation-state, and it found the terminology problematic because "self-determination" was typically reserved for subnational groups seeking independence. The USA was also concerned that provisions on lands, resources, and redress were "overly broad and inconsistent" and "impossible to implement." In what had quickly become an anglosphere pattern, the USA objected to the principle of free, prior, and informed consent, because it could be interpreted to "confer upon a sub-national group a power of veto over the laws of a democratic legislature."

"Observations" – the longest, most detailed argument against the Declaration – included two issues with content that were not present in other anglosphere explanations. First, the USA opposed the recognition of collective rights as part of the human rights consensus. If collective rights were recognized as human rights, it argued, individuals within those groups could become vulnerable to potential violations of individual human rights by the collective. Furthermore, if both individuals and collectives hold human rights, the two sets of rights could sometimes conflict. Second, the USA complained that the Declaration did not define "Indigenous peoples," noting that "this obvious shortcoming will subject application of the declaration to endless debate, especially if entities not properly entitled to such status seek to enjoy the special benefits and rights contained in the declaration."

Statement of endorsement

In early 2010, a few days after New Zealand's surprise announcement of support at the Permanent Forum on Indigenous Issues, the USA ambassador to the UN, Susan Rice, said that Washington was also launching a full review of the Declaration. Ultimately, that review included three nationwide tribal consultations in summer and fall, 2010. On December 16, 2010, near the end of his remarks to the White House Tribal Nations Conference, President Obama mentioned that the USA had decided to "lend its support" to the Declaration. As it had in 2007, the USA followed the brief announcement with a more detailed statement, issued by the White House.

The longer explanation of USA support included multiple qualifiers and exemptions. While Obama said that the Declaration affirmed Indigenous aspirations, the follow-up statement considered the issue of legal status in more detail. It argued that the Declaration was "not legally binding or a statement of current international law" but that it had "both moral and political force." It also emphasized the document's aspirational nature, as well as the government's intent to interpret it within the bounds of the Constitution:

> It expresses both the aspirations of indigenous peoples around the world and those of States in seeking to improve their relations with indigenous peoples. Most importantly, it expresses aspirations of the United States, aspirations that this country seeks to achieve within the structure of the US Constitution, laws, and international obligations, while also seeking, where appropriate, to improve our laws and policies.

In terms of content, the White House began with the concept of self-determination, and noted that the Declaration had initiated "a new and distinct international concept of self-determination specific to indigenous peoples" – a concept that is different from the prevailing interpretation in international law. The statement argued that provisions regarding Indigenous self-determination pertained to self-government arrangements within nation-states. And because tribal nations within the USA already enjoyed such a government-to-government relationship with the federal government, there was no need to make structural changes.

On the principle of free, prior, and informed consent, the USA noted that it already had such "a process of meaningful consultation with tribal leaders," but also noted that the principle of free, prior, and informed consent did not require the "agreement of those leaders, before the actions addressed in those consultations are taken." Here, the White House implicitly resolved the Declaration's lacking definition of "Indigenous," by saying that the government intended to "consult and cooperate in good faith with federally recognized tribes and, as applicable, Native Hawaiians, on policies that directly and substantially affect them."

Concerning land, resources, and redress, the USA made it clear that such provisions pertained to "full legal recognition of the lands, territories, and natural resources indigenous peoples currently *possess* by reason of traditional ownership, occupation, or use as well as those that they have otherwise acquired" (emphasis added). It also argued that nation-states should recognize appropriate "interests of indigenous peoples in traditional lands, territories, and natural resources." Again, the USA asserted that its existing legal framework was more than adequate in this context.

The USA did change its position between 2007 and 2010 in one substantial way – officially recognizing the existence of collective human rights. The White House explained that the USA "is committed to serving as a model in the international community in promoting and protecting the collective rights of indigenous peoples as well as the human rights of all individuals." It stated directly that "indigenous peoples possess certain … collective rights," in addition to the individual human rights possessed by everyone. The USA now interpreted the Declaration "in light of this understanding of human rights and collective rights." Although the statement drew a distinction between "human rights," which presumably adhere to individuals, and "collective rights" that Indigenous peoples possess, the mere acknowledgment of collective rights was notably historic: for the first time since the Cold War, the USA recognized such rights.[3]

Findings: selective endorsement

The anglosphere's selective endorsement of the Declaration on the Rights of Indigenous Peoples reveals several trends, which Table 4.1 indicates. First, it dropped concerns over process legitimacy and Indigenous rights. Initially, the anglosphere criticized the negotiations behind the Declaration; by 2010, states either refrained from commenting on the process or described the process in positive, complimentary terms. In revised statements of support, not one of the four faulted the negotiation process.

Second, the anglosphere underscored the normative importance of Indigenous rights while simultaneously qualifying the legal status of those rights. Issues of status remained remarkably consistent between 2007 and 2010. Each of the four states noted in 2007 that the Declaration was merely aspirational and non-binding – and would not affect their existing laws or policies. Each carefully reiterated its arguments in later statements of support. At the same time, each country emphasized the normative importance of Indigenous rights generally, and highlighted their global status as a supporter of Indigenous rights.

Third, Australia, New Zealand, and the USA initially enumerated similar content objections and later reassessed them – all regarding self-determination, land and resources, redress, and the principle of free, prior, and informed consent. Statements of support among these three states made it clear that previously objectionable provisions would not pose problems domestically as long as they were interpreted within existing laws and structures. Only Canada refrained from reinterpreting these provisions within the confines of existing laws and policies.

Outside of the historic USA shift on collective rights, there were no substantive changes around anglosphere commitments to Indigenous rights between

Table 4.1 Content analysis results

	Change on DRIP	*How announced*	*2007 statements*		*2009/2010 statements*	
Australia	"Support"	Public event, speech to Parliament	***Process:***	Objects	***Process:***	Highly complimentary
			Status:	Aspirational Non-binding Not reflective of existing law Not customary law	***Status:***	Aspirational Non-binding Not affecting existing law
			Content:	Problems with: • Self-determination • Lands and resources • Free, prior, and informed consent • Intellectual property	***Content:***	Clarifies: • Self-determination • Land and resources • Free, prior, and informed consent Frames as domestic issues where Indigenous and non-Indigenous citizens must be equal
New Zealand	"Support"	Public event, opening ceremony of UNPFII	***Process:***	Objects	***Process:***	Positive
			Status:	Aspirational Non-binding Fundamentally incompatible with domestic law and institutions	***Status:***	Aspirational Non-binding Consistent with spirit of Treaty of Waitangi
			Content:	Problems with: • Lands and resources • Redress • Indigenous involvement in decision making • Intellectual property	***Content:***	Lands and resources, and redress issues will continue to be handled through highly sophisticated domestic processes, Indigenous peoples to participate in domestic politics

Canada	"Endorse"	No public event, released on Ministry website	***Process:***	Disappointment	***Process:***	Absence of comment
			Status:	Aspirational Non-binding No legal effect in Canada Not customary international law	***Status:***	Aspirational Not legally binding Endorsed in a manner fully consistent with the Constitution and laws
			Content:	Problems with: Lands and resources Free, prior, and informed consent Fundamentally incompatible with parliamentary system	***Content:***	Supports the principles of the Declaration Declaration's principles are already consistent with Canada's approach to Aboriginal issues
USA	"Support"	Public event, Presidential remarks at Tribal Nations Conference	***Process:***	Flawed	***Process:***	Absence of comment
			Status:	Aspirational Non-binding Not reflective of international customary law	***Status:***	Aspirational Non-binding To be interpreted within the context of existing law and policy
			Content:	Problems with: Self-determination Lands and resources Redress Free, prior, and informed consent Collective rights Absence of definition	***Content:***	New understanding of self-determination is not inconsistent with existing US practice Lands, resources, and right to redress apply only to lands currently possessed and occupied Consultation does not mean agreement Define as federally recognized tribes and Native Hawaiians Acknowledges Indigenous collective rights

2007 and 2010. In fact, commitments, qualifications, and exclusions related to Indigenous rights remained remarkably consistent among the four states, whether they were opposing or supporting the Declaration. With their qualifications and exclusions, the countries strategically, collectively, and unilaterally wrote down international Indigenous rights norms so that they aligned with the anglosphere status quo – making further implementation efforts unnecessary.

Conclusions and implications of selective endorsement

Whether it is the Declaration on the Rights of Indigenous Peoples or another human rights doctrine, state commitment behavior exists beyond the traditional binary of ratification and non-ratification. By looking for other examples of selective endorsement we can contribute to a deeper understanding of the nuances of state commitment, compliance, and implementation of human rights norms.

Selective endorsement lies at the intersection of rationalist and constructivist expectations. When emerging international rights norms directly conflict with state interests and demand substantial changes to the status quo, states respond in some of the ways rationalists might expect: they strategically endorse those norms that align with their interests. Yet because the identities of liberal democratic states are co-constitutive of human rights, states also demonstrate behaviors that adhere more closely to what constructivists might predict: countries proclaim the normative importance of the rights in question and make great efforts to show how they already comply.

Selective endorsement, however, reveals a curious intersection of rationalist and constructivist behaviors: a state may strategically, collectively, and unilaterally write down international norms so that those rewritten norms align with its domestic interests, as well as the legal and institutional status quo, all the while shoring up its global standing as a supporter of human rights, without any intent of moving toward further implementation.

My findings suggest that the anglosphere may have attempted – and may still be continuing to attempt – to shift the conversation away from the legitimacy of international Indigenous rights toward the domestication of Indigenous issues, which preserves a (neo)liberal framework. Rather than substantively change their positions, these states actively engaged in self-exemption, by developing and utilizing a discourse of anglosphere exceptionalism. But self-exemption is not the only manifestation of selective endorsement. Indeed, the anglosphere collectively and unilaterally rewrote international norms: through selective endorsement of Indigenous rights, four settler states made pre-emptive political moves against full implementation, and thus preserved the legal and policy status quo while dodging transnational and domestic political pressure. Through selective endorsement, these states could plausibly profess the normative value of their commitment to Indigenous rights.

Australia, Canada, New Zealand, and the USA were able to maneuver themselves out of a human rights dilemma, in which they stood alone in the world in their expressed opposition to international Indigenous rights. Through selective endorsement, the countries attempted to appease critics – to dodge embarrassment, shame, political pressure, and moral persuasion campaigns – while maintaining their internal legal and institutional arrangements. In order to advance Indigenous rights in actual practice, moral and political campaigns must move beyond questions of endorsement and instead concentrate squarely on whether or not states implement and comply with Indigenous rights norms.

Notes

1 "Compliance" is defined as state conformity with a rule, following Raustiala and Slaughter's definition (2002).
2 The "anglosphere," a term and concept that is enjoying increased prominence in social and political discourse, implies much more than the use of a common English language. As James Bennett noted, membership in the anglosphere also "requires adherence to the fundamental customs and values that form the core of English-speaking countries" (2002).
3 Throughout the Cold War era, the USA firmly opposed collective rights, with the exception of the right of self-determination, out of fear of a communist or socialist agenda. The 2010 recognition of collective rights – in general and not just for Indigenous peoples – represents a major policy and attitude shift.

References

Anaya, S.J., 2010. *Statement by James Anaya, Special Rapporteur on the Rights of Indigenous Peoples on the Obligations of States to Implement the Declaration on the Rights of Indigenous Peoples, 18 October 2010.* New York: United Nations.

Banks, R., 2007. *Declaration on the Rights of Indigenous Peoples Explanation of Vote, 13 September 2007.* New York: United Nations.

Bennett, J., 2002. The Emerging Anglosphere. *Orbis*, 46(1), p. 111.

Canada Governor General, 2010. *A Stronger Canada. A Stronger Economy. Now and for the Future. Speech from the Throne: March 3, 2010.* Ottawa: Government of Canada.

Chayes, A. and Chayes, A., 1993. On Compliance. *International Organization*, 47(2), pp. 175–205.

Checkel, J.T., 2001. Why Comply? Social Learning and European Identity Change. *International Organization*, 55(3), pp. 553–588.

Downs, G.W., Rocke, D.M., and Barsoom, P.N., 1996. Is the Good News about Compliance Good News about Cooperation? *International Organization*, 50(3), pp. 379–406.

Farber, D.A. 2002. Rights as Signals. *The Journal of Legal Studies*, 31(1), pp. 83–98.

Franck, T.M., 1990. *The Power of Legitimacy Among Nations.* New York: Oxford University Press.

Hagen, R., 2007. *Explanation of Vote by Robert Hagen, U.S. Advisor, on the Declaration on the Rights of Indigenous Peoples, to the UN General Assembly, 13 September 2007.* New York: United Nations.

Hathaway, O.A., 2002. Do Human Rights Treaties Make a Difference? *The Yale Law Journal*, 111(8), pp. 1935–2042.

Hill, H.R., 2007. *Explanation of Vote by the Hon. Robert Hill, Ambassador and Permanent Representative of Australia to the United Nations, 13 September 2007.* New York: United Nations.

Indian and Northern Affairs Canada, November, 2010a. Last update, Backgrounder: Canada's Endorsement of the United Nations Declaration on the Rights of Indigenous Peoples. Available at: www.ainc-inac.gc.ca/ai/mr/nr/s-d2010/23429bk-eng.asp [last accessed January 10, 2011].

Indian and Northern Affairs Canada, 2010b. Last update, Canada Endorses the United Nations Declaration on the Rights of Indigenous Peoples. Available at: www.ainc-inac.gc.ca/ai/mr/nr/s-d2010/23429-eng.asp [last accessed January 10, 2011].

Keck, M.E. and Sikkink, K., 1998. *Activists Beyond Borders: Advocacy Networks in International Politics.* Ithaca, NY: Cornell University Press.

Kratchowil, F.V., 1989. *Rules, Norms, and Decisions on the Conditions of Practical and Legal Reasoning in International Relations and Domestic Affairs.* Cambridge; New York: Cambridge University Press.

Lasswell, H. 1950 [1936]. *Politics: Who Gets What, When, How.* New York: P. Smith.

Lightfoot, S.R., 2010. Emerging International Indigenous Rights Norms and "Over-compliance" in New Zealand and Canada. *Political Science*, 62(1), pp. 84–104.

Macklin, J., 2009. *Statement on the United Nations Declaration on the Rights of Indigenous Peoples, Speech to Australian Parliament, 2 April 2009.* Canberra, Australia.

Malezer, L., 2007. *Statement by the Chairman, Global Indigenous Caucus, United Nations, 13 September 2007.* New York.

McNee, J., 2007. *Statement by Ambassador McNee to the General Assembly on the Declaration on the Rights of Indigenous Peoples, 13 September 2007.* New York: United Nations.

Moravcsik, A., 2000. The Origins of Human Rights Regimes: Democratic Delegation in Postwar Europe. *International Organization*, 54(2), pp. 217–252.

Obama, B., 2010. *Remarks by the President at the White House Tribal Nations Conference, 16 December 2010.* Washington, DC: The White House.

Raustiala, K. and Slaughter, A., 2002. International Law, International Relations and Compliance. In W. Carlsnaes, T. Risse, and B.A. Simmons, eds, *Handbook of International Relations*, 1st edn. London: Sage, pp. 538–558.

Rice, S.E., 2010. *Remarks by Ambassador Susan E. Rice, U.S. Permanent Representative to the United Nations, at the UN Permanent Forum on Indigenous Issues, 20 April 2010.* New York: United Nations.

Risse-Kappen, T., Ropp, S.C., and Sikkink, K., 2013. *The Persistent Power of Human Rights: From Commitment to Compliance.* Cambridge: Cambridge University Press.

Sharples, H.D.P., 2010. *UNPFII Opening Ceremony New Zealand Statement, Speech to United Nations Permanent Forum on Indigenous Issues, 19 April 2010.* New York.

Shestack, J., 1997. The Legal Profession and Human Rights: Globalization of Human Rights Law. *Fordham International Law Journal*, 21, pp. 558–568.

Simmons, B.A., 2009. *Mobilizing for Human Rights: International Law in Domestic Politics.* Cambridge; New York: Cambridge University Press.

Tauli-Corpuz, V., 2007. *Message of Victoria Tauli-Corpuz, Chairperson of the UN Permanent Forum on Indigenous Issues, On the Occasion of the Adoption by the General Assembly of the Declaration on the Rights of Indigenous Peoples, 13 September 2007.* New York: United Nations.

United Nations, 2007. *News Release: Adoption of Declaration on the Rights of Indigenous Peoples a Historic Moment for Human Rights, UN Expert Says, 14 September 2007.* New York: United Nations.

United Nations Department of Public Information, 2007. *General Assembly Adopts Declaration on the Rights of Indigenous Peoples, 13 September 2007.* New York: United Nations Document GA/10612.

United Nations General Assembly, 2007. *News Release: General Assembly Adopts Declaration on the Rights of Indigenous Peoples, 13 September 2007.* New York: United Nations.

United Nations Permanent Forum on Indigenous Issues, 2007. *Frequently Asked Questions – Declaration on the Rights of Indigenous Peoples.* New York: United Nations Permanent Forum on Indigenous Issues.

United States Mission to the United Nations, 2007. *News Release: Observations of the United States with Respect to the Declaration on the Rights of Indigenous Peoples, 13 September 2007.* New York: United Nations.

White House, 2010. *Announcement of U.S. Support for the United Nations Declaration on the Rights of Indigenous Peoples, Initiatives to Promote the Government-to-Government Relationship and Improve the Lives of Indigenous Peoples, 16 December 2010.* Washington, DC: White House.

WindSpeaker, D.S., 2011. Last update, Luke Warm Endorsement Receives Tepid Response [Homepage of Aboriginal Multi-Media Society (AMMSA)]. Available at: www.ammsa.com/publications/windspeaker/luke-warm-endorsement-receives-tepid-response [last accessed January 11, 2011].

5 State compliance with Indigenous rights

Opening the binary of compliance/non-compliance

The Indigenous rights regime places political and moral demands on states by asking them to adopt constitutional, legislative, and domestic policies that recognize and protect the individual rights of Indigenous citizens, but also their collective rights as peoples, including over land and self-determination. Given the major if not subtly revolutionary challenges posed by the emerging regime, the high levels of commitment required to implement it, and its non-binding nature, states have predictably responded in numerous ways.

This chapter considers some of those responses, along with typical and unusual state compliance. In the first section, I analyze data from sixty countries with significant Indigenous populations to determine five prevailing patterns: compliance, non-compliance, under-compliance, partial compliance, and what I call "over-compliance." Paradoxically, an over-compliant state takes constitutional, legal, and policy steps which recognize specific Indigenous rights, or categories of rights, that go beyond its international treaty obligations or normative commitments. I seek to explain that paradox in the second section of this chapter.

State compliance in Indigenous rights

The International Work Group for Indigenous Affairs (IWGIA)[1] considers sixty countries around the world with significant populations of Indigenous peoples, and each year it compiles data from those countries in its report, *The Indigenous World*. Table 5.1 draws primarily from the 2011 to 2015 IWGIA reports (Wessendorf 2011; Mikkelson 2012, 2013, 2014, 2015) to provide a snapshot of Indigenous rights as of December 31, 2014.

In compiling Table 5.1, I followed the lead of the IWGIA and grouped countries by region, so that geopolitical trends can emerge across thirteen different categories. The first column to the right of each country lists percentages of Indigenous peoples. If the IWGIA gave a specific population for a country, rather than a percentage of population, I calculated that percentage using statistics from *The World Factbook 2014* (Central Intelligence Agency 2015). The second column identifies political systems as parliamentary, presidential, semi-presidential, or one-party. The third column codes legal systems as common law,

Table 5.1 Indigenous rights commitment and compliance

Country	*Indigenous population (%)*	*Political system*	*Legal system*	*Political structure*	*ICERD*	*ICCPR*	*ICESCR*	*ILO 107*	*ILO 169*	*UNDRIP*	*Commitment*	*Behaviour*	*Overall compliance*
THE ARCTIC													
Greenland (Denmark)	88.0	Parliamentary	Civil	Unitary	☑	☑	☑	☐	☑	For	High	Strong	Compliant
Finland	0.1	Parliamentary	Civil	Unitary	☑	☑	☑	☐	☐	For	High	Moderate	Partially Compliant
Norway	0.5	Parliamentary	Civil	Unitary	☑	☑	☑	☐	☑	For	High	Strong	Compliant
Russian Federation	0.1	Semi-presidential	Civil	Federal	☑	☑	☑	☐	☐	Abstain	Low	Weak	Non-compliant
Sweden	0.2	Parliamentary	Civil	Unitary	☑	☑	☑	☐	☐	For	High	Moderate	Partially Compliant
NORTH AMERICA													
Canada	3.6	Parliamentary	Common	Federal	☑	☑	☑	☐	☐	Against (qualified support as of 2010)	Low	Moderate	Overcompliant
United States	1.7	Presidential	Common	Federal	☑	☑	☐	☐	☐	Against (qualified support as of 2010)	Low	Moderate	Overcompliant
LATIN AMERICA													
Argentina	3.0	Presidential	Civil	Federal	☑	☑	☑	☑	☑	For	High	Weak	Undercompliant
Bolivia	62.0	Presidential	Civil	Unitary	☑	☑	☑	☑	☑	For	High	Moderate	Partially Compliant
Brazil	0.4	Presidential	Civil	Federal	☑	☑	☑	☑	☑	For	High	Weak	Undercompliant
Chile	7.0	Presidential	Civil	Unitary	☑	☑	☑	☐	☑	For	High	Moderate	Partially Compliant
Colombia	3.1	Presidential	Civil	Unitary	☑	☑	☑	☑	☑	Abstain (support as of 2011)	High	Moderate	Partially Compliant
Costa Rica	1.7	Presidential	Civil	Unitary	☑	☑	☑	☑	☑	For	High	Weak	Undercompliant
Ecuador	11.5	Presidential	Civil	Unitary	☑	☑	☑	☑	☑	For	High	Weak	Undercompliant
Guatemala	60.0	Presidential	Civil	Unitary	☑	☑	☑	☐	☑	For	High	Weak	Undercompliant
Mexico	14.0	Presidential	Civil	Federal	☑	☑	☑	☑	☑	For	High	Weak	Undercompliant
Nicaragua	5.0	Presidential	Civil	Unitary	☑	☑	☑	☐	☑	For	High	Moderate	Partially Compliant
Panama	12.7	Presidential	Civil	Unitary	☑	☑	☑	☑	☐	For	High	Moderate	Partially Compliant
Paraguay	2.0	Presidential	Civil	Unitary	☑	☑	☑	☑	☑	For	High	Weak	Undercompliant
Peru	48.0	Presidential	Civil	Unitary	☑	☑	☑	☑	☑	For	High	Weak	Undercompliant
Suriname	3.7	Presidential	Civil	Unitary	☑	☑	☑	☐	☐	For	High	Weak	Undercompliant
Venezuela	2.8	Presidential	Civil	Federal	☑	☑	☑	☐	☑	For	High	Moderate	Partially Compliant

continued

Table 5.1 Continued

Country	*Indigenous population (%)*	*Political system*	*Legal system*	*Political structure*	*ICERD*	*ICCPR*	*ICESCR*	*ILO 107*	*ILO 169*	*UNDRIP*	*Commitment*	*Behaviour*	*Overall compliance*
PACIFIC													
Australia	2.5	Parliamentary	Common	Federal	☑	☑	☑	☐	☐	Against (qualified support as of 2009)	Low	Moderate	Overcompliant
Guam	37.0	Unincorporated Territory	Common	Unitary	N/A	N/A	N/A	N/A	N/A	N/A	N/A	Weak	N/A
New Zealand-Aotearoa	17.0	Parliamentary	Common	Unitary	☑	☑	☑	☐	☐	Against (qualified support as of 2010)	Low	Moderate	Overcompliant
ASIA													
Bangladesh	2.0	Parliamentary	Common	Unitary	☑	☑	☑	☑	☐	Abstain	Low	Weak	Non-compliant
Burma	32.0	Parliamentary	Mixed	Unitary	☐	☐	☐	☐	☐	For	High	Weak	Undercompliant
Cambodia	1.2	Parliamentary	Civil	Unitary	☑	☑	☑	☐	☐	For	High	Weak	Undercompliant
China	8.5	One-Party	Civil	Unitary	☑	☐	☑	☐	☐	For	High	Weak	Undercompliant
India	8.2	Parliamentary	Common	Federal	☑	☑	☑	☑	☐	For	High	Weak	Undercompliant
Indonesia	17.0	Presidential	Civil	Unitary	☑	☑	☑	☐	☐	For	High	Weak	Undercompliant
Israel	2.5	Presidential	Mixed	Unitary	☑	☑	☑	☐	☐	Absent	Low	Weak	Non-compliant
Japan	0.1	Parliamentary	Civil	Unitary	☑	☑	☑	☐	☐	For	High	Moderate	Partially Compliant
Laos	60.0	One-Party	Civil	Unitary	☑	☑	☑	☐	☐	For	High	Weak	Undercompliant
Malaysia	12.0	Parliamentary	Common	Federal	☐	☐	☐	☐	☐	For	High	Moderate	Partially Compliant
Nepal	37.0	Parliamentary	Common	Federal	☑	☑	☑	☐	☑	For	High	Weak	Undercompliant
Philippines	10.0	Presidential	Mixed	Unitary	☑	☑	☑	☐	☐	For	High	Moderate	Partially Compliant
Sri Lanka	0.1	Presidential	Mixed	Unitary	☑	☑	☑	☐	☐	For	High	Weak	Undercompliant
Taiwan	2.2	Semi-presidential	Civil	Unitary	N/A	N/A	N/A	N/A	N/A	N/A	N/A	Weak	N/A
Thailand	0.2	Parliamentary	Civil	Unitary	☑	☑	☑	☐	☐	For	High	Weak	Undercompliant
Vietnam	14.0	One-Party	Civil	Unitary	☑	☑	☑	☐	☐	For	High	Weak	Undercompliant

AFRICA													
Algeria	30.0	Presidential	Civil/ Islamic	Unitary	☑	☑	☑	☐	☐	For	High	Weak	Undercompliant
Angola	<0.1	Presidential	Civil	Unitary	☐	☑	☑	☑	☐	For	High	Weak	Undercompliant
Botswana	3.3	Presidential	Civil	Unitary	☑	☑	☐	☐	☐	For	High	Weak	Undercompliant
Burundi	1.3	Presidential	Civil	Unitary	☑	☑	☑	☐	☐	Abstain	Low	Weak	Non-compliant
Cameroon	12.4	Presidential	Civil	Unitary	☑	☑	☑	☐	☐	For	High	Weak	Undercompliant
Congo, Dem. Rep of	3.0	Presidential	Civil	Unitary	☑	☑	☑	☐	☐	For	High	Weak	Undercompliant
Congo, Rep. of	2.3	Presidential	Civil	Unitary	☑	☑	☑	☐	☐	For	High	Weak	Undercompliant
Ethiopia	15.0	Parliamentary	Civil	Federal	☑	☑	☑	☐	☐	Absent	Low	Weak	Non-compliant
Gabon	1.3	Presidential	Civil	Unitary	☑	☑	☑	☐	☐	For	High	Moderate	Partially Compliant
Kenya	25.0	Presidential	Common/ Islamic	Unitary	☑	☑	☑	☐	☐	Abstain	Low	Weak	Non-compliant
Mali	10.0	Presidential	Civil	Unitary	☑	☑	☑	☐	☐	For	High	Weak	Undercompliant
Morocco	28.0	Parliamentary	Civil	Unitary	☑	☑	☑	☐	☐	Absent	Low	Weak	Non-compliant
Namibia	8.0	Presidential	Civil	Unitary	☑	☑	☑	☐	☐	For	High	Weak	Undercompliant
Niger	8.5	Semi-presidential	Civil	Unitary	☑	☑	☑	☐	☐	For	High	Weak	Undercompliant
Nigeria	<0.1	Presidential	Common	Federal	☑	☑	☑	☐	☐	Abstain	Low	Weak	Non-compliant
Rwanda	0.3	Presidential	Civil	Unitary	☑	☑	☑	☐	☐	Absent	Low	Weak	Non-compliant
South Africa	1.0	Presidential	Civil	Unitary	☑	☑	☑	☐	☐	For	High	Moderate	Partially Compliant
Tanzania	1.3	Presidential	Common	Unitary	☑	☑	☑	☐	☐	For	High	Weak	Undercompliant
Uganda	<0.1	Presidential	Common	Unitary	☑	☑	☑	☐	☐	Absent	Low	Weak	Non-compliant

Sources: All ratification information on International Labour Organization conventions No. 107 and No. 169 comes from the ILO's website. Voting status on UNDRIP is from the UN Department of Public Information.

civil law, mixed, common/Islamic, or civil/Islamic. Political structures are shown in the fourth column as federal or unitary. I relied on *The World Factbook 2014* for these three columns as well.

Table 5.1 also looks at three major human rights treaties: the International Convention on the Elimination of all Forms of Racial Discrimination (ICERD); the International Covenant on Civil and Political Rights (ICCPR); and the International Covenant on Economic, Social and Cultural Rights (ICESCR). Checkmarks indicate a country's ratification or accession of a particular convention, but do not appear if a country has merely signed that convention. For these columns, I drew upon the United Nations Treaty Collection (United Nations 2015).

The next three columns consider commitments to Indigenous rights instruments, specifically International Labour Organization conventions No. 107 and No. 169, and the United Nations Declaration on the Rights of Indigenous Peoples.[2] A check under ILO 107 indicates whether a state ever ratified the convention (countries like Colombia and Mexico that went on to ratify No. 169 implicitly denounced No. 107). General Assembly votes on the Declaration on the Rights of Indigenous Peoples (UNDRIP) are indicated as "for," "against," "abstain," or "absent." Since the 2007 vote, several countries have changed positions, and those changes are indicated. (As discussed in Chapter 4, Australia, New Zealand, Canada, and the USA all announced some type of qualified support for the Declaration between 2009 and 2010. Colombia, which abstained in 2007, announced its support in 2011.)

The next three columns indicate national commitments to and compliance with Indigenous rights. "Commitment" is based on ratification records. I marked countries as "high" if they have ratified ILO No. 169, voted for UNDRIP, or have since announced full, unqualified support for the Declaration. I coded countries as "low" if they have not ratified ILO No. 169, did not vote for UNDRIP, or have announced anything short of full support for the Declaration. This is because even qualified support constrains a country's actual commitment to Indigenous rights. For example, USA President Barack Obama briefly announced on December 16, 2010 that the United States would be "lending its support" to the Declaration. However, later that same day, the White House released a follow-up statement qualifying its support, including numerous exclusions on self-determination, free, prior, and informed consent, and land, resources, and redress. The statement also reconfirmed the USA's view that the Declaration was merely an "aspirational" document.

I based "Behavior" on how constitutions, laws, and policies address Indigenous rights. A country is deemed "strong" if it performs well in all three categories. It receives "moderate" if it complies constitutionally and legally, but has limited actual implementation. "Weak" indicates that a country falls short in all three areas. (I based "Behavior" levels on more extensive qualitative data, which appear in Appendix 5.1.)

I determined "Overall Compliance" based on the previous two columns, according to a framework outlined in Table 5.2 to Kal Raustiala and Anne-Marie

Table 5.2 Formula for compliance coding

Indigenous rights commitment	*Constitutional, legal, and policy behavior*	*Indigenous rights compliance*
High	Strong	Compliant
High	Moderate	Partially compliant
High	Weak	Under-compliant
Low	Weak	Non-compliant
Low	Moderate	Over-compliant
Low	Strong	Over-compliant

Slaughter's definition of compliance (Raustiala and Slaughter 2002). If a country is firmly committed to Indigenous rights and exhibits strong behavior, as is the case with Denmark (Greenland), it is compliant. That is to say, a country complies when its behavior matches the international standard. On the other hand, a country such as Morocco that does not commit to the international standard and does not alter its behavior is non-compliant. A high level of commitment and a low level of policy conduct results in under-compliance, which is true of many countries including Argentina, Peru, China, Indonesia, Cameroon, and Botswana. A partially compliant country, such as Bolivia or Japan, demonstrates a high level of commitment but has not fully implemented its own positive policies (Hawkins and Jacoby 2010).[3] A country is over-compliant if it exhibits strong or moderate behavior but a low level of commitment. In other words, a country such as New Zealand is curiously more committed in action than on paper.

The concept of "over-compliance" is new to IR theory. Both scholars and practitioners assume that states find it easier to sign or vote for conventions than to implement actual policies; commitment exceeds compliance if behavior lags. Under-compliance and more recently partial compliance have received theoretical and practical attention. I argue, however, that conduct can counter-intuitively exceed commitment.

I define over-compliant states as those that (1) recognize Indigenous land claims or self-determination rights beyond their legal obligations; or (2) recognize categories of Indigenous rights domestically while opposing those same categories internationally. For example, if a state has signed ILO No. 107 and behaves according to its provisions, then it is compliant. If it has signed the more advanced ILO No. 169 but its behavior reflects the previous standards, it is considered under-compliant or partially compliant. If, as in the case of the USA, it has signed neither ILO No. 107 nor ILO No. 169 but behaves more as if it has signed ILO No. 169, then it is considered over-compliant. While an over-compliant state goes beyond its legal or normative commitments, it still falls short of Indigenous demands and the expectations of the broader Indigenous rights consensus. My term "over-compliance" does not suggest that such states comply fully with or exceed international standards as articulated in the Declaration – they do not. It simply indicates that such states perform above the levels that their public commitments would otherwise suggest.

Because this is a qualitative study, I have analyzed Table 5.1 with an eye toward dominant trends. Table 5.3 summarizes compliance levels: 17.2 percent are non-compliant, 51.7 percent are under-compliant, 20.7 percent are partially compliant, 3.4 percent of countries are compliant, and 6.9 percent are over-compliant. (Taiwan and Guam are not UN member states, and have therefore not voted on international Indigenous rights instruments. This makes it difficult to assess their commitment levels, so I excluded them from my compliance figures.)

Table 5.4 breaks countries down by compliance level. Regionally, trends emerge.[4] Of the five circumpolar countries, two are compliant (Norway and Denmark), two are partially compliant (Sweden and Finland), and one is non-compliant (Russian Federation). Both North American countries (Canada and the USA) are over-compliant, as are the two Pacific countries in the dataset: Australia and New Zealand. Latin America appears to have high aspirations but a serious implementation gap. All fifteen countries have high levels of commitment, but actual behaviors range from weak to moderate. As a result, the region

Table 5.3 Indigenous rights compliance rates by compliance level

Level of compliance	*Countries exhibiting this level of compliance*	*(%)*
Non-compliant	10	17.2
Under-compliant	30	51.7
Partially compliant	12	20.7
Compliant	2	3.4
Over-compliant	4	6.9
	Total: 58 countries	

Table 5.4 Indigenous rights compliance by country

Level of compliance	*Countries exhibiting this level of compliance*
Non-compliant	Bangladesh, Burundi, Ethiopia, Israel, Kenya, Morocco, Nigeria, Russian Federation, Rwanda, Uganda
Under-compliant	Algeria, Angola, Argentina, Botswana, Brazil, Burma, Cambodia, Cameroon, China, Congo (Democratic Republic of), Congo, (Republic of), Costa Rica, Ecuador, Guatemala, India, Indonesia, Laos, Mali, Mexico, Namibia, Niger, Nepal, Paraguay, Peru, Sri Lanka, Suriname, Tanzania, Thailand, Vietnam
Partially compliant	Bolivia, Chile, Colombia, Finland, Gabon, Japan, Malaysia, Nicaragua, Panama, Philippines, South Africa, Sweden, Venezuela,
Compliant	Greenland (Denmark), Norway
Over-compliant	Australia, Canada, New Zealand/Aotearoa, USA
	Total: 58 countries

shows the lowest rate of compliance, with every country either under-compliant or partially compliant. Of the fifteen Asian countries, ten are under-compliant, two are non-compliant, and three are partially compliant. (Taiwan is not a UN member and cannot vote in the General Assembly, so I did not evaluate it here.) Asian countries tend toward high levels of commitment, but exhibit widespread resistance to recognizing Indigenous peoples within their borders – often considering them ethnic or national minorities instead. Compliance records among African countries are also mixed: seven of the nineteen countries assessed are non-compliant, ten are under-compliant, and two are partially compliant. Commitment levels vary substantially; as in Asia, African countries generally do not recognize self-identified Indigenous groups. Like other developing regions, Africa performs poorly in implementing Indigenous rights policies.

High rates of under-compliance and relatively low rates of compliance are not surprising given the novelty and policy implications of the emerging Indigenous rights regime. However, the rate of over-compliance – especially among developed countries – merits further investigation. Why do so many North American and Pacific countries exhibit a puzzling pattern of over-compliance, which effectively under-commits them to Indigenous rights?

Explaining "over-compliance"

Theoretical approaches to a state's compliance or non-compliance with international law, including human rights standards, fall into three general streams: rationalist, liberal, and constructivist. The existing literature does not sufficiently explain the phenomenon of over-compliance, although a constructivist explanation coupled with Hathaway's cost-of-commitment theory (Hathaway 2003) offers a start. Further examination of Table 5.1 bolsters my hypothesis for the existence of over-compliance.

Theoretical approaches

Rationalist explanations to state compliance are rule based and claim that nations, as rational actors, join and comply with international law regimes that meet their own interests. Numerous scholars have relied on this stream of thought (Keohane 1997; Snidal 1985; Abbott 1992; Setear 1996) to argue that "nation-states obey international law when it serves their short or long term self-interest to do so" (Koh 1997), or that "nations employ cooperative strategies to pursue a complex, multifaceted long-run national interest, in which compliance with negotiated legal norms serves as a winning long-term strategy in a iterated 'prisoner's dilemma' game" (Koh 1997).

Rationalists argue that states are unitary actors who pursue their best interests – constraints on their capacities and power notwithstanding. Within rationalist theory, compliance involves a strict calculation of interests within the existing distribution of power (Kingsbury 1998), or a positive cost–benefit calculation toward ratification (Cole 2005). Within this framework, there is little reason for a state to comply with human rights law vis-à-vis Indigenous rights. First, states have much greater material and discursive power than Indigenous peoples. Second, they view concessions to Indigenous peoples as zero-sum games, in which they stand only to lose power – domestic and otherwise. A rationalist approach can help explain the prevalence of non-compliance and non-adherence, especially among the world's most powerful nations, but it generally fails to explain why states would ever comply, much less over-comply with Indigenous rights.

Chayes and Chayes (1993) and Downs et al. (1996) offer somewhat limited explanations for state compliance. The Chayes approach, while not purely rationalist, is nonetheless rationalist leaning: non-compliance is actually deviant behavior and can be dealt with through effective management, enhanced communication, and technical assistance. They emphasize persuasion by international peers rather than enforcement. Downs et al. agree that non-compliance is deviant and unexpected behavior, and argue that states endorse and comply with international regimes that are not dissimilar to what they would have done on their own. Their argument also focuses on cooperation and technology to enhance compliance, with an eye toward collective benefits.

Ultimately, these theories fail to explain compliance – much less over-compliance. These theorists claim that a state joins a treaty regime out of self-interest alone, which accounts for the paucity of ILO No. 169 signatories but not the significant support for the Declaration. On the whole, then, rationalist approaches do not adequately explain Indigenous rights compliance, and offer no explanation for why a state would be reluctant to ratify an international instrument whose standards it may already exceed.

Liberal explanations downplay the rationalist assumption that the state is a unitary actor, and allow for its disaggregation into domestic components, each with individual considerations. The interest of the state, then, is a combination of varied, sometimes competing concerns – what Kingsbury (1998) describes as the aggregated preferences of relevant actors. This strand of liberal compliance theory also rests on the notion of rule legitimacy, as elaborated by Franck (1995).

Another strand of liberal thought casts the type of regime as a critical variable. Moravcsik (1997) and Slaughter (1995), for example, draw on democratic peace theory to argue that compliance with international law depends on the democratic character of the regime. Just as liberal democracies do not fight one another – they tend to be more transparent and more open to citizen and NGO influence – they are more apt to comply with international law than non-democracies.

If liberal theory can explain state compliance and non-compliance when it comes to Indigenous rights, then one should expect more committed, compliant liberal democracies than non-democracies. This is only partially the case. Australia, New Zealand, the USA, and Canada are liberal democracies with comparatively good compliance records but weak levels of commitment. Furthermore, liberal theory loses some of its explanatory purchase in failing to account for patterns of under-commitment. The USA, for example, has not ratified ILO No. 169, nor addressed its discrimination of Indigenous peoples through constitutional or legal reforms, under the ICCPR. It has participated in other aspects of the ICCPR, however; its lack of compliance – and its lackluster commitment to Indigenous rights in general – weakens liberal explanations.

Furthermore, liberal theory does not account for compliance among less liberal states. Consider support for ILO No. 169, which came largely from Latin American and African countries that are not clear liberal democracies. In addition, the quality of democracy that does exist is uneven. Many of these states, however, such as Colombia and Bolivia, have made bone fide attempts to improve their relationships with Indigenous peoples in order to comply with international norms.

While offering insight into compliance, liberal theories leave open a number of important questions. They do not explain why a state would recognize any collective rights, nor why a state would over-comply with its Indigenous rights obligations while concurrently attempting to block the Declaration and the emergence of an international rights norm.

Unlike rationalist and liberal theories, constructivist explanations take a process-oriented approach rather than a rule-oriented one, and prioritize "the social construction of identities and meanings among actors in the international system" in such a way that interests and identities are inter-subjectively constructed (Kingsbury 1998). Through this inter-subjective process, societies self-constitute themselves through laws; states thus become what they imagine themselves to be. In other words, norms do not have the regulative function that they do in liberal theories. Rather, they have constitutive functions – forming the identities of states and then driving their behavior. As Koh (1997) argues, "nations thus obey international rules not just because of sophisticated calculations about how compliance or noncompliance will affect their interests, but because a repeated habit of obedience remakes their interests so that they come to value rule compliance."

Other normative theories suggest that transnational legal processes help constitute state identities. Finnemore and Sikkink (1998), for example, argue that global standards emerge through the activities of transnational actors. Over time, a "norm cascade" develops and these *de jure* rules become institutionalized instruments that help guide state behavior. Accordingly, ratification and compliance reflect normative commitments as states adopt international norms (Bearce and Bondanella 2007). Risse et al. (1999) developed a five-stage "spiral model" to explain how a state moves from norm violator to norm follower. Simmons (2000) suggests that reputational concerns explain compliance patterns; states comply with international commitments in order to enhance or maintain positive reputations. In their 2013 revisit to the spiral model, Risse et al. (1999) identify five "scope conditions" that determine state compliance: democratic vs. autocratic regime type, consolidated vs. limited state capacity, centralized vs. decentralized rule implementation, material vulnerability, and social vulnerability.

Koh (1997) also offers a thick constructivist explanation for why states obey international law, and in so doing provides some theoretical footing for my concept of over-compliance. He argues that nations obey international law through a process of interaction, interpretation, and internalization within domestic legal systems. This process – at once transnational and domestic – sees nation-states, NGOs, multinational corporations, and private individuals make, interpret, and internalize laws through their various interactions. This "international legal process" is distinctive in that it is "transnational, normative, and constitutive" in character. Thus, it is through a dynamic process of making, interpreting, and complying with legal norms that all relevant actors' identities become inter-subjectively shaped and constituted.

Constructivist theory helps us understand the Indigenous rights movement of the late 1960s and early 1970s. At the time, Indigenous leaders in several countries joined together in a common struggle for the protection and recognition of their rights. As Keck and Sikkink (1998) point out, many Indigenous peoples had reached impasses with their respective states. The transnational movement, then, attempted to "boomerang" around the state to achieve domestic reforms through international pressure – and to correct crucial omissions and discriminatory aspects of international law and human rights norms. Concurrently, states engaged in a concerted effort to advance human rights in general. Indigenous leaders took advantage of this dynamic transnational legal process by framing their aims within the larger human rights movement.

Through their interactions, the Indigenous rights movement and various states came to constitute themselves over time. A new supranational identity called "Indigenous people" or "indigeneity" emerged (Ivison et al. 2000; Niezen 2003; Coates 2004); for some Indigenous peoples this added to already complicated patterns of kinship, tribal, and national minority identity formation. Likewise, some states came to be known as strong supporters of international human rights.

Domestically, political discourse during this period changed in two important ways. First, with regard to Indigenous people, some states shifted from completely needs-based discourse to increasingly rights-based dialogue (Maaka and Fleras 2002). Importantly, these states began to accept Indigenous peoples as "peoples" and even treaty nations, rather than seeing them as disadvantaged multicultural minorities not fully integrated into dominant society. In doing so, governments acknowledged uniquely Indigenous rights, especially those concerned with land and self-determination. Second, three of the four states that I identify as over-compliant distanced themselves from their British origins, and some enacted, or are now in the process of enacting, constitutional and electoral reforms that solidified their distinct national identities. Thus, in order to distinguish themselves in a globalized world, these countries found and articulated uniquely Australian, Canadian, and New Zealander characteristics – a process that required coming to terms with their imperial legacies.[5] As Tully (1995) puts it, emerging discourses of indigeneity entailed similarly discursive shifts in domestic constitutionalism that had historically supported colonial domination.

This dynamic interaction, coupled with Hathaway's cost-of-commitment theory (2003), helps explain why some states over-comply with Indigenous rights. The larger Indigenous movement framed its struggle within a more general human rights discourse, even though that discourse did not yet include the most sought-after Indigenous rights. At the same time, a number of states made domestic reforms that enhanced their identities as good stewards of human rights, which helped reconcile their colonial legacies.

Hathaway points out that we must also account for domestic enforcement mechanisms and the cost of international commitments when evaluating the effect of international law on state behavior. For treaties with low enforcement mechanisms (the case with most human rights treaties), states consider the costs of compliance along with the likelihood that those costs will be incurred. The result: countries that begin with better practices are more reluctant to commit to additional rights instruments, while those countries with poor domestic-enforcement mechanisms are less reluctant.

In the larger international context, settler states occasionally attempt to reconcile their colonial legacies and their self-fashioned post-colonial identities. For these states, commitment to Indigenous rights is often conflated with full compliance. In practice, however, the cost of fully committing to Indigenous rights is high – undoing an entrenched colonial legacy, revamping domestic enforcement mechanisms, and so forth – which translates to a high "cost of compliance." Consequently, a state may resist ratifying one set of Indigenous rights – even if it already acknowledges and supports some of those rights – to avoid any expectation that it will one day comply with other, more exhaustive sets of rights. By keeping its commitments low, a country can carefully cherry-pick rights with low compliance costs. Conversely, a state with no compelling need to reconcile its colonial past – or that does not constitute its international identity through a commitment to human rights – has to make fewer domestic reforms.

A constructivist theoretical approach helps account for the paradox of over-compliance: a state can exhibit over-compliant behavior while simultaneously resisting the full body of Indigenous rights. Because changes in domestic political discourse involve reconciliation with the colonial past, a liberal state has an upper limit on its tolerance of Indigenous rights, which falls short of the emerging norms. This upper limit is often constitutional: a nation such as Canada is founded on doctrines of individualism, equality, and multiculturalism, which ultimately are difficult to reconcile with collective land ownership and self-determination for Indigenous peoples, or especially the expectation of free prior and informed consent.

Liberal states are constrained by the very doctrines of liberalism. A polity that seeks to join other socially conscious nations – and to reject its colonial past while at the same time defending status quo power relations – can only concede so much to Indigenous peoples. The full recognition of rights requires a form of sovereignty sharing and nation-to-nation relationship. While the Indigenous rights discourse and the Declaration call for pluri-national countries, a state's liberal foundations negate or at least diminish that discursive possibility.

Similarly, the cost-of-compliance component, which predicts that countries with better practices are less likely to commit to international instruments due to perceived costs, accounts for the demonstrated reluctance among the four democracies with stronger domestic policies (Canada, the USA, Australia, and

New Zealand) to commit to the global Indigenous rights discourse. Hathaway theorizes that the internal costs of such commitments are simply too high, because full compliance comes with the expectation of full commitment. Her findings, however, suggest that democracy determines treaty ratification. Table 5.1 shows a wide variety of compliance among liberal democracies with strong internal enforcement mechanisms, so Hathaway's theory warrants refinement. In the following section, I return to Table 5.1 and seek to further identify domestic barriers to the emerging international Indigenous rights discourse.

Data

The advancement of Indigenous rights, or lack thereof, is often explained in terms of domestic demographics and politics. These explanations typically fall into one of four categories. First, large Indigenous populations lead to the advancement of rights. Although this appears to be a common argument anecdotally, it does not appear in the scholarly literature. Second, advancement comes about through parliamentary systems as found in Australia and Canada, or, further, a proportional representative parliamentary system as found in New Zealand (Lijphart 1999).[6] Third, federalism supports Indigenous rights (Abele and Prince 2006; Borrows 2002; Cairns 2000; Fletcher 1999; Henderson 1994; Ladner 2003; Papillon 2008; Tully 1995; White 2002). Fourth, compliance is achieved through a country's legal system – civil or common law (Simmons 2009).[7]

To test these standard accounts, I compared countries' rights compliance to percentages of Indigenous population, and analyzed political systems (presidential or parliamentary), political structure (federal or unitary), and legal systems (common or civil law). Simply put, Table 5.1 does not back up the four prevailing explanations, or supports only a partial explanation of over-compliant state behavior.

While it may seem plausible that large populations of Indigenous peoples lead to stronger Indigenous rights performance, the data show otherwise. In fact, as Table 5.5 shows, no significant difference exists between countries with relatively large and small Indigenous populations. Compliance among countries with smaller populations (less than 10 percent), as shown in Figure 5.1, is slightly greater than countries with larger populations (10 percent or more), as shown in Figure 5.2, but the differences are marginal while similarities in behavior are striking.

Its political system does, however, influence a country's commitment to Indigenous rights, as well as its overall compliance.[8] In presidential Panama, for example, the Constitution recognizes autonomous Indigenous territories, yet reports have emerged of forced displacements without free, prior, and informed consent along with land incursions by local farmers that the government does not enforce. Presidential Mexico is similar, with an amended constitution that declares Mexico a pluri-cultural country, and the 1996 San Andreas Accords included territorial and political rights for Indigenous peoples. Yet, land conflicts

Table 5.5 Distribution of Indigenous rights compliance by percentage of Indigenous population

Indigenous population (%)	*Level of Indigenous rights compliance*	*Countries demonstrating the level of compliance*	*(%)*
Fewer than 10 (37 countries)	Non-compliant	5	13.5
	Under-compliant	20	54.0
	Partially compliant	8	21.6
	Compliant	1	2.7
	Over-compliant	3	8.1
Equal to or greater than 10 (21 countries)	Non-compliant	3	14.3
	Under-compliant	12	57.0
	Partially compliant	4	19.0
	Compliant	1	4.8
	Over-compliant	1	4.8

and pockets of violence persist in the state of Chiapas and issues over water and cultural rights, including reports of violent military repression, come out of the state of Oaxaca. Meanwhile, parliamentary countries, especially throughout Africa and Asia, often keep their commitments low (e.g., Kenya and Nigeria), and do not recognize any group within their borders as "Indigenous," thus contributing to continued land insecurity and marginalization for groups that do self-identify as Indigenous. Table 5.6 shows that presidential countries are more likely to under-comply or partially comply than parliamentary ones. This, in turn, indicates that presidential countries tend to commit to Indigenous rights at

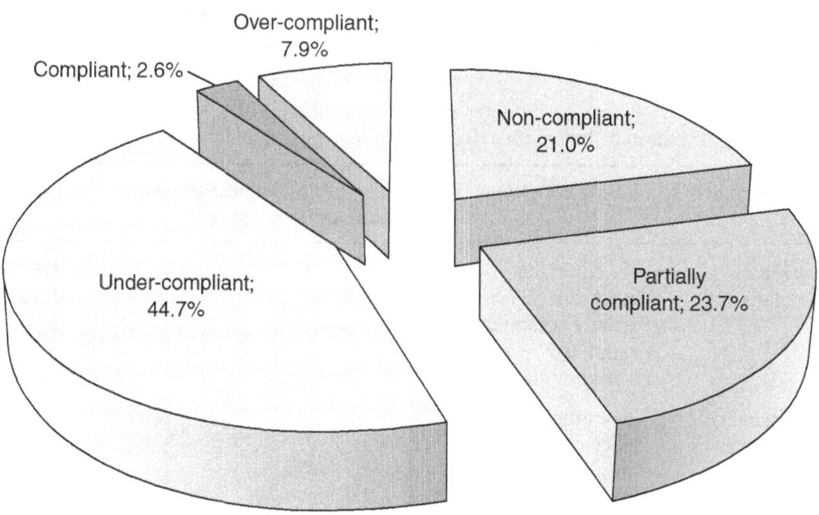

Figure 5.1 Compliance distribution with small Indigenous population.

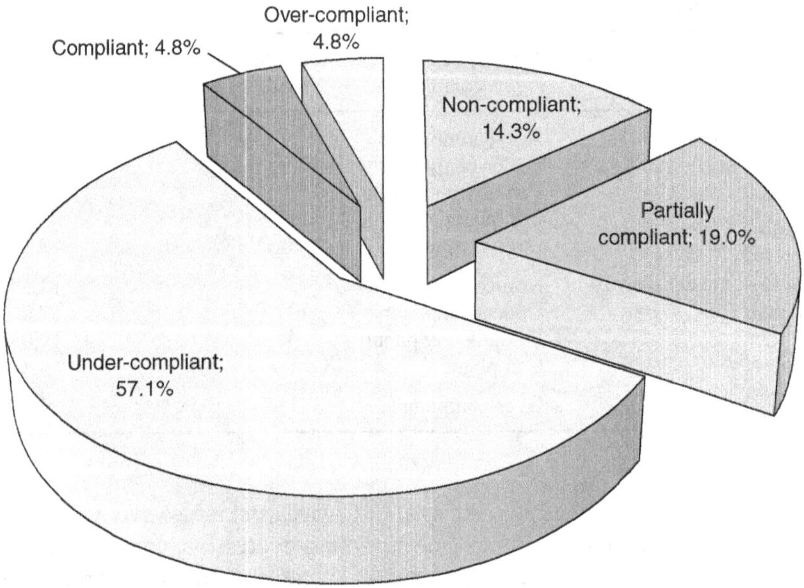

Figure 5.2 Compliance distribution with large Indigenous population.

higher levels. Indeed, commitment levels under presidential structures are significantly higher than under parliamentary systems. As Table 5.7 shows, only one of the four over-compliant countries, the USA, has a presidential system.

Compliance levels among parliamentary countries are fairly even and are thus less revealing. These countries are as likely to over-comply as to not comply, and they are almost as likely to partially comply as to under-comply. For example,

Table 5.6 Distribution of Indigenous rights compliance by political system

Political system	*Level of compliance*	*Countries demonstrating the level of compliance*	*(%)*
Presidential (36 countries)	Non-compliant	6	16.7
	Under-compliant	20	55.5
	Partially compliant	9	25.0
	Compliant	0	0
	Over-compliant	1	2.7
Parliamentary (17 countries)	Non-compliant	3	17.6
	Under-compliant	5	29.4
	Partially compliant	4	23.5
	Compliant	2	11.8
	Over-compliant	3	17.6

Table 5.7 Indigenous rights commitment by political system

Political system	*Level of Indigenous rights commitment*	*Number of countries with this level of commitment*	*(%)*
Presidential (36 countries)	High	29	80.1
	Low	7	19.4
Parliamentary (16 countries)	High	11	64.7
	Low	6	35.3

Greenland has been self-governing within the Danish realm since 1979, and in 2009, new self-government legislation provided even more self-determination, while the Finnish government refuses to address Saami land rights and refuses special legislation for Saami. Japan recognized the Ainu as an Indigenous people in 2008 and is working toward policy measures; while Nepal now recognizes some groups as Indigenous, these groups still experience substantial discrimination. Parliamentary governments' commitment to Indigenous rights skews high (64.7 percent of parliamentary countries have high levels), but not as high as presidential governments (80.1 percent). And three of the four over-complying countries are parliamentary (Canada, Australia, and New Zealand.)

That is to say, parliamentary governments tend to exhibit lower levels of commitment than do presidential systems. However, higher levels often coincide with limited compliance, with more than 80 percent of presidential countries partially complying or under-complying. Despite their lower levels of commitment, parliamentary countries comply more evenly. Approximately two-thirds of them commit at high levels; two out of seventeen (11.8 percent) actually comply with their commitments, while nine remain partially or under-compliant. Three parliamentary countries (17.6 percent) are non-compliant, meaning that they have made low commitments to Indigenous rights, and another three over-comply with their commitments. Thus, while parliamentary countries are typically restrained in their commitments, they are more likely than presidential countries to match or even exceed those commitments in actual practice – through constitutional, legal, and policy behavior. However, while over-compliance is most often seen in parliamentary countries, and lower commitments appear to correlate with such countries, a parliamentary system alone does not sufficiently explain over-compliance.

There is also little correlation between federalism and Indigenous rights commitment. As Table 5.8 shows, six out of thirteen federal countries (46 percent) make low commitments while the other seven (54 percent) make high commitments. Federalism has little bearing on compliance as well: eight countries (61.5 percent) rate low, and five countries (38.5 percent) rate medium. Not a single federal system exhibits high compliance behavior.

Legal systems do seem to correlate with Indigenous rights compliance. For example, Colombia, a civil law country, has a constitution that recognizes Indigenous rights and territories, including reserves, but conflicts over resource extraction are ongoing and recent legislation says that Indigenous peoples must

Table 5.8 Indigenous rights commitment and behaviour in 13 federal structures

Level of Indigenous rights commitment		
Low	6	46.0%
High	7	54.0%
	Total: 13	
Indigenous rights behavior		
Weak	8	61.5%
Moderate	5	38.5%
Strong	0	0%
	Total: 13	

permanently occupy their lands in order to retain them, leaving Colombia partially compliant. Meanwhile, in Argentina, another civil law country, development efforts continually encroach on Indigenous lands and Indigenous peoples are pressured or coerced into renouncing their lands, leaving Argentina under-compliant. Common law Malaysia has laws respecting Indigenous customary land rights, although they are regularly ignored by the government, leaving the country partially compliant. Table 5.9 breaks down Indigenous rights compliance by common law and civil law.[9] It shows that the rates of under-compliance and partial compliance are higher (57.1 and 26.2 percent, respectively) in civil law countries than in common law countries (33.3 and 8.3 percent, respectively). Rates of compliance are 4.8 percent in civil law countries, while no common law systems fully comply. Non-compliance runs at 11.9 percent in civil law countries and 25 percent in common law countries. All over-compliant countries fall entirely into a single category: common law systems. This suggests an association between common law and over-compliance, which is the case for a full one-third of such countries.

As with political systems, differences among common law and civil law compliance levels tend to reflect levels of commitment. Table 5.10 shows that high

Table 5.9 Distribution of Indigenous rights compliance by legal system

Legal system	*Level of compliance*	*Countries demonstrating the level of compliance*	*(%)*
Common law (12 countries)	Non-compliant	3	25.0
	Under-compliant	4	33.3
	Partially compliant	1	8.3
	Compliant	0	0
	Over-compliant	4	33.3
Civil law (39 countries)	Non-compliant	5	11.9
	Under-compliant	24	57.1
	Partially compliant	11	26.2
	Compliant	2	4.8
	Over-compliant	0	0

commitment among civil law countries is strong (88.0 percent), while two-thirds of common law countries exhibit low levels of commitment.

When political system and legal system are analyzed together, an even stronger relationship appears. As Table 5.11 displays, only common law countries are over-compliant (Canada, the USA, Australia, and New Zealand) and most of those countries have parliamentary systems (Canada, Australia, and New Zealand): a full 42.9 percent of parliamentary countries with common law foundations over-comply with their Indigenous rights responsibilities. Again, though, over-compliance goes hand-in-hand with low commitment, as Table 5.12 demonstrates.

Whether parliamentary or presidential, common law countries appear less committed to Indigenous rights than civil law countries do. But what about other

Table 5.10 Indigenous rights commitment by legal system

Legal system	*Level of Indigenous rights commitment*	*Countries with this level of commitment*	*(%)*
Common (12 countries)	High	4	33.3
	Low	8	66.6
Civil (42 countries)	High	37	88.0
	Low	5	11.9

Table 5.11 Indigenous rights compliance by political and legal system combined

Political and legal system	*Level of compliance*	*Countries demonstrating the level of compliance*	*(%)*
Parliamentary common law (7 countries)	Non-compliant	1	14.3
	Under-compliant	2	28.6
	Partially compliant	1	14.3
	Compliant	0	0
	Over-compliant	3	42.9
Parliamentary civil law (9 countries)	Non-compliant	2	22.2
	Under-compliant	2	22.2
	Partially compliant	3	33.3
	Compliant	2	22.2
	Over-compliant	0	0
Presidential common law (5 countries)	Non-compliant	3	60.0
	Under-compliant	1	20.0
	Partially compliant	0	0
	Compliant	0	0
	Over-compliant	1	20.0
Presidential civil law (28 countries)	Non-compliant	2	7.1
	Under-compliant	18	64.3
	Partially compliant	8	28.6
	Compliant	0	0
	Over-compliant	0	0

Table 5.12 Indigenous rights commitment by political and legal system combined

Political and legal system	*Level of commitment in Indigenous rights*	*Number of countries demonstrating this level of commitment*	*(%)*
Parliamentary common (7 countries)	High	3	42.8
	Low	4	57.1
Parliamentary civil (9 countries)	High	7	77.7
	Low	2	22.2
Presidential common (5 countries)	High	1	20.0
	Low	4	80.0
Presidential civil (28 countries)	High	26	92.9
	Low	2	7.1

human rights instruments? To see, I considered twelve governments that had signed or ratified other accords, specifically ICERD, ICCPR, and ICESCR. Table 5.13 clearly demonstrates their support of these instruments; common law reluctance to endorse human rights conventions is overwhelmingly limited to Indigenous issues.

Common law alone does not determine a country's commitment to Indigenous rights. Therefore, while there is a correlation between common law and a country's low commitment – and some relationship between common law and over-compliance – legal system alone insufficiently explains patterns of over-compliance.

The dataset discussed throughout this chapter challenges the four prevailing explanations for over-compliance, and shows that there is no discernible relationship between Indigenous population and Indigenous rights compliance, or between political structure and Indigenous rights. While arguments about political system and legal system have traction – some association between common law parliamentary systems and over-compliance does exist – they are nonetheless limited.

Conclusion

I examined various state responses to the emerging international Indigenous rights discourse, and observed four levels of compliance: compliance, partial

Table 5.13 Twelve common law countries and their high commitments to major human rights instruments

Human rights instrument	*Common law countries making high commitments*	*(%)*
ICERD	11	91.7
ICCPR	11	91.7
ICESCR	10	83.3
ILO 169	1	8.3
UNDRIP	3	25.0

compliance, under-compliance, and what I call over-compliance. I define "over-compliance" as legal, constitutional, or policy behavior that exceeds a state's commitment to international Indigenous rights instruments.

My analysis of the dataset shows that 3.4 percent of states comply with Indigenous rights, meaning that their behavior matches their high commitment; 17.2 percent are non-compliant, meaning that their commitments to Indigenous rights and their behavior are low; 72.4 percent of countries are partially compliant or under-compliant, meaning that their commitments outweigh their compliance; and 6.9 percent are over-compliant, meaning that their behavior exceeds their low levels of commitment.

Compliance is highest in Europe, North America, and the Pacific, although certain countries with moderate to strong levels of legal, constitutional, or policy behavior are reluctant to make a high commitment to Indigenous rights. Such countries are over-compliant. My concept of over-compliance has not been considered by international relations theory, and a brief review of the compliance literature shows that rationalist and liberal theories both fail to explain its existence. However, the cost of compliance, grounded in constructivist theory and coupled with Hathaway's cost-of-commitment theory, offers a partial explanation.

According to this explanation, over-compliance results when a common law settler state identifies as a strong supporter of human rights and must reconcile its colonial legacy with its own post-colonial image within the Indigenous rights discourse. In a shifting international order, this same state is reluctant to commit to the emerging standards because of the high cost of commitment – the result of domestic enforcement mechanisms left over from its colonial foundation.

What are other sources of high commitment costs for these common law countries? In the following two chapters, I seek to further refine my notion of over-compliance with case studies of Indigenous rights in New Zealand and Canada.

Notes

1 The International Work Group for Indigenous Affairs (IWGIA) is a non-governmental organization located in Copenhagen, Denmark which documents and disseminates information about Indigenous rights. It holds consultative status with the United Nations Economic and Security Council (ECOSOC) and observer status with the Arctic Council, which counts Canada, Denmark, Finland, Iceland, Norway, Russia, Sweden, and the USA among its members.

2 The first international treaty dealing with Indigenous issues, International Labor Organization (ILO) Convention No. 107, "Convention Concerning the Protection and Integration of Indigenous and Other Tribal and Semi-tribal Populations in Independent Countries," was passed in 1957. Drafted without Indigenous participation, it was later criticized for its paternalistic tone. States that ratified ILO No. 107 pledged to "protect" Indigenous populations from discrimination and other social ills, and also committed to assisting Indigenous populations toward "progressive integration into the life of their respective countries."

Convention No. 169, "Convention Concerning Indigenous and Tribal Peoples in Independent Countries," passed in 1989, represents a significant advance over the paternalistic tone of No. 107. Rather than presume the eventual disappearance or assimilation of Indigenous peoples, it includes provisions for collective land rights and political self-determination.

As a human rights declaration, UNDRIP is not an international convention or considered binding international law, but it does represent a normative global consensus on the rights of Indigenous peoples.

3 "Partial compliance" – the middle ground between compliance and non-compliance – is a term and a concept introduced by Hawkins and Jacoby (2010). They maintain that states can partially comply in a variety of ways, including (but not limited to) ratification without legislative implementation; ratification with partial implementation; and underfunding agencies that monitor compliance. I follow Hawkins and Jacoby's lead in attempting to break down the dichotomy of compliance and non-compliance, because doing so helps us better understand compliance behavior.

4 Simmons (2000) and Lutz and Sikkink (2000) have previously found region to be a determinant in state compliance behavior.

5 The USA case stands a little apart, because Americans actively pursued a unique national identity earlier and to a larger extent than Australia, Canada, and New Zealand. In addition, the level that the USA is concerned with its human rights identity and international reputation can shift dramatically, depending on political moment and presidential administration.

6 As Lijphart (1999) argues, minorities in parliamentary systems with proportional representation have stronger voices than those in presidential or single-member district plurality systems, such as those found in the USA and throughout Latin America.

7 Simmons (2009) finds that reluctance to commit to human rights treaties is greater among common law countries than among civil law systems.

8 I have excluded the semi-presidential regimes of the Russian Federation, Taiwan, and Niger, as well as the one-party regimes of China, Vietnam, and Laos, from this section of my analysis, which only considers presidential and parliamentary governments.

9 I have excluded the mixed legal systems of the Philippines, Burma, Sri Lanka, and Israel, as well as the Islamic legal systems of Algeria and Kenya, from this analysis, which examines only common and civil law systems.

References

Abbott, K.W., 1992. Elements of a Joint Discipline, International Law and International Relations Theory: Building Bridges. *American Society of International Legal Practice*, 86, pp. 167–168.

Abele, F. and Prince, M.J., 2006. Four Pathways to Aboriginal Self-government in Canada. *The American Review of Canadian Studies*, 36(4), pp. 568–595, 696.

Bearce, D.H. and Bondanella, S., 2007. Intergovernmental Organizations, Socialization, and Member-state Interest Convergence. *International Organization*, 61(4), pp. 703–733.

Borrows, J., 2002. *Recovering Canada: The Resurgence of Indigenous Law*. Toronto: University of Toronto Press.

Cairns, A., 2000. *Citizens Plus: Aboriginal Peoples and the Canadian State*. Vancouver: University of British Columbia Press.

Central Intelligence Agency, 2015. *The 2014 World Factbook*. Available at: www.cia.gov/library/publications/the-world-factbook [last accessed July 20, 2015].

Chayes, A. and Chayes, A., 1993. On Compliance. *International Organization*, 47(2), pp. 175–205.

Coates, K., 2004. *A Global History of Indigenous Peoples: Struggle and Survival*. London: Palgrave Macmillan.

Cole, W.M., 2005. Sovereignty Relinquished? Explaining Commitment to the International Human Rights Covenants, 1966–1999. *American Sociological Review*, 70(3), pp. 472–495.

Downs, G.W., Rocke, D.M., and Barsoom, P.N., 1996. Is the Good News about Compliance Good News about Cooperation? *International Organization*, 50(3), pp. 379–406.

Finnemore, M. and Sikkink, K., 1998. International Norm Dynamics and Political Change. *International Organization*, 52(4), pp. 887–917.

Fletcher, C., 1999. *Does Federalism Safeguard Indigenous Rights?* Mont-Tremblant: International Conference on Federalism.

Franck, T.M., 1995. *Fairness in International Law and Institutions*. New York: Clarendon Press.

Hathaway, O., 2003. The Cost of Commitment. *Stanford Law Review*, 55(5), pp. 1821–1862.

Hawkins, D. and Jacoby, W., 2010. Partial Compliance: A Comparison of the European and Inter-American Courts for Human Rights. *Journal of International Law and International Relations*, 6(1), pp. 35–86.

Henderson, J.Y., 1994. Empowering Treaty Federalism. *Saskatchewan Law Review*, 58, pp. 241–330.

International Labour Organization, 2015a. *Ratifications of C107 – Indigenous and Tribal Populations Convention, 1957 (No. 107)*. Available at: www.ilo.org/dyn/normlex/en/f?p=NORMLEXPUB:11300:0::NO:11300:P11300_INSTRUMENT_ID:312252:NO [last accessed May 26, 2015].

International Labour Organization, 2015b. *Ratifications of C169 – Indigenous and Tribal Peoples Convention, 1989 (No. 169)*. Available at: www.ilo.org/dyn/normlex/en/f?p=1000:11300:0::NO:11300:P11300_INSTRUMENT_ID:312314 [last accessed May 26, 2015].

Ivison, D., Patton, P., and Sanders, W., 2000. *Political Theory and the Rights of Indigenous Peoples*. London: Cambridge University Press.

Keck, M.E. and Sikkink, K., 1998. *Activists beyond Borders: Advocacy Networks in International Politics*. Ithaca, NY: Cornell University Press.

Keohane, R., 1997. International Relations and International Law: Two Optics. *Harvard Journal of International Law*, 38(2), pp. 487–501.

Kingsbury, B., 1998. The Concept of Compliance as a Function of Competing Conceptions of International Law. *Michigan Journal of International Law*, 19(2), pp. 345–372.

Koh, H.H., 1997. Why Do Nations Obey International Law? *The Yale Law Journal*, 106(8), pp. 2599–2659.

Ladner, K.L., 2003. Treaty Federalism: An Indigenous Vision of Canadian Federalisms. In F. Rocher and M. Smith, eds, *New Trends in Canadian Federalism*. Peterborough, ON: Broadview Press.

Lijphart, A., 1999. *Patterns of Democracy: Government Forms and Performance in Thirty-six Countries*. New Haven, CT: Yale University Press.

Lutz, E.L. and Sikkink, K., 2000. International Human Rights Law and Practice in Latin America. *International Organization*, 54(3), pp. 633–659.

Maaka, R. and Fleras, A., 2002. Engaging with Indigeneity: Tino Rangatiratanga in Aotearoa. In D. Ivison, P. Patton, and W. Sanders, eds, *Political Theory and the Rights of Indigenous Peoples*. London: Cambridge University Press.

Mikkelson, C., ed., 2012. *The Indigenous World*. Copenhagen: International Work Group for Indigenous Affairs.

Mikkelson, C., ed., 2013. *The Indigenous World*. Copenhagen: International Work Group for Indigenous Affairs.

Mikkelson, C., ed., 2014. *The Indigenous World.* Copenhagen: International Work Group for Indigenous Affairs.

Mikkelson, C., ed., 2015. *The Indigenous World.* Copenhagen: International Work Group for Indigenous Affairs.

Moravcsik, A., 1997. Taking Preferences Seriously: A Liberal Theory of International Politics. *International Organization*, 51(4), pp. 513–553.

Niezen, R., 2003. *The Origins of Indigenism: Human Rights and the Politics of Identity.* Berkeley: University of California Press.

Papillon, M., 2008. *Federalism from Below? The Emergence of Aboriginal Multilevel Governance in Canada: A Comparison of the James Bay Crees and Kahnawa:ke Mohawks*. Ph.D. thesis, University of Toronto.

Raustiala, K. and Slaughter, A., 2002. International Law, International Relations and Compliance. In W. Carlsnaes, T. Risse, and B.A. Simmons, eds, *Handbook of International Relations*. London: Sage.

Risse, T., Ropp, S.C. and Sikkink, K., 1999. *The Power of Human Rights: International Norms and Domestic Change.* Cambridge: Cambridge University Press.

Risse, T., Ropp, S.C., and Sikkink, K., 2013. *The Persistent Power of Human Rights: From Commitment to Compliance*. Cambridge: Cambridge University Press.

Setear, J.K., 1996. An Iterative Perspective on Treaties: A Synthesis of International Relations Theory and International Law. *Harvard International Law Journal*, 37, pp. 139–230.

Simmons, B.A., 2000. International Law and State Behavior: Commitment and Compliance in International Monetary Affairs. *American Political Science Review*, 94(4), pp. 819–835.

Simmons, B.A., 2009. *Mobilizing for Human Rights: International Law in Domestic Politics*. Cambridge: Cambridge University Press.

Slaughter, A., 1995. International Law in a World of Liberal States. *European Journal of International Law*, 6(4), pp. 503–538.

Snidal, D., 1985. The Game Theory of International Politics. *World Politics*, 38(1), pp. 25–57.

Tully, J., 1995. *Strange Multiplicity: Constitutionalism in an Age of Diversity*. Cambridge: Cambridge University Press.

United Nations, 2015. United Nations Treaty Collection. Available at: http://treaties.un.org [last accessed May 26, 2015].

Wessendorf, K., ed., 2011. *The Indigenous World.* Copenhagen: International Work Group for Indigenous Affairs.

White, G., 2002. Treaty Federalism in Northern Canada: Aboriginal–Government Land Claims Boards. *Publius: The Journal of Federalism*, 32(3), pp. 89–114.

6 Indigenous rights in New Zealand

> You can't be honourable in a fundamentally dishonourable process of dispossession.
>
> Moana Jackson, 2008

New Zealand is a country that takes its international reputation and its human rights obligations extremely seriously. The country played a major role in drafting the original Universal Declaration of Human Rights in 1948. It has also ratified numerous human rights instruments, including the ICERD, the ICCPR, the ICESCR, the Convention on the Elimination of Discrimination against Women (CEDAW), the Convention on the Rights of the Child, and the Convention on the Rights of Persons with Disabilities. Upon ratification, these instruments have a significant impact on domestic law. New Zealand has also passed a number of domestic legislative acts to uphold its international human rights obligations to non-discrimination, including the Race Relations Act 1971, the Human Rights Commission Act 1977, the Bill of Rights Act 1990, and the Human Rights Act 1993 (Office of the High Commissioner for Human Rights 2013; Magallanes 1999). Yet, New Zealand has not ratified the major Indigenous rights convention, ILO No. 169, and it actively campaigned and voted against the Declaration on Indigenous Rights in the UN General Assembly, later issuing a statement that "provisions in the Declaration are fundamentally incompatible with New Zealand's constitutional and legal arrangements, the Treaty of Waitangi, and the principle of governing for the good of all our citizens" (New Zealand Mission to the United Nations/Te Mangai o Aotearoa 2007). Although New Zealand did announce its support for the Declaration in May, 2010, as described in Chapter 4, this was "selective endorsement"; New Zealand exempted itself from a number of the Declaration's provisions on land, self-determination, and free, prior, and informed consent.

New Zealand is also known worldwide, and takes great pride in its reputation, as a beacon of hope for Indigenous citizens. It has added Māori as an official language, including renaming the country Aotearoa/New Zealand, as Aotearoa is the Māori language word for the islands known in English as New Zealand.[1] The government has mandated that all children learn some Māori language in school. It has renamed many place names from English back to their original Māori names. It has enacted extensive and expansive government programs to help reduce disparities and help "Māori achieve their full potential."[2] In fact, the disparities between Māori and non-Māori in New Zealand have been reduced to the lowest level anywhere in the world where Indigenous peoples live in non-Indigenous-dominated societies. In short, New Zealand has demonstrated a remarkable commitment to Māori and has been recognized around the world for its efforts. Yet, at the same time, New Zealand's commitments to international Indigenous rights are extremely low. Furthermore, activists for Māori political self-determination find themselves perpetually at odds with the New Zealand government, even coming under arrest in some extreme cases for their advocacy of Māori rights and sovereignty.[3] New Zealand, therefore, is a paradox in Indigenous rights. It is far ahead of other settler societies in some ways and yet it is one of the global leaders most consistent in resisting Indigenous rights advancement. How can this paradox, this conjunction of overt opposition to the codification of Indigenous peoples' rights and an "over-compliance" of practice in recognizing Indigenous "rights" be explained?

New Zealand's Indigenous rights high behavior/low commitment pattern defies the usual explanations of state compliance. In this chapter, I will explore the New Zealand case in light of the constructivist "cost of commitment" explanation presented in Chapter 5. My argument is that common law countries founded on the Doctrine of Discovery are caught in a particular tension of reconciling their colonial legacy and their post-colonial image within the larger context of the emerging Indigenous rights discourse. On the other hand, Indigenous rights, as articulated in the Declaration, compel a vision of Indigenous–state relationships – what I call Indigenous reconciliation – that is transformational and would reset the relationship to one grounded in a nation-to-nation relationship, with secure Māori land and self-determination rights. That is, a shift from the status quo of norm plane A to transformational norm plane B, as discussed in Chapter 1. However, the New Zealand government remains engaged in a process of reconciliation that I call Doctrine of Discovery reconciliation, the aim of which is to settle past grievances and move forward with Māori as equal citizens of New Zealand, under Crown sovereignty. In other words, New Zealand keeps its commitments to Indigenous rights low, to preserve the status quo, and to avoid moving along the transformational norm vector from norm plane A toward norm plane B.

There are several important factors at play in New Zealand that have led to its paradoxical Indigenous rights behavior under a constructivist cost-of-commitment argument, factors that rationalist, liberal, and common explanations either miss or under-emphasize. First, an extremely vocal Indigenous movement has been active in New Zealand since the 1970s and 1980s, a domestic movement that is well connected to the international Indigenous rights movement and often invokes an international human rights framework for Māori rights. Second, New Zealand demonstrates a high level of concern for its human rights reputation both overseas and in its own self-image. Third, the nation has a British colonial history, and, as I will argue, an implicit reliance on the Doctrine of Discovery as a means of colonization. New Zealand, like other Commonwealth countries, has become preoccupied with a search for identity, as it has increasingly separated from Britain in recent years. It has become a more multi-ethnic society in recent decades and, along with increased interactions with its Asian and Pacific neighbors, its ties with Britain have weakened. In its attempt to carve out a new international identity, New Zealand as a whole has begun taking on Māori identification.

Treaty settlements – that is, reconciliation efforts – in New Zealand began in the 1970s and have exposed a huge gap between two dominant yet different understandings of the single treaty signed between the British and Māori, the 1840 Treaty of Waitangi/Te Tiriti o Waitangi ("the Treaty"), and what the resulting governance structure of Aotearoa/New Zealand should look like in the post-settlement era. One understanding of the Treaty relationship, which is often a Pākehā[4] and New Zealand government position, is that under the Treaty of Waitangi, Māori ceded total sovereignty to the Crown under one unified parliamentary government. This understanding compels "Doctrine of Discovery reconciliation" efforts, where the Crown assumes its superiority and also presumes that, with the signing of the Treaty, Māori surrendered full and complete sovereignty over New Zealand to the Crown, while Māori then became full and equal British subjects. The goal of reconciliation under this vision requires only an adjustment to the lack of equality between Māori and the rest of New Zealand society. Past grievances must be settled appropriately so that the nation can move forward, unified and equal, under "one law."

The contrasting interpretation, Indigenous reconciliation, reflects an understanding of the Treaty relationship as one that preserves the "tino rangatiratanga" of Māori. Tino rangatiratanga is a Māori term that best translates into "full sovereignty," although this is not a purely accurate translation. This interpretation of the Treaty notes that in the Māori text of the Treaty they ceded only "kawanatanga." or governership, in the Treaty, and expressly retained tino rangitiratanga. This vision views the two Treaty parties – Māori and Pākeha – as equal partners, which then necessitates shared governance and, by extension, a reconfiguration of sovereignty in New Zealand. There are two language versions of the Treaty of Waitangi, and, under the Māori-language version, "tino rangatiratanga" was never ceded by Māori, a point validated by a 2014 Waitangi Tribunal report.[5] This interpretation of reconciliation necessitates a rearrangement of the Treaty relationship between Māori and Pākehā toward a plural sovereignty or shared sovereignty arrangement in governance. It is the gap between these two understandings of Indigenous reconciliation and the Treaty relationship that ultimately accounts for Indigenous rights over-compliance in New Zealand.

Conditions for reconciliation in New Zealand

Unlike neighboring Australia and many other places around the world that fell under colonial control, the relationship between Māori and the Crown has never been defined by the *terra nullius*, or the "empty land" doctrine. Whereas in the USA where the Doctrine of Discovery remains valid law and has been cited by the Supreme Court as recently as 2005 (United States Supreme Court 2005), the Doctrine of Discovery has never been an explicit component of New Zealand's domestic jurisprudence as the basis of the nation's foundation. Rather, the British signed a treaty with Māori in 1840, the Treaty of Waitangi, which is considered the founding document of the state of New Zealand. This treaty was not a peace treaty, as there was no state of war between Māori and the British at that time. Rather, this was a treaty intended to peacefully found the new settler territory of New Zealand and establish a relationship of governance between Māori and the Crown.

When the Treaty was signed in 1840, there were two versions: an English-language version and a Māori-language version. These two versions differed in one critical respect, a difference that has remained politically salient up until the present day. The English-language version stated that the Crown was granted *full and complete sovereignty* over all of New Zealand while Māori were to receive full possession of their traditional lands (Wiessner 1999). The Māori-language version, however, read that Māori granted *kawanatanga*, or governorship, but retained *tino rangatiratanga*, which means chieftainship, or is best translated as sovereignty. Māori have a different word, *rangatira*, which would have better reflected the English understanding of internal self-government over traditional lands, but this word was not utilized in the Māori-language version. There is a great deal of historical scholarship that delves into the differences between the English and Māori versions of the Treaty and whether or not the English Crown attempted to trick Māori into signing it.[6] In October, 2014, the Waitangi Tribunal issued a report (Wai 1040) which revealed the following:

- The rangatira (chiefs) who signed te Tiriti o Waitangi in February 1840 did not cede their sovereignty to Britain. That is, they did not cede authority to make and enforce law over their people or their territories.
- The rangatira agreed to share power and authority with Britain. They agreed to the Governor having authority to control British subjects in New Zealand, and thereby keep the peace and protect Māori interests.
- The rangatira consented to the Treaty on the basis that they and the Governor were to be equals, though they were to have different roles and different spheres of influence. The detail of how this relationship would work in practice, especially where the Māori and European populations intermingled, remained to be negotiated over time on a case-by-case basis.
- The rangatira agreed to enter land transactions with the Crown, and the Crown promised to investigate pre-treaty land transactions and to return any land that had not been properly acquired from Māori.
- The rangatira appear to have agreed that the Crown would protect them from foreign threats and represent them in international affairs, where that was necessary.

The report also found that "though Britain went into the Treaty negotiation intending to acquire sovereignty, and therefore the power to make and enforce law over both Māori and Pākehā, it did not explain this to the *rangatira*" (chiefs) and that, in the end, the chiefs had only agreed "to share power and authority with Britain." In a demonstration of the ongoing gap of interpretation, Government Treaty Negotiations Minister Chris Finlayson responded to the report by stating: "There is no question that the Crown has sovereignty in New Zealand. This report doesn't change that fact" (Bennett 2014). Despite the ongoing conflict, what is clear is that what was ceded to the Crown in the Māori language version of the Treaty was something far less than the "full and complete sovereignty" expressed in the English version. Common law, which is the basis for New Zealand law, is very clear, that when there is a dispute over translation it is the Indigenous understanding of a treaty that must be relied upon.[7] More important for analyzing the Indigenous rights behavior of New Zealand, however, is the fact that these two translations of the Treaty do exist, and that they continue to represent two entirely different schools of thought on Treaty interpretation in contemporary New Zealand, continuing to frame the debate over Indigenous rights, governance, and the relationship between Māori and the Crown.

General Hobson, the English General who presented the Treaty of Waitangi to Māori leaders at Waitangi in 1840, immediately proclaimed, "*He iwi tahi tatou*" or "We are all one people now" in the earliest expression of what would become the Doctrine of Discovery understanding of the Treaty. In 1840, the primary reason the British pursued a treaty was to "give legitimacy to the Crown to colonize the country" (Durie 2008). While the British approached Māori with the Treaty rather than explicitly invoking the Doctrine of Discovery to settle the islands of New Zealand, I argue that the Doctrine of Discovery and its presumption of European superiority has been and remains implicit in this understanding of the Treaty and Indigenous rights in general. For the ink was barely dry on the Treaty before the British began taking Māori lands illegally. Only three months after the Treaty was first signed at Waitangi, General Hobson was already frustrated by what he viewed as the slow pace of Māori leaders' acceptance of the Treaty on South Island. Rather than continuing to seek signatures from South Island Māori, he completely cast the Treaty aside, explicitly and exclusively invoking the Doctrine of Discovery to justify the taking of New Zealand's South Island for the British Crown. Using the words "on the grounds of discovery," Hobson proclaimed Crown sovereignty over the whole of South Island on May 21, 1840 (Evison 1990). In 1841, the colonial government again relied on the Doctrine of Discovery when it passed the Land Claims Ordinance stating that lands not actually occupied or used by Māori belonged to the Crown. The Māori land wars of 1845 to 1872 resulted in vast confiscations of Māori land by the Crown. Further Crown land acquisition and settler encroachment of Māori land became commonplace in subsequent decades. As more settlers arrived and their power grew, Māori became increasingly marginalized in their own country. The Treaty of Waitangi was even declared a "simple nullity" in 1877 by Judge Prendergast in his ruling in a major Māori land case (New Zealand Supreme Court 1877).

An active domestic Indigenous movement connected to the global Indigenous rights movement

Beginning in the 1970s, Māori political activism awoke with a vengeance, not only domestically but also internationally, shifting the relationship between Māori and the state of New Zealand from a needs-based to a rights-based relationship (Maaka and Fleras 2002). Māori from New Zealand have been powerful leaders in the international Indigenous rights movement, maintaining an extensive network of international Indigenous contacts, hosting numerous international conferences, and often adopting a leadership role in the United Nations Declaration process. In fact, one of the first transnational Indigenous peoples' meetings, the 1975 WCIP founding meeting in Port Alberni, British Columbia, comprised representatives of Māori and several Western Canadian First Nations (Anaya 2004). Some scholars consider that advances in Māori rights are solely domestic political victories (Magallanes 1999). However, the significant internationalization of the Indigenous rights movement, coupled with New Zealand's strong commitment to international human rights, provides evidence for a more multi-faceted and nuanced explanation. As international linkages have grown, so has Māori assertiveness. Since the international Indigenous movement helped constitute Indigenous identities and the struggle for rights around the world (Niezen 2003), Māori, like other Indigenous groups, began to bring home some of the language and protest techniques acquired at international fora for use in their domestic politics, and vice versa. The New Zealand government seemed to be aware of international scrutiny and was increasingly wary of making any move to reduce Māori rights. This interaction between the international and domestic realms resulted in significant changes to the discourse surrounding the Treaty of Waitangi, particularly the relationship between Māori and the New Zealand state. As the idea of self-determination evolved into a touchstone of Indigenous politics around the world, the phrase "tino rangatiratanga" simultaneously gained wide use in Māori discourse and protest, reflecting an increasing Māori emphasis on governance and self-determination in addition to anti-discrimination initiatives.

Beginning in the 1970s, and coincident with the rise of Indigenous transnational activity, the Tino Rangatiratanga understanding of the Treaty of Waitangi was increasingly asserted in domestic politics, producing not only an important shift in domestic political discourse regarding the foundational centrality of the Treaty in New Zealand, but it also marked an effort to remake the Treaty relationship between Māori and Pākehā into a new vision of sovereignty in New Zealand. The Te Papa National Museum of New Zealand, which opened in 1998 in the capital city of Wellington, was architecturally designed with a permanent exhibition of the Treaty of Waitangi, "Signs of a Nation," at its center, around which all other exhibitions circulate, clearly indicating the centrality the Treaty had come to represent in New Zealand political discourse by that time. During Waitangi Day celebrations and commemorations in February, 2008, Massey University Professor and Treaty expert Mason Durie stated during

Te Papa's Treaty Debate Series that "The Treaty is imbedded in the life of the nation," that "it is part of New Zealand's constitutional conventions," and that "the Treaty of Waitangi has come to equate with ... New Zealand values," and "that there is now a very high level of agreement that the Treaty of Waitangi ... signaled the emergence of New Zealand as a modern state" (Durie 2008). Human Rights Commissioner Joris de Bres also noted that the national school curriculum launched in 2008 "acknowledges the principles of the Treaty of Waitangi and the bicultural foundations of Aotearoa New Zealand" (de Bres 2008). Te Papa's Chief Executive Seddon Bennington alluded to the rise of the Tino Rangatiratanga understanding of the Treaty and the possibility of rearranging New Zealand's sovereignty in his comments as moderator of the debate, stating that the Treaty "provides a platform for the future, a unique platform in this country, not just for Māori but for all New Zealanders" (Bennington 2008). Professor, Treaty expert and Treaty negotiator Matthew Palmer agreed, stating that "there should be some ongoing relationship between the British Crown and Māori, *hapu*[8] and *rangatira*[9] concerning the exercise of public power," and that the Treaty should be inscribed in ordinary law so that it will "provide the basis for a healthy set of ongoing relationships between the Crown, Māori and other New Zealanders" (Palmer 2008a). Mason Durie expressed this sentiment as representing what he called an "Aotearoa tradition" whereby Māori interact with the rest of New Zealand in a partnership, based "on the skills, knowledge, resources, and values that they can bring." In his words, "the yet-to-be realized promise of the Treaty of Waitangi is about the way in which we will prepare for the future, and the unique stamp we will place on New Zealand" (Durie 2008).

Bone fide efforts to reconcile the Treaty with past behavior toward Māori began in 1975, the year the New Zealand Parliament passed the Treaty of Waitangi Act, which, after 135 years, finally "accorded some effect to the Treaty" (Wiessner 1999). The Act created the Waitangi Tribunal, which was charged with investigating violations of the Treaty, reporting findings and making recommendations for governmental action. This is not simply a land claims settlement tribunal. Reports and recommendations range from monetary settlement for old land claims to the return of disputed lands. Fishing claims have also featured heavily in Tribunal reports and recommendations. Although the Tribunal does not have direct enforcement powers, its recommendations impact the actions of all three branches of the New Zealand government. As further evidence of the domestic impact of the international Indigenous movement, the Tribunal often references Indigenous activities and developments in other countries, especially in treaty interpretations. There are also numerous references in Tribunal reports to the importance of upholding Indigenous self-determination under international law.

During the 1980s, various New Zealand courts handed down a series of decisions recognizing and upholding Māori fishing rights as part of their self-determination status, as articulated in the Treaty of Waitangi. Jurisprudence in these decisions relied extensively on similar Indigenous rights decisions in Canada, Australia, and the USA (Magallanes 1999). Thus, international developments in Indigenous rights had an impact on New Zealand jurisprudence as well.

Global human rights steward

In recent decades, New Zealand identity's has increasingly centered around the view of itself as a racially harmonious society based on fairness, tolerance, and respect for universal human rights. As stated in a 2006 Human Rights Commission submission regarding a revised national school curriculum, "In New Zealand, human rights underlie our expectations about life, education, health, work, personal security, equal opportunity and fair treatment, our ability to have a say and our system of government" (New Zealand Human Rights Commission/Te Kahui Tika Tangata 2006). This "global human rights steward" identity for New Zealand manifests itself in numerous ways.

The *New Zealand Handbook on International Human Rights*, published in 2008 by the Ministry of Foreign Affairs, extols the virtuous history of New Zealand as a global advocate and leading champion of international human rights. In the Foreword, former Prime Minster Helen Clark states: "our human rights record is one from which we can take great satisfaction and encouragement" (New Zealand Ministry of Foreign Affairs and Trade 2008). As the *Handbook* explains, New Zealand has always been a world leader in international human rights. In the drafting process for the United Nations Charter in 1944, New Zealand was one of a handful of outspoken states that called for stronger language on international human rights. In a joint New Zealand–Australian statement issued in 1944, New Zealand took exception to the narrow vision of human rights offered by the USA and the UK, taking a more progressive position on human rights, and arguing that human rights should occupy a stronger place in the UN Charter. New Zealand also played an important leadership role in the 1948 deliberations over the Universal Declaration of Human Rights. The *Human Rights Handbook* also highlights the strong position New Zealand takes against discrimination. Several sections highlight New Zealand's visible participation in contemporary human rights issues areas like women's rights, children's rights, and rights of refugees.

Another Ministry of Foreign Affairs document states clearly and unequivocally that "human rights considerations are central to the Government's foreign policy" based on the "*fundamental values and aspirations* that underpin our society" (emphasis in original) (New Zealand Ministry of Foreign Affairs and Trade 2000). The same document also asserts that New Zealand has "a strong commitment to upholding the universality and indivisibility of human rights" and that the government places a "high priority on human rights."

A 2004 report by the New Zealand Human Rights Commission (New Zealand Human Rights Commission/Te Kahui Tika Tangata 2004) found that "New Zealand meets international human rights standards in many respects, and often surpasses them" because "New Zealanders place a high value on harmonious race relations" and also on "fairness" (this is often expressed colloquially in terms of a "fair go"), and have a "well-developed tradition of tolerance and flexibility." This report also noted the pride New Zealanders should feel that New Zealand was instrumental in the development of international human rights law itself.

Interviews with Māori activists and New Zealand government officials during 2008 also attest to the importance of New Zealand's identity as a "good steward of international human rights," particularly where Indigenous peoples are concerned. These interviews also reveal how Māori activists connected with the international Indigenous rights movement attempt to leverage a strategy of shaming the nation in the area of Indigenous rights against the New Zealand government. Dr John Tamahori (2008), Chief Policy Advisor for the Te Puni Kōkiri agency, the Ministry for Māori Development, discussed how Māori who are connected to the international Indigenous movement attempt to gain leverage with the New Zealand government:

> [Māori who are active in international Indigenous rights] are the most vigorous critics of their own government.... So, they have earned their spurs by being critics of the New Zealand government; [they] demonize them overseas in all Indigenous forums.

As reported by Māori activists, the shaming strategy is not just criticism but is a deliberate attempt to expose the hidden racism and colonial mentality existing immediately under the surface of this emerging "good human rights steward" national identity. Exposing these stains on New Zealand's self-image is intended to change Indigenous rights policies domestically. One Māori activist said, "we are very happy to have that support from the United Nations because it validates our position and it supports our rights that we always believed were valid, and it shames the government" (Māori Activist #5 2008).

Many interviewees indicated that the results of these shaming campaigns often fall short of what is hoped. However, the government's various responses to the use of the shaming strategy do indicate that it is extremely sensitive when its human rights image is attacked. Typically, the government becomes defensive, sometimes trying to discredit the very same UN human rights apparatus that it extols so eloquently in other contexts. One activist described the actions of the New Zealand government vis-à-vis Indigenous rights issues:

> We had the UN's Special Rapporteur on Indigenous issues come and visit, issue a report, government dissed it, said he was a low-level bureaucrat in the UN system. We had the UN Committee on the Convention on the Elimination of Racial Discrimination write a report on New Zealand and question the Foreshore and Seabed Act and tell them that they really need more consultation and they dished the CERD. They just dismissed it.
>
> (Māori Activist #1 2008)

Another activist reported that in response to censures by any UN committee relating to Indigenous rights, the New Zealand government tries to:

> brush them off and tries to discredit those (UN) organizations or those committees and so they must be biased, they must have spoken to the wrong people, and they don't take the criticism on the chin really.
>
> (Māori Activist #2 2008)

Yet another Māori activist spoke to the racism and colonial mentality that remains in New Zealand, which is in direct conflict with, and even masked by, its positive human rights reputation and self-image. He said:

> I guess that the issue I have with the New Zealand government in terms of the way that it engages on Indigenous issues is that it tends not to deal with these issues with integrity. And I think that's different than the people across the way in Australia because for years and years the Indigenous people in Australia knew what the attitude of the Australian government was. They'd come right out and say certain things and do certain things, which are, quite frankly, racist. The cultural difference here is that they'll say and do whatever they can just to avoid the issue.... Mainstream culture here in New Zealand is not one that comes right out in front and says certain things, and I think that mainstream New Zealand is quite afraid of being called racist which is fair enough but what it doesn't do is allow you to actually deal with the issues and that's the problem.... On the one hand they are trying to hold up New Zealand as this really racially harmonious society while at the same time being quite underhanded and quite nasty to Indigenous peoples here as well.
>
> (Māori Activist #9 2008)

Māori Party Member of Parliament and long-time activist Hone Harawira (2008)[10] was rather more optimistic on the results of the shaming strategy in Indigenous rights. In his view,

> New Zealand's reputation in that area suffered hugely when they took away the foreshore and seabed because I think that for the first time, Māori appealed to the United Nations, to the CERD.[11] And we had a Rapporteur come over and basically caned the government for what they'd done, for the breach of the Treaty, for their denial of legal rights to us, etc. etc., which tended to lift everybody's vision to another level here.... New Zealand, I think, has started to suffer from Māori determining to take their case to the international stage. You know, they talk about this thing, the clean, green image and, oh, we treat our Māori so well ... yeah, yeah ... there's starting to be these cracks. Yeah, it's starting to crack.

Even though the government's response to UN criticism is often tepid and sometimes highly defensive, Harawira sees that there is actual embarrassment in the government and society when Indigenous issues are exposed at the international level. He said:

> Oh, the government was embarrassed, and it continues to be so, because we use it often in our speeches in the House, the Māori Party, and because the Rapporteur's report covered such a broad range of areas, we're able to use aspects of that report on numerous occasions, I'd say probably twenty times

> in twenty different speeches in the House last year we referred to the CERD report and different aspects of it. And the importance of New Zealand realizing that if they want to go down that track, we are here to remind them of this and that. And the world is now open and, of course, our speeches are on the Internet.

New Zealand's shifting identity: multiculturalism and an absorption of Māori identity

In the decades since the 1970s rebirth of Māori activism and international Indigenous activity, several discourses have developed that have together produced a shift in New Zealand's identity, focused in two areas: multiculturalism and an absorption of Māori identity. These discourses, coupled with the "global human rights steward" discourse, have intersected, converged, and together produced a desire to reconcile New Zealand's colonial past.

A multicultural society in a globalized world

New Zealand has undergone tremendous changes in recent decades that have also impacted the country's Indigenous rights behavior and its interpretation of the Treaty relationship. With an influx of immigration, particularly from Asia and the Pacific, New Zealand has become increasingly multi-ethnic. During the same period of time, the United Kingdom joined the European Union and began looking more toward Europe; as a result, many Commonwealth nations like New Zealand have moved steadily away from their British origins. In this post-colonial globalized world, the questions of what is New Zealand and what are its unique identifying features have become near-obsessions in this small, remote island nation in the South Pacific. Newspaper editorial pages are filled with columns and letters reflecting the national search for identity and place in the world. Politicians from all political parties also wrestle with the question of what defines the nationhood of New Zealand. In a famous 2004 speech entitled "Nationhood," National Party Leader Don Brash advocated that New Zealand's emerging national identity should reflect the nation's multiculturalism and principles of equality.

Prime Minister Helen Clark, Labour Party, also echoed this sentiment during her terms in office (1999–2008). In a speech to Parliament in early 2005, Clark stated that building national identity and pride was one of the primary objectives of her government and that a primary source of this identity and pride lies in "building a nation which offers fairness and opportunity, is tolerant and respectful of all." In her opening remarks for a symposium marking the centennial anniversary of New Zealand's Dominion status, Clark elaborated these priorities:

> Whether we're talking about the past, the present, or the future, the question of what constitutes this place we call home is important for how we see ourselves and how the world sees us. Ideas about what contributes to our country's identity have changed a great deal over the course of the past century, partly as

> we've positioned ourselves in the world in our own style, and partly as we've become more comfortable with ourselves. Of most significance, perhaps is our growing willingness to acknowledge ... our growing diversity as a key component of what defines 21st century New Zealand.... So many different peoples now contribute to New Zealand's identity, and we recognize, and should recognize, and celebrate each one of them.... And I would hope that the defining feature of 21st century New Zealand's identity will be that of inclusion and value of all who live here and make a contribution.

National Prime Minister John Key, elected in 2008, called for a highly controversial referendum in 2016 on changing the national flag, hoping to drop the design featuring Britain's Union Jack in favor of a new design that would be uniquely New Zealand, and is "about our place in the world and how we see ourselves ... confident, outward-looking, multicultural" (Anonymous 2014). During a March, 2014 speech at Victoria University in Wellington, Key said:

> It [is] time for us to take some decisions about how we represent ourselves to the world beyond 2015. For more than a hundred years the New Zealand flag has served us well.... It has given us an identity.... But the current flag represents the thinking by and about a young country moving from the 1800s to the 1900s.... A time when we had less of a role in the Pacific, and a time before Asia registered in our consciousness.
>
> It is my belief, and I think one shared by many New Zealanders, that the design of the New Zealand flag symbolises a colonial and post-colonial era whose time has passed. The flag remains dominated by the Union Jack in a way that we ourselves are no longer dominated by the United Kingdom.... I am proposing that we take one more step in the evolution of modern New Zealand by acknowledging our independence through a new flag.... We should be represented by a flag that is distinctly New Zealand's.

These public remarks from various leaders of the two largest political parties – Labour and National – not only discuss the ongoing search for New Zealand's identity, but also highlight one of the three distinct yet tightly interrelated identity discourses currently at play in New Zealand's social and political life. Clark, Brash, and Key all focused their remarks around the concept of multiculturalism and inclusion as defining features of New Zealand society, separate and independent from Britain.

Absorption of Māori identity

Māori lawyer and activist Moana Jackson (2008) described the identity struggle of New Zealand as "schizophrenic":

> because it always wants to be seen as honourable and good, but as colonizers, there is a fundamental contradiction because you can't be honourable in

> a fundamentally dishonourable process of dispossession. You can't show good faith while usurping the authority of others, an essentially bad faith act. And so I think there's a certain schizophrenia, not just in their human rights identity but in Pākehā identity which is why they struggle so much to identify who they are.

Jackson also sees this identity struggle as the source of the third major identity discourse at play in New Zealand: the adoption of Māori identity as a defining feature of the national New Zealand identity. Jackson notes that the schizophrenia of colonialism leads to the obsessive identity quest which, in turn, leads into the taking on of Māori identity by Pākehā New Zealand, as representing some formative part of Pākehā identity. Jackson says, "they steal from us to validate who they are, without recognizing that they are stealing from us."

This adoption or absorption of Māori cultural identity into the national identity – the indigenization of New Zealand society – is evident throughout New Zealand and particularly salient whenever New Zealanders represent themselves overseas. A vocabulary of about 500 Māori words is used commonly and routinely by all in New Zealand, and without translation. It is simply assumed that everyone understands the meaning and the nuance of the relevant Māori vocabulary. New Zealand sports teams typically do a *haka*[12] before beginning any international competition. Newspapers regularly publish photos of groups of Pākehā high school boys, or New Zealand troops in East Timor, or a graduating police class in Auckland, all doing the *haka*. Tourists flock to buy a piece of greenstone as a souvenir. New Zealanders traveling overseas will also typically wear a piece of greenstone in a Māori design prominently around their neck to demonstrate to the world that they are from New Zealand. A report by the Ministry for Māori Development, Te Puni Kokiri (2007), showed that Māori culture has a good reputation and is quickly growing internationally. The report advocated that New Zealand businesses should use Māori images to brand New Zealand's products and to differentiate them overseas. When New Zealand government officials travel overseas, they bring along a *kappa haka* group (troupe) of Māori not only to perform the *haka*, but also to engage other government officials in Māori rituals of encounter. Any official visitor – whether it be a minister, a head of state, or a diplomat – who comes to New Zealand will also go through a *powhiri*[13] when they come to present their credentials, as well as celebrities, musicians, etc. The *hongi*[14] is always used when New Zealanders greet foreigners in any official capacity. As one Māori activist noted, "It's just part of how things are done here. People do these things without even thinking" (Māori Activist #2 2008).

Pākehā are increasingly taking on a Māori identity because, as one activist noted:

> Māori culture is fashionable. Indigenous culture is fashionable. But, it's more vogue to be Māori overseas than it is to be Māori here. People overseas without all the baggage, they just see what they see and they like it.

> They like the beauty of the art. They like the sound of the language. They like the meaning of the culture.
>
> (Māori Activist #1 2008)

Another Māori activist mentioned:

> An interesting thing about New Zealanders is that the white settler population here even identifies itself with a Māori word, Pākehā.... I guess what it is, is that a lot of them are trying to find a way to connect with this place, Aotearoa/New Zealand.... It's often not until they leave this place that they realize that there are some really unique things about it and so they grasp on to Māori things. And I think that it's a really interesting thing because it's not about Māori identity, it's about white settler identity and they are trying to find a way to describe their connection.
>
> (Māori Activist #9 2008)

The Pākehā search for their identity and their connection to the land of New Zealand through the absorption of Māori identity reached a critical point in 1999 when Michael King published a book in which he argued that Pākehā are now every bit as Indigenous to New Zealand as are Māori, writing that "the people who live in New Zealand by choice as distinct from an accident of birth, and who are committed to this land and its people and steeped in their knowledge of both, are no less 'Indigenous' than Māori." Race Relations Minister Trevor Mallard made a speech in 2004 which echoed King's sentiments. His speech emphasized the need to put the difficulties of the past behind them, so that New Zealand can forge a collective sense of nationhood because Māori and Pākehā are both Indigenous people now. He even stated unabashedly that "I regard myself as an Indigenous New Zealander."

Many Māori not only took offense at these claims of the Indigeneity of Pākehā, but they also recognized the discursive maneuvering being done at the intersection of the three dominant discourses in New Zealand. One Māori activist pondered the possibility that declarations of Pākehā Indigeneity may actually be an attempt to pretend that colonization never happened. Moana Jackson (2008) was more explicit about the colonial undertones and overtones in the absorption of Māori identity by Pākehā:

> I always say, if you want an identity, then acknowledge the beginnings of your place in this country. And then build your identity on an honest acknowledgement of what that is. But it's actually easier to indigenize yourself because what colonization does is it allows Indigenous peoples to keep the safe and the exotic, but it denies the things that exercise real power. So we can sing our songs, and we can dance our dances. We can even speak our language, but we can't exercise the power that those songs and dances and language once expressed. And so I think that they feel very generous in allowing us to do that and in return for their generosity, they should be allowed to take those safe things as well and use them in whatever way they wish.

These three discourses – the search for a national identity, a positive human rights self-image, and a shift toward multiculturalism and Māori identity – have converged and intersected for the better part of four decades in New Zealand society and politics. Together, they have produced a desire to reconcile New Zealand's colonial past but, as Moana Jackson's remarks indicate, these discourses have produced a particular model of reconciliation: the Doctrine of Discovery understanding of both reconciliation and the Treaty of Waitangi. This model of reconciliation looks to settle past grievances but also to maintain unified Crown sovereignty in New Zealand. The contrasting Indigenous view of reconciliation and of the Treaty of Waitangi, the Tino Rangatiratanga understanding, focuses on land and self-determination rights. This understanding requires a reordering and renegotiation of sovereignty in New Zealand, which remains highly controversial. One of the major sources of political conflict in New Zealand is the gap and tension between these two understandings.

Two competing understandings of reconciliation and the Treaty of Waitangi

The Doctrine of Discovery understanding of reconciliation is based on the settlement and disposition of past grievances so that the nation can move forward under one law, as one people. One of the unquestioned assumptions in this understanding of reconciliation and the Treaty relationship is that the Crown legitimately holds and will retain full and exclusive sovereignty in New Zealand. Major political parties – centre-left and centre-right – both hold this assumption. Don Brash, the National Party leader in 2004, stated that New Zealand is "one country with many peoples," "a modern democratic society, embodying the essential notion of one rule for all in a single nation state." He claimed, "There are some Māori who claim that sovereignty never properly passed from Māori into the hands of the Crown. They are living in a fantasy world." Brash concedes that "where there has been a clear breach of the Treaty – where land has been stolen, for example – then it is right that attempts to make amends should be made," but he is clear that the Treaty "did not create a partnership: fundamentally, it was the launching pad for the creation of one sovereign nation." In this same speech, Brash also highlighted the many efforts New Zealand has made to "close the gaps" economically, socially, and educationally between Māori and Pākehā. He even addressed the importance of Māori culture and language in New Zealand and how much New Zealand society values it and takes great strides to protect it: "The Indigenous culture of New Zealand will always have a special place in our emerging culture, and will be cherished for that reason."

The Labour Party's position, as a centre-left party on the New Zealand political spectrum, places a high priority on social policy and workers' rights, but the underlying assumptions about power and the discourses surrounding Māori, reconciliation, and the Treaty are remarkably similar to the National Party. In her 2005 address to Parliament, Prime Minister Helen Clark talked about how the nation "has to keep moving ahead, to become an even more compelling place to live in, work in, bring children up in, invest in, and above all take pride in." Like Brash's focus on "closing the gaps," the Labour Party is also focused on correcting Māori disparities in society. Clark stated Labour's goal that "the decade and this century will see Māori emerge even more strongly as very significant stakeholders, asset holders and contributors to economic development" and, in fact, it is in this terrain that New Zealand has earned its pro-Māori reputation. Regarding reconciliation and the Treaty, however, Labour's position is that in order to achieve Māori potential, it "is important to get historical claims settled" because "both Māori and Pākehā want us to complete treaty settlements so we can move forward together." Like Brash, however, Clark does not allow any space for ongoing partnership in governance or anything but complete Crown sovereignty. She states, "There's no place for the kind of government that sets New Zealanders against each other." Rather, reconciliation with Māori is a process that has a discrete end point and will be successful when all Treaty settlements are finalized.[15] Clark told BBC reporters, "on historical claims, the time has come to seek finality" (Anonymous 2005). Labour's focus is on improving the positions of Māori as individual citizens of New Zealand. As the Minister of Customs Nanaia Mahuta, speaking on behalf of the Minister of Foreign Affairs, stated during Parliament's discussion of the UN Indigenous Rights Declaration, this "Government is committed to ensuring that Māori participate equally and successfully in New Zealand's economy and society" and has made it a priority to improve "outcomes for Māori" (New Zealand Parliament Debates 2007). Once Māori grievances are settled, Māori are expected to take their places next to other New Zealand citizens as "one people" under "one law" – the Crown's law.[16] The National Party, led by Prime Minister John Key, has continued the Treaty settlements effort under its government.

Since coming to power in 2008, the pace of Treaty settlements has remained brisk. Key has remained firmly resistant to any mention of Māori "sovereignty," considering it to be the equivalent of "separatism" (Young 2015). Yet, as will be discussed later, several Treaty settlements finalized in 2014 feature unprecedented levels of Māori self-government, and even co-governance, arrangements for territories and natural resources. This important shift in favor of the Tino Rangatiratanga understanding of the Treaty and Indigenous reconciliation is largely attributed to National's coalition relationship with the Māori party (Anonymous 2015).

The Doctrine of Discovery understanding of reconciliation attempts to effectively retain the colonial order in New Zealand and *presumes* the superiority of Pākehā culture and government. By contrast, the Tino Rangatiratanga understanding of the Treaty – the Indigenous view of reconciliation – centers on notions of respect, equality, cooperation, and co-governance between Treaty partners. As such, it presents a direct frontal challenge to the colonial order and assumptions. Another crucial difference is that the Tino Rangatiratanga/Indigenous understanding does not have an end date after which reconciliation will be complete. Rather, it sees reconciliation as an ongoing process of renegotiation and reordering of sovereignty in New Zealand. This process would replace unified Crown sovereignty with a Treaty partnership model of governance, as stated in the Māori-language version of the Treaty of Waitangi.

One activist described the Tino Rangatiratanga vision as "Māori control over Māori things" (Māori Activist #9 2008). Māori Party Member of Parliament (MP), Te Ururoa Flavell (2008), said Tino Rangatiratanga means that Māori *iwi* are able "to run our own affairs based on the Treaty of Waitangi, and we think we can do it better than the state." Others testified that "a significant transfer of land back to Māori" is required for a genuine reconciliation so that *iwi* can be self-sustaining and self-governing (Māori Activist #1 2008). Virtually all Māori activists interviewed advocated for some form of constitutional change in New Zealand that would entrench the Treaty, a move that would necessarily involve some sort of power sharing. Some, like Māori Party MP Hone Harawira (2008), have called for a two-house Parliament – a Māori house and a non-Māori house – with disputes resolved in an upper house. Bill Hamilton (2008), of the non-partisan Human Rights Commission, described a complex power-sharing proposal called "Paepae Rangatira" which is based on the principles of mutual recognition, respect, and negotiation between the two Treaty partners: the Crown and Māori. Under Paepae Rangatira, a partnership would be created that integrates a better Treaty relationship. Each Treaty partner, the Crown, and the *rangatira*[17] would maintain a set of human rights coupled with responsibilities on various levels of engagement. As Moana Jackson (2008) said in an interview, the only just path to reconciliation in New Zealand is a rejection of colonization, coupled with an honest process of renegotiation of power and governance in the country:

> One of the great myths in this country is that colonization has ended, but no one has yet been able to tell me when it ended. And if colonization is the systematic dispossession and the denial of rights and equality of Indigenous peoples, then it has definitely not ended. Politicians come up with various constitutional milestones in the Westminster tradition, like when the settlers presumed to take self-government from the governor, passage of the statute of Westminster Act and so on. Poets take it from the discovery of a Pākehā identity. Sports people take it from the first international tour by a rugby team to England. But, for me, it has not ended and will not end until the culture of colonization has been dismantled. And that means not just a government process of treaty settlements, but a whole constitutional reorganization which acknowledges that Māori are the first people of this land, not just as some quaint metaphorical description, but are the first people in terms of authority, of law, of jurisdiction.... And so part of ending the culture of colonization here is to have a proper and effective recognition of Māori jurisdiction and Māori law which then leads to a Māori-defined notion of Māori rights.

I now shift discussion to some political issues in recent decades that demonstrate the gap and tension between these two understandings of reconciliation and the

Treaty of Waitangi. The Waitangi Tribunal and the Treaty Settlements process, along with the Foreshore and Seabed legislation, both illustrate how the dominant Doctrine of Discovery understanding manifests itself in Indigenous policy, along with a more recent subtle shift toward the Tino Rangatiratanga understanding.

The Waitangi Tribunal and the Treaty Settlements process

The Waitangi Tribunal is a permanent commission of inquiry charged with making recommendations on Māori claims relating to actions or omissions by the Crown that breach the Treaty of Waitangi. It does not have the authority to adjudicate claims. Only the Crown can make Treaty settlements, and it is free to take the Tribunal's recommendations into account or to completely ignore them.

The Treaty Settlements process works as follows.[18] First, a claim is submitted by a claimant group to the Waitangi Tribunal. If the claim meets the requirements of the Treaty of Waitangi Act, it is registered and assigned a "WAI" number and all interested parties are notified. The claims are then carefully researched and Tribunal hearings are held. Evidence and submissions are presented first by claimants and then by the Crown, and then by anyone else with an interest in the claim. The hearings and researching phase can take an extremely long period of time; the average time is twenty-five years. Yet, several Māori reported that this can be a healing time for an *iwi*. One Māori leader said:

> In order to present to the Tribunal, you have to open up the knowledge to that entire *iwi* because you have to piece together all the little bits of history that maybe five individuals know a lot, but they need all the little bits that tie it all together. So when you are going through an actual hearing process, you'll get Auntie so and so whose whole job in life has been to work at the *marae* in the kitchen, but she has a story or she has a photograph, or she has a book and it has this really valuable piece of information, just a little piece, but it's really important. And so she gets to speak and everyone gets to hear her and it just changes the way that people feel about each other. It's a very inclusive process and everyone can participate.
>
> (Māori Activist #8 2008)

When the research and hearings are complete, the Waitangi Tribunal issues its report on the claims, including its recommendations. If both the claimants and the Crown agree, they can begin formal negotiations and the Crown may or may not decide to accept the Tribunal's recommendations. Once the claimants and the Crown agree on the terms of settlement, a deed of settlement is signed. The settlement can be implemented and legislation passed if necessary to give effect to the settlement. At any stage in this process, the claimants can elect to skip to the end of the process and simply negotiate directly with the Crown, which is the scenario preferred by the New Zealand government as this approach is most expedient.

Final Deeds of Treaty Settlement have three components. First, there is a Crown apology, which includes a full account of historical events and acknowledgment of the Treaty violations. These apologies are long (up to twelve pages), and they are read publicly at a *marae*[19] by an official representative of the Crown. Second, there must be cultural redress, which may include such topics as changing geographical placenames back to Māori or safeguarding rights of access to certain important areas for cultural or spiritual purposes. Finally, there is financial redress, which may be cash settlements and/or return of Crown land to Māori.

As of March, 2015, there were fifty-one completed settlements with enabling legislation, twelve with deeds of settlement awaiting legislation, and another forty-one in process at various stages (New Zealand Office of Treaty Settlements 2015a, 2015b). The total financial redress awarded in all of the completed settlements stood at more than NZ$1.8 billion as of the end of 2014.[20] Early settlements between 1992 and 1998 were some of the largest, with three major settlements each accounting for NZ$170 million (Ngāi Tahu, Waikato, and Commercial Fisheries) while Ngāti Porou ($110 million), Central North Island ($161 million), and Tūhoe ($169 million) were more recent large settlements, reached between 2008 and 2014. In recent years, small settlements are in the $1 to $6 million range, and most claimant groups are in the $10 to $25 million range. Settlements are now typically 3 percent or less than the market value of the land that was lost. Once a settlement is signed, it is agreed by all parties that it is full and final. No treaty claims may ever be made again by that claimant group against the Crown.

The Treaty Settlements process is highly reflective of the Doctrine of Discovery understanding of reconciliation and the Treaty relationship, although there are some early signs of a subtle shift toward the Tino Rangatiratanga or Indigenous understanding. The settlement process aims to settle past grievances, and often generously, providing a land and economic base so that Māori can prosper and the nation move forward together, under Crown sovereignty and authority. The superiority of the Crown and its government is presumed, and its power remains firmly intact. Hone Harawira, Māori Party MP, speaking in 2008, summed up his critique of the settlements process from a strong Tino Rangatiratanga perspective:

> I'm not a fan of the settlements process because the thief has written the rules, the thief set up the Tribunal, the thief determines who's on the Tribunal, the thief determines what the Tribunal can review, the thief determines what the Tribunal can decide, and at the end of it, the thief says, "Well, if we don't like what you've done, we can ignore it." We Māori are so engaged in achieving settlements that we seem to have missed the fact that no settlement to date has been settled for more than 3% of the value of the claim. And most of them are substantially lower. Not only are they substantially lower, but we are being conned into signing the clause that they are full and final, which means that we are effectively saying to our

> grandchildren that, "You don't have any Treaty claim after we are gone because we agreed to that." So when my grandson stands up and says, "You idiot! You settled for 2.5% and you want to roll over on that, no way." And he'll be right. He will be right. And so I try to say to people, look, if you must settle, then settle on the basis of compensation for that particular time, for that particular claim. And don't ever let it affect our Treaty rights, which are ongoing. Our ancestors didn't sign a Treaty so that it could be ended in 2008. Our ancestors signed the Treaty so that it would be a pluralistic management and governance of this nation forever. It's not reconciliation at all, it's just set up to make us Indigenous people feel like we're getting something back.

Two key settlements completed in 2014 demonstrate a subtle but important shift away from rigid adherence to the Doctrine of Discovery interpretation of reconciliation and a move toward some acceptance of the Tino Rangatiratanga interpretation that involves shared governance, or Treaty partnership, between Māori and governmental institutions in New Zealand. The Ngāruahine group, located in central Taranaki, signed a deed of settlement with the Crown on August 1, 2014, with a settlement package which included an agreed historical account and Crown apology, cultural redress, and financial redress in the amount of NZ$67.5 million. However, this settlement also includes protocols to be issued to the Minister for Arts, Culture and Heritage, the Minister for Primary Industries, and the Minister of Conservation on how "to consult with Ngāruahine when carrying out duties and functions" (New Zealand Office of Treaty Settlements 2014a). In addition, the deed proposes a shared governance arrangement in the form of designated *iwi* representation on the two standing committees of the Taranaki Regional Council so that the *iwi* will have the "opportunity to be at the decision-making table, including decisions that affect their rohe,[21] and the council and region to benefit the experience and input of the iwi of Taranaki." The Tūhoe settlement, with enabling legislation that was passed on July 24, 2014, also included Crown acknowledgments, an apology, and a financial redress package in the amount of NZ$170 million (New Zealand Office of Treaty Settlements 2014b). Furthermore, the settlement set out a new arrangement for the management of Te Urewera National Park, which is located in Tūhoe traditional territory. The deed provides that the National Park will be vested in a new separate legal entity that will be co-governed by Tūhoe and Crown nominees. In addition, the deed contains a provision for what is called Mana Motuake, which translates approximately as Māori self-rule. This is essentially a new relationship agreement between Tūhoe and the Crown designed to facilitate co-management of numerous government functions and service delivery for Tūhoe.

Foreshore and seabed issue

One of the most politically explosive issues in Indigenous rights in New Zealand's history came about in 2004, when the New Zealand Parliament passed the

Foreshore and Seabed Act. This Act effectively unilaterally extinguished Māori aboriginal title to the foreshore[22] and seabed coastal areas of New Zealand. When Parliament passed this act, Māori exploded into protest. Protest marches, or *hikoi*, were held throughout New Zealand, including a very large and famous march of 30,000 to 50,000 people on the New Zealand Parliament in Wellington. The Māori Party was birthed at this time, a direct result of Māori feeling betrayed and abandoned by the Labour Party that had pushed this Act through Parliament.

The issue of the foreshore and seabed began on June 19, 2003 with a Court of Appeal decision in the case of *Ngāti Apa v Attorney General*. In this case, the Court of Appeal departed from the previous understanding of the law regarding the foreshore and seabed, which was a presumption of Crown ownership. The Court of Appeal ruled that Māori native land title had never been extinguished and had survived the Crown's assumption of full sovereignty since 1840. This ruling opened up the legal possibility that Māori could seek freehold title on the foreshore and seabed through the Māori Land Court (Charters 2006). The fear expressed in the wider public discourse was that Māori could now pursue title to the entire coastline of New Zealand and potentially cut off access to non-Māori. In response to public concerns about access to the beaches, the Labour government announced that it would enact legislation to ensure public ownership and access to the coastline.

As soon as the Labour government's policy was announced, the case was immediately referred, as an urgent inquiry, to the Waitangi Tribunal. The Tribunal agreed to consider the case, noting that its resolution was important to New Zealand and its identity as a fair, human rights-supporting society:

> We proceed in the expectation that governments in New Zealand want to be good governments, whose actions, although carried by power are mitigated by fairness. Fairness is the value that underlies the norms of conduct with which good governments conform – legal norms, international human rights norms, and in the New Zealand context, Treaty norms.... We think that New Zealanders generally have an instinct for fairness, and that a policy that is intrinsically fair will, when properly explained, ultimately find favour.
>
> (Waitangi Tribunal 2004)

The Tribunal hearing took place over six days in January 2004, and a report was issued in February. The Tribunal report was highly critical of the government's policy, stating that "the policy clearly breaches the Treaty of Waitangi" but, more than that, the policy also "fails in terms of wider norms of domestic and international law that underpin good government in a modern, democratic state" and referred especially to principles of fairness and non-discrimination. The Tribunal recommended that the government "go back to the drawing board, and engage with Māori in proper negotiations about the way forward." The Tribunal Report was clear that there was a need to search for an outcome that "is faithful to the vision of the Treaty: two peoples living together in one nation, sharing authority and resources, with fundamental respect for each other."

This vision of the Treaty expressed by the Tribunal was antithetical to the government's understanding of its absolute and unfettered sovereignty. In response, Parliament passed the Foreshore and Seabed Act on November 18, 2004. This Act granted the Crown "absolute ownership of all foreshore and seabed land that is not held in fee simple, thereby extinguishing existing Māori common law aboriginal title" (Charters 2006).

A group of Māori organizations lobbied the United Nations Committee on the Elimination of Racial Discrimination (UN CERD) to consider the legislation, and it sent Special Rapporteur (UNSR) Rudolfo Stavenhagen to investigate and report on the situation in New Zealand. The Special Rapporteur's report, which was highly critical of the New Zealand government, was issued in March, 2005. The UNSR 2005 Report made several recommendations to the New Zealand government, including a recommendation to repeal or significantly amend the Foreshore and Seabed Act. The Report recognized some of the positive and significant achievements New Zealand can boast where the status of Indigenous people is concerned. However, the Report also stated that these achievements were not adequate to shield New Zealand from criticism, as the foreshore and seabed controversy could attest. The Special Rapporteur also made several additional recommendations, in light of emerging international human rights principles regarding Indigenous peoples, which directly challenged the government's presumption of full sovereignty. First, it called for a constitutional convention to "design a constitutional reform in order to clearly regulate the relationship between the Government and the Māori on the basis of the Treaty of Waitangi and the internationally recognized right of all peoples to self-determination." The Report stated that the Treaty should be constitutionally entrenched so that Māori can exist "as a distinct people, possessing an alternative system of knowledge, philosophy and law." Furthermore, the Special Rapporteur recommended that *iwi* and *hapu* should form the units for Māori self-governance.

In 2008, the National Party was elected with the support of the new Māori Party. National's Minister for Treaty Settlements Chris Finlayson regularly referred to the Act as unfair and discriminatory. As agreed between the National and the Māori Party, a review of the legislation was conducted in 2009, and in June, 2010 Prime Minister John Key announced that the legislation would be repealed and, in March, 2011, its replacement, the Marine and Coastal Areas Act, was passed (Finlayson 2011). This highly controversial legislation provides a path for Māori groups to prove customary marine title and space for co-governance between Māori groups and Crown authorities when such customary title is demonstrated. However, opponents complain that few Māori groups would be able to prove such title, given the long history of land and coastline dispossession of Māori in New Zealand (Anonymous 2010).

Conclusion

I have offered an explanation for New Zealand's Indigenous rights over-compliance which attempts to explain the paradox of New Zealand's excellence in soft Indigenous rights areas while simultaneously resisting the hard rights called for in international standards. Thus, the constructivist cost of commitment explanation succeeds where other explanations fail. Yet, at the same time, the New Zealand case also shows a subtle, yet important, shift in the direction of hard rights acceptance, above and beyond its technical international commitments.

According to the constructivist cost of commitment explanation, there are three discourses that have developed in New Zealand during the past four decades, intersecting and producing a reconciliation effort: (1) a highly vocal domestic Indigenous movement connected to the global Indigenous rights movement; (2) the nation's concern for its human rights reputation; and (3) a shift in the national identity, which is defining itself in terms of a super-tolerant liberal multiculturalism that is also increasingly integrating Māori identity as a central feature of the New Zealand national identity. Thus, New Zealand is propelled toward reconciliation while simultaneously remaining largely constrained within a particular framework of reconciliation and firmly resisting the full body of international Indigenous rights standards.

The first two discourses – a globally connected domestic Indigenous rights movement and a "global human rights steward" identity – work together to compel New Zealand to reconcile past grievances and deal with remnant colonial structures. The Indigenous rights movement, through campaigns of shame and embarrassment, exposes how New Zealand has not and does not live up to its "global human rights steward" identity when it comes to Māori. In order for New Zealand's "global human rights steward" identity to be cleansed of its settler-colonial stains, New Zealand engages, and often excels in, the realm of Indigenous soft rights; that is, rights such as culture, language, religion, and education or even economic opportunities to "close the gap" between Māori and others. Conventional explanatory theories can certainly account for this side of the compliance picture. A domestic movement presses for a policy change, and the New Zealand state makes accommodations. While these rights have often been difficult to attain in New Zealand, since many of these rights involve acceptance of collective rights by a country that has typically followed the British tradition of individual rights, this struggle has not been insurmountable, and, in terms of explanation, not particularly difficult or controversial.

These explanations do fail, however, to account for New Zealand's excellence in some areas of Indigenous rights *and* its simultaneous resistance to other Indigenous rights, and particularly to the codification of those rights in an international declaration. A constructivist cost of commitment explanation addresses this paradox by providing insight into the simultaneous positive and negative Indigenous rights behavior of New Zealand. The third discursive change – a shift in New Zealand's identity toward multiculturalism and absorption of Māori identity – when combined with the first two discourses, produces the paradoxical pattern.

When all three discourses conjoin, the impulse to reconcile the colonial past with the post-colonial present becomes constrained by a shift in New Zealand's identity, and then a particular tension develops between the two divergent understandings of reconciliation. First, the two identity shifts, namely multiculturalism and the "Māori-ization" of the nation, are both strong equalizing forces and both ultimately result in the negation of Indigeneity (defined in terms of being Indigenous to the land), in favor of placing Māori side by side, on an equal basis, with all other ethnic groups in New Zealand. In short, the identity shifts create a discursive environment that constrains the state from accepting "hard rights" of land or self-determination, because a multicultural "Māori-ized" nation would view these rights as "special rights" inappropriately recognized (or "granted") to a particular group of otherwise equal citizens. Second, the globally connected domestic Indigenous rights movement advocates for both hard rights and soft rights under the Tino Rangatiratanga/Indigenous understanding of reconciliation, yet a tension remains as New Zealand pursues reconciliation largely under the Doctrine of Discovery understanding that emphasizes soft rights. While there have been some early moves in this direction with treaty settlements in 2014 and the Marine and Coastal Area Act, the full cost of commitment for New Zealand to pursue Tino Rangatiratanga reconciliation is high, requiring an alteration in the arrangement of governance and sovereignty in New Zealand.

Notes

1 The usual translation of Aotearoa is "land of the long white cloud."
2 The main government agency charged with this mission is called Te Puni Kōkiri, which translates as "Realizing Māori Potential." It provides policy advice to the Minister for Māori Development and the Minister for Whānau Ora, which is an Indigenous health initiative.
3 On October 15, 2007, 300 paramilitary police raided houses and arrested seventeen Māori sovereignty activists under the Terrorism Suppression Act 2002 (TSA). It was the first time that the Act was invoked in a search warrant (Black 2007). Charges were later dropped against eleven of the seventeen activists. Four were eventually sentenced on weapons charges in 2012. One activist died before trial.
4 Pākehā is a Māori word which means those members of New Zealand's population that are not Māori. The word first referred to the settler population that had origins in the British Isles. The use of the term later expanded to refer to all settlers who were of European origin. Some New Zealanders still use the word in this context; however, in its common contemporary usage it generally refers to all members of the population who are not Māori or Polynesian, therefore encompassing all other populations in New Zealand. It is thus more a term of political and/or social categorization rather than strictly racial or ethnic. Māori also often refer to themselves as *tangata whenua*, meaning literally "people of the land" to describe their Indigeneity. Non-Māori are then referred to as *tangata tiriti*, meaning "people of the Treaty," to describe the populations that have come to live in New Zealand under the Treaty.
5 WAI 1040, released October 14, 2014, stated explicitly that the Māori rangatira, or chiefs, who signed the Treaty of Waitangi in 1840 did not cede their sovereignty to the Crown.
6 See, e.g., Belgrave et al. 2005; Brookfield 2006; Kawharu 1989; Orange 1987; Palmer 2008b.
7 The source of this international law principle lies in the 1905 US Supreme Court case *United States v Winans*, which established the principle of the "canons of treaty construction." The US Supreme Court ruled that "by rule of interpretation of agreements and treaties with Indians, ambiguities occurring will be resolved from the standpoint

of the Indians" (see also Pevar 2002). In New Zealand, the Waitangi Tribunal has adopted the canons of treaty construction when interpretation of the Treaty of Waitangi is in doubt. See especially the Montunui Waitora Report, WAI 6 (1983). In Canada, two Supreme Court cases have supported this legal principle: *Nowegijick v The Queen* (1983) and *Simon v The Queen* (1985) which together led to the Canadian Supreme Court's rule of treaty construction: treaties must be interpreted liberally and fairly and, most crucially, in line with how the Indians would have understood them.

8 A *hapu* is a Māori sub-tribe made up of a group of extended families, or *whanua*. An *iwi* is a Māori tribe; several *hapu* make up an *iwi*. Traditionally, Māori governance occurred at the *hapu* level.

9 "Rangatira" is the Māori word for chief or chiefs, as the word is the same whether it is used in the singular or plural. It also means a chieftainship, or leadership position.

10 In 2011, MP Harawira split with the Māori Party and resigned, forcing a by-election in his constituency. He formed a new party, the Mana Party, and won his seat under that party designation in the May, 2011 by-election. He was returned to Parliament in the November, 2011 general election. Harawira was defeated in the 2014 general election and the Mana Party failed to capture any seats in Parliament.

11 The CERD refers to the monitoring body of the Convention on the Elimination of Racial Discrimination. New Zealand is a signatory to this Convention and, as a result, is subject to its review.

12 The *haka* is a traditional Māori ritual of challenge to those who are entering a *marae*. It is characterized by foot stomping, chest beating, and extending tongues. The idea is to look fierce in order to repel those who may do harm, although it may also be seen as preparation for battle if necessary.

13 A Māori ritual of encounter.

14 Another Māori ritual of encounter and friendly greeting. It involves touching the bridge of one's nose to the bridge of the other person's nose, then taking a long, slow breath together.

15 The Labour Party's stated goal was to have all treaty claims settled by 2020.

16 Interviewees #1, #2 #5, #7, #8, and #9 (all Māori activists) expressed this sentiment, each in his or her own words. Interviews with government officials echoed the same sentiment; although the way they expressed it did differ, the meaning remained the same.

17 Māori word, both singular and plural, for chief, or the leadership of an *iwi*, a tribal group.

18 Procedural information and settlement statistics were obtained directly from the Waitangi Tribunal Office.

19 A *marae* is a communal ceremonial and social space.

20 This total was calculated based on data provided on the old Office of Treaty Settlements (OTS) website (New Zealand Office of Treaty Settlements 2015b) and also the new OTS website (New Zealand Government 2015a).

21 Rohe means traditional territories.

22 The foreshore is the area of land that emerges between high and low tide.

References

Anaya, S.J., 2004. *Indigenous Peoples in International Law.* New York: Oxford University Press.

Anonymous, 2005. NZ Labour to Limit Maori Claims. BBC News, August 4.

Anonymous, 2010. Foreshore Replacement Bill "Fraud." *New Zealand Herald*, December 6.

Anonymous, 2014. New Zealand's Identity Clashing with the Sunset. *The Economist*, November 1.

Anonymous, 2015. Editorial: Sovereignty – It's Nothing for Us to Fear. *New Zealand Herald*, February 11.

Belgrave, M., Kawharu, M. and Williams, D., eds, 2005. *Waitangi Revisited: Perspectives on the Treaty of Waitangi.* Oxford: Oxford University Press.

Bennett, A., 2014. Crown Still in Charge: Minister Chris Finlayson on Waitangi Treaty Ruling. *New Zealand Herald*, November 14.

Bennington, S., 2008. *"Finding Common Ground" Te Papa Treaty Debate Series 31 January 2008.* Wellington, NZ: Te Papa National Museum of New Zealand.

Black, E., 2007. New Zealand's Police Accused of Repressing Indigenous Maori. *McGill Daily*, October 25.

Brash, D., 2004. Speech by Don Brash, Leader of the National Party, Orewa Rotary Club, January 27.

Brookfield, F.M., 2006. *Waitangi and Indigenous Rights: Revolution, Law and Legitimation.* Auckland, NZ: Auckland University Press.

Canada Supreme Court, 1983. *Nowegijick v The Queen.* 1 SCR. 29. Ottawa: Canada.

Canada Supreme Court, 1985. *Simon v The Queen.* 2 SCR. 29. Ottawa: Canada.

Charters, C., 2006. An Imbalance of Powers: Maori Land Claims and an Unchecked Parliament. *Cultural Survival*, 30, pp. 32–35.

Clark, P.M.H., 2007. Opening Remarks at "Concepts of Nationhood: Marking 100 Years Since the Proclamation of Dominion Status for New Zealand", Parliament, September 26. Wellington, NZ.

De Bres, J., 2008. *"Finding Common Ground" Te Papa Treaty Debate Series 7 February 2008.* Wellington, NZ: Te Papa National Museum of New Zealand.

Durie, M., 2008. *"Finding Common Ground" Te Papa Treaty Series, 31 January 2008.* Wellington, NZ: Te Papa National Museum of New Zealand.

Evison, H.C., 1990. *The Treaty of Waitangi and the Waitangi Tribunal: Fact or Fiction.* Christchurch, NZ: Ngai Tahu Maori Trust Board.

Finlayson, C., 2011. *Press Release: Marine and Coastal Area (Takutai Moana) Bill Passes.* Wellington, NZ: New Zealand Office of Treaty of Settlements.

Flavell, T.U., 2008. Interview by author, March 6. Wellington, NZ.

Hamilton, B., 2008. Interview by author, February 26. Wellington, NZ.

Harawira, H., 2008. Interview by author, February 20. Wellington, NZ.

Jackson, M., 2008. Interview by author, March 11. Wellington, NZ.

Kawharu, I.H., 1989. *Waitangi: Maori and Pakeha Perspectives on the Treaty of Waitangi.* Auckland, NZ: Auckland University Press.

Key, J., 2014. Speech at Victoria University, March 11.

King, M., 1999. *Being Pakeha: Reflections and Recollections of a White Native.* Auckland, NZ: Penguin Books.

Maaka, R. and Fleras, A., 2002. Engaging with Indigeneity: Tino Rangatiratanga in Aotearoa. In D. Ivison, P. Patton, and W. Sanders, eds, *Political Theory and the Rights of Indigenous Peoples.* Cambridge: Cambridge University Press, pp. 90–109.

Magallanes, C.J.I., 1999. International Human Rights and their Impact on Domestic Law on Indigenous Peoples' Rights in Australia, Canada and New Zealand. In P. Havemann, ed., *Indigenous Peoples' Rights in Australia, Canada and New Zealand.* Oxford: Oxford University Press.

Mallard, T., 2004. Speech by Race Relations Commissioner, "We are all New Zealanders Now" at Victoria University, July 28. Wellington, NZ.

Māori Activist #1, 2008. Interview by author, February 13. Wellington, NZ.

Māori Activist #2, 2008. Interview by author, February 17. Wellington, NZ.

Māori Activist #5, 2008. Interview by author, February 27. Wellington, NZ.

Māori Activist #8, 2008. Interview by author, March 8. Wellington, NZ.

Māori Activist #9, 2008. Interview by author, March 10. Wellington, NZ.

New Zealand Government, 2015. Last update, Office of Treaty Settlements. Available at: www.govt.nz/organisations/office-of-treaty-settlements/ [last accessed July 30, 2015].

New Zealand Human Rights Commission/Te Kahui Tika Tangata, 2004. *Human Rights in New Zealand Today: New Zealand Action Plan for Human Rights.* Auckland, NZ: New Zealand Human Rights Commission.

New Zealand Human Rights Commission/Te Kahui Tika Tangata, 2006. *The New Zealand Draft Curriculum for Consultation 2006: Human Rights Issues.* Wellington, NZ: Human Rights Commission.

New Zealand Ministry of Foreign Affairs and Trade, 2000. *Inquiry in the Role of Human Rights in Foreign Policy: Submission by the Ministry of Foreign Affairs and Trade.* Wellington, NZ: New Zealand Ministry of Foreign Affairs and Trade.

New Zealand Ministry of Foreign Affairs and Trade, 2008. *New Zealand Handbook on International Human Rights.* Wellington, NZ: Ministry of Foreign Affairs and Trade.

New Zealand Mission to the United Nations/Te Mangai o Aotearoa, 2007. *Explanation of Vote by New Zealand Permanent Representative, Declaration on the Rights of Indigenous Peoples 13 September 2007.* New York: United Nations General Assembly.

New Zealand Office of Treaty Settlements, 2014a. Summary, Deed of Settlement between the Crown and Ngaruahine. Wellington, NZ.

New Zealand Office of Treaty Settlements, 2014b. Summary, Deed of Settlement between the Crown and Tuhoe. Wellington, NZ.

New Zealand Office of Treaty Settlements, 2015a. Last update, Progress of Claims. Available at: www.ots.govt.nz [last accessed July 30, 2015].

New Zealand Office of Treaty Settlements, 2015b. Year-to-date Progress Report, July 1, 2014 to March 31, 2015. Wellington, NZ.

New Zealand Parliament Debates, 2007. Transcript, Question Time in New Zealand Parliament, September 12. Document on file with author.

New Zealand Supreme Court, 1877. *Wi Parata v Bishop of Wellington.* 3 NZ Jur (NS) SC 72. Wellington, NZ: New Zealand Supreme Court.

Niezen, R., 2003. *The Origins of Indigenism: Human Rights and the Politics of Identity.* Berkeley: University of California Press.

Office of the High Commissioner for Human Rights, 2013, Status of Ratification of Human Rights Instruments (as of February 13). Available at: www.ohchr.org/Documents/HRBodies/HRChart.xls [last accessed July 15, 2015].

Orange, C., 1987. *The Treaty of Waitangi.* Wellington, NZ: Bridget Williams Books.

Palmer, M., 2008a. *"Finding Common Ground" Treaty Debate Series 31 January 2008.* Wellington, NZ: Te Papa National Museum of New Zealand.

Palmer, M.S.R., 2008b. *The Treaty of Waitangi in New Zealand's Law and Constitution.* Wellington, NZ: Victoria University Press.

Pevar, S.L., 2002. *The Rights of Indians and Tribes*, 3rd edn. Carbondale: Southern Illinois University Press.

Stavenhagen, R., 2006. *Report of the Special Rapporteur on the Situation of Human Rights and Fundamental Freedoms of Indigenous Peoples UN Doc E/CN.4/2006/78/Add.3.* New York: United Nations.

Tamahori, J., 2008. Interview by author with Dr. John Tamahori, Chief Advisor, Policy, Te Puni Kokiri. Wellington, NZ.

Te Puni Kokiri, New Zealand Government, 2007. *Te wa o te ao hurihuri ki te Ohanga Whanaketanga Maori/A Time for Change in Maori Economic Development.* Wellington, NZ.

United States Supreme Court, 1905. *United States v Winans 198 U.S. 371*. Washington, DC: US Supreme Court.

United States Supreme Court, 2005. *City of Sherrill v Oneida Nation of New York 544 U.S. 197.* Washington, DC: US Supreme Court.

Waitangi Tribunal, 1983. *WAI 6: Montunui Waitora Report.* Wellington, NZ: Waitangi Tribunal.

Waitangi Tribunal, 2004. *WAI 1071: Report on the Crown's Foreshore and Seabed Policy.* Wellington, NZ: Waitangi Tribunal.

Waitangi Tribunal, 2014. *WAI 1040: The Report on Stage 1 of the Te Paparahi o Te Raki Inquiry.* Wellington, NZ: Waitangi Tribunal.

Wiessner, S., 1999. Rights and Status of Indigenous Peoples: A Global Comparative and International Analysis. *Harvard Human Rights Journal*, 12, p. 57.

Young, A., 2015. Key: Little's Waitangi Comments Push "Separatism." *New Zealand Herald*, February 9.

7 Indigenous rights in Canada

> [Canadians] must humble themselves and be prepared to move beyond their mythology and the politics of multiculturalism in order to deal with Indigenous peoples in an honourable way.
>
> Indigenous Activist from Canada, 2008

Canada is often viewed very positively internationally for its "Canadian way" of various cultures living side by side harmoniously within Canadian society. At the same time, however, Canada is highly criticized for failing to match its ideals with reality when it comes to respecting the rights of Indigenous peoples. Indigenous peoples in Canada do have constitutional protection of some treaty rights, Canada engages multiple land claims settlement processes, and Canada has issued an apology in Parliament, and launched a six-year Truth and Reconciliation Commission for its century-long policy of placing Native children into residential schools.[1] Yet, at the same time, Canadian police are regularly accused of abusing Aboriginal people (Human Rights Watch 2013), the Canadian government consistently and repeatedly refused demands for a public inquiry on the issue of missing and murdered Indigenous women in spite of multiple domestic and international reports exposing the issue[2] (Inter-American Commission on Human Rights (IACHR) 2014; Royal Canadian Mounted Police (RCMP) 2014), Aboriginal people remain consistently at the bottom of all socio-economic indicators (Statistics Canada 2012a), and First Nations peoples face continual pressures on their traditional lands from the government and from corporations seeking resource extraction and development.[3] Furthermore, as mentioned in earlier chapters, Canada was one of only four countries to vote against the Declaration on the Rights of Indigenous Peoples, although it announced its official change in position in late 2010 while including a broad set of caveats and exclusions. In fact, Canada is reported to have been the most active lobbyist against the Declaration amongst UN member states from June, 2006 to September, 2007 (Continuing Legal Education Society of British Columbia 2008); it claimed that the Declaration was inconsistent with and "unworkable in a Western democracy under a constitutional government" (Edwards 2007).[4] In short, the Indigenous rights situation in Canada may best be described as a paradox, and far from settled for a country that is known around the world as a leader in human rights.

Like New Zealand, Canada takes its international reputation in human rights very seriously. The Government of Canada's 2005 *Action Plan Against Racism* touted the extent of Canada's commitment to international human rights, noting that Canada "is recognized internationally as a leader in human rights" (Multiculturalism National Office 2005). As the report pointed out, Canada is the birthplace of John Peters Humphrey, one of the authors of the 1948 Universal Declaration on Human Rights. In addition to serving as one of the driving forces behind the Universal Declaration on Human Rights, Canada's human rights record includes ratification of all the major international human rights treaties: the International Covenant on Civil and Political Rights (ICCPR); the International Covenant on Economic, Social and Cultural Rights (ICESC); the International Covenant on the Elimination of Racial Discrimination (ICERD); the Convention on the Rights of the Child; the Convention on the Elimination of all Forms of Discrimination Against Women (CEDAW); the Convention against Torture and Other Cruel, Inhuman or Degrading Treatment or Punishment; and the Convention on the Rights of Persons with Disabilities (United Nations 2015). Canada has also signed and ratified numerous other international human rights instruments, making it one of the world leaders in human rights treaty ratification (University of Minnesota Human Rights Library 2008). Canada served as a member of the United Nations Human Rights Council from 2006 to 2009. The Human Rights Council is charged primarily with "promoting universal respect for the protection of all human rights and fundamental freedoms for all" and with making "recommendations with regard to the promotion and protection of human rights" (United Nations General Assembly 2006).

The international community often references Canada's domestic Aboriginal rights record as impressive and progressive, and there is some evidence to support this position. During the British colonial period, when straightforward Doctrine of Discovery logic was typically applied by colonizing European powers, the Royal Proclamation of 1763 was a significant and notable departure from the global norm. Rather than asserting *terra nullius* and full Crown ownership of lands in North America, the Royal Proclamation "acknowledges the Indians as continuing to own the lands which they have used and occupied" (Tennant 1990). The Royal Proclamation thus acknowledged some degree of Indian title very early in Canada's history, although precisely how much and to what extent is still a matter of ongoing jurisprudence.[5] Yet, due to the Royal Proclamation's recognition of Indian title, the British generally did not take land arbitrarily in North America, but rather they negotiated and signed treaties – "the primary means by which diplomatic relations were conducted between Britain and the aboriginal peoples" (Borrows and Rotman 1998).

The treaty-making norm continued after Canada's Confederation in 1867. Canada recognized Indian treaties signed by the British pre-Confederation, and then it negotiated and signed eleven numbered treaties with Aboriginal peoples in the prairies and the west (except most of British Columbia) between 1871 and 1923.[6] Yet, in 1876, Canada unilaterally imposed the highly paternalistic Indian Act, which defined and controlled nearly every aspect of the lives of Indigenous peoples: from defining Indian status, to banning all traditional ceremonies and forms of governance; from forcing children into residential schools, to limiting any off-reserve movement of status Indians without a pass from the Indian agent; and much more.[7] The Indian Act remains valid law in Canada today. While it has been subject to significant modifications over the years, and today in many respects provides greater levels of freedom for status Indians than in years past, such aspects as the reserve system, status definitions, and band council governments under federal control remain firmly in place. While Aboriginal title continued to exist throughout the twentieth century, it was rarely asserted. This was largely because, until it was revised in 1951, the Indian Act prohibited status Indians from hiring attorneys or engaging in legal action.

As revisions began to loosen some of the Indian Act restrictions on status Indians, including the prohibition against legal action, land claims cases against the Canadian government became a possibility. The Supreme Court's landmark *Calder* decision of 1973 "recognized that Aboriginal title over unceded lands could possibly have survived the assertion of sovereignty by the crown and the creation of the overlapping federal and provincial jurisdictions in British Columbia" (Cassidy 2005). Now confronted with uncertainty of Aboriginal title and its implications, the Canadian federal government was compelled to act. The federal government launched a series of land claims settlement negotiations, which culminated in such notable achievements as the modern-day British Columbia treaties and land claims settlements as well as the 1999 establishment of Nunavut, an Inuit territory in the far north. The landmark 2014 *Tsilhqot'in* decision (Canada Supreme Court 2014) advanced Aboriginal title issues in favor of First Nations. While some have hailed it a "game-changer" (Hildebrandt 2014), American Indian law professor Robert A. Williams, Jr. notes that while the decision does recognize Aboriginal title, it simultaneously limits it and provides a means for governmental infringement if its justifications are compelling enough, particularly if those justifications have an economic – that is, resource extraction – base (Pottie 2014).

In 1982, Canada ratified its new Constitution, which included Section 35(1), providing constitutional protection for "any existing Aboriginal right." However, from an Indigenous perspective, the constitutional protection, while valuable, does not go far enough, since it only protects the rights secured up until that point in history. It does not include protections for Indigenous collective land ownership and self-determination; these Aboriginal rights continue to be negotiated or litigated on a case-by-case basis. The land claims process in Canada "has been widely criticized as being unfair, costly, time-consuming, unresponsive and, ultimately, unjust" (Assembly of First Nations). Therefore, many Aboriginal peoples in Canada have worked in the international sphere since the 1970s, in addition to domestic ones, attempting to use international pressure to encourage the Canadian government to recognize further Indigenous rights to land and self-determination. The Canadian and international press report numerous roadblocks and other forms of protest as Aboriginal groups attempt to cast light on Canada's shortcomings in Indigenous rights.[8] In late 2012 and early 2013, the

#IdleNoMore movement sparked numerous protests against Canadian policies and proposed legislation, particularly omnibus bill C-45, which loosened a significant number of environmental protections for forests and waterways. The movement received substantial international attention as allied movements in multiple countries held protests of their own in support.

On the international level, Canada has not ratified the advanced Indigenous rights convention ILO No. 169. Canada also campaigned and voted against the Draft Declaration in the Human Rights Council in late 2006 and was one of the four states to vote against the Declaration on the floor of the UN General Assembly in September 2007. Even as Canada cast its vote against the Declaration, Ambassador John McNee's statement to the General Assembly touted Canada's "commitment to actively advancing indigenous rights at home and internationally;" a poignant illustration of Canada's paradoxical behavior in Indigenous rights. Canada, he said, "take[s] effective action, at home and abroad, to promote and protect the rights of indigenous peoples" (McNee 2007). While leaving the distinct impression that Canada's vote against the Declaration was rooted in its already superior domestic law, the Ambassador's statement concludes by curtly asserting that the Declaration is not legally binding, has no effect in Canada, and does not represent customary law. In the months following the UN General Assembly vote on the Declaration, the Canadian House of Commons passed a resolution to endorse the Declaration (Parliament of Canada 2008), and a group of more than 100 legal scholars issued an open letter asserting that no legal or constitutional barrier existed to prevent Canada from endorsing the Declaration (Amnesty International 2008). Rather, they wrote, the Declaration "is consistent with the Canadian Constitution and Charter and is profoundly important for fulfilling their promise." In 2009, the Human Rights Council in its Universal Periodic Review (United Nations Human Rights Council 2009) recommended that Canada endorse and fully implement the Declaration, and reiterated its recommendation for a Canadian national implementation plan in its 2013 report (United Nations Human Rights Council 2013). Both reports also recommended that Canada ratify ILO No. 169.

Since Canada never ratified ILO No. 169, voted against the Declaration, and issued numerous caveats and self-exemptions when it did eventually support the Declaration, it seems that Canada's tendency is to ensure that its international commitments to Indigenous rights remain at only a very low level. Yet, Canada's record indicates that it has enacted certain domestic policies that have brought it into at least partial compliance with some of the provisions of ILO No. 169 and the Declaration. In addition to a constitutional recognition of treaty rights, a number of land and self-government agreements have been negotiated across Canada, including the establishment of the Inuit territory of Nunavut. Further, in 1995 the Canadian government adopted a policy that recognized the inherent right of First Nations to self-government (Government of Canada 1995). While all of these policies contain problematic elements from Indigenous perspectives, and do not achieve nationhood or sovereignty goals as asserted by many Indigenous activists and leaders, the focus of this chapter is a comparison of Canada's international commitments with its behavior, and to find an explanation for its "over-compliance."

I argue that Canada's paradoxical behavior in Indigenous rights has resulted from a convergence of several factors that have led to the Doctrine of Discovery model of reconciliation. As is the case in New Zealand, there is a vocal Indigenous movement in Canada that has been actively involved in the global Indigenous rights movement and has invoked the international human rights discourse in its domestic struggles. Also like New Zealand, Canada demonstrates a high level of concern for its world reputation in human rights advancement and even relies on this reputation for the construction of its self-image. As a medium power in a globalized world, Canada is on an almost constant quest to find and assert its identity, again in a very similar way to that in which New Zealand struggles with national identity. While there are structural, legal, and societal elements that distinguish Canada from New Zealand in terms of Indigenous rights, the models of reconciliation are remarkably similar in both countries. While Canada has the structural and legal opportunity to create space for Indigenous rights as articulated by the emerging global Indigenous rights consensus, it remains constrained by a particular model of reconciliation, which emphasizes absolution for past actions as well as certainty of both land tenure and Crown sovereignty in the future. In other words, Canada is resisting the challenges to liberalism and Westphalian sovereignty that are presented by the emerging global Indigenous rights consensus and what would be an Indigenous vision of reconciliation. As a result, Canada's behavior in Indigenous rights, while advanced in certain respects, often ends with confusing, inconsistent, and paradoxical policy outcomes.

In this chapter, I explore Canada's Indigenous reconciliation discourse and demonstrate how it is ultimately constrained by the liberal framework within which it operates, namely that Canada's Doctrine of Discovery reconciliation results from the emerging Canadian national identity narrative that forecloses the possibility of an alternative model of reconciliation advanced by Indigenous leaders in Canada. This alternative, an Indigenous model of reconciliation, would renounce the Doctrine of Discovery and adopt the principle of Indigenous self-determination (as distinct from self-governance), both central features of the emerging global Indigenous rights regime. In the end, the Doctrine of Discovery model of reconciliation, while demonstrating over-compliance in certain Indigenous rights areas, is also an effort to resist Indigenous rights in other areas.

Following the reconciliation context, I foreground three cases that illustrate the Canadian Doctrine of Discovery model of reconciliation and over-compliance at work. Each case demonstrates how a Canadian Aboriginal policy initially appears to advance Indigenous rights but, in actuality, represents *resistance* to Indigenous land and self-determination rights. First, I will examine the legal establishment of the territory of Nunavut. Second, I will explore the state apology for the Indian Residential School program, and the Truth and Reconciliation Commission that followed. Third, I will consider the British Columbia Treaty Process, with particular emphasis on the 1998 Nisga'a Treaty and the 2009 Tsawwassen Treaty.

Indigenous reconciliation in Canada

The Canadian version of Indigenous reconciliation differs notably from New Zealand's experience, yet they share certain commonalities. Like Māori from New Zealand, Indigenous groups from Canada have been extremely active in international Indigenous politics for as long as there has been such a movement. One of the very first transnational Indigenous organizations was the World Council on Indigenous Peoples, founded in 1975 by George Manuel (Shuswap). The World Council on Indigenous Peoples, which focused exclusively on the international struggle for Indigenous rights, was one of the first two Indigenous organizations to attain consultative status at the UN as an NGO and took part in the first NGO conference in Geneva in 1977. First Nations, Métis, and Inuit groups from Canada have always been present and play a highly visible role in Indigenous peoples' meetings at the United Nations. They have also brought the human rights framework of Indigenous rights back to Canada and have used it as leverage against the Canadian state.

Also like New Zealand, Canada has, in recent decades, become somewhat obsessed with its search for national identity as a medium power in a globalized world, and it has also experienced a rapid shift in the diversity of its population, a fact that continues to distance Canada from its British past. As in New Zealand, Canada has increasingly become a nation of diverse immigrants. As recently as the 1960s, most immigration to Canada came from Northern and Western Europe, but in recent decades Canada has accepted large numbers of immigrants from many parts of the world, typically accepting upward of 250,000 immigrants per year (Statistics Canada 2012b). According to data from the Canadian government (Statistics Canada 2012c), 47 percent of Canada's citizens have ethnic origins other than British, French or Native-born Canadian. In 2011, over 20 percent of Canada's population, or one in five persons, were foreign born – the highest proportion in the G8 – and international migration accounted for almost two-thirds of Canada's population growth. Between 2006 and 2010, well over 60 percent of Canada's immigration was from Asia with increasing numbers from Africa, the Caribbean, and Central and South America. In the cities of Vancouver and Toronto, more than one-third of the population is a visible minority and one out of every five schoolchildren in each of these cities is a new immigrant to Canada. For more than half of these children, the language spoken in the home is neither English nor French. These massive population changes over the past several decades have necessitated a renewed search for a definitive Canadian identity.

Whether the issue is Quebec or Asian immigration, the Canadian challenge has long been to find unity in its diversity. As Kernerman observes:

> The defining narrative of Canada is of an unwieldy political project, always in search of unity and forever attempting to constitute itself as a political community.... The results are a continued preoccupation with

> determining their common identity *as Canadians* and a fixation on the sources of cohesion that will, at minimum, hold them together as members of a single political community.
>
> (Kernerman 2005, emphasis in original)

Governor General Michaëlle Jean also referred to the Canadian need to find unity in diversity during her 2005 installation speech: "We must eliminate the spectre of all the solitudes and promote solidarity among all citizens who make up the Canada of today" (Jean 2005).

The popular press in Canada often reports the elusive nature of Canadian identity, and defining Canadian identity even became a stated goal of the Harper government.[9] Prime Minister Harper created a new sub-ministerial cabinet position dedicated to the search for Canadian identity, naming Jason Kenney as Secretary of State for Multiculturalism and Canadian Identity in 2007 (Anonymous 2007a). In the summer of 2015, the *Globe and Mail* newspaper ran an essay series calling for a national conversation about Canadian identity and "shared story" because "no one really knows what that is." The series concluded that the primary Canadian narrative, which is the strength it can offer the rest of the world, is "mutual accommodation," although it was noted several times in the series that the main population group which has yet to benefit from mutual accommodation is Aboriginal peoples (MacDonald 2015).

Canadians aim to stake out their unique place in the world in part by separating themselves from their British colonial heritage, but they also spend a great deal of energy trying to separate their identity from the USA (Resnick 2005). A 1999 Maclean's/CBC survey reported that half of Canadian respondents believed that Canada was becoming more like America, and nearly one-third felt that a full political union with the USA was likely at some point in the future. By the end of 2002 however this sentiment had changed, with Canadians expressing a desire to distinguish themselves from their southern neighbor, and those who stated that Canadians were "essentially different" from Americans increased to 57 percent (Canadian Encyclopedia 2008). As one commentator on Canadian national identity observed, "The real story is Canadians' need to be perceived, and to perceive themselves, as more tolerant than Americans" (Barsch 2005).

Tolerance and diversity, most often represented in the language of "multiculturalism," has come to symbolize a key theme of the emerging Canadian national identity. As Chief Justice Beverley McLachlin states on the Supreme Court of Canada website:

> Canadians are privileged to live in a peaceful country. Much of our collective sense of freedom and safety comes from our community's commitment to a few key values: democratic governance, respect for fundamental rights and the rule of law, and accommodation of difference.

Prime Minister Jean Chrétien echoed these sentiments about the centrality of multiculturalism to the national identity in a speech in June, 2000:

> We have established a distinct Canadian way, a distinct Canadian model: Accommodation of cultures. Recognition of diversity. A partnership between citizens and state. A balance that promotes individual freedom and economic prosperity while at the same time sharing risks and benefits.

A federal government statement on diversity and multiculturalism states unequivocally that "Canada's experience with diversity distinguishes it from most other countries" (Canadian Heritage) and that multiculturalism "is viewed as one of Canada's most important attributes, socially and economically."

In 1971, Canada was the first country in the world to adopt multiculturalism as an official government policy, which meant that it would provide programs and services for different cultural associations. The Pierre Trudeau government viewed multiculturalism as a way to diffuse the bilingual "duopoly" problem between English- and French-speaking Canada, arguing that cultural rights were an element of individual freedom (Mackey 1999). Since 1972, the cabinet in Canada has included a Minister for Multiculturalism. In the 1982 Canadian Constitution, multiculturalism gained constitutional recognition in Section 27 of the Charter of Rights and Freedoms, which specified that Canadian courts were to make rulings "in a manner consistent with the presentation and enhancement of the multicultural heritage of Canada." In June 1988, the Canadian Multiculturalism Act passed, which legislatively established the official government policy of multiculturalism (Government of Canada 1988). These initiatives by government reflect a growing sentiment that multiculturalism has become a defining feature of Canadian national identity. In fact, by 2006 a poll of Canadians reported that approximately 40 percent viewed multiculturalism as the core of Canadian identity (Geddes 2006).

Of course, Canada has always been a nation of diversity, with its history of bilingualism and biculturalism between the English- and French-speaking settler populations alongside, and often blending with, extremely diverse Aboriginal peoples, although not always readily or comfortably. As the above discussion has illustrated, the search for the Canadian identity in recent decades has shifted the national narrative away from its historical bilingual/bicultural emphasis toward an emerging Canadian identity that focuses around two important features: Canada's image as a global steward of human rights; and multiculturalism. While the global steward of human rights identity has compelled Canada to reconcile its colonial relationship with Indigenous peoples, the multiculturalism aspect of Canadian identity has impacted the character of that reconciliation.

"Global steward of human rights"

As a "good global steward of human rights" it is important for Canada to be perceived as a global leader in human rights and also in Indigenous rights, since in order to maintain its global reputation as a peacemaker and honest broker in international politics it must also be a world leader in Indigenous rights and demonstrate that it has reconciled with Aboriginal peoples and moved beyond its own colonial past. Anything less is a stain on its self-image. Interviews with Indigenous leaders from Canada during 2007 and 2008 document how Canada's reputation and positive self-image in human rights is consciously utilized by Indigenous activists as a tool to expose Canada's shortcomings in Indigenous rights in order to compel Canada to act in ways that advance Indigenous reconciliation.

One First Nations leader reported that "Canada has a constitutional guarantee of the rights of Indigenous peoples. However, even with this guarantee, the protection of our rights is not easy" (Indigenous Interviewee in Canada #5 2008). Another leader added, "It is essential to show the world that Canada is not a paradise in relation to human rights because Canada does not take seriously the situation of First Nations" (Indigenous Interviewee in Canada #2 2008). Indigenous interviewees in Canada spoke often about how they attempted to embarrass Canada about its vote against the Declaration of Indigenous Rights at the UN General Assembly, using Canada's "good human rights steward" identity against it on an international level. One First Nations leader said:

> We must denounce the Canadian government, which chose to vote against the Declaration. We welcome the passage of the Declaration, but Canada has let us down. The Declaration is not the end of a process but is the beginning. There is a need for urgent action. We must bring shame upon Canada. Canada changed its reputation with respect to international human rights when it voted against the Declaration. Canada cannot be considered a great nation until it supports the Declaration.
>
> (Indigenous Interviewee in Canada #2 2008)

Another Indigenous activist from Quebec stated:

> Canada offers a rich society. It offers new immigrants the chance of a job, health care and reasonable housing. It makes reasonable attempts to integrate new cultures into the Canadian fabric. How then can we explain the desperate situation of us Indigenous peoples in Canada?
>
> (Indigenous Interviewee from Canada #4 2008)

Indigenous groups used the shaming strategy liberally in the Canadian press to call Canada's human rights self-image into question after the government voted against the Declaration. In a press release from the First Nations Leadership Council, Grand Chief Stewart Philip, President of the Union of British Columbia Indian Chiefs, was quoted as saying:

> Canada no longer enjoys a "blue beret" reputation at the United Nations. Canada's disgraceful and disgusting conduct against Indigenous People at both the national and international level is being noted. It is simply shameful that, as a member of the Human Rights Council, Canada pretends to espouse the highest standards and protection of Human Rights.
>
> (First Nations Leadership Council 2007)

A year later, on the first anniversary of the Declaration's passage, the First Nations Leadership Council issued another press release, urging "all political parties [in the upcoming Canadian election] to publicly demonstrate their commitment to the Declaration and to the human rights of Indigenous peoples across Canada" (First Nations Leadership Council 2008a).

The shaming strategy is also evident in UN meetings. Speaking at the Seventh Session of the UN Permanent Forum on Indigenous Issues, Chief Ghislain Picard (2008) of the Assembly of First Nations of Quebec and Labrador called out Canada's human rights reputation:

> I would like to shed new light on Canada which boasts being a model country on the international scene and encourages others to adopt its high standards on human rights, yet it refuses to endorse the Declaration on Indigenous Rights, which shows its minimal norms for Indigenous peoples.

On another day of the Seventh Session of the Permanent Forum on Indigenous Issues, both Wilton Littlechild, speaking on behalf of the Assembly of First Nations, and Beverley Jacobs of the Native Women's Organization of Canada addressed the failure of Canada to endorse the Declaration as a minimum standard of Indigenous rights. Both speakers called upon Canada to immediately implement the Declaration in order to salvage its global human rights reputation. The representative from the Canadian Ministry of Foreign Affairs was quick to respond and publicly defend Canada's human rights and Indigenous rights record. She stated:

> Canada has long demonstrated its commitment to advancing Indigenous peoples' rights both domestically and internationally. Canada did not support the Declaration because it could not support this particular set of political commitments. Canada continues to have concerns about the Declaration, but it is not our intention to stand in the way.... Canadian policies will continue to remain based on existing human rights obligations and commitments.
>
> (Canadian Ministry of Foreign Affairs 2008)

As a state party to the Convention on the Elimination of Racial Discrimination (CERD), Canada is obligated to submit periodic reports of its efforts against racial discrimination and is subject to biannual review. The CERD Committee then evaluates and makes recommendations to a state party. While CERD recommendations are not legally binding, they do, as CERD Committee member Francisco Calí (2007) said, "carry considerable weight and are meant to guide state parties as to their obligations under the Convention. No country wants to be condemned by this committee." As part of its review procedure, the CERD accepts "shadow reports" from groups representing affected minority populations. First Nations groups have made effective use of this option. When Canada was up for review by the CERD in 2007 and again in 2012, a number of groups representing First Nations submitted shadow reports, all of which attempted to demonstrate to the world that Canada was not the "good human rights steward" it purported to be.

The 2007 shadow report submitted by the International Indian Treaty Council and the Confederation of Treaty 6 First Nations firmly accused Canada of "racism and racial discrimination towards the Indigenous Peoples whose traditional homelands are considered to be located within that country." The IITC submission argued that Canada's failings included:

> ongoing institutional racism and discrimination within the criminal justice and court systems, Treaty violations, a range of inequities in social services and living conditions ... and the imposition of development projects impacting Indigenous Peoples' lands, waters, and traditional means of subsistence undertaken without their free, prior and informed consent.

The Lubicon Lake First Nation (2007) also submitted a shadow report to the CERD regarding Canada's periodic review. This submission also charged Canada with international dishonesty regarding the rights of Indigenous peoples:

> Canada has been the subject of several UN decisions regarding the abuse of the human rights and aboriginal rights of the Lubicon Lake Indian Nation under ... international human rights covenants to which Canada is a signatory. Canada has not only ignored these decisions but has misrepresented them to both Canadians and to members of the international community.

These efforts by Indigenous groups achieved the desired effect of calling into question Canada's "good human rights steward" self-image and international reputation. On March 8, 2007, the UN CERD Committee called upon Canada to reverse its position on the Draft Declaration on the Rights of Indigenous Peoples. It also "voiced concerns" about the actions of transnational mining companies registered in Canada and urged Canada to "take measures" to ensure their accountability with regard to the human rights of Indigenous peoples (Confederacy of Treaty Six First Nations and International Indian Treaty Council 2007). This was the first time the CERD had held multinational corporations accountable when it ruled that the state is responsible for the actions of corporations both within and operating outside the boundaries of the state (Carmen 2007). As Ron Lameman (Beaver Creek First Nation), representative of the Confederation of Treaty Six First Nations, stated:

> We learned the process and we helped set new standards.... When we present shadow reports, then we have the ability to stand up to these lawyers. They have all this machinery; we don't have that.... But, our efforts at the United Nations help hold Canada accountable to the international community. We have forced the government of Canada to change its actions.
>
> (Lameman 2007)

In 2013, the United Nations Special Rapporteur on the Rights of Indigenous Peoples, S. James Anaya, conducted an official visit to Canada. His report, issued in July, 2014, recognized the highly developed legal framework and a number of noteworthy policies dealing with Indigenous peoples' rights but also noted the persistent socio-economic gap between Indigenous and non-Indigenous populations in Canada, unresolved treaty and Aboriginal claims, the vulnerability of Aboriginal women and girls, as well as the high levels of distrust among Indigenous peoples toward both the federal and provincial governments. He called on Canada to live up to its international reputation and fully respect the constitutional, treaty, and internationally recognized rights of Indigenous peoples.

Multiculturalism

Multiculturalism, both as a policy and a discourse, has also helped shape reconciliation in two important and problematic ways. First, it exerts an equalizing force, essentially moving to erase Indigeneity in Canada. Second, it encourages Indigenous policies that focus primarily on correcting socio-economic disparities between Aboriginal peoples and non-Aboriginal Canadians.

Multiculturalism, as an equalizing force in government and societal discourse that serves to erase Indigeneity in favor of universal immigrant status, is manifested most commonly in statements such as one that appears in a Mount Allison University publication on Multiculturalism in Canada:

> Canada is often described as a multicultural nation. But what does that mean? Simply stated, it means that Canadians are not of any one cultural background, race or heritage. Instead, Canadians today reflect a vast diversity of cultural heritages and racial groups. This multicultural diversity is a result of centuries of immigration. *All Canadians, including the Native People, can trace their origins to an immigrant past.*
>
> (Canadian Studies, Mount Allison University 2007, emphasis added)

Another poignant example of this discursive move is from *First Nations? Second Thoughts*, written by Thomas Flanagan, political science professor and former advisor to Conservative Prime Minister Stephen Harper. Flanagan (2000) argues that Aboriginal peoples are no different than other "ethnic groups" in Canada, the only difference being the timing of their arrival in North America, ahead of other immigrant groups:

> In that somewhat qualified sense, Canada treats status Indians as a separate racial group. Call them Siberian-Canadians. The attribution of privileges to Siberian-Canadians on the basis of ancestry is anomalous in a liberal democracy because it contradicts a fundamental aspect of the rule of law – treating people for what they do rather than who they are.

He continues by asserting that Aboriginal sovereignty is actually reverse racism:

> Why not consider the coming of the Europeans as a fourth migration, a new set of tribes pushing others in front of them?… At bottom, the assertion of an inherent right of aboriginal self-government is a kind of racism.… But Europeans had no similar right to push their way in.

The essential component of each statement is the assertion that all Canadians, Aboriginal or not, are immigrants. This discursive move implies that Aboriginal people are not really "Indigenous" to Canada, and "Aboriginal Canadians" are simply another instance of multiple cultures arriving from other places. When emphasis is placed on multiculturalism, all "cultures" can become equivalent and then the erasure of Indigeneity comes from the logic of multiculturalism itself. Under this logic, "Aboriginal Canadians" are in no way entitled to treaty rights, land claims, or self-determination rights as peoples indigenous to the land, since these would all be considered "special rights" unfairly granted to one group over others.

Multiculturalism also encourages policies that prioritize focus on the socio-economic disparities between Aboriginal and non-Aboriginal populations. *A Canada for All: Canada's Action Plan Against Racism* (Department of Canadian Heritage 2005) demonstrates this impulse. This 2005 report presents a Six Point Action Plan to "close the gaps in social and economic outcomes" for all: women, visible minorities, and Aboriginal people. The action plan included the following components: (1) combat discrimination; (2) promote diversity; (3) strengthen civil society; (4) strengthen regional and international cooperation; (5) diversity education, and (6) counter hate and bias. While Aboriginal people are mentioned throughout the report, the context is always related to their socio-economic deficiencies and the need to reduce disparities. Land rights and self-determination for Indigenous peoples and communities are notably absent from this fifty-six-page report. The report concludes that, by implementing this plan, Canadians will "achieve a shared vision of an inclusive society – a Canada for all – where everyone is treated with respect and dignity, and … no one is left behind." In other words, multiculturalism will be successful when the socio-economic gaps between all groups – Aboriginal and otherwise – are closed.

As the above discussion has demonstrated, the two defining features of emerging Canadian identity are shaping Indigenous rights and the reconciliation discourse in particular ways, a set of dual impulses that have together created the Canadian model of reconciliation. The "good human rights steward" image encourages Canada to make positive actions in Indigenous rights, in order to reconcile its colonial past and maintain its positive image. Multiculturalism then pushes that action into a particular framework which emphasizes equality and correcting socio-economic disparities as an end goal. These dual impulses create the Canadian model of Indigenous reconciliation which centers on two primary goals: (1) to provide absolution to Canada for its past actions related to Indigenous peoples; and (2) to create certainty for the future by securing land tenure and state sovereignty, keeping all groups equal within the existing power structure.

The Doctrine of Discovery vision of reconciliation looks vastly different from the Indigenous model of reconciliation that has been advanced by the international Indigenous rights movement and often advocated by Aboriginal peoples in Canada. The central feature of the Indigenous model is a call for states to renounce the Doctrine of Discovery in their laws, policies, and thought patterns, and, in its place, to negotiate or renegotiate, in good faith, land and self-determination agreements and partnerships that embody the principle of free, prior, and informed consent. As Chief Oren Lyons (Haudenosaunee) stated at the Seventh Session of the UN's Permanent Forum on Indigenous Peoples (2008), "Canadian law always works against us. There is a barrier there that, for years, we couldn't see. The answer is that the Doctrine of Discovery is foundational to law. Canadian law and jurisprudence help legitimize colonial doctrines." Regarding a renegotiated, treaty-based, nation-to-nation relationship between Aboriginal peoples and Canada, one Indigenous activist commented,

> Canadian society is built on a foundation of theft. In order for a real reconciliation to occur, Canadians must first apologize for their collective actions in the past. Then, they must humble themselves and be prepared to move beyond their mythology and the politics of multiculturalism in order to deal with Indigenous peoples in an honorable way.
>
> (Indigenous Interviewee from Canada #3 2008)

Chief Wabananick (2008), speaking at the UN Permanent Forum on Indigenous Issues, also addressed the Indigenous model of reconciliation:

> We have the right to co-management. First Nations have been fighting about access to resources but First Nations never gave up the right to access territories. Under Canadian law, ancestral occupation gives us underlying title to the land. This means that provinces never had exclusive rights on public land. Their property right depends on Aboriginal title which can only be given up through negotiation.... First Nations can only give up their inherent sovereignty under treaties.... Treaties provide the opportunity to reconcile Indigenous sovereignty and the sovereignty of the Crown.

Although there are many similarities between Canada's and New Zealand's visions of reconciliation, there are several structural and societal elements that distinguish the Canadian model of Indigenous reconciliation from New Zealand's Doctrine of Discovery understanding of the Treaty of Waitangi, as discussed in the previous chapter. First of all, Canada is a federal system while New Zealand has a unified national government. As a result, Canada would seem to be better prepared structurally to accommodate various layers of sovereignty, as demanded by Indigenous advocates for self-determination. Second, although Canada and New Zealand are both engaged in a constant search for national identity, Canada has not absorbed Aboriginal identity into the national identity in the same way that Maori identity has come to represent the New Zealand identity. Even with these significant differences, however, the end product – that is, the model of reconciliation employed – looks remarkably similar in Canada and New Zealand, suggesting that there is another element, common to both countries, that encourages them to resist the Indigenous model of reconciliation.

In the following section, three cases of reconciliation in Canada will be briefly examined: the legal establishment of the territory of Nunavut; the Harper government's apology for residential schools and the resulting Truth and Reconciliation Commission; and the British Columbia treaty process. Each of these three cases illustrates how Canada excels within the framework of the Canadian model of reconciliation, even to the point of accepting the existence of collective rights for Indigenous peoples. However, this framework ultimately forecloses the possibility of the Indigenous model of reconciliation grounded in land rights, self-determination, and free, prior, and informed consent.

The creation of the territory of Nunavut

> A bold attempt to right past wrongs and bring hope to an entire region was launched as this day began and the map of Canada was redrawn to make room for the new territory of Nunavut.
>
> At midnight, with the wind chill here hovering around 45 below zero, and a rare blue moon encircled by a halo of light, Ottawa divided the old Northwest Territories in two and Nunavut, which means, "our land" was created from the eastern 60% of the region.
>
> ... "What we affirm today, with the stroke of a pen, is the end of a very long road," said Prime Minister Chretien.
>
> (DePalma 1999)

In April, 1999, the territory of Nunavut was created. It was the first time the map of Canada has been redrawn in fifty years, and was widely heralded in the Canadian and international press as a significant Canadian achievement in Indigenous rights. As the article quoted above implies, Canada "gave" the Inuit "a land of their own." A division of the Northwest Territories was first discussed in 1976 during land claims negotiations between the Inuit Tapiriit Kanatami and the Canadian government. A referendum on the possible division of the Northwest Territories was held in 1982, which passed with a majority of Northwest Territories residents voting in favor of the division. The final land claims agreement was reached in September, 1982 and ratified by nearly 85 percent of the voters in Nunavut. On July 9, 1993, the Canadian Parliament passed both the Nunavut Land Claims Agreement Act and the Nunavut Act. The territory of Nunavut was officially created on April 1, 1999. Paul Okalik, the first premier of the newly launched territory, proudly proclaimed, "We have regained control of our destiny and will now determine our own path" (Okalik 1999).

Certain features of the cultural and political landscape of Nunavut demonstrate Canada's tolerance for an advanced level of soft Indigenous rights, particularly in language, cultural arts, and even in relation to internal governance.

For example, the territory of Nunavut has two official languages, in addition to English and French: Inuktitut and Inuinnaqtun. Inuit in Nunavut have "their inherent right to use the Inuit language in full equality with other Official Languages.... This exceeds any other legal protection in place for any other Aboriginal group in Canada" (Government of Nunavut 2008). In addition, Canada now, as a whole, widely utilizes the *Inukshuk*[10] as a cultural symbol, even dedicating it as the symbol for the 2010 Winter Olympics in Vancouver. Nunavut's internal governance structure reflects Canada's accommodation of Inuit culture. There are no parties in the Nunavut Legislative Assembly and the legislature operates on a consensus basis, in accordance with Inuit culture (Anonymous 2008). There is also an advisory council of elders whose task it is to help incorporate Inuit culture into the Nunavut government.

While, on the surface, it appears that Nunavut demonstrates an advanced level of Canadian Indigenous rights compliance in language, culture, and even self-government, a more in-depth examination shows that the Nunavut land claims settlement and the creation of the public Government of Nunavut are more reflective of the Doctrine of Discovery model of reconciliation than of the Indigenous model of reconciliation. Rather than accommodating the hard rights of Indigenous land and self-determination, Nunavut actually demonstrates a pattern of Canadian *resistance* to these rights. First of all, the land claims settlement, like other Aboriginal land claims settlements in Canada, moved land from Aboriginal title to fee simple title. In other words, Inuit lands, which were formerly held in collective Aboriginal title, were placed into individual ownership with the completion of a land claims settlement. Far from recognizing the Indigenous form of collective land rights, Canada demands that land claims be settled in a way which results in land ownership by individuals or Aboriginal corporate entities. Since Canada serves both as defendant and arbiter in the land claims settlement process, it is in the position to make such demands, regardless of what type of land title is desired by Indigenous peoples. Aboriginal title is tied conceptually to Indigeneity, implying attachment to and responsibility for certain lands. Fee simple title lands can be bought and sold to anyone. Therefore, the Nunavut land claims settlement erased, rather than recognized, land-based Indigeneity.

Second, through the Nunavut land claims process, Canada also sought certainty of land tenure for the future. With all Aboriginal title eradicated, and all lands in Nunavut converted to fee simple title, Canada could move forward with development and resource extraction plans, unimpeded by possible title obstructions by the Supreme Court.

Third, the public government in Nunavut has remained strictly under Canadian federal control, particularly since the territory is almost completely dependent upon Ottawa to fund its governmental operations. In the end, Canada has tightly maintained Crown sovereignty over Nunavut. "By negotiating both the real estate deals simultaneously but separately, Ottawa was able to avoid creating an ethnic state," said former Northwest Territories premier Dennis Patterson. "And by setting up Nunavut as a territory, constitutionally on par with the other two territories (the Yukon and remaining Northwest Territories), the creation of a fourth level of government was avoided" (DePalma 1999). Even though the Nunavut territory is expensive for Ottawa, Inuit leader John Amagoalik said that "it has been money well spent because the building up of Nunavut and its communities has been an effective way for Canadians to assert Arctic sovereignty, a pressing issue for the Harper government" (O'Neill 2009).

Apology followed by Truth and Reconciliation Commission

On June 11, 2008, Prime Minister Stephen Harper stood up before the Canadian House of Commons and delivered an apology to the former students of Indian residential schools in Canada. The residential school system, which had operated in Canada from the 1880s until the 1970s, had been a key part of the government's cultural assimilation policy for Aboriginal peoples during that period. More than 160,000 Native children passed through the residential school system during its years of operation, many of them the victims of physical, emotional, and sexual abuse. All of them were victims of a harsh educational program that removed Native children from their homes and communities and forbade them from speaking their languages or practicing their cultures so that they would assimilate as quickly as possible into Canadian society, as a servile second class of laborers.

Harper's apology relied heavily on both Canada's "good human rights steward" and multiculturalism identity discourses: "These objectives were based on the assumption that aboriginal cultures and spiritual beliefs were inferior or unequal.... Today we recognize that this policy of assimilation was wrong, has caused great harm and has no place in our country" (Harper 2008). Noting that "the absence of an apology has been an impediment to healing and reconciliation," Harper offered the apology on behalf of the government and society "to Aboriginal peoples for Canada's role in the Indian residential schools system." Again, near of the end of the text, Harper declared, "There is no place in this country for the attitudes that inspired the Indian residential school system."

Directly invoking the reconciliation impulse, Harper next stated that in order to move in the direction of "healing, reconciliation and resolution of the sad legacy of Indian residential schools," the Indian Residential Schools Settlement Agreement from 2007 had offered compensation to the victims of abuse, along with the establishment of a Truth and Reconciliation Commission, whose five-year work plan would revolve around a series of public hearings. This settlement agreement, he said, is "a positive step in forging a new relationship between aboriginal peoples and other Canadians." He then characterized this new relationship in multicultural terms, as one in which "Aboriginal and non-Aboriginal Canadians" will "move forward together with a renewed understanding that ... vibrant cultures and traditions will contribute to a stronger Canada for all of us."

A number of alternative voices in Canada offered critical reactions to the apology, noting in particular that it did not live up to the renegotiated power relationship envisioned in the Indigenous model of reconciliation. Under this vision, the apology was flawed because it was limited to the residential schools issue and did not make any mention of land loss, continued institutionalized racism, or, most importantly, a renegotiated land and power arrangement. As Kahentinetha Horn (2008) wrote in *Mohawk Nation News*:

> There has finally been an official apology.... This is a start. Now we have to deal with other big issues, sovereignty and resources.... Don't be fooled! The evil program is still in full swing. Canada has no intention to stop. They continue to drive us off our land, to criminalize us, incarcerate us and refuse to return control of our land and resources to us.... Saying sorry doesn't cut it.... Real reconciliation means restoring the traditional homelands and resources of the various indigenous people who have been dispossessed. Anything less is a farce.

The text of this apology reflects the Doctrine of Discovery model of reconciliation, combining the discourses of multiculturalism and the "good steward of human rights." Driven by the desire to maintain this image, Canada was compelled to act in some way to remove the stain from its conscience, as residential school survivors had begun airing the issue publicly during the 1990s. Beginning in the 1990s and continuing until 2005, a series of class action lawsuits were filed against the federal government and the Catholic and Anglican churches that had operated the schools. In 2005, the Assembly of First Nations filed a massive class action lawsuit against the federal government, citing the scope of abuse that had been perpetrated against Aboriginal children. Seeking to stop the lawsuits and, of course, salvage Canada's human rights image, the Canadian government approved a settlement package for residential school survivors. Survivors had until August, 2007 to accept a government settlement or pursue an individual case. The government offered a common experience settlement to all survivors with a supplemental settlement if there had been abuse. The common settlement was $10,000 for the first year of residence and $3000 for each additional year of residence after the first year.[11] Again, like the Nunavut settlement, this was a Canadian effort to individualize a collective Aboriginal issue.

The text of the residential school apology is also an effort to seek reconciliation, framed in terms of Canada's multicultural identity, mentioning that "the vibrant cultures" of Canadian society would now be able to "move forward together." The implication here is that now that this apology has been offered, Aboriginal peoples can rightfully take their place alongside other cultures in Canada. This is another discursive effort by Canada to erase the land-based uniqueness of the Indigenous experience in Canada.

The release, in June, 2015, of the Summary of the Final Report of the Truth and Reconciliation Commission of Canada, continues to demonstrate the ongoing tension between the two competing visions of reconciliation in Canada. After six years of operation, the TRC issued its summary report. During these six years, the TRC held national events in Winnipeg, Inuvik, Halifax, Saskatoon, Montreal, Vancouver, and Edmonton, as well as regional and community events, and collected statements from over 6700 survivors and their families. Survivors' groups brought several court actions to compel the federal government of Canada to turn over all of its relevant documents to the TRC. The report summary proclaimed explicitly, "it is time to abandon the colonial policies of the past, to address the legacy of the school and to engage in a process of reconciliation with the Aboriginal people of Canada." The report included ninety-four specific calls to action and made clear that any effective and meaningful process of reconciliation would necessarily be comprehensive, and "must move beyond residential schools to encompass all aspects of Aboriginal and non-Aboriginal relations and connections to the land."

In short, the report made plain that the old colonial ways of doing business would not result in reconciliation between Aboriginal and non-Aboriginal peoples in Canada; reconciliation requires a complete shift in social, legal, and political relations. Call to Action 43 in the summary report stated clearly: "We call upon federal, provincial, territorial and municipal governments to fully adopt and implement the United Nations *Declaration on the Rights of Indigenous Peoples* as the framework for reconciliation" (emphasis in original). Further Calls to Action (44–49) stated that colonial legal concepts like the Doctrine of Discovery and *terra nullius* be repudiated, and Canadian constitutional and legal orders be reconciled with these repudiated doctrines and principles in a new, jointly developed "Royal Proclamation of Reconciliation." "Treaty relationships based on principles of mutual recognition, mutual respect, and shared responsibility" must also be renewed or established. The Prime Minister's reaction to the TRC's recommendations demonstrates Canadian recalcitrance to accept the more comprehensive Indigenous view of reconciliation; in spite of the TRC's recommendations, the Prime Minister continued to favor the Doctrine of Discovery view, which highlights the Canadian self-image as an existing leader in Indigenous rights and protects the legal and political status quo of power relations in Canada. In the first parliamentary question period following the release of the TRC's recommendations, Prime Minister Stephen Harper refused to commit to any of the ninety-four recommendations, and stated, "Canada is one of the very few countries in the world where aboriginal and treaty rights are recognized, and that's one of the reasons why the government accepts the UN declaration as an aspirational document" (Walters 2015). He also referenced his 2008 apology as evidence of his commitment to reconciliation, albeit a reconciliation without structural change in political, social, or legal relationships. The TRC's recommendations became a major issue in the October, 2015 federal election. The New Democratic Party pledged, very early on, to fully implement all ninety-four TRC recommendations, including repudiation of the Doctrine of Discovery and full implementation of the Declaration. In the last few weeks of the campaign, the Liberal Party, headed by Justin Trudeau, likewise promised to "enact" the TRC's recommendations (Liberal Party). While it is not known what Trudeau and the victorious Liberal Party mean by the phrase "enact the TRC's recommendations," it is clear that those ninety-four recommendations became an important campaign issue.

The British Columbia treaty process

As discussed in an earlier section, the Royal Proclamation of 1763 had established the principle of Aboriginal title in Canada, which differed from fee simple title.[12] Even though the Royal Proclamation claimed to extend British sovereignty over all of North America, it also maintained that British sovereignty was not incompatible with Indian land ownership under Aboriginal title. Aboriginal title remained intact unless it was specifically transferred to the Crown. These principles were largely followed in eastern Canada, but were mostly ignored in British Columbia (Tennant 1990).

Vancouver Island and British Columbia Governor James Douglas made a total of fourteen land agreements with Indigenous nations on Vancouver Island during his tenure (1851–1864) (Morales 2006). These agreements, later referred to as the Douglas Treaties, were similar to treaties in other parts of Canada, which left Aboriginal title intact. Governor Douglas mysteriously stopped making treaties in 1854 in favor of a Doctrine of Discovery approach which denied Aboriginal title and assumed Crown sovereignty and ownership of land (Tennant 1990). This approach generated the "Aboriginal land problem" in British Columbia that would last for the next century and a half.

While First Nations had engaged in low-level protests and resistance since the 1850s, the official land claims process in British Columbia emerged during the early 1970s era of heightened domestic and global Indigenous activism following the 1969 White Paper as well as the Supreme Court's *Calder* ruling in 1973.[13] Although the Nisga'a nation in the Nass Valley of northwestern British Columbia lost the actual case in *Calder*, the Court's opinion did acknowledge the concept of Aboriginal title; that is, the idea that Aboriginal title existed pre-contact, rather than deriving solely from statutory law. The Supreme Court opinion threw into question most of the land tenure in British Columbia. As such, the Trudeau government asked the Nisga'a and other First Nations groups to negotiate directly with the federal government rather than litigating. The federal government began direct negotiations with the Nisga'a in 1976 and the provincial government later joined the negotiations in 1990.

The independent British Columbia Treaty Commission (BCTC) was established in 1993 in order to manage and monitor the British Columbia treaty negotiation process. Completely funded by the federal and BC governments, its full range of functions include: beginning negotiations; allocating funding to Aboriginal groups; reporting on the progress of negotiations, and assisting in resolving differences. The treaty process is composed of six stages, beginning with the "Statement of Intent to Negotiate" and including the "Negotiation Of An Agreement in Principle," Treaty Finalization, and Treaty Implementation (British Columbia Treaty Commission b).

The establishment of the BCTC marked the beginning of the modern-day treaty making in British Columbia, reflected in the province's official "New Relationship" policy. According to a joint statement issued by the Province of British Columbia and the First Nations Leadership Council, the "New Relationship" policy reflects a commitment "to a new government-to-government relationship based on respect, recognition and accommodation of aboriginal title and rights and to reconciliation of Aboriginal and Crown titles and jurisdictions" (Union of BC Indian Chiefs 2009). According to Mike deJong, Aboriginal Relations Minister for British Columbia, "Treaties which include self-governing provisions that include a treaty settlement land base are a further expression of the new relationship" (Anonymous 2007b). As of mid-2015, the BCTC reported that sixty-five First Nations were participating in or had already completed negotiations, representing 104 of British Columbia's 203 Indian Act bands (British Columbia Treaty Commission a).

The absence of treaties in British Columbia created a great deal of uncertainty for government and industry regarding the use and management of lands; as a result, a central feature of the BC treaty process has been the quest for "certainty" in land title (Blackburn 2005). The "certainty" quest places the BC treaty process largely within the Doctrine of Discovery model of reconciliation, a model that seeks absolution for past actions and assurance for the future of state sovereignty and power relations. However, elements of the Indigenous model of reconciliation may also be detected: the Final Agreements of both the Nisga'a Nation, in the Nass Valley of northwestern British Columbia, and the Tsawwassen First Nation in the southwestern corner of Metro Vancouver contain evident nods toward accommodation of new and multiple types of sovereignties.

The first modern BC treaty was the 1998 Nisga'a Final Agreement, which provided CAN$196 million in government transfers over a five-year period. The Final Agreement recognized Nisga'a ownerships and legal entitlements, including: ownership of certain mineral resources; entitlement to a share of salmon and other fish and seafood; and legal jurisdiction over Nisga'a children. The Agreement also repatriated artifacts, and protected certain Nisga'a sites. With the Final Agreement, Nisga'a was removed from the Indian Act and became a self-governing entity within Canada. The Indian Act Band Council government was replaced with the Nisga'a Lisims government and Nisga'a were declared "citizens" of the Nisga'a Nation rather than status Indians under the Canadian Indian Act. The Nisga'a Lisims government operates under the Canadian Constitution and the Charter of Rights of Freedoms. The Nisga'a Lisims government has the right to pass many laws independent of federal oversight, particularly concerning local control over local artifacts. But its power to govern does have certain limitations, negotiated and agreed upon during the treaty process. Residential lots on reserve lands can be converted to private ownership, although strictly under the Nisga'a Nation's registry of land title, not through provincial registration. The Nisga'a Lisims government also now has the authority to set up and collect taxes in its territory, as well as to determine how the revenue will be spent; it will eventually surrender all Indian Act tax exemptions. Salmon fishing in Nisga'a Nation territory is managed by the Nisga'a Lisims government, while all non-salmon fishing is co-managed with the province. The Nass Wildlife Committee, a tripartite body of Nisga'a, federal, and provincial authorities, created by the Nisga'a Final Agreement, manages wildlife in the entire Nass Valley. In addition, the Nisga'a Nation now owns and manages 2000 km^2 of forested land, as well as maintaining the rights to all the associated natural resources, although the Final Agreement specifically states that Nisga'a Nation must "meet or exceed" provincial standards of forest management.

Canadian Indian Affairs Minister Jane Stewart, who signed the agreement on behalf of Canada, referred to it as a "treaty of recognition and reconciliation" (Lockyer 1998). In a newspaper statement, Nisga'a President Joseph Gosnell, Sr. praised the Nisga'a Final Agreement as a document that makes "history as we correct the mistakes of the past [and] … talk about reconciliation and a new understanding between cultures" (Lockyer 1998). The Nisga'a President's equation of reconciliation with correcting (some) past mistakes reflects the first part of the Canadian model: absolution for past actions. This also shows how the two models of reconciliation, which I call Canadian and Indigenous, are not necessarily mutually exclusive and do not imply that one must be Indigenous or Canadian to ascribe to the different visions of reconciliation. In fact, the tension between the two visions of reconciliation remains evident. Here, the leader of an Indigenous nation clearly supports the Canadian vision of reconciliation, at least in part. Gosnell continued, in the same newspaper statement, to assert the importance of the certainty of land tenure and state sovereignty as well. He stated, "Today we join Canada and BC as free citizens, full and equal participants in the social, economic and political life of this country." Yet, at the same time, the negotiated Nisga'a Final Agreement essentially created a new level of governance within the Canadian state: an Indigenous nation government with self-rule under Canadian federal authority but apart from provincial authority, with levels of self-government and co-management previously unseen in the Canadian settler state.

As with the Nisga'a Final Agreement, the Tsawwassen Final Agreement, effective from April 3, 2009, removed the Tsawwassen First Nation (TFN) from the federal Indian Act and provided for self-government, defined as the ability to make its own laws, without federal approval or oversight. Under the agreement, TFN has the right to pass and enforce its own laws "relating to governance, natural resources, land management, and social programming, including health care, education, secondary education, social assistance, child and family services, and others" (Tsawwassen First Nation). As with the Nisga'a Agreement, the Tsawwassen Final Agreement included the conversion of reserve lands to individual, private ownership. However, the TFN's land ownership rights are much more extensive than those of Nisga'a Nation. The Tsawwassen Final Agreement included the transfer of 207 hectares of land from the Agricultural Land Reserve to TFN ownership and control, including subsurface rights, and made clear that TFN members had certain hunting and fishing rights over an additional 1000 km^2 of traditional Tsawwassen territory. In addition, individual TFN members have the right to develop or lease their individually held lands, although under the Tsawwassen Land Act they are not allowed to sell to anyone other than another TFN member or entity. In a famous speech before the BC Legislature on October 15, 2007 as it was preparing to debate the Tsawwassen Final Agreement, then Chief Kim Baird focused attention on reconciliation and the forging of new forms of relationships. She said:

> In my view, one of the important things this treaty achieves is a new relationship between Tsawwassen, British Columbia and Canada. It achieves reconciliation. I mean true reconciliation. To me, true reconciliation signifies real action and tangible change.

Noting how difficult and complex fourteen years of such negotiations can be, Baird looks to a future of new and improved relationships, commenting that the final agreement was "born of hard work and hard-fought compromises," including mutual accommodation that may "often be painful and rocky" and not fully satisfactory to all parties. Yet, overall, Baird sees the treaty as a success, that the TFN, British Columbia, and Canada are "decolonizing through accommodation of our differences – not assimilation" which she sums up as "the ultimate benefit of true reconciliation" (Anonymous 2007c).

As many critical voices have observed, the certainty aspect in BC treaty negotiations is often heavily slanted in the direction of the government. Robert Morales, Chair of the Chief Negotiators of the First Nations Summit, pointed out that the BC treaty process through the BCTC represents not a "New Relationship" between the government and First Nations, but merely an "extinguishment policy" with regard to First Nations peoples. By insisting on a framework of Crown sovereignty, the Canadian vision of reconciliation thus also has the practical effect of closing down the possibility of a true nation-to-nation relationship that the Indigenous model of reconciliation would compel. In short, it re-inscribes the Doctrine of Discovery in existing state sovereignty, by implying that the Canadian state has the sole right to hold full and complete sovereignty while Indigenous nations' place is to "join Canadian society." The BC treaty process does this in several ways. First of all, return of any larger Aboriginal title lands to First Nations is not open for negotiation. There is also no possibility of co-management of these lands or resources, or any sharing of revenue generated from those larger lands. Since the treaty process is meant to be "forward looking," there is not to be any compensation for the earlier illegal taking of Aboriginal lands. In addition, if a First Nation finds itself frustrated by the negotiations and wishes to resort to litigation, the treaty negotiation process will immediately and permanently cease. Finally, since the objective of the process is to achieve "certainty," all agreements are to be full and final settlement regarding Aboriginal title and rights claims (Morales 2006).

Several other characteristics of the BC treaty process, specifically the privatization of land ownership, and the model of governance, that the treaty process compels, reflect the ongoing tensions between the Doctrine of Discovery and Indigenous models of reconciliation. But these characteristics also move further, pre-empting any possible future renegotiation of sovereignty and power relations. Under both the Nisga'a and Tsawwassen Final Agreements, for example, *all* Nisga'a and TFN lands convert to individualized and privatized fee simple title. Thus, in order to be removed from the Indian Act, First Nations need to accept full privatization and individualization of their lands.

Second, the model of governance for both Nisga'a and the TFN also changed character. The Nisga'a Tribal Council was replaced by the Nisga'a Lisims government and a new Tsawwassen Constitution was ratified in 2007. Both new governments have the power to make certain laws related to internal self-governance (for instance, membership/citizenship, language, culture, marriages, and social services) but are subject to provincial and federal authority within the larger constitutional order. Notably, the Nisga'a Final Agreement stated that "the Nisga'a Government will be quite recognizable as a local government compatible with other local governments in Canada." As one Indigenous commentator observed, "This is a form of self-government that imitates municipal government. It's being portrayed as Nisga'a government but it's not. If it was, it would have involved the hereditary chiefs. It didn't" (Barnsley 1998). In the Final Agreement, elected Nisga'a President Joseph Gosnell acknowledged, "We are negotiating our way into Canada, not out of it." Nevertheless, many of the self-governance and co-management features of both the Nisga'a and the Tsawwassen Final Agreements indicate that a new level of governance for BC First Nations may be emerging out of the process, one that accords them duties and authorities similar to municipalities in some respects, but also grants them rights and powers (such as rights to natural resources, hunting and fishing rights, rights to provide education and social programming) normally reserved to provincial and/or federal authority.

Conclusion

Canada is a country that wishes to create and maintain an image of itself as a harmonious multicultural society and "good human rights steward." As the above discussion has illustrated, the "good human rights steward" image propels Canada toward reconciliation, although that reconciliation remains largely constrained by a particular framework: the Canadian model of reconciliation. Under this model, Canada seeks to be fully absolved of its "past" egregious behavior against Indigenous peoples, and it also seeks certainty for the future, especially in land tenure and Crown sovereignty. At the same time, elements of the Indigenous model of reconciliation are also evident, promoting self-determination of Indigenous nations and new, negotiated relationships with various levels of government. The ongoing tensions between these two models are palpable.

Canada's emerging multicultural identity also helps shape the character of reconciliation as many efforts in Canada are focused on "closing the gaps" between Aboriginal peoples and non-Aboriginal Canadians, framed strictly in socio-economic terms. Multiculturalism has created space for Aboriginal rights as collective rights, and has thus allowed Canada to become a world leader in such "soft rights" areas as language and culture while simultaneously foreclosing or limiting the "hard rights" of land, self-determination, and free, prior, and informed consent. Reconciliation efforts in Canada, from the creation of the Territory of Nunavut, to the Apology for Residential Schools, to the British Columbia treaty process, are all substantial achievements when considered from an international perspective Nevertheless, these efforts operate predominantly within the framework of the Doctrine of Discovery model of reconciliation, albeit with hints of the Indigenous model in play. In short, Canadian over-compliance is a symptom of underlying state *resistance* to the emerging global consensus in Indigenous rights. Canada is willing to move forward in certain "soft rights" areas in order to resist developments in "hard rights" areas that would threaten the liberal framework and the sovereignty status quo.

Notes

1 The Canadian Constitution recognizes three groups of Indigenous peoples as "Aboriginal": First Nations, Inuit, and Métis.

2 The Liberal Trudeau government, elected in October, 2015, announced such an inquiry in December, 2015.

3 See, e.g., Leslie 2008; First Nations Leadership Council 2008a.

4 Footnote 156 states:

> For the first eight months, Canada denied lobbying States on the *Declaration*. States, who asked that they remain anonymous, confided that this simply was not true. They indicated to representatives of Indigenous and human rights organizations that Canada was devoting more financial and human resources to oppose the *Declaration* than any other State.

5 The term "Indian title" has since given way to "Aboriginal title."

6 These treaties are literally called Treaty 1, Treaty 2, etc. It is noteworthy that no treaty was negotiated and signed in British Columbia during this period, and the vast majority of territory in British Columbia remains non-treaty; that is, unceded.

7 Indian Act, S.C. 1876, c.18. This Act defines who is an Indian, recognizes reserves and how they are to be managed, specifies the benefits payable to Indians as well as articulating exemptions from taxation. The Indian Act identifies those Indians with "status" as distinct from those without "status." According to the Indian Act, only status Indians are eligible for benefits or exemption from taxation. This Act remains widely criticized as paternalistic.

8 See, e.g., Johal 2006; Anonymous 2007a.

9 Examples of media coverage include: Zolf 2002; Anonymous 2002, 2004. CBC also compiled a series of instructional materials for Canadian educators focused specifically on the search for Canadian identity. A non-governmental website has also emerged which is dedicated to defining the Canadian identity (www.canadianidentity.com).

10 An Inukshuk is a piece of Inuit art composed of a series of stacked stones which resembles a human figure. The name itself means "likeness of a person." Inukshuks are widely available wherever tourist souvenirs are sold in Canada, even in places far away from Inuit territory. It has come to be a cultural symbol of Canada.

11 Information on the class action lawsuits and the government settlement was provided by Cohen Highley Lawyers, London, Ontario, and the Assembly of First Nations.

12 This concept has been previously referred to as Indian title.

13 The 1969 White Paper was a policy paper released by Prime Minister Pierre Trudeau and Minister of Indian Affairs Jean Chrétien which proposed to end the special legal relationship between the Canadian state and Aboriginal peoples. Among its proposals were the dissolution of the Indian Act and the Department of Indian Affairs, conversion of reserve lands to private property, and the gradual termination of treaties. Release of the White Paper sparked outrage among Aboriginal peoples and encouraged a strong wave of Aboriginal political organization.

References

Amnesty International, 2008. Last update, Open Letter, May 1. "UN Declaration on the Rights of Indigenous Peoples: Canada Needs to Implement This New Human Rights Instrument" [Homepage of Amnesty International]. Available at: www.amnesty.ca/index_resources/open_letters/un_ip_declaration_experts_letter.pdf [last accessed October 18, 2014].

Anonymous, 2002. Queen "Treasures" Her Role in Canadian Identity. *CBC News*, October 8.

Anonymous, 2004. A Changing Identity. *CBC Radio One*, May 18.

Anonymous, 2007a. The 39th Parliament: Stephen Harper's First Shuffle. *CBC News*, January 4.

Anonymous, 2007b. Armed Native Protesters Block Ontario Highway. *Toronto Sun*, June 29.

Anonymous, 2007c. Historic B.C. Treaty Opens the Often Caustic B.C. Legislature with a Party. *United Native News*, October 15.

Anonymous, 2008. On the Nunavut Campaign Trail. *CBC News*, March 5.

Assembly of First Nations. Available at: www.afn.ca/index.php/en/policy-areas/land-rights-and-claims/key-issues-activities/specific-claims [last accessed July 25, 2015].

Barnsley, P., 1998. Final Agreement Debated Across the Country. *Windspeaker*, August 10.

Barsch, R.L., 2005. Aboriginal Peoples and Canada's Conscience. In D.R. Newhouse and C.J. Voyageur, eds, *Hidden in Plain Sight: Contributions of Aboriginal Peoples to Canadian Identity and Culture, Volume 1.* Toronto, ON: University of Toronto Press, pp. 270–291.

Blackburn, C., 2005. Searching for Guarantees in the Midst of Uncertainty: Negotiating Aboriginal Rights and Title in British Columbia. *American Anthropologist*, 107(4), pp. 586–596.

Borrows, J.J. and Rotman, L.I., 1998. *Aboriginal Legal Issues: Cases, Materials and Commentary.* Toronto, ON: Butterworth.

British Columbia Treaty Commission a. Negotiation Update. Available at: http://bctreaty.net/files/updates.php [last accessed July 15, 2015].

British Columbia Treaty Commission b. Six Stages: Policies and Procedures. Available at: http://bctreaty.net/files/sixstages.php [last accessed August 1, 2015].

Calí, F., 2007. Presentation by Francisco Calí (Maya), Member of the CERD Committee. Human Rights Training Session held by the International Indian Treaty Council. Mille Lacs Indian Museum, Mille Lacs Reservation, Minnesota, September 27.

Canada Supreme Court, 1973. *Calder v Attorney-General of B.C. [1973] S.C.R. 313.* Ottawa, ON: Canada Supreme Court.

Canada Supreme Court, 2014. *Tsilhqot'in Nation v British Columbia [2014] SCC 44.* Ottawa, ON: Canada Supreme Court.

Canadian Encyclopedia. Becoming More American. Available at: www.thecanadianencyclopedia.com [last accessed January 10, 2008].

Canadian Heritage. Multiculturalism. Canadian Diversity: Respecting Our Differences [Homepage of Government of Canada]. Available at: www.cic.gc.ca/english/multiculturalism/index.asp [last accessed June 13, 2010].

Canadian Ministry Of Foreign Affairs, 2008. Statement by Canadian Ministry of Foreign Affairs. Seventh Session of the UN Permanent Forum on Indigenous Issues, New York, April 28.

Canadian Studies, Mount Allison University. About Canada: Multiculturalism in Canada. Available at: www.mta.ca/canadianstudies/ [last accessed October 10, 2007].

Carmen, A., 2007. Statement by Andrea Carmen, Executive Director of the International Indian Treaty Council. Human Rights Training Session held by the International Indian Treaty Council. Mille Lacs Indian Museum, Mille Lacs Reservation, Minnesota, September 27.

Cassidy, M., 2005. Treaties and Aboriginal–Government Relations, 1945–2000. In D.R. Newhouse, C.J. Voyageur, and D. Beavon, eds, *Hidden in Plain Sight: Contributions of Aboriginal Peoples to Canadian Identity and Culture*. Toronto, ON: University of Toronto Press, pp. 38–60.

Chrétien, J., 2000. *"The Canadian Way in the 21st Century." Speech of Prime Minister Jean Chrétien to Conference on "Progressive Governance for the 21st Century", 2 June 2000*. Ottawa, ON: Government of Canada.

Confederacy of Treaty Six First Nations and International Indian Treaty Council, 2007. Press Release: The UN Committee on the Elimination of Racial Discrimination Calls Upon Canada to Immediately Endorse the United Nations Declaration on the Rights of Indigenous Peoples, March 8.

Continuing Legal Education Society of British Columbia, 2008. *Aboriginal Law Conference 2008, Paper 2.1: United Nations Declaration on the Rights of Indigenous Peoples*. Vancouver, BC: Continuing Legal Education Society of British Columbia.

DePalma, A., 1999. Canada's Eskimos Get a Land of Their Own. *New York Times*, April 2.

Department of Canadian Heritage, 2005. *A Canada for All: Canada's Action Plan Against Racism*. Gatineau, QC: Government Of Canada.

Department of Indian and Northern Affairs, 1999. *Fact Sheet: Nisga'a Treaty*. Ottawa, ON: Government of Canada.

Edwards, S., 2007. Tories Defend "No" in Native Rights Vote. *Montreal Gazette* A16, September 14.

First Nations Leadership Council, 2007. Press Release: First Nations Leadership Council Troubled by Today's Vote at the United Nations; Inaction on Declaration on the Rights of Indigenous Peoples Inexcusable, September 13.

First Nations Leadership Council, 2008a. Press Release: First Nations Pressure Canada to Endorse the United Nations Declaration on the Rights of Indigenous Peoples on the Eve of the Anniversary of its Adoption, September 12.

First Nations Leadership Council, 2008b. Press Release: First Nations Mining Summit Set for October in Prince George, July 8. Available at: www.fns.bc.ca/pdf/NR_BC_FN_MiningSummit0708.pdf [last accessed July 15, 2015].

Flanagan, T., 2000. *First Nations? Second Thoughts*. Montréal, QC: McGill-Queen's University Press.

Geddes, J., 2006. Canadian Nationalism in Decline, Says Poll. *Maclean's*, January 23.

Government of Canada, 1988. *Canadian Multiculturalism Act, R.S.C., 1985, c. 24 (4th Supp.)*. Ottawa, ON: Government of Canada.

Government of Canada, 1995. *Aboriginal Self-government: The Government of Canada's Approach to Implementation of the Inherent Right and the Negotiation of Self-government*. Ottawa, ON: Minister of Public Work and Government Services.

Government of Canada, 2015. *Indian Act, R.S.C., c. I-5*. Ottawa, ON: Canada.

Government of Nunavut, 2008. Statement to the Seventh Session of the UN Permanent Forum on Indigenous Issues, New York, April 29.

Harper, S., 2008. *Statement of Apology to Former Students of Indian Residential Schools, 11 June 2008*. Ottawa, ON: Aboriginal Affairs and Northern Development Canada.

Hildebrandt, A., 2014. Last update. Supreme Court's Tsilqot'in First Nation Ruling a Game-changer for all, June 27 [Homepage of CBC News]. Available at: www.cbc.ca/news/aboriginal/supreme-court-s-tsilhqot-in-first-nation-ruling-a-game-changer-for-all-1.2689140 [July 30, 2015].

Horn, K., 2008. Canada Confesses to Part of its Crimes Against Humanity. *Mohawk Nation News*, June 14.

Human Rights Watch, 2013. *Those Who Take Us Away: Abusive Policing and Failures in Protection of Indigenous Women and Girls in Northern British Columbia.* Toronto: Human Rights Watch.

Indigenous Interviewee in Canada #1, 2008. Interview by author, May 10.

Indigenous Interviewee in Canada #2, 2008. Interview by author, May 18.

Indigenous Interviewee in Canada #3, 2008. Interview by author, May 24.

Indigenous Interviewee in Canada #4, 2008. Interview by author, May 19.

Indigenous Interviewee in Canada #5, 2008. Interview by author, May 31.

Inter-American Commission on Human Rights (IACHR), 2014. *Missing and Murdered Indigenous Women in British Columbia, Canada.* Washington, DC: Organization of American States.

International Indian Treaty Council (IITC), 2007. Submission to the United Nations Committee on the Elimination of Racial Discrimination (CERD), dated February 14. Regarding the Report of the Government of Canada to the Committee on the Elimination of Racial Discrimination, concerning Canada's Seventeenth and Eighteenth Periodic Reports to the CERD (CERD/C/CAN/18) to be considered at its Seventh session, February 19 to March 9.

Jean, M., 2005. *Installation Speech – The Right Honourable Michaëlle Jean Governor General of Canada on the Occasion of Her Installation, 27 September 2005.* Ottawa, ON: Government of Canada.

Johal, A., 2006. Native Tribes Fight to Block New Pipeline. *IPS News*, September 22.

Kernerman, G., 2005. *Multicultural Nationalism: Civilizing Difference, Constituting Community.* Vancouver, BC: University of British Columbia Press.

Lameman, R., 2007. Presentation at IITC's Human Rights CERD Training Session, September 27.

Leslie, K., 2008. First Nations Vow to Occupy Eastern Ontario Site to Block Uranium Mining. *The Canadian Press*, January 11.

Liberal Party of Canada. Truth and Reconciliation. Available at: www.liberal.ca/real-change/truth-and-reconciliation-2/ [last accessed October 20, 2015].

Lockyer, D., 1998. Nisga'a Celebrate Final Agreement. *Windspeaker*, August 4.

Lubicon Lake Indian Nation, 2007. Submission to the Seventieth Session of the UN Committee on the Elimination of Racial Discrimination with Regard to the Lack of Canadian Compliance with UN Human Rights Decisions and General Recommendation No. 23 of the Committee on the Elimination of Racial Discrimination, February 19 to March 9.

Lyons, O., 2008. Statement by Chief Oren Lyons, Haudenosaunee, Seventh Session of the UN Permanent Forum on Indigenous Issues. New York, April 29.

MacDonald, W., 2015. The Magic of the Canadian Ideal. *Globe and Mail*, June 10.

Mackey, E., 1999. *The House of Difference: Cultural Politics and National Identity in Canada.* London: Routledge.

McNee, J., 2007. *Statement by Ambassador McNee to the General Assembly on the Declaration on the Rights of Indigenous Peoples, 13 September 2007.* New York: United Nations.

Morales, R., 2006. New Treaty, Same Old Problems. *Cultural Survival*, 30(1). Available at www.culturalsurvival.org/publications/cultural-survival-quarterly/canada/new-treaty-same-old-problems [last accessed August 1, 2015].

Multiculturalism National Office, 2005. *Canada's Action Plan Against Racism: A Canada for All.* Gatineau, QC: Government of Canada. Department of Canadian Heritage.

Okalik, P., 1999. For Canada's Inuits, this Land is 'Our Land' (Nunavut). *Christian Science Monitor*, April 5.

O'Neill, K., 2009. Nunavut's Birthday Sparks Debate about its Future. *Globe and Mail*, March 31.

Parliament Of Canada, 2008. *Motion presented to the House of Commons on 7 April 2008 – "That the government endorse the United Nations Declaration on the Rights of Indigenous Peoples as adopted by the United Nations General Assembly on 13 September 2007 and that Parliament and Government of Canada fully implement the standards contained therein" (Third Report of the Standing Committee on Status of Women).* Ottawa, ON: Parliament of Canada.

Picard, G., 2008. Statement by Chief Ghislain Picard, Assembly of First Nations of Quebec and Labrador, Seventh Session of the UN Permanent Forum on Indigenous Issues. New York, April 30.

Pottie, E., 2014. American Law Professor: Aboriginal Title Decision is No Game-changer. *Herald News*, July 23.

Reid, I., 2008. *Defining Canada: A Nation Chooses The 101 Things That Best Define Their Country.* Ottawa, ON: Citizenship and Immigration Canada; Dominion Institute.

Resnick, P., 2005. *The European Roots of Canadian Identity.* Peterborough, ON: Broadview Press.

Royal Canadian Mounted Police (RCMP), 2014. *Missing and Murdered Aboriginal Women: A National Operational Overview.* Ottawa, ON: Her Majesty the Queen in Right of Canada as represented by the Royal Canadian Mounted Police.

Statistics Canada, 2012a. Last update, The Canada Yearbook [Homepage of Government of Canada]. Available at: www.statcan.gc.ca/pub/11-402-x/11-402-x2012000-eng.htm [last accessed July 15, 2015].

Statistics Canada, 2012b. Last update, Ethnic Diversity and Immigration [Homepage of Government of Canada]. Available at: www.statcan.gc.ca/pub/11-402-x/2012000/chap/imm/imm-eng.htm?fpv=30000 [last accessed August 14, 2015].

Statistics Canada, 2012c. Last update, Immigration and Ethnocultural Diversity in Canada [Homepage of Government of Canada]. Available at: www12.statcan.gc.ca/nhs-enm/2011/as-sa/99-010-x/99-010-x2011001-eng.cfm [last accessed August 15, 2105].

Supreme Court Of Canada, Word of Welcome from the Chief Justice of Canada. Available at: www.scc-csc.gc.ca/home-accueil/index-eng.aspx [last accessed August 18, 2015].

Tennant, P., 1990. *Aboriginal Peoples and Politics: The Indian Land Question in British Columbia, 1849–1989.* Vancouver, BC: University of British Columbia Press.

Truth and Reconciliation Commission of Canada, 2015. *Honouring the Truth, Reconciling the Future: Summary of the Final Report of the Truth and Reconciliation Commission of Canada, 31 May 2015.* Ottawa, ON: Truth and Reconciliation Commission of Canada.

Tsawwassen First Nation, Our Treaty. Available at: http:tsawwassenfirstnation.com/general-info/reports [last accessed August 15, 2015].

Union of BC Indian Chiefs, 2009. Joint Statement from Leaders of the First Nations Summit, BC Assembly of First Nations, and the Union of BC Indian Chiefs, March 12.

United Nations, 2015. Last update, United Nations Treaty Collection. Available at: https://treaties.un.org/Pages/Treaties.aspx?id=4&subid=A&lang=en [last accessed July 15, 2015].

United Nations Committee on the Elimination of Racial Discrimination, 2007. *Consideration of Reports Submitted by States Parties under Article 9 of the Convention, Concluding Observations of the Committee on the Elimination of Racial Discrimination, Canada UN Doc CERD/C/CAN/CO/18.* New York: United Nations.

United Nations General Assembly, 2006. *Resolution Adopted by the General Assembly: Human Rights Council, UN Doc A/Res/60/251.* New York: United Nations.

United Nations Human Rights Council, 2009. *Report of the Working Group on the Universal Periodic Review, Canada, UN Doc A/HRC/11/17.* New York: United Nations.

United Nations Human Rights Council, 2013. *Report of the Working Group on the Universal Periodic Review, Canada, UN Doc A/HRC/24/11.* New York: United Nations.

United Nations Human Rights Council, 2014. *Report of the Special Rapporteur on the Rights of Indigenous Peoples, James Anaya: The Situation of Indigenous Peoples in Canada, UN Doc A/HRC/27/52/Add.2.* New York: United Nations.

University Of Minnesota Human Rights Library, 2008. Last update, Ratification of International Human Rights Treaties. Available at: www.umn.edu/humanrts/research/ratification-index.html [last accessed July 30, 2015].

Wabanonick, L., 2008. Statement of Grand Chief Lucien Wabanonik (Tribal Council of the Anishinabeg Algonquin Nation), Assembly of First Nations of Quebec and Labrador, Seventh Session of the UN Permanent Forum on Indigenous Issues. New York, May 1.

Walters, H., 2015. Stephen Harper Defends Aboriginal Affairs Record in Wake of Residential Schools Report. *CBC News*, June 2.

Zolf, L., 2002. Peacekeeping and the Canadian Identity. *CBC News*, February 7.

8 The transformative potential of Indigenous rights

Let us return to where we began: September 13, 2007, the day upon which Indigenous delegates sat at the back of the General Assembly Hall watching the voting lights turn overwhelmingly green, indicating that the Indigenous Rights Declaration would be adopted by the UN. There was one important individual who had been part of this process from the very beginning who was not in New York that day. IITC Board Member Bill Means was in Minneapolis, having a lunch meeting with me, officially launching this research project. I had known Bill as a member of AIM, a founding member of IITC, a leader in the urban American Indian community, and a friend of my mother's since I was a small child growing up in Minneapolis. By coincidence, the day upon which we set up our first meeting, the day I offered Bill some tobacco and asked him for his stories of the Indigenous rights movement at the UN, turned out to be very same day upon which the General Assembly adopted the Declaration on the Rights of Indigenous Peoples. Over lunch, we discussed what a noteworthy victory it was. It was the first time that a group of marginalized non-state actors, with no real bargaining chips in the power politics game, had achieved any sort of international human rights standard for themselves. We celebrated the victory. Yet, as Bill explained, the Declaration adopted by the UN that day was certainly not a perfect document; the text had changed in some ways from what they had initially envisioned in the 1970s and 1980s. But, even with its limitations and the lack of support from English-speaking settler states, this day nevertheless represented an important turning point, he said. This Declaration was the first widespread commitment by UN member states to make important changes to their relationships with Indigenous peoples and to complete the UN's decolonization project begun decades earlier but which had so unjustly and unfairly excluded Indigenous peoples. However, Bill said, this was only the beginning of the long, real struggle yet to come.

In the words of Onondaga Faith-keeper Oren Lyons (2015), the Indigenous Rights Declaration was significant because "for the first time, we became human." He is referring to the history of UN decolonization that, for years, deliberately excluded Indigenous peoples from the human right of self-determination, which all other peoples enjoyed as an inherent aspect of their humanity. With this Declaration, Indigenous peoples finally enjoyed human rights on equal terms. My research also finds, however, that global Indigenous politics is much more than the mere correction of an unjust historical exclusion. Rather, I contend that global Indigenous politics, by seeking a space of accommodation for Indigenous peoples, actually poses much larger challenges to the structure and practice of global politics than international relations theorists typically recognize. Indeed, Indigenous peoples' struggles are often hardly noticed in a world characterized by issues like terrorism, nuclear proliferation, economic distress, climate change, and the like. In 2007, news of the UN's adoption of the Declaration on the Rights of Indigenous Peoples was barely a blip on the international media radar. Furthermore, those viewing the Declaration from a conservative, formal-legal perspective often dismiss it as non-binding and merely aspirational. States often also view the Declaration in this way. However, those regarding the Declaration from the critical end of Indigenous scholarship also tend to under-appreciate and dismiss it, overlooking its grassroots origins and the ways in which it can potentially be deployed to benefit Indigenous peoples.

In contrast to both of these positions, this book has argued that, in spite of its limitations, the Declaration was a significant achievement and represents an important transformational moment in global politics. A universal standard of Indigenous rights has been set, those standards represent significant change in the structure and practice of global politics, and there is at least rhetorical support for those standards coming from the vast majority of the world's nation-states. However, the real power and potential of Indigenous rights lies in how they will be deployed and implemented, especially since multiple forms of state resistance remain firmly in place.

According to the UN, the decolonization project is 99.75 percent completed, with 750 million people from former colonies having gained independence and only two million remaining in "non self-governing territories" waiting to be decolonized (United Nations). Even eight years after the UN Indigenous Rights Declaration's adoption, the UN's official decolonization figures still do not consider the world's 300 million Indigenous peoples to be "colonized" or their territories to be "non-self-governing." Clearly, a tension remains between the UN (that is, nation-states) and Indigenous peoples regarding what decolonization means and who has already attained it. Global Indigenous politics is the world's post-colonial completion project, and the Declaration is the guiding framework.

Indigenous rights aim to eradicate the discursive, normative, and, ultimately, material remnants of the colonial project and complete the unfinished business of decolonization. However, global Indigenous politics seeks a post-colonialism that is markedly different from that which has come before, because a world that accommodates Indigenous nationhood, Indigenous ontologies, and Indigenous political practices will be a world characterized by an entirely different set of values and power relations than exists in the current international order. Previous chapters have shown that by advocating for Indigenous rights, global Indigenous politics is leading a set of global changes that are hardly small and inconsequential, but rather represent important moments of transformation.

First, adoption of the Indigenous Rights Declaration represents the first time that a broad set of collective rights was accepted within the human rights consensus. By constituting Indigenous rights in both individual and collective terms, global Indigenous politics creates a type of politics distinctive from other rights movements. Indigenous rights battle two sets of violences simultaneously: (1) discrimination/marginalization; and (2) the dispossession and assimilation of Indigenous peoples. Individual human rights standards could only address the first; collective rights standards were essential to beginning to address the second.

By successfully adding collective rights to the international human rights consensus, the Declaration opens a wider door to collective rights acceptance, which had previously been firmly closed. English-speaking states have all expressed long-standing misgivings about and opposition to collective rights, arguing that a fundamental incompatibility exists between collective and individual rights, and that recognition of collective rights leaves individuals within groups overly vulnerable to harm.

Indigenous activists widely report that throughout the Cold War years, the USA always vociferously opposed any international instrument which included collective rights provisions, out of fear that collective rights represented some part of the communist agenda. So, when the Indigenous Rights Declaration, a broad statement supporting collective rights, passed the UN General Assembly by an overwhelming margin, voted on by the UK and later endorsed by the USA, it was a clear transitional moment in post-Cold War world politics. Other nations had eventually come to accept that collective rights in general could and should exist as part of the human rights consensus, but the USA was a strong holdout, specifically citing its opposition to collective rights in its 2007 explanation of opposition to the Declaration. Thus, in 2010, when the USA issued an explicit statement of support for collective rights in its endorsement, it was the first time in history that the USA had supported collective human rights in any form, representing an important shift in the long-held USA position. It thus completes the global consensus on collective rights, forcing a future global conversation about how to accommodate collective rights alongside, and without disrupting or undermining, individual rights.

Second, global Indigenous politics focuses attention on a particular global dilemma: how to apply universals that simultaneously allow for difference? Global Indigenous politics reveals how injustice can result from the application of universals. For example, during its first six decades, the international human rights regime aimed for the universal application of individual human rights in an effort to protect persons from abuse by their governments. However, by exclusively individualizing human rights, the system created a particular injustice for Indigenous peoples who also needed their collective rights (for instance, to land, religion, language, culture, political, and social institutions) protected from the violence caused by dispossession and assimilation. Indigenous rights problematize the exclusive individual rights construction of human rights that, in their effort to protect all persons equally, can actually *cause* discrimination by overlooking or failing to recognize *all* of the sources of ongoing oppression.

Global Indigenous politics also challenges the universal of sovereignty, since the existing nation-state framework has performed a specific injustice against Indigenous peoples' rights to land, resources, and self-determination by recognizing only state sovereignty as fully legitimate. Global Indigenous politics ultimately rests on a universal right to maintain difference – a new and potentially transformational idea in global politics. Yet, the Declaration does not include any universal prescriptive solution for what various rights, including self-determination, should come to mean in practice. In fact, it is the antithesis of a universal prescriptive solution. Rather, the Declaration provides space for the negotiation of a multitude of political arrangements with stated options ranging from autonomy and self-government to participation within the state. Presumably, other options could also come to exist in a future imagining of shared or plural sovereignty.

Third, global Indigenous politics imagines and practices international relations differently, incorporating Indigenous culture, spirituality, worldviews, and decision-making processes into international politics. Further, it shows that movements which begin from grassroots-level ideas and conversations do have the opportunity and the potential for impact at the global level. Unity and solidarity in movements can be maintained over an extended period of time and through extremely difficult circumstances. Much of the success of the transnational Indigenous rights movement may be attributed to pure tenacity, but more than some of the credit belongs to the manner in which the Indigenous movement conducts global politics. The consensus decision-making style, grounded in spirituality and rooted in a respect for the diversity of Indigenous cultures, strengthens the solidarity of the Indigenous rights movement and also presents an alternative, non-hierarchical model of international relations to the world.

Fourth, Indigenous rights push the meanings of decolonization and self-determination into new terrain, beyond purely statist conceptions. The meanings of both self-determination and decolonization are evolving on the international level, and Indigenous rights have an important role to play in the ongoing global conversation surrounding that evolution. Article 3 of the Declaration states, "Indigenous peoples have the right to self-determination," but, at the same time, the Declaration also offers protections for existing state sovereignty and territorial integrity in Article 46. Indigenous rights are therefore not a threat to the existence of states per se, but they are a direct threat to any doctrine, discourse, law, norm, political institution, or system that denies Indigenous peoples equal individual and collective rights, especially the rights associated with Indigenous nationhood: land and self-determination. Global Indigenous politics seeks the peaceful accommodation of Indigenous nationhood, with or without state structures, on a trajectory that inevitably leads toward more pluralistic conceptions of sovereignty and territoriality.

It is this move toward non-statist conceptions of decolonization and self-determination that nation-states, especially settler states, most actively resist. Since the 1970s, the transnational Indigenous rights movement has been shifting the international conversation on Indigenous peoples away from one focused solely on anti-discrimination toward one that also focuses on Indigenous nations' right to self-determination. This international conversation necessarily and inevitably leads to discussions about plural sovereignty and power-sharing arrangements *if* Indigenous nationhood is to be recognized and protected in a peaceful way, without disrupting or presenting any threat to existing states. Global Indigenous politics thus forces a rethinking of relationships between Indigenous peoples and states away from hierarchical, colonial relations and toward a new, fair, and just relationship that allows Indigenous peoples to freely determine their political status with, within, or across the borders of nation-states. The Declaration could represent an early, nascent articulation of an entirely new international order, a new way of living and being in the world. In lieu of hierarchical orders that include domination, extraction, exploitation, and colonial control, Indigenous rights represent the cutting edge of a radically new order based on principles brought forward by the Indigenous rights movement, such as mutual respect, sustainability, reciprocal relationships, and the ongoing negotiation of political questions.

Finally, the reason for such strong resistance to Indigenous rights from a set of states that are otherwise rights-advocating, liberal, and democratic emanates from a dual problem: the illegitimate foundation of their rule over Indigenous peoples and lands, based either explicitly or implicitly on the Doctrine of Discovery, coupled with their strong investment in the status quo of the international order. At heart, Indigenous rights present settler colonial states with a legitimacy problem. The more the power of a state rests on a colonial – and now illegitimate – foundation, the greater the sense of threat that state is likely to feel from Indigenous rights.

Some states, like the former European imperial powers, demonstrate virtually no sense of threat from Indigenous rights, since the dismantling of their empires is more or less a *fait accompli*. Some of these former colonial powers may even see a certain degree of justice as the decolonizing gaze now shifts away from their colonial histories and toward the present situation of settler colonial states. Most of Africa and Asia are made up of post-colonial states created from national independence movements and the first wave of UN decolonization. Some have Indigenous peoples and some do not. Their biggest fear tends to be secession or even the dismantling of the post-colonial state, and so the late addition of Article 46 to the Declaration, which protects state sovereignty from Indigenous rights claims, generally assuages their concerns. With large numbers of Indigenous peoples, the threat of Indigenous movements to Latin American countries is violence and political instability, and so these countries tend to employ a strategy of rhetorical support for Indigenous rights in an effort to keep Indigenous peoples pacified, even if the actual implementation of Indigenous rights lags significantly behind their normative commitments.

Settler colonial states stand apart and exhibit threat at a much deeper level. These states have prospered and staked out their place in the global power structure as a direct result of their dispossession and domination of Indigenous peoples. These foundations are under direct threat by the Indigenous rights regime, which demands an entirely different Indigenous–state relationship. Western philosophy tends to view questions of land, self-determination, and power in strictly zero-sum terms. As viewed through this Western philosophical lens, Indigenous rights present the biggest threat to those English-speaking settler colonial states with the most to lose by reallocating land, self-determination, and power. While there are hints of co-management and power-sharing arrangements emerging in these countries, reconciliation there still represents continued efforts on the part of these countries to individualize Indigenous peoples and bring them into their multicultural societies – the effective maintenance of an assimilative model – rather than working through a genuine conversation on resetting those relationships to nation-to-nation, treaty-based ones that could accommodate Indigenous difference. Worst of all, these countries' reconciliation models are leaving the Doctrine of Discovery firmly intact, in both legal and discursive senses. Indigenous rights, therefore, strike at the heart of the foundational legitimacy of these states. The greatest challenge confronting Indigenous movements, in both domestic and global contexts, is to push for the transformative agenda of global Indigenous politics in an atmosphere where settler colonial states feel and exhibit such an intense level of threat and engage in resistance to Indigenous rights in multiple, often cunningly manipulative, ways.

Global Indigenous politics as a subtle revolution

Global Indigenous politics forces states and global society to grapple with a set of fundamental transformations and challenging new problems. With a global consensus on Indigenous rights, the old hierarchical international order which created and enabled both colonialism and settler colonialism has been delegitimized. For states that still depend on colonialism or settler colonialism as the basis of their political and economic power, this delegitimation forces a palpable practical and moral dilemma. Such states wish to preserve the illusion of compliance with or support for Indigenous rights without giving up their actual power. States perform a number of contortions in order to appear to support this post-colonial completion project without actually engaging in the changes called for by the project. Taken seriously, Indigenous rights norms present a set of fundamental challenges and questions to human rights, liberalism, the state, and even the concept of sovereignty itself. As Indigenous rights norms continue to emerge and diffuse, all states, the international system, and international relations theory will be forced to cease their contortions and confront these challenges head-on.

English-speaking settler colonial states generally highly prize Lockean liberal notions regarding individuals' natural rights of equality and private property. They tend to experience arguments for state recognition of Indigenous collective rights as direct challenges to these values. Indigenous rights claims create certain fundamental tensions within liberal, democratic, Lockean-based, liberal conceptions of democratic politics and rights in settler colonial states. How can states recognize collective rights, or the rights of groups, without undermining, disrupting, or endangering the rights of individuals? How should society deal with the reality that liberalism's emphasis on rights of the individual, especially individual rights to private property, actually *creates* a state of inequality for certain groups, like Indigenous peoples, whose ways of life, and continued existence as peoples, depend on the recognition of their collective rights alongside their rights as individuals? At the same time, how can states protect such groups while also providing equal protections to the individual members of those groups? How can states create protections for groups that do not risk exposing members of those groups to certain tyrannies?

The second, related, set of questions around Indigenous rights concerns how states and the international system can accommodate difference while also maintaining commonality. As Inayatullah and Blaney (2004) argue, international relations in both practice and theory aim to "contain, domesticate, or destroy difference," particularly through prevailing theories of modernization and understandings of global order. Drawing on Todorov's (1984) work on the European discovery of America, Inayatullah and Blaney describe the "double movement" that emerged at first contact when Europeans were confronted with the fundamental differences of Indigenous peoples yet also recognized certain common human characteristics. The double movement rectifies the cognitive dissonance of otherness and commonality, as "difference becomes inferiority, and the possibility of a common humanity requires assimilation." In practice, this set of dual impulses pushed in two directions: it impelled the creation of colonial state structures that exercised domination over and expected assimilation of Indigenous peoples; and it also led to the creation of a hierarchical international system of dominant or powerful states, and subordinate colonial territories that were viewed as needing help toward modernization. In the modern/colonial era, difference has been viewed as "a dangerous aberration," responsible for disorder, and thus compelling the need for an "empire of uniformity" (Tully 1995). But Indigenous rights force an answer to the question of how to justly accommodate difference and equality both between and within states (Inayatullah and Blaney 2004) in ways that serve to rectify colonial relations of domination and subordination. Further, by framing decolonization as simply the creation of new Westphalian states out of former colonial territories, not only were Indigenous peoples unequally excluded, but, in addition, the hierarchical structures of both states and the international system were also inequitably retained. The post-colonial completion project of global Indigenous politics thus forces a questioning and rectification of such exclusions as well as the social, cultural, economic, and political hierarchies that have enabled and sustained them.

Finally, while human rights, humanitarian intervention, globalization, and the growth of supranational institutions have all limited or constrained Westphalian sovereignty (Donnelly 2003; Krasner 1999; Rues-Smit 2001), Indigenous rights now force a rethinking of it. Westphalian sovereignty – typically understood to mean the exclusive ability to exercise control over the affairs of a territorially bounded space (Ruggie 1983)– is a relatively recent form of human political organization. Many different forms of political organization preceded Westphalian sovereignty and, presumably, different forms of political organization will replace it. For, as Thomas Biersteker and Cynthia Weber (1996) have argued, sovereignty is a social construct and thus in a continual process of negotiation and renegotiation. Therefore, with transformative elements that include collective rights alongside individual rights, equal accommodation of difference, non-hierarchical power relations, and respect for the self-determination of Indigenous peoples without disrupting existing states, Global Indigenous politics necessarily forces an important global question to the surface: how to negotiate and redesign new plural, overlapping, and multiple types of sovereignties – state and Indigenous – within and across state borders, including sovereignties that may or may not be tied to exclusive authority over territories?

Further, global Indigenous politics will also help provide alternative understandings of what sovereignty can mean in the future by taking some "pre-modern" Indigenous principles of political relations that include respect for difference alongside a common commitment to equality, mutual respect, and peaceful co-existence within a malleable space, all of which together potentially provides a roadmap for a post-Westphalian world. As Lorie Graham and Siegfried Wiessner (2011) have articulated, Indigenous understandings of sovereignty/self-determination do not mean power over others but are focused on the maintenance of unique cultures and societies. Indigenous understandings of political relations recognize the interconnectedness of human beings and the land, emphasizing a concept of a human duty toward and stewardship of the land, as opposed to its control, ownership, and exploitation. In order to equally recognize the self-determination of all peoples, understood as the right of a people to exist and make decisions for themselves, the state would also need to recognize the fact that no one has the right to interfere with the right of any people to do so. Such a mutual recognition of self-determination will replace aggression and exploitation with cooperation and respect. However, at the same time, in societies where different peoples – Indigenous and non-Indigenous – live in overlapping and cross-border spaces, mutual recognition of self-determination will inevitably also lead to the negotiation of parallel and overlapping sovereignties. Global Indigenous politics, then, forges global change both by creating a set of challenges *and* providing a potential pathway for resolution. It not only fundamentally challenges the existing problematic international order, but also presents a set of alternative understandings and political practices, grounded in an entirely different set of values and worldviews, that provide an answer to those challenges. In short, the implementation of Indigenous rights will mean that patterns of exploitation, conquest, extraction, and inequality must give way to entirely different, more just, and sustainable forms of global political and economic relations.

Implementation of Indigenous rights

Implementation of Indigenous rights, as articulated in the Declaration, necessitates change – significant change – on both international and domestic levels.

Because Indigenous rights essentially calls for a restructuring of Indigenous–state relationships, it expects states to enact and implement a significant body of legal, constitutional, legislative, and policy changes that can accommodate such things as Indigenous land rights, free, prior, and informed consent, redress, and a variety of self-government, autonomy, and other such arrangements. Several possible implementation tools present themselves, which may be considered as being situated along two paths: *institutional remedies* and *active deployment*, giving effect to the Declaration's dual legal and political character.

Institutional remedies, or the legal path

Implementing the Declaration through institutional remedies involves utilizing existing systems and structures, on both international and domestic levels, to enhance rights protections for Indigenous peoples. Each of these remedies offers a particular advancement in Indigenous rights protections, but, it must be noted, each also comes with a set of attendant limitations that must be carefully considered, especially in light of creative, and constantly evolving, state resistance to Indigenous rights.

First, some Indigenous organizations seek enhanced international instruments to support Indigenous rights, especially in light of the non-binding, aspirational, and legally unenforceable nature of the UN Declaration. In the early days of the UN Working Group on Indigenous Popluations (WGIP), conversations were held about eventually working toward an international treaty or convention as a follow-up to the Declaration. This issue re-emerged after the Declaration was passed in 2007, when some Indigenous rights organizations noted state emphasis on the Declaration's non-binding character and state misuse of that non-binding character as the freedom to ignore and dismiss it. Thus, some Indigenous organizations felt the need to develop a mechanism to monitor and coordinate implementation of the Declaration, as well as to help interpret it in international law. In response, in 2012, the United Nations Permanent Forum on Indigenous Issues (UNPFII) launched a special study on an optional protocol to the Declaration, to examine the potential for such a mechanism. Consideration of an optional protocol was an unusual step, since an optional protocol is normally attached as a supplementary agreement to a human rights *treaty*, "which may either provide for procedures with regard to the treaty or address a substantive area related to the treaty"; optional protocols are not typically used as a follow-up to a human rights *declaration* (United Nations Entity for Gender Equality and the Empowerment of Women). Optional protocols are binding under international law and often contain terms that are more strict than the treaty itself. They are, as the name suggests, optional – a state may sign a treaty and then may or may not sign an optional protocol attached to that treaty.

The UNPFII released the study report on the optional protocol in 2014, recommending that such a mechanism should be voluntary, confined to only a handful of critical issues, and negotiated between states and Indigenous peoples (United Nations Permanent Forum on Indigenous Issues 2014). The report highlighted the need for enhanced implementation efforts, particularly since the "non-binding" nature of the Declaration could be interpreted by states to mean that they could ignore it. On the contrary, the report noted, human rights declarations carry significant normative weight for all countries, since they reflect international commitments attained through global consensus. After substantial discussion on this topic during the 2014 session of the UNPFII, the Global Indigenous Caucus issued its call for complete withdrawal of the proposal – its concerns rested on lack of historical precedent, and the voluntary character of an optional protocol. Because states could opt in or opt out of such an enforcement mechanism, the normative weight of the Declaration could be seriously undermined by the very mechanism intended to enhance it (Global Indigenous Caucus 2014).

Another implementation strategy is to use and cite the Declaration in domestic and international legal actions. This was first done in the Belize Supreme Court almost immediately after the Declaration passed the General Assembly. Ruling in favor of Mayan land rights, the Court cited the Declaration specifically, in addition to national law. Belize is a former British colony, and a common law country. The potential significance of a Belize court applying the Declaration domestically is that the court's decision might be persuasive and exert some precedential weight on judges in other common law jurisdictions. However, as Lumbee scholar David Wilkins (1997) has demonstrated, domestic court rulings, even Supreme Court rulings, can be easily undermined by subsequent legislation or executive action. In fact, this has been the case in Belize.

Some Indigenous peoples pursue constitutional change to support Indigenous rights in domestic contexts. Canada was the first to do so in 1982, when it included Section 35 in the repatriated Constitution in response to a massive campaign by Aboriginal organizations and activists who advocated for recognition of their rights and title in the new Constitution. Section 35 states specifically: "the existing aboriginal and treaty rights of the aboriginal peoples of Canada are hereby recognized and affirmed" (Canada 1982). Section 35 does not define Aboriginal rights and limits them to those that were already in existence in 1982. Since the Declaration in 2007, an increasing number of countries, such as Bolivia and Ecuador, have recognized Indigenous peoples and rights in their constitutions; others, like Kenya and Australia, are engaged in active discussions toward that end. This constitutional recognition of Indigenous peoples and rights is sometimes quite weak, like a non-binding instrument that merely recognizes the existence of Indigenous peoples within a state, while at other times it takes a much stronger constitutional form and entrenches treaty rights, land rights self-government.

Even the strongest constitutional protections, however, come with limitations. For example, strong constitutional protections or even enshrinement of the Declaration into national law, including the provision for free, prior, and informed consent, did not prevent resource extraction projects in Bolivia and Ecuador from proceeding without the consent of the Indigenous communities directly impacted by the projects. Further, as Dene political theorist Glen Coulthard argues in his 2007 article "Subjects of Empire," liberal states increasingly engage in policies and practices that "recognize" Indigenous cultural rights, rights to self-determination, and treaty rights, but such recognition is highly problematic at its core. Coulthard writes,

> one need not expend much effort to elicit the countless ways in which the liberal discourse of recognition has been limited and constrained by the state, the courts, corporate interests, and policy makers so as to help preserve the colonial *status quo*.

In his 1974 book *Behind the Trail of Broken Treaties*, Vine Deloria, Jr. presented concrete suggestions for a full-scale redesign of the USA–Indian relationship, including: (1) giving First Nations international protectorate status, meaning that tribal nations would be small nations under the protectorate status of the USA, but with full international status. The government would externally protect these tribal nations, but would have no right to interfere or intervene in their affairs; (2) USA surrender of its right to extinguish Aboriginal land title; (3) elimination of the USA claim to "first-purchase rights of tribal lands" so that no further sales of tribal lands would be permitted; (4) shifting the trust relationship between the USA government and tribal nations to a passive, rather than an active, trust; and (5) restore the treaty relationship. Decades later, neither the USA nor any other country has moved forward with any of these proposals.

Each of these institutional remedies certainly advance or protect Indigenous rights in some way. However, each of these strategies operates within norm plane A, the existing international order. As Cherokee political scientist Jeff Corntassel (2012) notes, Indigenous rights struggles that are premised on existing structures, discourses, and institutions have serious shortcomings and can only be taken so far. Such rights are conditional and risk "mimicking state functions." According to Corntassel, such Indigenous rights mobilization "will not lead to a sustainable self-determination process that restores and regenerates Indigenous nations." While such efforts can be a valuable start toward achieving Indigenous rights, they must all be considered carefully, with measured optimism and acknowledgement of their risks and limitations.

Active deployment, or the political path

The Indigenous Rights Declaration is increasingly invoked and deployed discursively and politically in a multitude of international and domestic contexts. The active deployment path is where the real potential lies to move along the transformational norm vector to a higher stage of Indigenous rights implementation. Indigenous rights may thus only be implemented to their full transformational potential when they are used as political and moral tools by Indigenous movements, often in alliance with other non-Indigenous groups, such as environmental and human rights movements.

Active deployment means invoking Indigenous rights principles in domestic and transnational political and social movements as well as in political and social discourses. A recent example is the Idle No More movement that sprang up in Canada in the winter of 2012/2013 in response to a series of parliamentary bills intended to erode Indigenous sovereignty, and land and water rights. It quickly became one of the largest Indigenous mass movements in history, characterized by teach-ins, protests, and rallies across Canada and then extending globally. But Idle No More was not an isolated or discrete movement. Rather, it was one flashpoint of a long and underlying Indigenous resistance to colonialism – a larger resistance that is non-violently assertive and operates from the same grassroots principles that form the core of the Declaration.

Furthermore, the discourse of Indigenous rights may be invoked in other contexts and in allied movements in a manner that, over time, becomes regularized and normalized, thus creating expectations of implementation through a process of repeated iteration. For example, in 2015, in Canada alone, the Declaration enjoyed widespread, repeated, and diverse deployment. In May's provincial elections in Alberta, the New Democratic Party won a surprise victory, explicitly promising to implement the Declaration in Alberta, a province with a number of ridings where the Indigenous vote can swing elections (Anonymous 2015). In June, the Truth and Reconciliation Commission released the summary of its final report along with ninety-four recommendations for government action, including a specific set of recommendations to fully implement the Declaration (Truth and Reconciliation Commission of Canada 2015). The Declaration also sprang up in the federal election launched in late July, with all major parties, except for the Conservatives, pledging to implement the Declaration directly, or by promising to implement the TRC recommendations, which then includes implementation of the Declaration. Indigenous voices in the campaign called for greater political party attention to Indigenous issues, including implementation of the UN Declaration (Innes 2015). In September, Treaty 6 Grand Chief Tony Alexis and Treaty 8 Grand Chief Steve Courtoreille held a press conference in Edmonton, Alberta to draw attention to how the police practice of "carding," or stopping individuals to ask them for identification, was inequitably impacting Aboriginal people in Edmonton (Huncar 2015). The grand chiefs specifically cited this practice as a violation of the UN Declaration. In the same week, a coalition of Canadian authors, artists, national leaders, and activists announced a declaration called the Leap Manifesto, which lays out a bold vision to transition the country off of fossil fuels. The Leap Manifesto portrays climate change not only as an existential crisis but an opportunity, or more of an imperative, to re-create political and economic systems that are more just and fair. The manifesto is also centered specifically on implementation of the Indigenous Rights Declaration. It states:

> This leap must begin by respecting the inherent rights and title of the original caretakers of this land. Indigenous communities have been at the forefront of protecting rivers, coasts, forests and lands from out-of-control industrial activity. We can bolster this role, and reset our relationship, by fully implementing the United Nations Declaration on the Rights of Indigenous Peoples.
>
> (The Leap Manifesto)

Global Indigenous politics, which involves Indigenous rights and the political movements to implement those rights, challenges states and the international system to complete the post-colonial project, reclaim moral legitimacy, and restructure themselves along lines that promote justice, fairness, and human dignity for all. States are not going to implement this multifaceted and complex set of changes on their own. They will require significant political and moral pressure to hold them accountable to the rhetorical commitments they have made. The repeated assertion of Indigenous rights will lead to wider transformative processes that will require sustained political will and commitment over the very long term, but the inevitable end result of this enhanced decolonization project will be radical systemic change. Walter Echo-Hawk (2013) argues that the Declaration is "planting the seeds of change." He writes,

> This harbinger of change asks every nation to restore the human rights of Native peoples that fell by the wayside during the colonial era. If that call is answered, the Declaration will someday be seen as the Magna Carta for the world's indigenous peoples. If implemented, those measures will change the world and fundamentally alter the way that humanity views some 350 million indigenous peoples who reside in over 70 nations.

These transformative processes will encounter many challenges along the way, and some of the answers to thorny problems will not be easy. But, ultimately, the UN Declaration on the Rights of Indigenous Peoples helps point the way toward a new and infinitely more fair, just, and hopeful global future.

References

Anonymous, 2015. Alberta Election 2015 Results: NDP Wave Sweeps Across Province in Historic Win. *CBC News*, May 5.

Bierstecker, T. and Weber, C., eds, 1996. *State Sovereignty as Social Construct*. Cambridge: Cambridge University Press.

Canada, 1982. Constitution Act, 1982. Being Schedule B to the Canada Act 1982 (UK). Canada.

Corntassel, J., 2012. Cultural Restoration in International Law: Pathways to Indigenous Self-determination. *Canadian Journal of Human Rights*, 1(1), pp. 93–125.

Coulthard, G.S., 2007. Subjects of Empire: Indigenous Peoples and the "Politics of Recognition" in Canada. *Contemporary Political Theory*, 6, pp. 437–460.

Deloria, Jr., V., 1974 [1985]. *Behind the Trail of Broken Treaties: An Indian Declaration of Independence*. Austin: University of Texas Press.

Donnelly, J., 2003. *Universal Human Rights in Theory and Practice*, 2nd edn. Ithaca, NY: Cornell University Press.

Echo-Hawk, W.R., 2013. *In the Light of Justice: The Rise of Human Rights in Native America and the UN Declaration on the Rights of Indigenous Peoples*. Golden, CO: Fulcrum Publishing.

Global Indigenous Caucus, 2014. Statement of May 12.

Graham, L. and Wiessner, S. 2011. Indigenous Sovereignty, Culture, and International Human Rights Law. *South Atlantic Quarterly*, 110, pp. 403–427.

Huncar, A., 2015. Police Carding Undermines Reconciliation, Treaty 6 Grand Chief Says. *CBC News Edmonton*, September 17.

Inayatullah, N. and Blaney, D.L. 2004. *International Relations and the Problem of Difference*. New York; London: Routledge.

Innes, R.A., 2015. Last update, The Indigenous Vote. Available at: https://uofmpress.ca/blog/entry/the-indigenous-vote [last accessed February 10, 2015].

Krasner, S., 1999. *Sovereignty: Organized Hypocrisy*. Princeton, NJ: Princeton University Press.

Leap Manifesto. A Call or a Canada Based on Caring for the Earth and One Another. Available at: https://leapmanifesto.org/en/the-leap-manifesto/ [last accessed January 10, 2015].

Lyons, O., 2015. Conversation. Available at: www.earthisland.org/journal/index.php/eij/article/oren_lyons_onondaga/edn. Berkeley, CA: Earth Island Journal.

Rues-Smit, C., 2001. Human Rights and the Social Construction of Sovereignty. *Review of International Studies*, 27, pp. 1–20.

Ruggie, J.G., 1983. Continuity and Transformation in the World Polity: Toward a Neorealist Synthesis. *World Politics*, 35, pp. 261–286.

Todorov, T., 1984. *The Conquest of America: The Question of the Other*. New York: Harper & Row.

Truth and Reconciliation Commission of Canada, 2015. *Honouring the Truth, Reconciling the Future: Summary of the Final Report of the Truth and Reconciliation Commission of Canada, 31 May 2015*. Ottawa, ON: Truth and Reconciliation Commission of Canada.

Tully, J., 1995. *Strange Multiplicity: Constitutionalism in an Age of Diversity*. Cambridge; New York: Cambridge University Press.

United Nations. The United Nations and Decolonization. Available at: www.un.org/en/decolonization/ [last accessed August 15, 2015].

United Nations Entity for Gender Equality and the Empowerment of Women. What is an Optional Protocol? Available at: www.un.org/womenwatch/daw/cedaw/protocol/whatis.htm [last accessed September 20, 2015].

United Nations Permanent Forum on Indigenous Issues, 2014. *Study on an Optional Protocol to UNDRIP Focusing on a Voluntary Mechanism 4 March 2014 UN Doc. E/C.19/2014/7*. New York: United Nations.

Wilkins, D.E., 1997. *American Indian Sovereignty and the U.S. Supreme Court: The Masking of Justice*, 1st edn. Austin: University of Texas Press.

Appendix 2.1

Draft Declaration of Principles for the Defense of the Indigenous Nations and Peoples of the Western Hemisphere, 1977

**Declaration of Principles
for the Defense
of the Indigenous Nations and Peoples
of the Western Hemisphere**

PREAMBLE:

Having considered the problems relating to the activities of the United Nations for the promotion and encouragement of respect for human rights and fundamental freedoms,

Noting that the Universal Declaration of Human Rights and related international covenants have the individual as their primary concern, and

Recognizing that individuals are the foundation of cultures, societies, and nations, and

Whereas, it is a fundamental right of any individual to practice and perpetuate the cultures. societies and nations into which they are born, and

Recognizing that conditions are imposed upon peoples that suppress, deny or destroy the culture, societies or nations in which they believe or of which they are members,

Be it affirmed that,

1. RECOGNITION OF INDIGENOUS NATIONS

Indigenous peoples shall be accorded recognition as nations, and proper subjects of international law, provided the people concerned desire to be recognized as a nation and meet the fundamental requirements of nationhood, namely:

a. Having a permanent population
b. Having a defined territory
c. Having a government
d. Having the ability to enter into relations with other states

2. SUBJECTS OF INTERNATIONAL LAW
Indigenous groups not meeting the requirements of nationhood are hereby declared to be subjects of international law and are entitled to the protection of this Declaration, provided they are identifiable groups having bonds of language, heritage, tradition, or other common identity.

3. GUARANTEE OF RIGHTS
No indigenous nation or group shall be deemed to have fewer rights, or lesser status for the sole reason that the nation or group has not entered into recorded treaties or agreements with any state.

4. ACCORDANCE OF INDEPENDENCE
Indigenous nations or groups shall be accorded such degree of independence as they may desire in accordance with international law.

5. TREATIES AND AGREEMENTS
Treaties and other agreements entered into by indigenous nations or groups with other states, whether denominated as treaties or otherwise, shall be recognized and applied in the same manner and according to the same international laws and principles as the treaties and agreements entered into by other states.

6. ABROGATION OF TREATIES AND OTHER RIGHTS
Treaties and agreements made with indigenous nations or groups shall not be subject to unilateral abrogation. In no event may the municipal laws of any state serve as a defense to the failure to adhere to and perform the terms of treaties and agreements made with indigenous nations or groups. Nor shall any state refuse to recognize and adhere to treaties or other agreements due to changed circumstances where the change in circumstances has been substantially caused by the state asserting that such change has occurred.

7. JURISDICTION
No state shall assert or claim to exercise any right of jurisdiction over any indigenous nation or group or the territory of such indigenous nation or group unless pursuant to a valid treaty or other agreement freely made with the lawful representatives of the indigenous nation or group concerned. All actions on the part of any state which derogate from the indigenous nations' or groups' right to exercise self-determination shall be the proper concern of existing international bodies.

8. CLAIMS TO TERRITORY
No state shall claim or retain, by right of discovery or otherwise, the territories of an indigenous nation or group, except such lands as may have been lawfully acquired by valid treaty or other cessation freely made.

9. SETTLEMENT OF DISPUTES
All states in the Western Hemisphere shall establish through negotiations or other appropriate means a procedure for the binding settlement of disputes, claims, or other matters relating to indigenous nations or groups. Such procedures shall be mutually acceptable to the parties, fundamentally fair, and consistent with international law. All procedures presently in existence which do not have the endorsement of the indigenous nations or groups concerned, shall be ended, and new procedures shall be instituted consistent with this Declaration.

10. NATIONAL AND CULTURAL INTEGRITY

It shall be unlawful for any state to take or permit any action or course of conduct with respect to an indigenous nation or group which will directly or indirectly result in the destruction or disintegration of such indigenous nation or group or otherwise threaten the national or cultural integrity of such nation or group, including, but not limited to, the imposition and support of illegitimate governments and the introduction of non-indigenous religions to indigenous peoples by non-indigenous missionaries.

11. ENVIRONMENTAL PROTECTION

It shall be unlawful for any state to make or permit any action or course of conduct with respect to the territories of an indigenous nation or group which will directly or indirectly result in the destruction or deterioration of an indigenous nation or group through the effects of pollution of earth, air, water, or which in any way depletes, displaces or destroys any natural resource or other resources under the dominion of, or vital to the livelihood of an indigenous nation or group.

12. INDIGENOUS MEMBERSHIP

No state, through legislation, regulation, or other means, shall take actions that interfere with the sovereign power of an indigenous nation or group to determine its own membership.

13. CONCLUSION

All of the rights and obligations declared herein shall be in addition to all rights and obligations existing under international law.

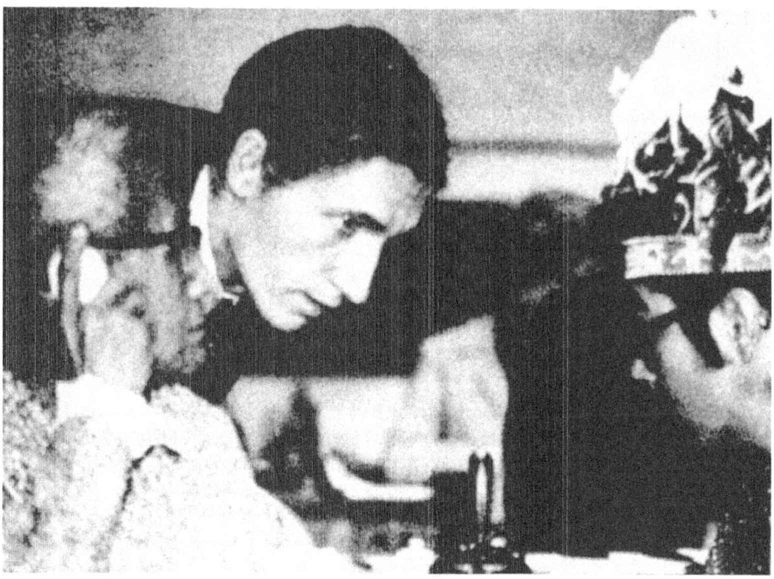

Tim Coulter, Institute for the Development of Indian Law, provided documentation and arguments in the Legal Commission. Here he confers with Iroquois delegates in the Commission.

Appendix 2.2

Working Group on Indigenous Populations Draft Principles (preliminary wording), 1985

UNITED NATIONS

Working Paper No. 4/Addendum 4 — 29 July 1985
E/CN.4/Sub.2/AC.4/1985/WP.4/Add.4 — Original: ENGLISH/SPANISH
GE.85–12538

COMMISSION ON HUMAN RIGHTS
Sub-Commission on Prevention of Discrimination and Protection of Minorities

Working Group on Indigenous Populations
Fourth session
Geneva
29 July–2 August 1985
Item 5 of the agenda

STANDARD-SETTING ACTIVITIES: EVOLUTION OF STANDARDS CONCERNING THE RIGHTS OF INDIGENOUS POPULATIONS

DRAFTING OF A BODY OF PRINCIPLES ON INDIGENOUS RIGHTS, BASED ON RELEVANT NATIONAL LEGISLATION, INTERNATIONAL INSTRUMENTS AND OTHER JURIDICAL CRITERIA

Material received from non-governmental organizations in consultative status with the Economic and Social Council

A special assembly of indigenous NGOs including the Indian Law Resource Center, Four Directions Council, National Aboriginal and Islander Legal Service, National Indian Youth Council, Inuit Circumpolar Conference, and International Indian Treaty Council, as well as other indigenous national and organizational delegations from Australia, Brazil, Canada, Chile, Ecuador, India, Mexico, Norway, Peru, and the United States, was held at the Palais des Nations, Geneva, from 22 to 26 July 1985. The purpose of this meeting was to seek consensus on action to be taken at the fourth session of the Working Group on Indigenous Populations.

The development of a United Nations declaration on the rights of indigenous peoples was the principal topic of discussion, and it was generally agreed that progress depended on the Working Group's adoption and dissemination of a working text or outline of principles for refinement at its future sessions.

The assembly reviewed with particular interest the draft principles prepared by various indigenous organizations and previously tabled with the Working Group, and invited a small drafting group to incorporate participants' comments into a revised text. The assembly reviewed, amended and adopted this revised text by consensus on 26 July, and agreed to table it with the Working Group on Indigenous Populations as a possible working text.

English and Spanish versions of the draft principles are equally authoritative.

DECLARATION OF PRINCIPLES

1. Indigenous nations and peoples have, in common with all humanity, the right to life, and to freedom from oppression, discrimination, and aggression.
2. All indigenous nations and peoples have the right to self-determination, by virtue of which they have the right to whatever degree of autonomy or self-government they choose. This includes the right to freely determine their political status, freely pursue their own economic, social, religious and cultural development, and determine their own membership and/or citizenship, without external interference.
3. No State shall asset any jurisdiction over an indigenous nation or people, or its territory, except in accordance with the freely expressed wishes of the nation or people concerned.
4. Indigenous nations and peoples are entitled to the permanent control and enjoyment of their aboriginal ancestral-historical territories. This includes surface and subsurface rights, inland and coastal waters, renewable and non-renewable resources, and the economies based on these resources.
5. Rights to share and use land, subject to the underlying and inalienable title of the indigenous nation or people, may be granted by their free and informed consent, as evidenced in a valid treaty or agreement.
6. Discovery, conquest, settlement on a theory of TERRA NULLIUS and unilateral legislation are never legitimate bases for States to claim or retain the territories of indigenous nations or peoples.
7. In cases where lands taken in violation of these principles have already been settled, the indigenous nation or people concerned is entitled to immediate restitution, including compensation for the loss of use, without extinction of original title. Indigenous peoples' desire to regain possession and control of sacred sites must always be respected.

8. No State shall participate financially or militarily in the involuntary displacement of indigenous populations, or in the subsequent economic exploitation or military use of their territory.
9. The laws and customs of indigenous nations and peoples must be recognized by States' legislative, administrative and judicial institutions and, in case of conflicts with State laws, shall take precedence.
10. No State shall deny an indigenous nation, community, or people residing within its borders the right to participate in the life of the State in whatever manner and to whatever degree they may choose. This includes the right to participate in other forms of collective action and expression.
11. Indigenous nations and peoples continue to own and control their material culture, including archeological, historical and sacred sites, artifacts, designs, knowledge, and works of art. They have the right to regain items of major cultural significance and, in all cases, to the return of the human remains of their ancestors for burial in accordance with their traditions.
12. Indigenous nations and peoples have the right to be educated and conduct business with States in their own languages, and to establish their own educational institutions.
13. No technical, scientific or social investigations, including archeological excavations, shall take place in relation to indigenous nations or peoples, or their lands, without their prior authorization, and their continuing ownership and control.
14. The religious practices of indigenous nations and peoples shall be fully respected and protected by the laws of States and by international law. Indigenous nations and peoples shall always enjoy unrestricted access to, and enjoyment of sacred sites in accordance with their own laws and customs, including the right of privacy.
15. Indigenous nations and peoples are subjects of international law.
16. Treaties and other agreements freely made with indigenous nations or peoples shall be recognized and applied in the same manner and according to the same international laws and principles as treaties and agreements entered into with other States.
17. Disputes regarding the jurisdiction, territories and institutions of an indigenous nation or people are a proper concern of international law, and must be resolved by mutual agreement or valid treaty.
18. Indigenous nations and peoples may engage in self-defense against State actions in conflict with their right to self-determination.
19. Indigenous nations and peoples have the right freely to travel, and to maintain economic, social, cultural and religious relations with each other across State borders.
20. In addition to these rights, indigenous nations and peoples are entitled to the enjoyment of all the human rights and fundamental freedoms enumerated in the international Bill of Rights and other United Nations instruments. In no circumstances shall they be subjected to adverse discrimination.

Appendix 2.3

Draft Declaration on the Rights of Indigenous Peoples (Sub-Commission Text), 1994

Draft United Nations Declaration on the Rights of indigenous Peoples
Sub-Commission Resolution 1994/45

The Sub-Commission on Prevention of Discrimination and Protection of Minorities,

Recalling its resolutions 1985/22 of 29 August 1985, 1991/30 of 29 August 1991, 1992/33 of 27 August 1992, 1993/46 of 26 August 1993,

Taking into account, in particular, paragraph 3 of its resolution 1993/46, in which it decided to postpone until its forty-sixth session consideration of the draft United Nations declaration on the rights of indigenous peoples agreed upon by the members of the Working Group on Indigenous Populations, to request the Secretary-General to submit the draft declaration to the appropriate services in the Centre for Human Rights for its technical revision, and to submit, if possible, the draft declaration to the Commission on Human Rights with the recommendation that the Commission adopt it at its fifty-first session,

Recalling Commission on Human Rights resolution 1994/29 of 4 March 1994, in which the Sub-Commission was urged to complete its consideration of the draft United Nations declaration at its forty-sixth session and to submit it to the Commission at its fifty-first session together with any recommendations thereon,

Bearing in mind General Assembly resolution 47/75 of 14 December 1992, paragraph 12 of Commission on Human Rights resolution 1993/30 of 5 March 1993, paragraph 6 (a) of Commission resolution 1993/31 of 5 March 1993 and paragraph II.28 of the Vienna Declaration and Programme of Action (A/Conf.157/23),

Having considered the report of the Working Group on Indigenous Populations on its twelfth session (E/CN.4/Sub.2/1994/30 and Corr.1), in particular the general comments on the draft declaration and the recommendations contained in chapters II and IX respectively of the report,

Taking into account the technical review of the draft declaration prepared by the Centre for Human Rights (E/CN.4/Sub.2/1994/2 and Add.1),

1. Expresses its satisfaction at the conclusion of the deliberations on the draft United Nations declaration on the rights of indigenous peoples by the Working Group on Indigenous Populations and the general views of the participants as reflected in the report of the Working Group on its twelfth session;
2. Expresses its appreciation to the Chairperson-Rapporteur of the Working Group, Ms. Erica-Irene Daes, and to the present and former members of the Working Group for their contributions to the process of elaboration of the draft declaration;
3. Expresses its appreciation to the Centre for Human Rights for its technical revision of the draft declaration;
4. Decides:

   (a) To adopt the draft United Nations declaration on the rights of indigenous peoples agreed upon by members of the Working Group as contained in the annex to the present resolution;
   (b) To submit the draft declaration to the Commission on Human Rights at its fifty-first session with the request that it consider the draft as expeditiously as possible;
   (c) To request the Secretary-General to transmit the text of the draft declaration to indigenous peoples and organizations, Governments and intergovernmental organizations and to include in the note of transmittal the information that the draft declaration is to be submitted to the Commission on Human Rights at its fifty-first session;

5. Recommends that the Commission on Human Rights and the Economic and Social Council take effective measures to ensure that representatives of indigenous peoples are able to participate in the consideration of the draft declaration by these two bodies, regardless of their consultative status with the Economic and Social Council.

36th meeting
26 August 1994
[Adopted without a vote]

Annex

DRAFT UNITED NATIONS DECLARATION ON THE RIGHTS OF INDIGENOUS PEOPLES

Affirming that indigenous peoples are equal in dignity and rights to all other peoples, while recognizing the right of all peoples to be different, to consider themselves different, and to be respected as such,

Affirming also that all peoples contribute to the diversity and richness of civilizations and cultures, which constitute the common heritage of humankind,

Affirming further that all doctrines, policies and practices based on or advocating superiority of peoples or individuals on the basis of national origin, racial, religious, ethnic or cultural differences are racist, scientifically false, legally invalid, morally condemnable and socially unjust,

Reaffirming also that indigenous peoples, in the exercise of their rights, should be free from discrimination of any kind,

Concerned that indigenous peoples have been deprived of their human rights and fundamental freedoms, resulting, inter alia, in their colonization and dispossession of their lands, territories and resources, thus preventing them from exercising, in particular, their right to development in accordance with their own needs and interests,

Recognizing the urgent need to respect and promote the inherent rights and characteristics of indigenous peoples, especially their rights to their lands, territories and resources, which derive from their political, economic and social structures and from their cultures, spiritual traditions, histories and philosophies,

Welcoming the fact that indigenous peoples are organizing themselves for political, economic, social and cultural enhancement and in order to bring an end to all forms of discrimination and oppression wherever they occur,

Convinced that control by indigenous peoples over developments affecting them and their lands, territories and resources will enable them to maintain and strengthen their institutions, cultures and traditions, and to promote their development in accordance with their aspirations and needs,

Recognizing also that respect for indigenous knowledge, cultures and traditional practices contributes to sustainable and equitable development and proper management of the environment,

Emphasizing the need for demilitarization of the lands and territories of indigenous peoples, which will contribute to peace, economic and social progress and development, understanding and friendly relations among nations and peoples of the world,

Recognizing in particular the right of indigenous families and communities to retain shared responsibility for the upbringing, training, education and well-being of their children,

Recognizing also that indigenous peoples have the right freely to determine their relationships with States in a spirit of coexistence, mutual benefit and full respect,

Considering that treaties, agreements and other arrangements between States and indigenous peoples are properly matters of international concern and responsibility,

Acknowledging that the Charter of the United Nations, the International Covenant on Economic, Social and Cultural Rights and the International Covenant on Civil and Political Rights affirm the fundamental importance of the right of self-determination of all peoples, by virtue of which they freely determine their political status and freely pursue their economic, social and cultural development,

Bearing in mind that nothing in this Declaration may be used to deny any peoples their right of self-determination,

Encouraging States to comply with and effectively implement all international instruments, in particular those related to human rights, as they apply to indigenous peoples, in consultation and cooperation with the peoples concerned,

Emphasizing that the United Nations has an important and continuing role to play in promoting and protecting the rights of indigenous peoples,

Believing that this Declaration is a further important step forward for the recognition, promotion and protection of the rights and freedoms of indigenous peoples and in the development of relevant activities of the United Nations system in this field,

Solemnly proclaims the following United Nations Declaration on the Rights of Indigenous Peoples:

PART I

Article 1

Indigenous peoples have the right to the full and effective enjoyment of all human rights and fundamental freedoms recognized in the Charter of the United Nations, the Universal Declaration of Human Rights and international human rights law.

Article 2

Indigenous individuals and peoples are free and equal to all other individuals and peoples in dignity and rights, and have the right to be free from any kind of adverse discrimination, in particular that based on their indigenous origin or identity.

Article 3

Indigenous peoples have the right of self-determination. By virtue of that right they freely determine their political status and freely pursue their economic, social and cultural development.

Article 4

Indigenous peoples have the right to maintain and strengthen their distinct political, economic, social and cultural characteristics, as well as their legal systems, while retaining their rights to participate fully, if they so choose, in the political, economic, social and cultural life of the State.

Article 5

Every indigenous individual has the right to a nationality.

PART II

Article 6

Indigenous peoples have the collective right to live in freedom, peace and security as distinct peoples and to full guarantees against genocide or any other act of violence, including the removal of indigenous children from their families and communities under any pretext.

In addition, they have the individual rights to life, physical and mental integrity, liberty and security of person.

Article 7

Indigenous peoples have the collective and individual right not to be subjected to ethnocide and cultural genocide, including prevention of and redress for:

(a) Any action which has the aim or effect of depriving them of their integrity as distinct peoples, or of their cultural values or ethnic identities;
(b) Any action which has the aim or effect of dispossessing them of their lands, territories or resources;
(c) Any form of population transfer which has the aim or effect of violating or undermining any of their rights;
(d) Any form of assimilation or integration by other cultures or ways of life imposed on them by legislative, administrative or other measures;
(e) Any form of propaganda directed against them.

Article 8

Indigenous peoples have the collective and individual right to maintain and develop their distinct identities and characteristics, including the right to identify themselves as indigenous and to be recognized as such.

Article 9

Indigenous peoples and individuals have the right to belong to an indigenous community or nation, in accordance with the traditions and customs of the community or nation concerned. No disadvantage of any kind may arise from the exercise of such a right.

Article 10

Indigenous peoples shall not be forcibly removed from their lands or territories. No relocation shall take place without the free and informed consent of the indigenous peoples concerned and after agreement on just and fair compensation and, where possible, with the option of return.

Article 11

Indigenous peoples have the right to special protection and security in periods of armed conflict.

States shall observe international standards, in particular the Fourth Geneva Convention of 1949, for the protection of civilian populations in circumstances of emergency and armed conflict, and shall not:

(a) Recruit indigenous individuals against their will into the armed forces and, in particular, for use against other indigenous peoples;

(b) Recruit indigenous children into the armed forces under any circumstances;
(c) Force indigenous individuals to abandon their lands, territories or means of subsistence, or relocate them in special centres for military purposes;
(d) Force indigenous individuals to work for military purposes under any discriminatory conditions.

PART III

Article 12

Indigenous peoples have the right to practise and revitalize their cultural traditions and customs. This includes the right to maintain, protect and develop the past, present and future manifestations of their cultures, such as archaeological and historical sites, artifacts, designs, ceremonies, technologies and visual and performing arts and literature, as well as the right to the restitution of cultural, intellectual, religious and spiritual property taken without their free and informed consent or in violation of their laws, traditions and customs.

Article 13

Indigenous peoples have the right to manifest, practise, develop and teach their spiritual and religious traditions, customs and ceremonies; the right to maintain, protect, and have access in privacy to their religious and cultural sites; the right to the use and control of ceremonial objects; and the right to the repatriation of human remains.

States shall take effective measures, in conjunction with the indigenous peoples concerned, to ensure that indigenous sacred places, including burial sites, be preserved, respected and protected.

Article 14

Indigenous peoples have the right to revitalize, use, develop and transmit to future generations their histories, languages, oral traditions, philosophies, writing systems and literatures, and to designate and retain their own names for communities, places and persons.

States shall take effective measures, whenever any right of indigenous peoples may be threatened, to ensure this right is protected and also to ensure that they can understand and be understood in political, legal and administrative proceedings, where necessary through the provision of interpretation or by other appropriate means.

PART IV

Article 15

Indigenous children have the right to all levels and forms of education of the State. All indigenous peoples also have this right and the right to establish and control their educational systems and institutions providing education in their own languages, in a manner appropriate to their cultural methods of teaching and learning.

Indigenous children living outside their communities have the right to be provided access to education in their own culture and language.

States shall take effective measures to provide appropriate resources for these purposes.

Article 16

Indigenous peoples have the right to have the dignity and diversity of their cultures, traditions, histories and aspirations appropriately reflected in all forms of education and public information.

States shall take effective measures, in consultation with the indigenous peoples concerned, to eliminate prejudice and discrimination and to promote tolerance, understanding and good relations among indigenous peoples and all segments of society.

Article 17

Indigenous peoples have the right to establish their own media in their own languages. They also have the right to equal access to all forms of non-indigenous media.

States shall take effective measures to ensure that State-owned media duly reflect indigenous cultural diversity.

Article 18

Indigenous peoples have the right to enjoy fully all rights established under international labour law and national labour legislation.

Indigenous individuals have the right not to be subjected to any discriminatory conditions of labour, employment or salary.

PART V

Article 19

Indigenous peoples have the right to participate fully, if they so choose, at all levels of decision-making in matters which may affect their rights, lives and destinies through representatives chosen by themselves in accordance with their own procedures, as well as to maintain and develop their own indigenous decision-making institutions.

Article 20

Indigenous peoples have the right to participate fully, if they so choose, through procedures determined by them, in devising legislative or administrative measures that may affect them.

States shall obtain the free and informed consent of the peoples concerned before adopting and implementing such measures.

Article 21

Indigenous peoples have the right to maintain and develop their political, economic and social systems, to be secure in the enjoyment of their own means of subsistence and development, and to engage freely in all their traditional and other economic activities. Indigenous peoples who have been deprived of their means of subsistence and development are entitled to just and fair compensation.

Article 22

Indigenous peoples have the right to special measures for the immediate, effective and continuing improvement of their economic and social conditions, including in the areas of employment, vocational training and retraining, housing, sanitation, health and social security.

Particular attention shall be paid to the rights and special needs of indigenous elders, women, youth, children and disabled persons.

Article 23

Indigenous peoples have the right to determine and develop priorities and strategies for exercising their right to development. In particular, indigenous peoples have the right to determine and develop all health, housing and other economic and social programmes affecting them and, as far as possible, to administer such programmes through their own institutions.

Article 24

Indigenous peoples have the right to their traditional medicines and health practices, including the right to the protection of vital medicinal plants, animals and minerals.

They also have the right to access, without any discrimination, to all medical institutions, health services and medical care.

PART VI

Article 25

Indigenous peoples have the right to maintain and strengthen their distinctive spiritual and material relationship with the lands, territories, waters and coastal seas and other resources which they have traditionally owned or otherwise occupied or used, and to uphold their responsibilities to future generations in this regard.

Article 26

Indigenous peoples have the right to own, develop, control and use the lands and territories, including the total environment of the lands, air, waters, coastal seas, sea-ice, flora and fauna and other resources which they have traditionally owned or otherwise occupied or used. This includes the right to the full recognition of their laws, traditions and customs, land-tenure systems and institutions for the development and management of resources, and the right to effective measures by States to prevent any interference with, alienation of or encroachment upon these rights.

Article 27

Indigenous peoples have the right to the restitution of the lands, territories and resources which they have traditionally owned or otherwise occupied or used, and which have been confiscated, occupied, used or damaged without their free and informed consent. Where this is not possible, they have the right to just and fair compensation. Unless otherwise freely agreed upon by the peoples concerned, compensation shall take the form of lands, territories and resources equal in quality, size and legal status.

Article 28

Indigenous peoples have the right to the conservation, restoration and protection of the total environment and the productive capacity of their lands, territories and resources, as well as to assistance for this purpose from States and through international cooperation. Military activities shall not take place in the lands and territories of indigenous peoples, unless otherwise freely agreed upon by the peoples concerned.

States shall take effective measures to ensure that no storage or disposal of hazardous materials shall take place in the lands and territories of indigenous peoples.

States shall also take effective measures to ensure, as needed, that programmes for monitoring, maintaining and restoring the health of indigenous peoples, as developed and implemented by the peoples affected by such materials, are duly implemented.

Article 29

Indigenous peoples are entitled to the recognition of the full ownership, control and protection of their cultural and intellectual property.

They have the right to special measures to control, develop and protect their sciences, technologies and cultural manifestations, including human and other genetic resources, seeds, medicines, knowledge of the properties of fauna and flora, oral traditions, literatures, designs and visual and performing arts.

Article 30

Indigenous peoples have the right to determine and develop priorities and strategies for the development or use of their lands, territories and other resources, including the right to require that States obtain their free and informed consent prior to the approval of any project affecting their lands, territories and other resources, particularly in connection with the development, utilization or exploitation of mineral, water or other resources. Pursuant to agreement with the indigenous peoples concerned, just and fair compensation shall be provided for any such activities and measures taken to mitigate adverse environmental, economic, social, cultural or spiritual impact.

PART VII

Article 31

Indigenous peoples, as a specific form of exercising their right to self-determination, have the right to autonomy or self-government in matters relating to their internal and local affairs, including culture, religion, education, information, media, health, housing, employment, social welfare, economic activities, land and resources management, environment and entry by non-members, as well as ways and means for financing these autonomous functions.

Article 32

Indigenous peoples have the collective right to determine their own citizenship in accordance with their customs and traditions. Indigenous citizenship does not impair the right of indigenous individuals to obtain citizenship of the States in which they live.

Indigenous peoples have the right to determine the structures and to select the membership of their institutions in accordance with their own procedures.

Article 33

Indigenous peoples have the right to promote, develop and maintain their institutional structures and their distinctive juridical customs, traditions, procedures and practices, in accordance with internationally recognized human rights standards.

Article 34

Indigenous peoples have the collective right to determine the responsibilities of individuals to their communities.

Article 35

Indigenous peoples, in particular those divided by international borders, have the right to maintain and develop contacts, relations and cooperation, including activities for spiritual, cultural, political, economic and social purposes, with other peoples across borders.

States shall take effective measures to ensure the exercise and implementation of this right.

Article 36

Indigenous peoples have the right to the recognition, observance and enforcement of treaties, agreements and other constructive arrangements concluded with States or their successors, according to their original spirit and intent, and to have States honour and respect such treaties, agreements and other constructive arrangements. Conflicts and disputes which cannot otherwise be settled should be submitted to competent international bodies agreed to by all parties concerned.

PART VIII

Article 37

States shall take effective and appropriate measures, in consultation with the indigenous peoples concerned, to give full effect to the provisions of this Declaration. The rights recognized herein shall be adopted and included in national legislation in such a manner that indigenous peoples can avail themselves of such rights in practice.

Article 38

Indigenous peoples have the right to have access to adequate financial and technical assistance, from States and through international cooperation, to pursue freely their political, economic, social, cultural and spiritual development and for the enjoyment of the rights and freedoms recognized in this Declaration.

Article 39

Indigenous peoples have the right to have access to and prompt decision through mutually acceptable and fair procedures for the resolution of conflicts and disputes with States, as well as to effective remedies for all infringements of their individual and collective rights. Such a decision shall take into consideration the customs, traditions, rules and legal systems of the indigenous peoples concerned.

Article 40

The organs and specialized agencies of the United Nations system and other intergovernmental organizations shall contribute to the full realization of the provisions of this Declaration through the mobilization, inter alia, of financial cooperation and technical assistance. Ways and means of ensuring participation of indigenous peoples on issues affecting them shall be established.

Article 41

The United Nations shall take the necessary steps to ensure the implementation of this Declaration including the creation of a body at the highest level with special competence in this field and with the direct participation of indigenous peoples. All United Nations bodies shall promote respect for and full application of the provisions of this Declaration.

PART IX

Article 42

The rights recognized herein constitute the minimum standards for the survival, dignity and well-being of the indigenous peoples of the world.

Article 43

All the rights and freedoms recognized herein are equally guaranteed to male and female indigenous individuals.

Article 44

Nothing in this Declaration may be construed as diminishing or extinguishing existing or future rights indigenous peoples may have or acquire.

Article 45

Nothing in this Declaration may be interpreted as implying for any State, group or person any right to engage in any activity or to perform any act contrary to the Charter of the United Nations.

Appendix 2.4

Declaration on the Rights of Indigenous Peoples, 2007

General Assembly

Distr.: General
2 October 2007

Sixty-first session
Agenda item 68

Resolution adopted by the General Assembly
[*without reference to a Main Committee (A/61/L.67 and Add.1)*]

61/295. United Nations Declaration on the Rights of Indigenous Peoples

The General Assembly,

Taking note of the recommendation of the Human Rights Council contained in its resolution 1/2 of 29 June 2006,[1] by which the Council adopted the text of the United Nations Declaration on the Rights of Indigenous Peoples,

Recalling its resolution 61/178 of 20 December 2006, by which it decided to defer consideration of and action on the Declaration to allow time for further consultations thereon, and also decided to conclude its consideration before the end of the sixty-first session of the General Assembly,

Adopts the United Nations Declaration on the Rights of Indigenous Peoples as contained in the annex to the present resolution.

107th plenary meeting
13 September 2007

Annex

United Nations Declaration on the Rights of Indigenous Peoples

The General Assembly,

Guided by the purposes and principles of the Charter of the United Nations, and good faith in the fulfilment of the obligations assumed by States in accordance with the Charter,

Affirming that indigenous peoples are equal to all other peoples, while recognizing the right of all peoples to be different, to consider themselves different, and to be respected as such,

Affirming also that all peoples contribute to the diversity and richness of civilizations and cultures, which constitute the common heritage of humankind,

Affirming further that all doctrines, policies and practices based on or advocating superiority of peoples or individuals on the basis of national origin or racial, religious, ethnic or cultural differences are racist, scientifically false, legally invalid, morally condemnable and socially unjust,

Reaffirming that indigenous peoples, in the exercise of their rights, should be free from discrimination of any kind,

Concerned that indigenous peoples have suffered from historic injustices as a result of, inter alia, their colonization and dispossession of their lands, territories and resources, thus preventing them from exercising, in particular, their right to development in accordance with their own needs and interests,

Recognizing the urgent need to respect and promote the inherent rights of indigenous peoples which derive from their political, economic and social structures and from their cultures, spiritual traditions, histories and philosophies, especially their rights to their lands, territories and resources,

Recognizing also the urgent need to respect and promote the rights of indigenous peoples affirmed in treaties, agreements and other constructive arrangements with States,

Welcoming the fact that indigenous peoples are organizing themselves for political, economic, social and cultural enhancement and in order to bring to an end all forms of discrimination and oppression wherever they occur,

Convinced that control by indigenous peoples over developments affecting them and their lands, territories and resources will enable them to maintain and strengthen their institutions, cultures and traditions, and to promote their development in accordance with their aspirations and needs,

Recognizing that respect for indigenous knowledge, cultures and traditional practices contributes to sustainable and equitable development and proper management of the environment,

Emphasizing the contribution of the demilitarization of the lands and territories of indigenous peoples to peace, economic and social progress and development, understanding and friendly relations among nations and peoples of the world,

Recognizing in particular the right of indigenous families and communities to retain shared responsibility for the upbringing, training, education and well-being of their children, consistent with the rights of the child,

Considering that the rights affirmed in treaties, agreements and other constructive arrangements between States and indigenous peoples are, in some situations, matters of international concern, interest, responsibility and character,

Considering also that treaties, agreements and other constructive arrangements, and the relationship they represent, are the basis for a strengthened partnership between indigenous peoples and States,

Acknowledging that the Charter of the United Nations, the International Covenant on Economic, Social and Cultural Rights[2] and the International Covenant on Civil and Political Rights,[2] as well as the Vienna Declaration and Programme of Action,[3] affirm the fundamental importance of the right to self-determination of all peoples, by virtue of which they freely determine their political status and freely pursue their economic, social and cultural development,

Bearing in mind that nothing in this Declaration may be used to deny any peoples their right to self-determination, exercised in conformity with international law,

Convinced that the recognition of the rights of indigenous peoples in this Declaration will enhance harmonious and cooperative relations between the State and indigenous peoples, based on principles of justice, democracy, respect for human rights, non-discrimination and good faith,

Encouraging States to comply with and effectively implement all their obligations as they apply to indigenous peoples under international instruments, in particular those related to human rights, in consultation and cooperation with the peoples concerned,

Emphasizing that the United Nations has an important and continuing role to play in promoting and protecting the rights of indigenous peoples,

Believing that this Declaration is a further important step forward for the recognition, promotion and protection of the rights and freedoms of indigenous peoples and in the development of relevant activities of the United Nations system in this field,

Recognizing and reaffirming that indigenous individuals are entitled without discrimination to all human rights recognized in international law, and that indigenous peoples possess collective rights which are indispensable for their existence, well-being and integral development as peoples,

Recognizing that the situation of indigenous peoples varies from region to region and from country to country and that the significance of national and regional particularities and various historical and cultural backgrounds should be taken into consideration,

Solemnly proclaims the following United Nations Declaration on the Rights of Indigenous Peoples as a standard of achievement to be pursued in a spirit of partnership and mutual respect:

Article 1

Indigenous peoples have the right to the full enjoyment, as a collective or as individuals, of all human rights and fundamental freedoms as recognized in the Charter of the United Nations, the Universal Declaration of Human Rights[4] and international human rights law.

Article 2

Indigenous peoples and individuals are free and equal to all other peoples and individuals and have the right to be free from any kind of discrimination, in the exercise of their rights, in particular that based on their indigenous origin or identity.

Article 3

Indigenous peoples have the right to self-determination. By virtue of that right they freely determine their political status and freely pursue their economic, social and cultural development.

Article 4

Indigenous peoples, in exercising their right to self-determination, have the right to autonomy or self-government in matters relating to their internal and local affairs, as well as ways and means for financing their autonomous functions.

Article 5

Indigenous peoples have the right to maintain and strengthen their distinct political, legal, economic, social and cultural institutions, while retaining their right to participate fully, if they so choose, in the political, economic, social and cultural life of the State.

Article 6

Every indigenous individual has the right to a nationality.

Article 7

1. Indigenous individuals have the rights to life, physical and mental integrity, liberty and security of person.
2. Indigenous peoples have the collective right to live in freedom, peace and security as distinct peoples and shall not be subjected to any act of genocide or any other act of violence, including forcibly removing children of the group to another group.

Article 8

1. Indigenous peoples and individuals have the right not to be subjected to forced assimilation or destruction of their culture.
2. States shall provide effective mechanisms for prevention of, and redress for:

   (a) Any action which has the aim or effect of depriving them of their integrity as distinct peoples, or of their cultural values or ethnic identities;
   (b) Any action which has the aim or effect of dispossessing them of their lands, territories or resources;
   (c) Any form of forced population transfer which has the aim or effect of violating or undermining any of their rights;
   (d) Any form of forced assimilation or integration;
   (e) Any form of propaganda designed to promote or incite racial or ethnic discrimination directed against them.

Article 9

Indigenous peoples and individuals have the right to belong to an indigenous community or nation, in accordance with the traditions and customs of the community or nation concerned. No discrimination of any kind may arise from the exercise of such a right.

Article 10

Indigenous peoples shall not be forcibly removed from their lands or territories. No relocation shall take place without the free, prior and informed consent of the indigenous peoples concerned and after agreement on just and fair compensation and, where possible, with the option of return.

Article 11

1. Indigenous peoples have the right to practise and revitalize their cultural traditions and customs. This includes the right to maintain, protect and develop the past, present and future manifestations of their cultures, such as archaeological and historical sites, artefacts, designs, ceremonies, technologies and visual and performing arts and literature.

2. States shall provide redress through effective mechanisms, which may include restitution, developed in conjunction with indigenous peoples, with respect to their cultural, intellectual, religious and spiritual property taken without their free, prior and informed consent or in violation of their laws, traditions and customs.

Article 12

1. Indigenous peoples have the right to manifest, practise, develop and teach their spiritual and religious traditions, customs and ceremonies; the right to maintain, protect, and have access in privacy to their religious and cultural sites; the right to the use and control of their ceremonial objects; and the right to the repatriation of their human remains.
2. States shall seek to enable the access and/or repatriation of ceremonial objects and human remains in their possession through fair, transparent and effective mechanisms developed in conjunction with indigenous peoples concerned.

Article 13

1. Indigenous peoples have the right to revitalize, use, develop and transmit to future generations their histories, languages, oral traditions, philosophies, writing systems and literatures, and to designate and retain their own names for communities, places and persons.
2. States shall take effective measures to ensure that this right is protected and also to ensure that indigenous peoples can understand and be understood in political, legal and administrative proceedings, where necessary through the provision of interpretation or by other appropriate means.

Article 14

1. Indigenous peoples have the right to establish and control their educational systems and institutions providing education in their own languages, in a manner appropriate to their cultural methods of teaching and learning.
2. Indigenous individuals, particularly children, have the right to all levels and forms of education of the State without discrimination.
3. States shall, in conjunction with indigenous peoples, take effective measures, in order for indigenous individuals, particularly children, including those living outside their communities, to have access, when possible, to an education in their own culture and provided in their own language.

Article 15

1. Indigenous peoples have the right to the dignity and diversity of their cultures, traditions, histories and aspirations which shall be appropriately reflected in education and public information.
2. States shall take effective measures, in consultation and cooperation with the indigenous peoples concerned, to combat prejudice and eliminate discrimination and to promote tolerance, understanding and good relations among indigenous peoples and all other segments of society.

Article 16

1. Indigenous peoples have the right to establish their own media in their own languages and to have access to all forms of non-indigenous media without discrimination.

2. States shall take effective measures to ensure that State-owned media duly reflect indigenous cultural diversity. States, without prejudice to ensuring full freedom of expression, should encourage privately owned media to adequately reflect indigenous cultural diversity.

Article 17

1. Indigenous individuals and peoples have the right to enjoy fully all rights established under applicable international and domestic labour law.
2. States shall in consultation and cooperation with indigenous peoples take specific measures to protect indigenous children from economic exploitation and from performing any work that is likely to be hazardous or to interfere with the child's education, or to be harmful to the child's health or physical, mental, spiritual, moral or social development, taking into account their special vulnerability and the importance of education for their empowerment.
3. Indigenous individuals have the right not to be subjected to any discriminatory conditions of labour and, inter alia, employment or salary.

Article 18

Indigenous peoples have the right to participate in decision-making in matters which would affect their rights, through representatives chosen by themselves in accordance with their own procedures, as well as to maintain and develop their own indigenous decision-making institutions.

Article 19

States shall consult and cooperate in good faith with the indigenous peoples concerned through their own representative institutions in order to obtain their free, prior and informed consent before adopting and implementing legislative or administrative measures that may affect them.

Article 20

1. Indigenous peoples have the right to maintain and develop their political, economic and social systems or institutions, to be secure in the enjoyment of their own means of subsistence and development, and to engage freely in all their traditional and other economic activities.
2. Indigenous peoples deprived of their means of subsistence and development are entitled to just and fair redress.

Article 21

1. Indigenous peoples have the right, without discrimination, to the improvement of their economic and social conditions, including, inter alia, in the areas of education, employment, vocational training and retraining, housing, sanitation, health and social security.
2. States shall take effective measures and, where appropriate, special measures to ensure continuing improvement of their economic and social conditions. Particular attention shall be paid to the rights and special needs of indigenous elders, women, youth, children and persons with disabilities.

Article 22

1. Particular attention shall be paid to the rights and special needs of indigenous elders, women, youth, children and persons with disabilities in the implementation of this Declaration.
2. States shall take measures, in conjunction with indigenous peoples, to ensure that indigenous women and children enjoy the full protection and guarantees against all forms of violence and discrimination.

Article 23

Indigenous peoples have the right to determine and develop priorities and strategies for exercising their right to development. In particular, indigenous peoples have the right to be actively involved in developing and determining health, housing and other economic and social programmes affecting them and, as far as possible, to administer such programmes through their own institutions.

Article 24

1. Indigenous peoples have the right to their traditional medicines and to maintain their health practices, including the conservation of their vital medicinal plants, animals and minerals. Indigenous individuals also have the right to access, without any discrimination, to all social and health services.
2. Indigenous individuals have an equal right to the enjoyment of the highest attainable standard of physical and mental health. States shall take the necessary steps with a view to achieving progressively the full realization of this right.

Article 25

Indigenous peoples have the right to maintain and strengthen their distinctive spiritual relationship with their traditionally owned or otherwise occupied and used lands, territories, waters and coastal seas and other resources and to uphold their responsibilities to future generations in this regard.

Article 26

1. Indigenous peoples have the right to the lands, territories and resources which they have traditionally owned, occupied or otherwise used or acquired.
2. Indigenous peoples have the right to own, use, develop and control the lands, territories and resources that they possess by reason of traditional ownership or other traditional occupation or use, as well as those which they have otherwise acquired.
3. States shall give legal recognition and protection to these lands, territories and resources. Such recognition shall be conducted with due respect to the customs, traditions and land tenure systems of the indigenous peoples concerned.

Article 27

States shall establish and implement, in conjunction with indigenous peoples concerned, a fair, independent, impartial, open and transparent process, giving due recognition to indigenous peoples' laws, traditions, customs and land tenure systems, to recognize and adjudicate the rights of indigenous peoples pertaining to their lands, territories and resources, including those which were traditionally owned or otherwise occupied or used. Indigenous peoples shall have the right to participate in this process.

Article 28

1. Indigenous peoples have the right to redress, by means that can include restitution or, when this is not possible, just, fair and equitable compensation, for the lands, territories and resources which they have traditionally owned or otherwise occupied or used, and which have been confiscated, taken, occupied, used or damaged without their free, prior and informed consent.
2. Unless otherwise freely agreed upon by the peoples concerned, compensation shall take the form of lands, territories and resources equal in quality, size and legal status or of monetary compensation or other appropriate redress.

Article 29

1. Indigenous peoples have the right to the conservation and protection of the environment and the productive capacity of their lands or territories and resources. States shall establish and implement assistance programmes for indigenous peoples for such conservation and protection, without discrimination.
2. States shall take effective measures to ensure that no storage or disposal of hazardous materials shall take place in the lands or territories of indigenous peoples without their free, prior and informed consent.
3. States shall also take effective measures to ensure, as needed, that programmes for monitoring, maintaining and restoring the health of indigenous peoples, as developed and implemented by the peoples affected by such materials, are duly implemented.

Article 30

1. Military activities shall not take place in the lands or territories of indigenous peoples, unless justified by a relevant public interest or otherwise freely agreed with or requested by the indigenous peoples concerned.
2. States shall undertake effective consultations with the indigenous peoples concerned, through appropriate procedures and in particular through their representative institutions, prior to using their lands or territories for military activities.

Article 31

1. Indigenous peoples have the right to maintain, control, protect and develop their cultural heritage, traditional knowledge and traditional cultural expressions, as well as the manifestations of their sciences, technologies and cultures, including human and genetic resources, seeds, medicines, knowledge of the properties of fauna and flora, oral traditions, literatures, designs, sports and traditional games and visual and performing arts. They also have the right to maintain, control, protect and develop their intellectual property over such cultural heritage, traditional knowledge, and traditional cultural expressions.
2. In conjunction with indigenous peoples, States shall take effective measures to recognize and protect the exercise of these rights.

Article 32

1. Indigenous peoples have the right to determine and develop priorities and strategies for the development or use of their lands or territories and other resources.
2. States shall consult and cooperate in good faith with the indigenous peoples concerned through their own representative institutions in order to obtain their free and informed consent prior to the approval of any project affecting their lands or territories and other resources, particularly in connection with the development, utilization or exploitation of mineral, water or other resources.
3. States shall provide effective mechanisms for just and fair redress for any such activities, and appropriate measures shall be taken to mitigate adverse environmental, economic, social, cultural or spiritual impact.

Article 33

1. Indigenous peoples have the right to determine their own identity or membership in accordance with their customs and traditions. This does not impair the right of indigenous individuals to obtain citizenship of the States in which they live.
2. Indigenous peoples have the right to determine the structures and to select the membership of their institutions in accordance with their own procedures.

Article 34

Indigenous peoples have the right to promote, develop and maintain their institutional structures and their distinctive customs, spirituality, traditions, procedures, practices and, in the cases where they exist, juridical systems or customs, in accordance with international human rights standards.

Article 35

Indigenous peoples have the right to determine the responsibilities of individuals to their communities.

Article 36

1. Indigenous peoples, in particular those divided by international borders, have the right to maintain and develop contacts, relations and cooperation, including activities for spiritual, cultural, political, economic and social purposes, with their own members as well as other peoples across borders.
2. States, in consultation and cooperation with indigenous peoples, shall take effective measures to facilitate the exercise and ensure the implementation of this right.

Article 37

1. Indigenous peoples have the right to the recognition, observance and enforcement of treaties, agreements and other constructive arrangements concluded with States or their successors and to have States honour and respect such treaties, agreements and other constructive arrangements.
2. Nothing in this Declaration may be interpreted as diminishing or eliminating the rights of indigenous peoples contained in treaties, agreements and other constructive arrangements.

Article 38

States in consultation and cooperation with indigenous peoples, shall take the appropriate measures, including legislative measures, to achieve the ends of this Declaration.

Article 39

Indigenous peoples have the right to have access to financial and technical assistance from States and through international cooperation, for the enjoyment of the rights contained in this Declaration.

Article 40

Indigenous peoples have the right to access to and prompt decision through just and fair procedures for the resolution of conflicts and disputes with States or other parties, as well as to effective remedies for all infringements of their individual and collective rights. Such a decision shall give due consideration to the customs, traditions, rules and legal systems of the indigenous peoples concerned and international human rights.

Article 41

The organs and specialized agencies of the United Nations system and other intergovernmental organizations shall contribute to the full realization of the provisions of this Declaration through the mobilization, inter alia, of financial cooperation and technical assistance. Ways and means of ensuring participation of indigenous peoples on issues affecting them shall be established.

Article 42

The United Nations, its bodies, including the Permanent Forum on Indigenous Issues, and specialized agencies, including at the country level, and States shall promote respect for and full application of the provisions of this Declaration and follow up the effectiveness of this Declaration.

Article 43

The rights recognized herein constitute the minimum standards for the survival, dignity and well-being of the indigenous peoples of the world.

Article 44

All the rights and freedoms recognized herein are equally guaranteed to male and female indigenous individuals.

Article 45

Nothing in this Declaration may bc construed as diminishing or extinguishing the rights indigenous peoples have now or may acquire in the future.

Article 46

1. Nothing in this Declaration may be interpreted as implying for any State, people, group or person any right to engage in any activity or to perform any act contrary to the Charter of the United Nations or construed as authorizing or encouraging any action which would dismember or impair, totally or in part, the territorial integrity or political unity of sovereign and independent States.

2. In the exercise of the rights enunciated in the present Declaration, human rights and fundamental freedoms of all shall be respected. The exercise of the rights set forth in this Declaration shall be subject only to such limitations as are determined by law and in accordance with international human rights obligations. Any such limitations shall be non-discriminatory and strictly necessary solely for the purpose of securing due recognition and respect for the rights and freedoms of others and for meeting the just and most compelling requirements of a democratic society.
3. The provisions set forth in this Declaration shall be interpreted in accordance with the principles of justice, democracy, respect for human rights, equality, non-discrimination, good governance and good faith.

Notes

1 See *Official Records of the General Assembly, Sixty-first Session, Supplement No. 53* (A/61/53), part one, chap. II, sect. A.
2 See resolution 2200 A (XXI), annex.
3 A/CONF.157/24 (Part I), chap. III.
4 Resolution 217 A (III).

Appendix 5.1

Compliance detail by country

Country	*Status of Indigenous rights, as of December 31, 2014*	*Behavior*
THE ARCTIC		
Greenland (Denmark)	Self-governing within Danish realm since 1979. Has been equal part of Danish realm and has had representatives in Danish Parliament since 1953. In 2009, new Act on Self-Government provided increased political self-determination. Internal political issues in Greenland. Greenland established own Human Rights Commission in 2013.	Strong
Finland	Negotiations planned regarding a new land use model. Finnish government refuses to address Saami land rights. Treats Saami as a minority, refuses special legislation for Saami. Focus of state is on equality for all. Finland sees itself as neutral in negotiations.	Moderate
Norway	Saami status recognized by constitutional amendment. Saami Parliament has consultation agreement with Norwegian Parliament. Government plan to map land rights. Land under pressure. Government will base new decisions on UN DRIP.	Strong
Russian Federation	Article 69 of Russian Constitution establishes cultural, political, and territorial rights for some small Indigenous groups. Land rights denied. Multiple issues with implementation due to natural resource legislation. Indigenous peoples lack access to natural resources and participation in decision making. Law allowing subsistence hunting and fishing not followed in practice. Law guaranteeing participation in decision making adopted but without procedures. Indigenous peoples not recognized by Russia, although some small populations of Northern peoples have certain rights.	Weak
Sweden	Saami Parliament Act but Saami Parliament acts under Swedish Parliament. Change made to Swedish Constitution to recognize Saami but as a people. Recognizes reindeer herding areas, but no designated lands for Saami. Saami Parliament criticizes Sweden for lack of self-determination. Saami Language Act to protect its use as an official language.	Moderate

continued

Appendix 5.1 Continued

Country	*Status of Indigenous rights, as of December 31, 2014*	*Behavior*
NORTH AMERICA[1]		
Canada	First Nations have reserves and self-governance although limited by Indian Act. Section 35 of 1982 Constitution recognizes and affirms existing Aboriginal and treaty rights. Self-governing Inuit territory of Nunavut established 1999. Land claims negotiations ongoing; many settled. Many government programs and initiatives to reduce socio-economic disparities. Land and resources rights for Indigenous peoples limited. Canada recognizes cultural rights as collective rights. Ongoing disputes over nature of consultation and consent, especially with regard to natural resource extraction. In 2014 Tsilhqot'in case, Supreme Court affirms existence of Aboriginal title.	Moderate
USA	566 federally recognized Indigenous nations, many with treaty rights, although treaty rights are largely ignored by the federal government. American Indian law often subject to inconsistent rulings by US Supreme Court. Tribal sovereignty theoretically exists but is limited by plenary power of US Congress. US government trust status, so federal government hold land title in trust, thus limiting self-determination. Financial trust accounts severely mismanaged by federal government. Collective rights of Indigenous peoples acknowledged in 2010.	Moderate
LATIN AMERICA		
Argentina	Thirty-five Indigenous peoples are recognized. Development efforts are encroaching on Indigenous land, violating their collective rights. Indigenous peoples are pressured or coerced into renouncing their lands. Law of 2006 prevents land evictions yet forced evictions continue. Indigenous education initiatives not implemented. Autonomies not respected.	Weak
Bolivia	Indigenous hold collective land title under legal concept of Native Community Lands. UN DRIP ratified as law in country. New Constitution recognizes multinational state and pre-existence of Indigenous peoples. Indigenous peoples defined as nationalities with language and cultural rights. Indigenous languages are official languages along with Spanish. Community democracy is accepted as equal with elective democracy. New Constitution has special chapter on Indigenous rights, including collective cultural rights, self-determination, collective ownership of territories, autonomous management of territories, and exclusive use of natural resources in their territories. Conflicts over highway construction in Indigenous territory. Indigenous autonomies law of 2010, yet progress is slow. Morales government elected to third term in 2014. Mining law of 2014 has no provision for free, prior, and informed consent.	Moderate

Brazil	Government increasingly refuses to recognize Indigenous territories in favor of development and natural resource extraction projects as economic growth remains the government's priority. Conflicts especially over land loss related to hydroelectricity, mining, and deforestation. Biofuel production is placing pressure on Indigenous land, which is delaying demarcation. Some hydro projects and associated roads will negatively impact Indigenous peoples living in voluntary isolation. Efforts to increase social services and language preservation. Land evictions, sometimes violent, for purposes of resource extraction. No recognized Indigenous autonomy. Limited to no consultation on development projects.	Weak
Chile	Constitution does not recognize Indigenous peoples or their rights, although government has called for Indigenous consultation on institutional and legal reforms. Slow land return has sparked protest and violent police repression. Indigenous protest criminalized. Heavy protest and repression in Rapa Nui. Indigenous consultation fails to meet standards, so protest often results.	Moderate
Colombia	Constitution of 1991 recognizes ethnic and cultural diversity as well as Indigenous rights and territories. One-third of national territory titled as Indigenous reserves, owned collectively by Indigenous communities. Free Trade Agreements with USA, Canada, and Switzerland encourage privatization of Indigenous lands and resources. Ongoing internal war negatively impacts Indigenous peoples. Government initiatives to guarantee rights of the displaced. Conflicts over resource extraction on Indigenous territories. Many gains in Indigenous rights have been lost in recent years. Recent regulation that Indigenous must permanently occupy their land in order to retain it. Law of 2014 created system to operationalize Indigenous administration in their territories.	Moderate
Costa Rica	Indigenous "reserves" set up in 1956. Indigenous Law enacted in 1977 but territorial rights in it have never been respected. ILO 169 has constitutional status. Yet, ongoing dispossession of lands and natural resources. Widespread discrimination in public institutions. Conflicts over Indigenous land repressed by police who protect business interests. Current government rejects Indigenous rights. Obligation to consult, yet government ignores. Government favors multiculturalism agenda in education rather than respecting Indigenous specific education.	Weak
Ecuador	Constitutional recognition of intercultural and multinational character of country. Lack of enforcement and enabling legislation for Indigenous rights. Conflicts over oil and mining. Indigenous leaders accused of terrorism and security-related crimes. Forms of Indigenous protest criminalized. Nueva Loja court found Chevron-Texaco guilty of environmental damage to Amazon, awarded $8 billion in damages, call for public apology. Case against government in Inter-American Court of Human Rights over oil concession granted in Indigenous territory. Demands for prior consultation.	Weak

continued

Appendix 5.1 Continued

Country	*Status of Indigenous rights, as of December 31, 2014*	*Behavior*
Guatemala	Indigenous population is majority but treated as minority. Conditions not improved substantially since Peace Accords signed in 1996. National policy against racism and discrimination. Many political constituencies resist Indigenous land rights in favor of status quo power structure and ethnic integration. Resource extraction licenses in Indigenous areas is an issue, as these projects threaten the Indigenous way of life in these areas. Government held consultations with Indigenous communities over these licenses and then ignored the results, claiming that the consultations were not legally valid. Land registry office has produced regulations for titling of communal Indigenous lands, but no system yet implemented. Conflicts over natural resource development projects encroaching on Indigenous territories without adequate consultation. Violent evictions of Indigenous leaders protesting development projects. One municipality returned title and rights to Indigenous community.	Weak
Mexico	Article 6 of amended Constitution declares Mexico a pluri-cultural country. San Andreas Accords of 1996 included territorial and political rights for Indigenous peoples. In 2001 Mexican Congress passed Law on Indigenous Rights and Culture, but did not integrate rights from San Andreas Accords. Some states have recognized and are implementing portions of San Andreas Accords. Land conflicts and pockets of violence continue in Chiapas. Issues in Oaxaca over water and cultural rights, including reports of violent military repression. Conflicts over natural resource development projects encroaching on Indigenous territories. Increased militarization of development project areas as well as over illegal drug trade. Deepening of conflicts in Indigenous territories as Indigenous peoples are more actively asserting self-determination and their own views of development.	Weak
Nicaragua	Constitution of 1987 recognizes collective rights of Indigenous communities, including some communal land title. Some recent legislation to improve regional autonomy. Autonomous education system recognized. Indigenous rights advances closely linked to volatile political situation. Conflicts remain over Indigenous land ownership. Army plays major role in managing natural resource development projects. Government agencies interfere with Indigenous governments and autonomous territories.	Moderate

Panama	Constitution recognizes collective right to autonomous Indigenous territories, although government has declined to recognize some communities. Recognizes Indigenous congresses as autonomous government entities. Some forced displacements without free, prior, and informed consent have been reported, especially related to hydroelectric power. Some reports of land incursions by local farmers which the government does not enforce. Police repression in Indigenous communities, especially over natural resource extraction and control of the drug trade. Dam construction flooded Indigenous lands, without compensation.	Moderate
Paraguay	Few national policies for Indigenous peoples, although ILO 169 has been transposed into legislation and Article 64 of Constitution says communal lands are inalienable. Inter-American Court of Human Rights has intervened in cases related to land, food, water, and medical care; resources allocated for resolution. Atmosphere of discrimination remains. Indigenous lands often taken through coerced consent for agribusiness. Gap between recognition of rights and implementation.	Weak
Peru	Right to communal lands in 1979 Constitution, but recent government actions have eroded these rights in favor of economic development. Attempts to create an institutional structure to deal with Indigenous issues. No enshrinement of Indigenous rights in Constitution. Law passed on prior consultation with Indigenous peoples but does not specify when consent needs to be obtained and final decision rests with state. Government has distributed draft regulations. Law to return "unused and unoccupied" to the government to be released for development. Conflicts over mining and bilingual education.	Weak
Suriname	Legislative system does not recognize Indigenous peoples. No legislation on Indigenous peoples' land or other rights. Only country in Western hemisphere that does not recognize Indigenous peoples in any way. In 2007, an Indigenous community won material damages over logging and mining through the Inter-American Court of Human Rights but government has not complied and implementation has lagged. Without any legal protection, violations of Indigenous peoples' rights and territories continue. Development projects go forward without Indigenous consultation or participation.	Weak
Venezuela	Recognizes more than forty Indigenous peoples. Constitution of 1999 enshrines Indigenous rights and enhances Indigenous participation in national politics. Collective land titles have been issued to Indigenous communities. Ministry for Indigenous Peoples. Indigenous movement within country has shifted focus to implementing Indigenous rights in governmental policies; much frustration over lack of progress, especially in land demarcation and consultation. Government passes paternalistic laws that emphasize welfare provision (e.g., Organic Law on Indigenous Peoples and Communities) rather than Indigenous rights. Conflicts over illegal mining.	Moderate

continued

Appendix 5.1 Continued

Country	*Status of Indigenous rights, as of December 31, 2014*	*Behavior*
PACIFIC		
Australia	*Terra nullius* doctrine overturned in 1980s. Policy of reconciliation in place since 1990s. Ministry for Reconciliation. Apology offered by new Rudd government in 2008. Some recognition of collective rights of Indigenous people and partial autonomy for Aboriginal communities, although government in 2007 conducted "Emergency Intervention" in Northern Territories by suspending the Racial Discrimination Act. In 2011, government launched consultations on possible recognition in Constitution. In 2011, independent National Congress of Australia's First Peoples established to advance Indigenous rights. Huge socio-economic gap between Indigenous and non-Indigenous populations.	Moderate
Guam	Unorganized, unincorporated territory of the USA. Longest colonized possession in the world. Does not have own constitution but does have an Organic Act that grants US citizenship. Only part of US Constitution applies. Has been on UN list of Non-Self-Governing Territories since 1946. US re-militarization activity threatens Indigenous territory. Some decolonization discussions ongoing.	Weak
New Zealand-Aotearoa	Excels in language, cultural, and educational rights. Waitangi Tribunal and treaty settlements process underway since 1990s; many settlements finalized, although self-determination outcomes are limited. Maori is official language, alongside English. Extensive government programs to reduce socio-economic disparities, yet large gaps remain. Marine and Coastal Area Act of 2011 highly detrimental to Maori rights over foreshore and seabed. Petroleum surveying done without consultation. UN Special Rapporteur's recommendations ignored. Maori Party holds seats in Parliament. Waitangi Tribunal affirmed in 2014 that Maori never ceded sovereignty in Treaty of Waitangi.	Moderate
ASIA		
Bangladesh	No constitutional recognition of Indigenous peoples. Widespread persecution and discrimination. Violent conflicts in Chittagong Hill Tracts. Peace Accord in 1997 recognized traditional governance and autonomy, although it remains largely unimplemented. Implementation of Chittagong Hill Tracts Accord very slow.	Weak
Burma	Military regime oppresses ethnic nationalities. Some ceasefire agreements have provisions for special regions with some degree of autonomy. In 2010 election, no voting held in many ethnic nationality areas. Intensified conflict in ethnic nationality areas. Extensive human rights violations reported.	Weak

Cambodia	Land Law of 2001 recognized collective Indigenous rights to land by offering communal land titles, although implementation is very slow and Indigenous land loss regularly occurs. Forestry Law of 2002 also references Indigenous land rights. Policy on Registration Right to Use of Land in Indigenous Communities in 2009. Indigenous peoples arrested for protesting development projects.	Weak
China	Government recognizes fifty-five ethnic minorities with protected rights under Constitution but does not recognize national minorities as Indigenous peoples. Ethnic minorities have autonomous regions, local administrative governance, and right to practice own language and culture. Five Year Plan for Ethnic Minorities to increase their socio-economic status. Conflicts over land and religion. Tibet issue remains unresolved. Repression against Uyghur people in Xinjiang.	Weak
India	Four hundred and sixty-one "scheduled tribes" recognized by the government. Some areas recognize Indigenous rights to land and self-governance. Many Indigenous experience land violations, civil and political rights violations, displacement, and false prosecution. Frequent violent conflicts. Land confiscations and displacements for development purposes. Serious implementation gap in laws intended to protect Indigenous peoples.	Weak
Indonesia	Amendment to Constitution recognizes Indigenous peoples' rights, but the government denies the existence of Indigenous peoples in the country. UN CERD has made recommendations regarding Indigenous rights. Widespread agrarian conflict and many Indigenous communities deprived of their lands as a result of government actions. Cases reported of religious discrimination. National Program for the Recognition and Protection of Indigenous Peoples launched in 2014.	Weak
Israel	Government restricted Bedouins to a specific area in 1950s with a promise that they could return to their original lands – a promise that has not yet come to fruition. Live in recognized townships and unrecognized villages. Focus on land restitution claims as government attempts to forcibly resettle the Bedouin. Unrecognized villages considered illegal by the government and constant threat of demolition is present.	Weak
Japan	Ainu recognized as Indigenous people in 2008. Council on Ainu Policy Promotion working to develop policy measures, although Indigenous rights framework not being invoked in reports released thus far. Discriminatory attitudes prevalent and serious socio-economic gaps remain. Conflicts over US military presence in Okinawa.	Moderate

continued

Appendix 5.1 Continued

Country	*Status of Indigenous rights, as of December 31, 2014*	*Behavior*
Laos	Indigenous peoples not recognized but all ethnic groups officially equal in status. No specific legislation regarding Indigenous peoples or rights. Land concessions associated with development projects negatively impact ethnic minorities most. A few communities have temporary communal land title. Government resettlement of some groups for poverty alleviation.	Weak
Malaysia	British colonial laws recognizing customary land rights and customary law still exist; however, the government widely ignores them. Recent court cases have recognized communal Indigenous rights to land. Land rights task force completed inquiry in 2014. Encroachments and loss of land regularly occur, especially in favor of economic development initiatives. Regular protests against land loss. In 2014, government rejected all recommendations under Universal Periodic Review.	Moderate
Nepal	Some Indigenous nationalities recognized by the government but many are not. Indigenous experience substantial discrimination. New Constitution recognizes cultural diversity and mentions enhancing skills, knowledge, and rights of Indigenous peoples. Conflicts ongoing over development projects.	Weak
Philippines	Indigenous Peoples Rights Act passed in 1997 which calls for respect of Indigenous cultural rights as well as rights to lands and self-determination. Gaps in implementation especially related to land and resource development. Harassment of Indigenous peoples' schools by the military, political incarceration of Indigenous activists, and extra-judicial killings. Some autonomous regions. Ongoing issues over resource extraction and free, prior, and informed consent.	Moderate
Sri Lanka	Tribal groups not recognized by legislation or in Constitution. Displacement practices ongoing. Traditional livelihood practices prohibited in many areas due to forest protection legislation. Some rights protected for people who live in forest areas.	Weak
Taiwan	Fourteen Indigenous peoples recognized. Some laws to protect Indigenous rights, especially related to language and culture. Little legislative progress on self-governance/autonomy.	Weak
Thailand	Tribal peoples often considered security threat. Many still lack Thai citizenship. Constitution of 2007 does not recognize Indigenous peoples. Forest protection laws in recent years have dispossessed Indigenous peoples of land, including forced evictions. Communal land titling and other reform initiatives stalled.	Weak

Vietnam	Government does not recognize any groups as Indigenous, only ethnic minorities. No group possesses its own territory and no collective rights to land for ethnic minorities. Large socio-economic gaps between majority and ethnic minorities. Much land important to ethnic minorities is classified as forest land. Land law also ignores ethnic minorities' traditional forest governance practices. Tensions over development projects. Hmong have demanded autonomous region, staged protest that was repressed by the army.	Weak
AFRICA		
Algeria	Constitution recognized Tamazight Indigenous language but Amazigh Indigenous people remain unrecognized by government and marginalized. No regulative implementation mechanisms for these laws. Sharia law governs all, ignoring Amazigh tradition and customary law. No benefits from natural resource extraction in their territories. Tight military security and freedoms tightly restricted due to terrorism concerns.	Weak
Angola	No national policy or laws to protect Indigenous peoples. Poverty and discrimination extreme.	Weak
Botswana	Government does not recognize any groups as Indigenous. No specified laws protecting Indigenous peoples. Unresolved issues over game reserve and talk of more relocations of Indigenous peoples. Mines established in Indigenous territories but no benefits to the San. Community trusts being discussed. Severe poverty and discrimination.	Weak
Burundi	Indigenous peoples have been completely dispossessed of traditional lands. Constitution of 2005 provides designated seats in National Assembly and Senate for Indigenous group. Government has initiated a land reform process but progress is slow. Large number of human rights violations reported. Severe poverty and rampant discrimination.	Weak
Cameroon	Series of legislative acts adopted in 2011 to protect populations from development projects. Law on Forest and Fauna revised in 2011 to permit sale of forest products by Indigenous peoples. Pastoral Code adopted in 2011 to help demarcate lands and articulate access to water and roads. Parliamentary dialogue held with Indigenous peoples in 2011. Poverty and land access are ongoing issues.	Weak

continued

Appendix 5.1 Continued

Country	*Status of Indigenous rights, as of December 31, 2014*	*Behavior*
Congo, Democratic Republic of	Discrimination widespread. Systemic violations of Indigenous rights. No government recognition or protection of Indigenous lands. Due to logging and forest reform, Indigenous peoples increasingly displaced from forest and forced to adopt a sedentary life. In 2009, government issued a report delineating a strategic framework for a development plan for Indigenous peoples. In 2011 government held a National Forum on Indigenous peoples' land and rights.	Weak
Congo, Republic of	Law of 2011 adopted to protect Indigenous peoples' rights but not yet being enforced and no implementing regulations yet in place. Discrimination and forced labor and slavery widespread and poverty extreme. Land registration system under land law negatively impacts Indigenous peoples.	Weak
Ethiopia	No national policy to protect Indigenous peoples. Massive land evictions and "resettlement" of Indigenous peoples for overseas investment leases and development projects.	Weak
Gabon	In 2005, government recognized existence of Indigenous people in an Indigenous Peoples' Plan, which was part of a World Bank policy loan. A few projects focused on Indigenous communities are in the planning stages. President has promised that the revised Forest Code will take Indigenous peoples' rights into account. Logging threatens Indigenous peoples' traditional territories. Government launched special census initiative to identify Indigenous peoples. Indigenous peoples heavily involved in forest mapping. Indigenous organizations regularly liaise with government.	Moderate
Kenya	Constitution of 2010 includes collective rights of minorities and marginalized communities, and definition of "marginalized" encompasses most groups that identify as Indigenous. A few pieces of enabling legislation for constitutional rights, although none specifically for Indigenous rights. Land and resource tenure insecurity, poor political representation, discrimination, and exclusion. Revamped judiciary offers hope for better implementation of laws and regulations, and Indigenous groups are increasingly using judiciary to assert their rights. Violence against Indigenous rights defenders.	Weak
Mali	Constitution recognizes cultural diversity, but does not implement Indigenous rights.	Weak
Morocco	Indigenous peoples under constant threat of assimilation. New Constitution recognizes Amazigh identity and gives official status to the language. Use of Amazigh names still banned in practice.	Weak

Namibia	No constitutional or national legislation to protect Indigenous peoples. Eighty percent of San dispossessed of traditional lands. Some rural San have access and land and recognized communal control. Land reform program underway aimed at poor and marginalized populations. Extreme poverty and marginalization. Some San entering tourist industry. Government launched an agency for San development in 2010.	Weak
Niger	No constitutional recognition of Indigenous peoples' existence. Pastoral Code passed in 2010, protecting rights of pastoralists, although no law for implementation as yet.	Weak
Nigeria	Government does not recognize any group as Indigenous. Exclusion and marginalization of Indigenous groups *from political system. Language discrimination in educational system in favor of majority languages.* Land tenure insecurity for Indigenous and nomadic groups. Indigenous groups charge that petroleum laws are discriminatory due to land tenure differences.	Weak
Rwanda	Indigenous peoples have been completely dispossessed of traditional lands. Discrimination widespread. Government refuses to recognize Indigenous identity, as all ethnic identification has been banned since 1994 genocide. No laws to protect Indigenous peoples. Poverty of Indigenous peoples extreme and discrimination rampant. Government policy to destroy traditional huts in favor of modern houses is ongoing and occurs without consultation.	Weak
South Africa	No constitutional recognition of Indigenous peoples, although redress for past discrimination is included. Amended Traditional Leadership and Governance Framework Act in 2009 and National Traditional Leadership Bill of 2011 accommodate a measure of political self-determination and recognition of customary law. Both were adopted with substantial consultation. Major Supreme Court victory for land and resources rights in 2003. Various language and cultural preservation programs. Land reform is slow.	Moderate
Tanzania	Does not recognize any group in country as Indigenous. No national policy or legislation for Indigenous rights. Land and resource tenure insecurity. Engaged in constitutional process, and Indigenous groups are attempting to engage in process. "Certificates of Village Land" may be obtained, recognizing collective ownership, with individuals obtaining certificates of occupancy. Ongoing conflicts over land use.	Weak

continued

Appendix 5.1 Continued

Country	*Status of Indigenous rights, as of December 31, 2014*	*Behavior*
Uganda	No government recognition of Indigenous peoples. Constitution of 1995 does not offer specific protections, although it does mention protection of historically marginalized groups. Land Act of 1998 protects customary use of land and traditional use of forests but same act also allows government to exclude human beings from a protected area, thus nullifying Indigenous land rights to forest areas. Significant socio-economic gaps with non-Indigenous population and discrimination rampant. Batwa, who were evicted from the forest in the past, would like to return. Government program to settle pastoral communities.	Weak

Note

1 While both Canada and the United States have substantial Arctic regions, they are classified here as North American countries, since the majority of Indigenous peoples in both countries are outside of the Arctic region. Both countries' Arctic behavior has been included in their evaluation.

Index

Page numbers in *italics* denote tables, those in **bold** denote figures.